The Americanization of the Jews

REAPPRAISALS IN JEWISH SOCIAL AND INTELLECTUAL HISTORY

GENERAL EDITOR: ROBERT M. SELTZER

THE AMERICANIZATION
OF THE JEWS

Edited by Robert M. Seltzer
and Norman J. Cohen

NEW YORK UNIVERSITY PRESS
NEW YORK AND LONDON

NEW YORK UNIVERSITY PRESS
New York and London

Library of Congress Cataloging-in-Publication Data
The Americanization of the Jews / edited by Robert M. Seltzer and
Norman J. Cohen
p. cm.—(Reappraisals in Jewish social and intellectual history)
Includes bibliographical references and index.
ISBN 0-8147-8000-8 (cloth).—ISBN 0-8147-8001-6 (pbk.)
1. Jews—United States—Identity—Congresses. 2. Jews—Cultural
assimilation—United States—Congresses. 3. Jews—United States—
Politics and government—Congresses. 4. Judaism—United States—
Congresses. 5. United States—Ethnic relations—Congresses.
I. Seltzer, Robert M. II. Cohen, Norman J. III. Series.
E184.J5A618 1995
305.892'4073—dc20   94-36160
                                CIP

New York University Press books are printed on acid-free paper,
and their binding materials are chosen for strength and durability.

Manufactured in the United States of America

10   9   8   7   6   5   4   3   2   1

To Naomi W. Cohen and Eugene B. Borowitz,
cherished colleagues and models
to younger generations of scholars

Contents

ix

PART THREE
Zionism in an American Setting

PART FOUR
Traditional Religion in an American Setting

PART FIVE
The Impact of the Women's Movement

Foreword

Norman J. Cohen

The aim of this book is to assess the current state of American Jewish life, drawing on the research and thinking of scholars from a variety of disciplines and diverse points of view. The groundwork was laid at a conference entitled "American Jews: Dreams and Realities," held in New York City in the spring of 1991. Cosponsored by the Hebrew Union College–Jewish Institute of Religion and the Joseph and Ceil Mazer Institute for Research and Advanced Study of Judaica of the Graduate School of the City University of New York, the three-day gathering took place at the Brookdale campus of H.U.C.–J.I.R. and at the Roosevelt House of Hunter College. The sessions drew large audiences of academics and professionals working in Jewish agencies as well as laypeople, and the presentations elicited vigorous response and interchange of ideas.

We are grateful to the staffs of the New York School of the College–Institute, in particular to Linda Jaffe, and of the Mazer Institute and the Hunter Jewish Social Studies Program, especially Rosalie K. Bachana and Marilyn J. Sladowsky, for making the myriad of arrangements for the conference. It could not have taken place and this volume would not have seen the light of day without the generous support of the Judy and Michael Steinhardt Foundation. The Steinhardts' concern for the future vitality of American Jewish life led them to subvent the conference and the preparation of this book, along with a plethora of other activities in the Jewish community.

We are grateful, too, for the support and encouragement of the leadership of the College–Institute, especially President Alfred Gottschalk and Stanley P. Gold, Chair of the Board of Governors, as well as of members of the administration of the CUNY Graduate Center, especially Solomon Goldstein, former Dean of Research and University Programs.

Above all, our gratitude goes to Naomi W. Cohen, Distinguished Service Professor of American Jewish History at the Jewish Theological Seminary of America, and to Eugene B. Borowitz, Sigmund L. Falk Distinguished Professor of Education and Jewish Religious Thought at the New York School of H.U.C.–J.I.R., both of whom served with me and Robert M. Seltzer on the planning committee. We benefited greatly from Naomi Cohen's careful reading of all the papers and her indispensable advice in shaping the manuscript. The project owes much to her acumen and friendship.

Our special thanks is extended to Dennis M. Dreyfus for all that he did in helping to transform these presentations into a unified book. He was a full partner in bringing this work to press, going far beyond normal editorial duties. He spent many hours with each article and each contributor, sharpening content and polishing style. We cannot overstate his thoughtfulness, cooperation, skill, and remarkable ability to work effectively in an area that was not his own specialization.

We would like to express our appreciation to the Lucius N. Littauer Foundation for a grant that helped defray publication costs and the preparation of the index.

We would also like to thank our editors at New York University Press, Niko Pfund and Despina Papazoglou Gimbel, for their gracious and patient encouragement, gentle but determined coaxing, and, in Bob's case, for the warm friendship that has developed through this and other projects over the years.

Through this volume, we expect to bring to a wider audience the disparate insights and overall issues that permeated these papers and the discussion accompanying them. In so doing, we hope to contribute to a deeper understanding of the unique nature of American Jewish life, its past and present, and to the key questions that shape our future on this continent.

Contributors

JEROLD S. AUERBACH, author of *Rabbis and Lawyers: The Journey from Torah to Constitution*, is professor of history at Wellesley College. His other books include *Labor and Liberty, Unequal Justice*, and *Justice without Law*, and his articles have appeared in *Commentary, Judaism, Midstream*, and *Present Tense*.

NORMAN J. COHEN is Dean of the Hebrew Union College–Jewish Institute of Religion, New York School, and professor of midrash. He is the author of numerous articles in the field of midrash and of *Self, Struggle and Change—The Family Conflict Stories in Genesis and Their Meaning for Our Lives*.

STEVEN M. COHEN is a professor in the Melton Center for Jewish Education in the Diaspora at the Hebrew University of Jerusalem. He is author or editor of many books on contemporary Jewish sociology, including *American Modernity and Jewish Identity, Two Worlds of Judaism: The Israeli and American Experiences* (with Charles Liebman), and *Cosmopolitans and Parochials: Modern Orthodox Jews in the United States* (with Samuel Heilman).

DAVID G. DALIN is professor of American Jewish history at the University of Hartford. His publications include *From Marxism to Judaism: The Collected Essays of Will Herberg* and *American Jews and the Separationist Faith: The New Debate on Religion and Public Life*, as well as many articles and book reviews.

DENNIS M. DREYFUS is an editor, copywriter, and translator in more than a dozen languages.

ARNOLD EISEN is a professor of religious studies and Aaron-Roland Fellow at Stanford University. He is author of *The Chosen People in America* and *Galut: Modern Jewish Reflection on Homelessness and Homecoming* and writes on contemporary Jewish theology and religious life.

DAVID ELLENSON is Anna Grancell Professor of Jewish Religious Thought at Hebrew Union College–Jewish Institute of Religion, Los Angeles. He is author of *Rabbi Esriel Hildeshemier and the Creation of a Modern Jewish Orthodoxy* and *Tradition in Transition: Orthodoxy, Halakha, and the Boundaries of Modern Jewish Identity*.

HENRY L. FEINGOLD is professor of history, Baruch College and the Graduate Center of the City University of New York, author of *The Politics of Rescue: The Roosevelt Administration and the Holocaust, 1938–1945*, and other books and essays on American Jewish history and the Holocaust. He was general editor of *The Jewish People in America*, a series sponsored by the American Jewish Historical Society, and author of volume 4, *A Time for Searching: Entering the Mainstream, 1920–1945*.

NATHAN GLAZER is professor emeritus of education and social structure, Harvard University, and author of *American Judaism* and many books on issues of social concern, including *Ethnic Dilemmas, Affirmative Discrimination: Ethnic Inequality and Public Policy*, and *The Limits of Social Policy*. He is coeditor of the quarterly journal *The Public Interest*.

ARTHUR A. GOREN is the Russell and Bettina Knapp Professor of American Jewish History at Columbia University and professor emeritus of American history at the Hebrew University of Jerusalem. He is author of *New York Jews and the Quest for Community: The Kehilla Experiment, 1908–1922, The American Jews*, and editor of *Dissenter in Zion: From the Writings of Judah L. Magnes*.

JEFFREY S. GUROCK is Libby M. Klaperman Professor of Jewish History at Yeshiva University, author of *When Harlem Was Jewish:*

1870–1930, *American Jewish History: A Bibliographic Guide*, and other studies of American Judaism.

JUDITH HAUPTMAN is a professor of Talmud at the Jewish Theological Seminary. She is the author of *Development of the Talmudic Sugya: Relationship of Tannaitic and Amoraic Sources* and other writings on Talmud, Midrash, and feminist methodologies for reading rabbinic texts.

SAMUEL C. HEILMAN is Proshansky Professor of Jewish Studies at Queens College and the Graduate Center of the City University of New York and author of *Synagogue Life, The People of the Book, The Gate behind the Wall,* and other sociological studies of contemporary Jewish religious life.

PAULA E. HYMAN is the Lucy Moses Professor of Modern Jewish History at Yale University. Among her books are *From Dreyfus to Vichy: The Remaking of French Jewry, 1906–1939* and *The Emancipation of the Jews of Alsace.* She is coauthor of *The Jewish Woman in America: Images and Reality* and coeditor, with Steven M. Cohen, of *The Jewish Family.* Her most recent book is *Gender and Assimilation in Modern Jewish History.*

JENNA WEISSMAN JOSELIT is a visiting professor in the Department of Religion and a fellow of the Center for the Study of American Religion at Princeton University. She is author of *Our Gang: Jewish Crime and the New York Jewish Community* and *New York's Jewish Jews: The Orthodox Jewish Community of the Interwar Years* and coeditor of *Getting Comfortable in New York: The American Jewish Home, 1880–1950,* and *The Wonders of America: Reinventing Jewish Culture, 1880–1950.*

JACOB KABAKOFF is professor emeritus of Hebrew and Jewish studies at Lehman College of the City University of New York. He is editor of the *Jewish Book Annual* and author and editor of works in Hebrew and English on modern Hebrew literature, including *Master of Hope: Selected Writings of Naphtali Herz Imber.*

EDWARD K. KAPLAN is professor of French and comparative literature at Brandeis University, fellow of the Taubler Institute, and author of works on French literature, twentieth-century Jewish theology, and studies on the life and thought of Abraham Joshua Heschel.

CHARLES S. LIEBMAN is a professor of political science at Bar-Ilan University. His extensive work on American Jews was the subject of a retrospective in *American Jewish History* 80, no. 4 (Summer 1991). His most recent book, coauthored with Steven M. Cohen, is *Two Worlds of Judaism: The Jewish Experience in Israel and the United States*.

STEVEN M. LOWENSTEIN is Isadore Levine Professor of Jewish History at the University of Judaism, Los Angeles, and author of numerous books and articles on German-Jewish social and cultural history, including *Frankfurt on the Hudson: The German-Jewish Community of Washington Heights, 1933–1983*.

EGON MAYER is professor of sociology at Brooklyn College and Director of the Center for Jewish Studies of the Graduate School of the City University of New York. He is author of *From Suburb to Shtetl*, on the Orthodox and Hasidic communities of Boro Park, and of many studies on intermarriage, including *Love and Tradition: Marriage between Jews and Christians*.

PAUL RITTERBAND is professor of sociology and Jewish studies at the City College and Graduate Center of the City University of New York, director of the Institute on Jewish Communal Life, and former director of the Center for Jewish Studies at the Graduate Center of CUNY. He is author of *Jewish Learning in American Universities: The First Century* and of studies on Israeli migration to the United States and the demography of New York's Jewish community over the last one hundred years and is editor of *Modern Jewish Fertility* and *Contemporary Jewish Philanthropy*.

JONATHAN D. SARNA is the Joseph H. and Belle R. Braun Professor of American Jewish History at Brandeis University. His books include *Jacksonian Jew: The Two Worlds of Mordecai Noah, JPS: The Americanization of Jewish Culture, The Jews of Cincinnati* (with Nancy H. Klein) and *The American Synagogue: A Bibliography and State-of-the-Field Survey* (with Alexandra S. Korros).

MEL SCULT is a professor of Jewish thought at Brooklyn College. His essays have appeared in *Judaism, Modern Judaism,* and the *Reconstructionist.* He is coeditor of *Dynamic Judaism: The Essential Writings of Mordecai M. Kaplan.* He is author of *Judaism Faces the Twentieth Century: A Biography of Mordecai Kaplan.*

ROBERT M. SELTZER is professor of history at Hunter College and the Graduate School of the City University of New York, chair of the Hunter Jewish Social Studies Program, former director of the Joseph and Ceil Mazer Institute for Research and Advanced Study in Judaica at the CUNY Graduate School, and author of *Jewish People, Jewish Thought* and of studies on East European Jewry and modern Jewish thought.

ELLEN M. UMANSKY is Carl and Dorothy Bennett Professor of Judaic Studies at Fairfield University. She is coeditor of *Four Centuries of Jewish Women's Spirituality* and author of *Lily Montagu and the Advancement of Liberal Judaism* and *From Christian Science to Jewish Science: Spiritual Healing and American Jews.*

MELVIN I. UROFSKY is professor of history at Virginia Commonwealth University. The author of more than two dozen books and over a hundred articles, his works include *A Mind of One Piece: Brandeis and American Reform, Louis D. Brandeis and the Progressive Tradition, A March of Liberty: American Constitutional and Legal Development, A Conflict of Rights: The Supreme Court and Affirmative Action,* and *Felix Frankfurter: Judicial Restraint and Individual Liberties.* His studies of Zionism include *We Are One: American Jews and Israel* and *American Zionism from Herzl to the Holocaust.*

STEPHEN J. WHITFIELD occupies the Max Richter Chair in American Civilization at Brandeis University and is author of

Voices of Jacob, Hands of Esau: Jews in American Life and Thought, *American Space, Jewish Time,* and other books on American culture and thought.

RUTH R. WISSE is professor of Yiddish literature at Harvard University. She is senior editor of the *Library of Yiddish Classics,* editor of volumes of Yiddish stories and poems, author of *The Schlemiel as Modern Hero, I. L. Peretz and the Makings of Modern Jewish Culture,* and other works, and a regular contributor to many magazines of Jewish and general affairs.

CHAPTER I

Introduction: The Ironies of American Jewish History

Robert M. Seltzer

Jewish history is singular, not least because of its incongruities. The migrations, invasions, defeats, and myriad other crises of the ancient Israelites, a small people that was among the least of the kingdoms, became the matrix of the cosmic historiography that came to dominate Europe, North Africa, and western Asia after late antiquity. Not exceptionally distinguished in art, technology, or warfare, the Jewish impact flowed from a handful of surviving oracles, hymns, legal codes, and tales of ancestors and from an abiding drive to metabolize the symbolic forms of nearby cultures according to an obsession that only the God of Israel was truly divine. Few in number relative to the populations alongside whom they lived, the Jews generated a collective image that loomed preternaturally large throughout the medieval and early modern centuries in the minds of Christendom and Islam and, of course, in the Jewish conception of the significance of their group existence. Modern Jewry has sought in various ways to reduce that incongruous image to manageable proportions—to normalize and humanize it—with limited success and considerable failure. Because of the powerful valence of the image of the Jews, modern Jewish history, far from being one more chapter appended to a chronicle of many centuries, has become an intellectual world in itself, a complex series of encounters and adjustments in which, ironically, the Jews are both a paradigm for many other small groups and a special case.

Jewry's record of reactions, initiatives, and restructurings in the last two centuries is often said to be prototypical of vulnerable religious, ethnic, and social minorities responding to accelerating and sometimes cataclysmic change. Yet it is a story like no other. In the mid-eighteenth century, the preponderance of a marginalized but proud Jewish people, defined by loyalty to the Torah and its God, lived in a diaspora stretching from Alsace and the western German and northern Italian states to the eastern reaches of Poland-Lithuania and, in a second swath, from Morocco across North Africa and the southern Balkans to the Middle East, Iran, and beyond. Farther out, harbingers of immense shifts about to be set in motion were the newest Jewish communities on the Atlantic— Amsterdam, London, Hamburg, Bordeaux, Curacao, Charleston, Philadelphia, New York, Newport. Less than two and one-half centuries later, the Jewish people had become transformed into an incomparably more complex social grouping living in a handful of economically advanced countries, marked by an ideological and behavioral diversity virtually unparalleled in Jewish history such that "who is a Jew" became a question that concerned even the Jews themselves.

Yet another way Jews found themselves to be prototypical and exceptional is that they underwent, before many other minority groups, the possibilities and metamorphoses summoned by the rampant urbanization, mobility, and secularization that accompanied modern education, economic change, and political upheaval. On the one hand, sectors of the Jewish people confronted early what wider elements of the population experienced later, making Jews pioneers in the self-transformations forced on minorities in the last ten or fifteen decades of modernity. On the other hand, the desire to avoid total rupture with the past and to maintain continuity evoked a series of creative responses by Jewish elites. Bound together in new arrangements and modes of self-awareness, modern Jewry's exertions to maintain order and cohesion constitute a many-sided drama not usually given its due in comparative history. Efforts to achieve conclusive liberation led to the prolonged struggle for Jewish emancipation in the European diaspora, to a preoccupation with revolutionary politics in some countries, and to movements for Jewish self-emancipation and return to the ancient homeland. Catching up to a European Enlightenment that was embarked in new humanistic and universalistic directions led to a new continuum of Jewish denominations and theologies and eventually to the inclusion in it of secular ideologies of Jewishness. The Haskalah, *Wissenschaft des Judentums*, Neo-Orthodox Judaism, Classical Reform, Positive-Historical Judaism, Bundism, Diaspora Nationalism, Political Zionism, Spiritual Zionism, Labor Zionism, Revisionist Zionism, and other programs of thought and act were all symptoms of the power over Jews of calls for justice, equality, fraternity, and hope. Yet none of the programs of re-formation ended up as their initiators intended. They and the other ideologies of Jewish regeneration turned out to have critical limits, leaving the Jews just as vulnerable as they had always been to the deracinating lures of integration and assimilation on the one hand and to campaigns of vilification and extermination on the other hand. Whatever modernity may turn out to be, it has never stood still.

Locating this kaleidoscope of reactions and counterreactions in its proper context calls for a special academic field: the comparative study of modern Jewish diasporas. Jews in most lands have found themselves on the edge of social and intellectual change but confronting different givens. As a result of the economic and political development (and revolutions) of the nation-states in which Jews live, each Jewry had to respond to its own set of challenges in its own way.

Four especially creative Jewries have contributed most to the remaking of the Jewish people: those of Germany, Russia and Poland, Israel, and America. From German Jewry came a tripartite denominational structure that has marked modernized Judaism since the mid-nineteenth century, as well as most of the fecund schools of modern Jewish philosophy, from the Enlightenment of Moses Mendelssohn to the existentialism of Franz Rosenzweig. Russia and Poland constituted a greenhouse of secular Judaism—literary, nationalist, and socialist—and became the home of vibrant forms of traditional religious Judaism, especially the yeshivah world and later Hasidism. The Yishuv and the State of Israel has been the exemplary setting for social experimentation and redemptive ingathering, as well as the means for Jews to take a new stance as a nation and find a voice in the international arena.

It is more difficult, however, to delineate what American Jewry has accomplished in relation to its special environment.

Although the Jewish population of the United States has numbered in the millions since about World War I, the Jewish encounter here with modernity is actually one of the longest: in the year 2004 it will have lasted three and one-half centuries. (Jews have lived as long in North America as they have in postmedieval Britain and France and only sixty years less than in Amsterdam—and English, French, and Dutch Jewries are usually considered the principal harbingers of modern Jewry.) The tale most often told is that of immigrants arriving in America to escape the disabilities and misfortunes of the Old World: how they, their children, and their grandchildren sunk roots in a land that seemed to promise an end to the degradations of poverty and exile. Another well-established story is that of the creation by American Jewry of a host of new organizations, institutions, and agencies to cope with the religious and political milieu of the United States. But there is much more. In the last four decades American Jewish studies has become a full-fledged branch of American ethnic and social history, exploring such themes as the presence of Jews in far-flung parts of the continent and disparate sectors of the economy, the migration of Jews from region to region of North America, their impact on the polity and popular culture of the United States, the growth of Jewish educational institutions, and the politics of American Zionism. The resulting picture indicates how an Americanized Jewry emerged from a melting pot of Old World Jewish subcultures and became internally divided along new fault lines, producing its own dialectic of vectors and forces pointing . . . where? We will return to that question later.

This book is a selection of recent work by some of the most accomplished scholars and researchers in a burgeoning field. The committee that invited these essays was interested in the interplay between Jews and the ideal of America, that is, between dreams and realities: between the Jewish dreams of America and what happened to the Jews as they became part of the mainstream to a degree that did not occur elsewhere. For Jews, America was a land of immense opportunities and, for Judaism, immense dangers. It offered Jews as individuals the opportunity to live free of the restrictions that often persisted in the Old World and Jews as a group the opportunity to find a safe home. But America threatened personal disorientation and collective disintegration, corrosion of family ties and the demise of a distinctive Jewish culture, with a rapidity much greater than almost anywhere else in the world. Rumors of the promise and risk of America arrived on the other side of the Atlantic not long after the initial groups of Sephardic Jews landed here. By the late eighteenth century, America as a brave new land of freedom and equality became a key constituent of the ideal of a place where Jews could live with complete dignity and new self-respect. Hopes and perceptions are, after all, autonomous forces in the calculus of intentions and acts. First-generation German-speaking Jewish immigrants from Central Europe and first-generation Yiddish-speaking Jews from Eastern Europe were lured by a *novus ordo seclorum* where revolutionary developments were creating a new nation. Not a few of the younger immigrants took advantage of the plasticity afforded by immigration to throw off the shackles of tradition and recreate themselves as dejudaized Americans. Others saw the amorphousness of America as summoning them to lay the foundations for forms of Jewish association and identity that, though modified in the Depression and the war years, persisted in the golden age of American Jewry that lasted to the midsixties.

The essays in this book illustrate the paradoxical effect of the Americanization of the Jews: America undermined and energized Jewish commitment. Much was discarded and much was saved. Acculturation (in the sociological use of the term presupposed in these papers) did not always lead to assimilation: sometimes the most acculturated were among the most conscious of their Jewish identity and the most preoccupied with Jewish affairs. Despite rapid and severe acculturation, Jewishness was honed as an independent variable in the motivations of more than a few of its American adherents—and has remained so, even though Jewish institutions, ideologies, and even Jewish values have been reshaped by America to such a degree that many Jews of the past might not recognize as Jewish some of what constitutes American Jewishness.

How the American environment differed has been repeatedly analyzed by the historians of American Jewry. Jewish immigrants came to an America populated largely by Europeans who had created a society with only traces of medievalism. Negative stereotypes of the Jews were offset by a Puritan identification with the history of biblical Israel so that, in American Christianity, disdain for a long-superseded Judaism was countered by esteem for the living descendants of the people of the Old Testament. From the beginning, the Jewish situation was more propitious even than in England (and the legal status of the Jews there was more benign than for Jews in most of the lands of continental Europe). In colonial British America there were no restrictions on Jewish economic activity and religious life so that, in the era of the American Revolution, there were no ghettos to be razed, no limits on how many Jews could be married, no Jewish taxes to be abolished, no Pale of Settlement to be demolished; likewise, there were no autonomous *batei din*, no venerable *yeshivot*, no government-recognized *gemeinde* or *landesrabbiner* to sustain an established community. Restrictions on the election of Jews to public office were rapidly abolished by most states; in some localities Jews were not particularly welcome (New England until the mid-nineteenth century), but there were no explicit limits on the freedom of Jews to live where they chose, to engage in any business or profession, and to consider themselves citizens of a country that, for all its bursts of nativism and decades of rejection of nonwhites and non-Nordics, was still more hospitable to immigrants than any other.

History, of course, offers instances of other frontiers where Jews have been welcomed because of their mobility and entrepreneurial skills. In industrializing nineteenth-century America, Jewish immigrants came to be not only peddlers and shopkeepers but also workers in expanding industries, such as clothing manufacture, that other Jews had largely created. The growing economy of the new nation lured Jews as it did other immigrants, but the image of America as the land of freedom was compelling: the United States promised liberty and justice, the chance to be people of worth and dignity, the opportunity to start life anew and rise to respectability and even prominence.

Arguably, the most remarkable feature of the America polity from the Jewish perspective is the Enlightenment ethos of its foundational documents. The universalist rationalism in the Declaration of Independence appealed to the rights of human beings as such, so that this charter of the American social contract was rooted in a notion of natural reason that by implication included non-Christians without caveat. The constitutional prohibition of an established church provided for a sweeping separation of religion and state that made the United States the political order most neutral to competing or friendly denominations. Although as a religion and an ethnic group Jews were legally invisible on the federal level, Clermont-Tonnerre's 1789 dictum that "the Jews should be denied everything as a nation, but granted everything as individuals" was realized earlier in America than in revolutionary France, where it was enunciated. Yet in America the Jewish religion was able eventually to attain a greater degree of informal legitimation as one of a plurality of publicly recognized faiths than Judaism achieved in any other diaspora; given the relative paucity of Jews involved, it is all the more remarkable that the Jewish tradition managed finally to gain equal status in the trinity of Protestantism-Catholicism-Judaism that has given a special tone to recent American life.

In the first phase of American Jewish history there was an overarching Jewish communal structure in each place where Jews settled in sufficient numbers. After the American Revolution it became clear that Jewry was free, within certain parameters, to reorganize itself the way it wanted. By the middle of the nineteenth century, American Judaism was structured according to the model of denominational Protestantism: larger communities had an increasing number of independent congregations, each conducting its affairs according to its own bylaws, relying solely on dues and contributions of its members, and selecting its officers and spiritual leader according to its own standards and desires. Membership in the Jewish community was stripped of any legal sanctions in America earlier than elsewhere and became even more a matter of personal choice as each new generation matured and as American Jewry increased in number and geographical distribution. American individualism has been commented on extensively from Alexis de Tocqueville's *Democracy in America* to Robert N. Bellah's *Habits of the Heart:* the radical individualism of America meant that Jews could choose as they wished among the Jewish options that appeared in the nineteenth century, that they could decide whether they would be Jewish in a strong way, or even be Jewish at all.

Nineteenth-century American Jewry gradually created a broad range of new intercommunal institutions to supplement the multiple congregations that had come into being on a local level: fraternal and charitable organizations, federations of philanthropies and synagogues, rabbinical schools, newspapers in German, Yiddish, and English, settlement houses, labor unions, *landsmanshaften*. By the early twentieth century most of the present Jewish defense agencies had emerged, each imbued by an ideal of America and dedicated to protecting the Jews at home and abroad. The formation of new national organizations confirmed the fragmentation of the community, as well as the minority status within American Jewry of traditional Old World Judaism. Only in America did the vast majority of Jews identify themselves with the various forms of liberal, non-Orthodox Judaism. Never had a Jewish community been to such an extent voluntary and so divided.

Meanwhile, by the end of the nineteenth century a restrictive definition of America was beginning to crystallize in the antisemitism of the Gilded Age that eventuated in the social exclusions, educational quotas, immigration allotments, and public expressions of aversion to Jews that became more conspicuous in the twenties and thirties. This exclusivism was emphatically not the Jewish image of America, and Jewish leaders, organizations, and voters gave their support to those positions that represented an America that embraced all its constituent races, religions, ethnic groups, and social classes. According to some historians, the overlapping, competing, and fractious Jewish organizational network may have contributed to the difficulties American Jewry encountered in forging a coherent policy to deal with the upsurge of American antisemitism in the thirties and with the blatant threat of Nazi Germany. The same voluntaristic pluralism, however, may have amplified the vitality of American Jewry after World War II on a series of fronts. In a postwar era of renewed social mobility, revival of respect for religion, and eclipse of anti-Jewish prejudice, Jews moved in large numbers to the suburbs, where many joined synagogues and reacquired at least a minimum of Jewish practice. All American Jewish religious organizations were energized in some fashion, and Jews were increasingly united by a surge of support for Israel as a symbol of determination to survive after the Holocaust, as a necessary means of achieving Jewish autonomy independent of a hostile majority, and as a self-chosen Jewish way of life. While American culture became fascinated with the complex ethnic roots of its heterogeneous population, a concomitant interest in Jewish roots arose. A Jewish community had probably never enjoyed such a positive image as that of American Jewry in the fifties and sixties, nor felt more accepted.

In light of post–World War II developments, it has become possible to perceive yet another way in which America stood out in the course of Jewish history: as Jews have become Americanized, they had contributed much to the liberal ideal of Americanism itself. American culture was remarkably absorbent of certain of the ethnic features of the groups that constituted the American populace: in popular culture (foods, humor, music, slang) and in politics and intellectual life (the American labor movement, New Deal and Fair Deal liberalism, racial desegregation, civil liberties, avant-garde arts, new directions in literary criticism), Jews were quite conspicuous. Just as Jews had remade themselves and their religion in light of their ideal of America, so they projected into the American dream Jewish values and yearnings. If American cultural forms were reshaping Jewishness, Jews helped shape America's conception of itself.

In the late sixties, however, there began to appear signals that called into question whether or not Jewish continuity and integration in America had been truly stabilized. Muting of antisemitism and enthusiasm for Israel were countered by fascination with Israel's purported failings and by disparagements that, to sensitive ears (perhaps hypersensitive, perhaps prescient), seemed close to antisemitism in new dress. Of broader impact on the Jewish situation were the changes becoming increasingly apparent as a result of Jewish acceptance, changes that were rapidly and dramatically remaking most of American Jewry in the absence of a continued stream of immigrants from traditional Old World Jewish backgrounds and upbringings. The decline of social barriers went hand in hand with a weakening of inhibitions against marriage outside the faith. The Jewish birthrate declined and the divorce rate soared.

Conversion to Judaism increased, as did disaffiliation. Was American Jewry headed for drastic shrinkage in numbers, if not outright extinction? The established denominational pattern seemed about to fragment. Feminism challenged age-old Jewish assumptions about gender and family. Changing sexual mores and yearnings for personal fulfillment threatened to disrupt the indirect, already tenuous connections of much of American Jewry to venerable values. The impact of a cohort of children raised part-Jewish and part-Christian posed dilemmas of principle and tactics for Jewish institutions. Was the Jewishness of many American Jews on the way to becoming a secondary or even a tertiary loyalty—a "postassimilation" Jewishness that faded in and out of the individual's consciousness along with involvements in other categories now considered cultural identities of their own? Was cyclical Jewishness the next stage in a new reality in the making? One group of Jewish sociologists has been labeled the "transformationists" because they emphasize not the cumulative attenuation of Jewishness from one generation to another but the protean nature of American Jewishness as unexpected forms of Jewish self-expression appear. Another group, often called the "assimilationists," dismisses the transformationalists as misguided Pollyannas.

American Jewish studies as seen from the nineties, therefore, is faced with questions different from those that predominated in the fifties, when American Jewish history came into its own as a distinct area of scholarly research and academic analysis. Is America still to be held exceptional to generalizations derived from all of Jewish history? Do recent developments indicate that broader diaspora-wide processes governing acculturation, marginalization, and decline are beginning to take hold, so that nineteenth-century Old World fears of America as corrosive to the integrity of Judaism are proving to be valid? Is the Jewish image of America as a uniquely benevolent home of an emancipated, normalized Judaism fated to be drastically modified or even abandoned, or will American Jewry be shown capable of generating its own self-perpetuation in yet another era of Jewish history?

Perhaps it is most helpful to pursue American Jewish dreams and realities as they relate to different glimpses of transformations in process. That is what we have tried to do in this book.

The first group of articles deals with the Jewish imagination. The essays of Steven M. Lowenstein and Jacob Kabakoff examine German and East European images of America in Jewish literature, including the literature produced by the Hebrew renascence of the turn of the century. European anticipations of the challenges that America would pose for Jewish immigrants were not so inaccurate as one might think; the New World was extolled as a land of liberty and equality but the travails of departure and arrival were widely recognized. American Jewish literature frequently conveys the experience of uprooting and settling, but what does the depiction of the grandchildren and great-grandchildren of those New Americans by American Jewish writers show of the character and incongruities of American Jewish life? Ruth R. Wisse points out that Jews have been grateful for the benefits of America—the material well-being and the freedom possible here—and that America has become the test case for modern Jewish resistance to dissolution (just as Judaism has been a test case for American tolerance). But American Jewish writers have often found the "hunted" (the European refugees) far more interesting than fully acculturated Jews. Is postimmigration American Jewish life so bland as to offer nothing of interest to creative Jews who shape American intellectual and cultural history? Stephen J. Whitfield suggests that, as America has overcome its negativity about the Jewish people, a point has been reached where the Jews can barely be distinguished from the non-Jews. American movies captured dramatically the old nervousness of American Jews with their Jewishness during the Depression and war years just as they chronicle the decline in the power of anti-Jewish images to intimidate the filmmaker since the fifties. If the old stereotypes are no longer potent, does this herald the obliteration of Jewish specialness? Indeed, the fate of American Jewry may be an ultimate test of the compatibility of acculturation with the preservation of meaningful historical distinctiveness in the diaspora.

The second group of articles concerns Jews and American politics in the twentieth century. According to Henry L. Feingold, the consistency with which American Jews (especially of East European origin) support liberal causes is exceptional, but it may obscure the changing components of that allegiance since the New Deal. David G. Dalin presents the intellectual biography of Will Herberg, who moved from radical politics to Neo-Orthodox crisis theology after World War II, as a case history in the evolution of Jewish ideological commitment. Nathan Glazer and Jerold S. Auerbach both examine the possibility that passage to an era where support of the State of Israel is no longer unquestionably part of the liberal agenda may mark another crossroads in American Jewish political sentiments— or it may not.

The propensity of twentieth-century American Jews to universalistic liberalism is so exceptional as to be a Jewish particularism. Conversely, growing American Jewish support for Zionist particularism took the form of an almost exaggerated universalism. Melvin I. Urofsky, Arthur A. Goren, and David Ellenson note that American Zionists defended their cause overwhelmingly in religious terms. Goren concludes that the political assumptions of classical Zionism—that a Jewish homeland was urgently needed as a refuge and shelter—applied to all Jewish diasporas except the American; Zionism's function for American Jews was to be a bulwark against assimilation and a cultural inspiration for this diaspora threatened with loss of its soul. Ellenson shows that during a crucial decade (the forties), Orthodox, Conservative, and Reform rabbis all defined Zionism as thoroughly compatible with the symbols and values of Protestantism and Americanism. Urofsky observes that the success of Zionism in winning support in America was directly related to the successful Americanization of Zionism itself.

The next part of this book deals with the adaptation of Jewish religious life to the American environment. The history of the American synagogue is the story of the by-and-large successful transformation of this key Jewish institution according to American religious patterns. Jonathan D. Sarna analyzes the evolution of synagogue life as it changed from century to century. Jeffrey S. Gurock describes a failed attempt to create a model synagogue for the children of turn-of-the-century Lower East Side immigrants; his case history reveals the deep-seated rivalry between Reform and the other branches of American Judaism, just as Ellenson's study of rabbinical defenders of Zionism indicates the commonalities shared by the branches three decades later. Jenna Weissman Joselit describes the process by which the Jewish food practices were Americanized: even something as seemingly particularistic and intractable to the American ethos as *kashrut* became a fountain of New World Jewish sentiment and an expression of an emerging American Jewish middle-class aesthetic.

The three essays on the women's movement in American Jewry hearken back to the impact of liberalism on Judaism (inasmuch as feminism is a manifestation at present of liberal egalitarianism) and to the changes that America has stimulated in the workings of the synagogue. Ellen M. Umansky traces growing sensitivity to equal status of women in Reform Judaism; Paula E. Hyman chronicles a key group in the 1970s that put feminist issues high on the Jewish agenda; Judith Hauptman analyzes Conservative feminism as it has led this branch of Judaism to confront the problematics of Jewish continuity in new ways.

Feminism seeks to spur the development of new forms of Jewish spirituality in the non-Orthodox denominations. Orthodoxy has its own forms of modern spirituality, and the various traditionalist movements often called "fundamentalist" constitute an assertive reaction to what are perceived as dangerous accommodations to modernity. Samuel C. Heilman uses the concept of "contra-acculturation" and the method of ethnographic narration to illustrate the rejection of secular American culture among traditionalist Jews who have learned to exploit mass media techniques to heighten their self-awareness and morale. In recent decades attempts have been made, especially through the formation of intimate groups for worship, study, and Jewish celebration *(havurot)*, to counteract the banalization of faith and community. Mel Scult shows that Mordecai M. Kaplan grappled early in his career with the weakening of communal bonds. Kaplan admired Americanism as a civic ideology, yet he viewed the Roman Catholic Church (*not* American Protestantism) as a model of group discipline and social cohesion for Jews. Edward K. Kaplan describes Abraham Heschel's quite different way of presenting twentieth-century European Jewish spirituality and of invigorating it with the American social conscience. Kaplan and Heschel are antipodes of American Jewish theology in the mid-twentieth century. Kaplan's ideology of Reconstructionism, noted for its didactic lucidity, scientism, and sociology, has been called the informal content of much of American Judaism and, on an overt level, has garnered an enthusiastic if circumscribed following. Heschel's poetical, rhetorical, and suggestive style has been an influential model among the Jewish religious leadership in the post-Holocaust age for regaining a sense of the sacred. America admires science but is susceptible to nostalgia, the evocative, and the prophetic.

Where then is American Jewry headed? The last group of essays offers contrasting commentaries on the Jewish future by four sociologists and a historian of American Judaism. According to Paul Ritterband, the scattering of the Jews and other hard factors may make massive assimilation inevitable. Yet, Steven M. Cohen points out, there is a consensus that results in continued affiliation among the moderately affiliated. Egon Mayer examines options available to an American Jewish leadership willing to revise its agenda in light of the changed composition of the community. Despite various recent departures, American Jewry just might be pushed back into a direction more recognizably Jewish, according to Charles S. Liebman, and Arnold Eisen points to new religious tendencies that constitute signals of hope for the future.

These studies show that the adaptation of Jewry to America represents a more nuanced phenomenon than was thought to be the case a generation ago. One of the most quickly Americanized of immigrant groups, American Jewry has grown deep roots in America and has cultivated a wider range of forms than any other diaspora, so that an objective evaluation of its achievements and of its probable future is difficult.

In recent years the dominant attitude, especially in the American Jewish leadership, is a compound of pride and disquietude. This paradoxical mix of self-confidence and anxiety may reflect a working out of what Reinhold Niebuhr called the "irony of history." "Irony consists of apparently fortuitous incongruities in life which are discovered, upon closer examination, to be not merely fortuitous" (Reinhold Niebuhr, *The Irony of American History* [New York: Scribner's, 1962], viii). Historical ironies flow from hidden limitations or defects at the heart of significant achievements that are rightful objects of pride. Exposure of illusions lurking in these successes can result in cynical fatalism but also, perhaps, to a better-focused sense of responsibility and, therefore, a more realistic idealism.

It is ironical that the Jewish accomplishments in America have contributed to a malaise about the future because success is often evaluated according to standards that obscure what has actually been attained. The American Jewish experience has indeed been different from any other. In America being a Jew is respected, and American Jews have been remarkably free to decide what of their heritage to conserve, reform, and reconstruct. For some, Judaism has elicited depths of personal and social involvement and a degree of commitment that is all the more intense for being freely chosen. Although continuing to measure itself by the burden of the past, religious and ethnic, American Jewry has responded to the openness of its options in a series of unparalleled achievements and by assuming a leadership in world Jewry the burden of which it seldom fully acknowledges to itself.

The era when Jewish survival could be galvanized by ideological certitude is over: most Jews only take seriously an idealism that does not promise panaceas and a messianic age here and now. Innocent optimism that centuries-old tensions (Jewish exile and alienhood in the Diaspora) have reached a final resolution runs up against the endless process of adapting to an America always in a state of flux. Communal self-isolation is surely not an option for the overwhelming majority of American Jews; they are firmly enthralled by American individualism and secularity. America may become more sharply subdivided into ethnic and linguistic entities if the ideology and reality of cultural diversity makes headway, but most Jews possess only symbolic remnants of Jewish ethnicity, meaningful as these may be. There is evidence in American Jewish history, however, of being able to cope quite well by drawing on resources and abilities honed by the diaspora environment.

In the absence of a seamless ideology of modern Jewishness, American Jews will have to become more comfortable with their particular dualities (duality of one kind or another being inherent in every pluralistic situation). There will always be immensely more Christians in America than Muslims, Buddhists, or Jews; Jews will have to find new ways to define themselves in juxtaposition to immersion in a consumer society on the one hand and to the non-Jewish faiths on the other hand. Whether being Jewish will continue to be of the highest priority may depend not on only one form of American Judaism but on the vitality of the religious continuum as a whole to demonstrate in everyday reality the historic, cosmic, and intimate significance of Judaism and in so doing to offer guidance to world Jewry.

The forces working to sustain American Jewry are all the stronger for the voluntarism and pluralism of American religion and the unique American combination of particularism and universalism. Of course, voluntarism can lead to assimilation or trivialization, and pluralism to fragmentation and internecine rivalry. But American Jewry has not just been acted upon; it has also acted in this milieu, at times quite effectively. Judaism has redefined itself according to the ideals of America and has helped shape those ideals in ways that have benefited itself and other groups. Could it be that the forthcoming test of American Jewry to confront its predicament can further demonstrate that the Jewish situation is paradigmatic of human beings as appropriators of identities that, because they transcend modernity, may prove to be its essence?

PART ONE

Imagining America

CHAPTER 2

The View from the Old World:
German-Jewish Perspectives

Steven M. Lowenstein

The topic of German-Jewish perceptions of America is a subject about which little that is specific has been written. Much greater interest has been shown in immigration from Germany, the Americanization of the immigrants once they arrived, and, to a lesser extent, the attitudes of American Jews of German background toward their former homeland. The attitude toward America of those Jews who remained behind, however, has received relatively little scholarly attention.

Much of the material for this essay, especially that concerning the nineteenth century, comes from the Jewish newspapers printed in Germany. Although these documents tell us what information was available to German-Jewish readers, they do not, strictly speaking, all come from European sources. Much of this material was written by Jews living in America to the editors in Germany, who then decided that it was worth publishing.[1] Although some individuals expressed idiosyncratic opinions, many of the sentiments are repeated over and over again, so that we can speak of them with some confidence as German-Jewish perceptions.

Still, the documentation on German-Jewish attitudes is relatively sparse, scattered, and hard to find. This raises the question of how much German Jews knew or cared to know about America. Although our American perspective would lead us to see America as a central focus in world history, it would seem that Jews in Germany did not necessarily see it that way. The great nineteenth-century histories of the Jews written in Germany by Jost and Graetz give American Jewry only very limited space and see America as rather peripheral.[2] In certain German-Jewish journals it was difficult to find many references to America, and even in those that refer to America quite frequently, such as the *Allgemeine Zeitung des Judentums*, these references are far fewer than those to Jews in European countries. In fact, American stories are seen as exotic and in the same category as stories about Jews in Argentina, North Africa, or New Zealand.

The degree of interest in America seems to have fluctuated considerably. In times of trouble for German Jews, it suddenly flourished; in times when they were satisfied with conditions in their own country, it decreased. Sometimes their reports on America were really intended to be commentaries on conditions in Europe.[3]

Interest in America was not unique to German Jews. Indeed, many of the images found in the writings of German Jews repeat themselves in those of Eastern European Jews and of non-Jews as well. The extent to which there is anything distinctive in the German-Jewish views is a question worth exploring. There seems to be a kind of generic myth of America that suited the needs of Europeans seeking either political liberty or economic opportunity. This generic myth helps explain why America was sought after as a land of immigration by so many waves of Europeans.

Nevertheless, despite their sharing in so much of the same picture of America as others, two factors, at least, might be said to be distinctive in the attitudes of German Jews. One is the peculiar position of German Jews. On the one hand, to a far greater degree than Eastern European Jews were affected by the culture of their neighbors, German Jews were affected by German cultural attitudes, quoting and being influenced by statements of German Christians. On the other hand, their position as Jews made them different from the majority of Germans, so that they could not share in the frequently anti-Jewish and anticommercial writings of Germans and German Americans about America.[4]

The other, related factor is the special political spectrum within German Jewry throughout much of its modern history. Because classical liberal ideas tended to predominate in German Jewry throughout much of the nineteenth century, German Jews may have had a more positive view of America than did either Eastern European Jews, affected by socialism with its implied criticism of capitalist America, or conservative Germans, who disapproved of the freewheeling liberal, capitalist, and tradition-breaking America.[5]

The liberal philosophy of equality before the law, freedom of opportunity, and separation of church and state, which most Europeans saw as exemplified by America, thus seems to have had fewer opponents among German Jewry than among Eastern European Jews. It could therefore be projected as a cure for the Jewish situation more easily in Germany than in Eastern Europe, where it had to compete with Zionism, which placed the solution in a totally different geographical setting, and Jewish socialism, which saw the solution in changing the situation at home. Although approximately the same proportion of Eastern European Jews left their homes for America as did German Jews,[6] the former were less likely to make an ideology of coming to America than were the latter.

The image of America as a solution to the problems of Europe was a powerful one in German culture as well as more specifically among German Jews. The most famous statement of this attitude, quoted frequently by both Christian and Jewish German writers, is Goethe's famous poem first published in 1831:[7]

America you have it better
Than our old continent.
You have no ruined castles
And no basalt ones.

. . . .
You are not disturbed from within
by useless memories
and wasted disputes.

This poem projected the image of an America free from both European feudalism and the weight of the past. America would combine freedom for the individual and unlimited possibilities for the future. Another aspect of the relationship of Germany to America expressed in this poem and repeated later was the juxtaposition of America and Europe, with the freedom of America being used as a veiled or open criticism of European conditions.

The comparison between freedom in America and lack of freedom in Germany is a frequent motif in German-Jewish writings on America. Whenever the position of the Jews of Germany deteriorated or the limitation on their rights seemed to be intolerable, the vision of freedom in America appeared on the horizon.

The first famous expression of this connection occurred in 1822 at the time of Mordecai Noah's famous and abortive founding of the Ararat Jewish colony near Buffalo. This event seems to have impressed some German-Jewish intellectuals, most notably the small coterie of the founders of *Wissenschaft des Judentums* in Berlin (including Leopold Zunz, Eduard Gans, and Heinrich Heine). At a time when the Prussian government was putting limits on the promised access of Jews to academic posts, the Society for Culture and Science of Judaism wrote a letter to Noah from Berlin. The society wished to explore the possibility of mass emigration. Their enthusiasm for the new opportunities in America was intimately linked to their disappointments in the Old World. They spoke of Noah's call as "animating the abject spirits of members of an abject nation, by summoning them from an ungrateful and unjust country, to that part of the globe which they style the *new*, but would yet with greater reason, name the *better*." They expressed the desire to "exchange the miseries of their native soil for public freedom," which America "granted to every religion."[8] The plans implied in the letter never came to fruition and later Heine engaged in ironic comments at the expense of the project, speaking of the day when "a happier generation will bless the lulav and chew matzes on the banks of the Mississippi."[9] Nevertheless, the hopeful tone of the 1822 letter would be repeated in many later statements.

A second, and much more influential, ideological call for migration to America came during the Revolution of 1848 from the pen of the Bohemian Jewish writer Leopold Kompert. When the revolution was accompanied by anti-Jewish riots, Kompert, in his famous articles entitled "Auf und nach Amerika" (Up and to America), called for the organizing of mass emigration. Quoting the Bible, Kompert compared those held back in the fatherland to the Israelites attracted by the fleshpots of Egypt. He despaired of the Old World: "For us no help has come. Seek it out in far-off America." He also argued against those who counseled waiting for the triumph of liberalism in Europe: "Ten thousand people who gain freedom for themselves immediately through their departure to America are a greater gain for us than if hundreds of thousands eat their hearts out for long years to come, in yearning and tribulation, helpless or gnashing their teeth." For Kompert, emigration means "to become free at once, without any delay, without parliamentary pros and cons, without sympathies and antipathies, right there and then on the spot as soon as the ship drops its anchor."[10]

The link between emigration and criticism of the situation in Europe becomes even clearer when we read the response to Kompert by David Mendl, who called upon Jews to remain and aid the revolution in bringing liberalism to triumph in Europe. Mendl combined criticism of America with hope for Europe. "Where slavery is tolerated as a right, there is no guarantee for the equality-rights of the free. . . . Here, however, the conditions are better; old prejudices are disappearing, law and justice are unfurling their banners in the land; the spirit is free of every fetter and will forcibly smash all other oppressive bonds to smithereens. The Jew also will be given back his human dignity."[11]

Many other examples of the link between conditions in Europe and America are found in the pages of the Jewish press. Some come from the pens of famous emigrants like Max Lilienthal, former head of modern schools in Russia, later rabbi in New York and Cincinnati. Others come from German-speaking Jews with no intention of leaving, who use the American situation as a weapon to attack conditions in their native land. (It should be remarked that Kompert himself, like the earlier *Wissenschaft* circle, never left Europe.)

Lilienthal's first report from New York, written in November 1845, is a paean to the new land. It opens with a flourish: "My greetings as a brother and friend from New York, from the God-blessed land of freedom, from the beautiful soil of civic equality. Old Europe with its restrictions lies behind me like a dream."[12] The editor of the leading Jewish newspaper in Germany, Ludwig Philippson, who had no intention of leaving, wrote several pieces using emigration as a criticism of the limitations on German-Jewish rights. One interesting piece of this type deals with the case of Schulm Moses.[13] In an article entitled "The Departure of Schulm Moses from Germany," Philippson describes how Schulm Moses must leave the country because his birth had never been properly registered. He writes, "Be thankful! You became famous and got to America for free, and all this because you were a German Jew without a birth certificate—you are to be envied!" Much of the article is a condemnation of Germany and its unfair laws that cause it to expel its own people. It ends, "I have cried enough in you, therefore I will not cry over you. . . . I want to forget you like you forgot me. You have your work . . . till you become a land where they don't ask about religion, estate, place of birth and birth certificate. . . . Just as I am going to a land where they don't ask anything more than 'are you a human being?' "[14]

Fifteen years later, when the position of Jews in Germany had improved greatly, Philippson linked conditions in Germany and emigration, in a totally different way. In 1860 he condemned calls for mass emigration, saying that the improvement in the political situation of German Jews that had taken place would have been impossible if they had emigrated. "No, the destiny of our race seems to be a different one. It should collaborate with countries and nations, so that freedom of religion and humaneness may win."[15]

Still another use of the stereotyped vision of America as a land of freedom was made without either condemnation or support of emigration. In 1845 Ignaz Schulhoff, speaking of the lack of freedom of Bohemian Jews, asks, "Should all those who feel their chains, pack up and move to the land of the unlimited spirit?" He suggests a third alternative to emigration or staying behind, namely, "Whoever feels the need for freedom, let them free themselves and found their America in themselves."[16]

The image of America as a land of freedom and an example of the shortcomings of Europe was often challenged by some of the factual reports coming out of the United States. The news that America, too, had its share of anti-Jewish feeling and narrow-minded religionists came as a shock to Europeans. Both the frequent reporting of such incidents in the German-Jewish press and the frequent prefacing of the reports with the comment that "even in America" such things could happen show how much emotional capital was expended on seeing America as the land of freedom for the Jews.[17] Almost every anti-Jewish incident in mid-nineteenth-century America that one finds in the standard histories of American Jewry is also reported at length in the *Allgemeine Zeitung des Judentums*.[18] The question of whether America was free of blots on its freedom seemed quite important to the editors of the German-Jewish newspapers and received conflicting interpretations from their correspondents in America.

Besides pointing to anti-Jewish feelings in America, some German-Jewish observers described other blemishes on America's freedom—not only slavery but also the extermination of the American Indian.[19] German Jews, and Europeans in general, were also interested in other aspects of the American experiment and its travails. Philippson wrote that the freeing of the slaves in America and of the serfs in Russia were the most important events in the nineteenth century.[20]

The issue of American freedom and its possible application to Germany were not the only ingredients in the picture German Jews had of America. Two other very important aspects of life were also of great interest to them and were reported upon frequently—economic life and the future of Jewish religious and cultural life.

The search for better economic conditions was one of the chief reasons for the German-Jewish emigration to America in the nineteenth century. The freewheeling economic life of America was therefore of great interest to those who remained behind and were perhaps themselves considering emigration. Reports in the press stressed both the great opportunities in the new land and the pitfalls for those expecting an easy time. Some spoke of the possibility of starting a new life for all, since the human soul was "so elastic." Other reports, however, warned in so many words that the streets of New York were not paved with gold, and that desire and ability were needed to succeed in America. For those who did not want to try anything new, one article warned, "If you think like that, stay in Germany patiently and sit with your beer stein. If you come, don't think you are too good to work."[21]

There were frequent warnings against "unsuitable people" emigrating, whether they were young people running away from stepparents or "half idiots." Most frequent of all was the warning against potential teachers and religious leaders who did not speak

English.[22] These warnings against underestimating the economic difficulties in America became much more urgent in years of economic slowdown.[23]

The reports on economic life shade over into consideration of the effects of economic activity on the world of the spirit. A frequent judgment on the American character found in German-Jewish reports as in many other European images was that Americans were both practical minded and materialistic. The fact that Americans seemed so busy trying to make a living and pursuing material success led some observers to fear that they might lose interest in the higher things of life. Some felt that this explained why American Jews seemed interested neither in intellectual pursuits nor in religious matters. One observer in the 1850s said that American Jews preferred to drink beer and play cards rather than attend lectures.[24] The view of Americans as practical rather than theoretical was given as an explanation for other American shortcomings. Since Americans were interested "more in the concrete institution than the idea behind it," American-Jewish religious institutions were said to be ideologically inconsistent.[25] The view of Americans and American Jews as anti-intellectual seems to have been widely held.

The supposed materialism, practicality, and restless activity of America were among the reasons why European observers often worried about the viability of Jewish religion in America. Although I could find no explicit reference in German-Jewish sources to America as a "*trefe* land," as is said to be a common motif in Eastern European images of America, there were certainly plenty of fears about the future of Judaism in the United States.[26]

Writers in the German-Jewish press gave several additional grounds for their fears for the Jewishness of the emigrants to America. One factor was the scattering of Jews to isolated settlements—a fact that induced the editor of the *Allgemeine Zeitung* to write a lead article expressing fear that they would not even be able to circumcise their sons.[27] Many described a falling off of traditional religious practice, although they did not all agree that this was a sign of decline. In what would later be a familiar criticism, a correspondent in 1864 wrote that the building of beautiful synagogue edifices couldn't cure the "cancer" of indifference he saw exemplified by the lack of attendance at Saturday services.[28]

Another aspect of America unfamiliar to German Jews was the total voluntarism of American religious life. German law had required all Jews in a town to belong to a single community. This community controlled all religious institutions in the locality. In America, on the other hand, there was a multiplicity of totally independent congregations with no centralizing force. European observers felt that this voluntarism and independence would lead to splintering of the community—a splintering that they saw as aided and abetted by the vanity and pursuit of honor by organizational leaders, each of whom wanted to be independent of all the others.[29]

Although some German Jews feared that American Jews, lacking a central authority, possessing few intellectual interests, and being immersed in the business world, might lose their religion, others were more confident. They spoke of the United States as a country in which the religious spirit was very strong. This would help preserve Judaism in America. Still others, however, feared this very power of religion as the source of a potential Christianization of the country and a restriction of Jewish rights. Articles told of the danger of the Sunday Blue Laws and even made uncomplimentary comparisons between the prayer styles of some evangelical Christians and that of the Hasidim.[30]

Implied in the tone of some of the reports in the press and sometimes stated quite explicitly is a view of America as the land of quackery and "humbug" (the latter word used untranslated in German texts). German-Jewish readers were told to take American newspaper reports (especially about numbers) with a grain of salt.[31]

This negative tone about American fakery is especially noticeable in reports in Philippson's newspaper about the activities of the American Reform leader Isaac Meyer Wise. Philippson frequently complained about the lack of gratitude of Jewish leaders who went off to America and never stayed in touch with their benefactors. He was disturbed by their lack of interest in and support for any German institution or cause. Instead they tried to estrange their fellow American Jews from Germany. Wise was singled out for criticism. The *Allgemeine Zeitung* accused Wise of plagiarism from Jewish newspapers in Germany, of fanning agitation against German Jewry, and of trying to make himself the autocrat of American

Jewry.[32] Correspondents even used the ultimate insult by referring to Wise as "this Polish or Hungarian Jew."[33]

Wise replied to his European critics in kind, saying that German Jews were half-hearted and hypocritical in their reforms. He said that all Europe was dead and going the way of fossilized China, and that Judaism in Europe was way behind Judaism in America. Finally he remarked, "What they say about us on the other side of the ocean is of no interest to us since they don't understand our circumstances."[34]

Some of the conflict between Philippson and Wise came about because Jews in Germany and Jews in America had opposite interests when it came to the process of Americanization. In America it seemed to many that the only means for Judaism to continue in the next generation was for it to be English in language and American in attitude and values. For those who shared such views, it was important for American Jews to cease to be dependent on Europe and to produce their own leaders and ideologies. For the Jews who remained in Germany (and for some in America as well),[35] the issue was seen differently. Many German Jews took pride in the fact that their coreligionists were bearers of German culture and language in America and (through Yiddish) in Eastern Europe as well. They certainly wanted to see American Jewry flourish, but they thought that without the intellectual power of the German language and German ideology, the Americans would be without an anchor. They could not understand why American Jews wished to cut off their ties with their origins. Similar sentiments were expressed by German Christians about their countrymen who had emigrated to America.

Despite the mutual recriminations of some leaders, however, there were several reasons for Jews in Germany and America to be interested in each other during the second and third quarters of the nineteenth century. During most of this time the two groups still shared the German language as a link. Secondly, they shared close family ties. A large proportion of German Jews must have had at least some close relatives in America. The continued bond between American and German Jews was also demonstrated by the fact that American congregations continued to seek German rabbis and cantors and to advertise for them in Jewish newspapers in Germany well into the 1870s at least.[36]

Close personal ties notwithstanding, the German-Jewish press at times promoted the image of America as an exotic land, offering readers stories of strange or humorous events taking place there. One tells of an American Christian converting to Judaism to marry a Jewish woman who cried out during his circumcision, "Oh Jesus Christ you killed me." In another story, an American Jewish newspaper suggested Jewish "reverends" strike for higher pay.[37] Most common of all—and this too may tell us much about the perception of American Jewry in Europe—are stories about the building of institutions and the raising of money.[38]

Between the end of the mass German-Jewish immigration to the United States in the latter part of the nineteenth century and Hitler's rise to power, America played a smaller part in the consciousness of German Jews. Most German Jews were quite satisfied to remain where they were and had no intentions of going to America. With the passing of generations, the relatives in America were no longer so closely related and probably no longer knew German. Besides, both German Jewry and American Jewry changed greatly during the period. German Jews were now financially better off, less religiously observant, more conversant with German high culture, and, at least according to the law books, equal citizens of Germany. American Jewry was transformed by the huge Eastern European wave of immigration beginning in the 1880s, which made Jews of German origin a small minority in American Jewry.

Perhaps equally influential in changing attitudes was the fact that the relationship between America and Europe in general changed, especially in the years after World War I. America was now a major world power, and influence was more likely to come from west to east than in the opposite direction. The Americanization of Germany through modern, efficient business methods, advertising, new forms of art and music (jazz, for instance), and a general speedup in the pace of life was a frequent theme during the Weimar Republic. Much of the comment about these trends was negative, especially at the right and left fringes of the German cultural scene.[39] On occasion such disparaging views of America were even to be found in the German-Jewish press during the Weimar period, though less pervasively than among non-Jews.[40]

By the 1920s communications between the New and Old worlds had improved considerably. The German-Jewish press of the 1920s seems to have been better informed about American Jewry than it had been half a century earlier. Nevertheless, America was still a rather peripheral interest for the German-Jewish newspapers, and reports sometimes still contained serious misunderstandings. Mainstream Jewish liberal newspapers like the *C.V. Zeitung* tended to show less interest in and to be more critical of American Jewry than the Zionist *Jüdische Rundschau*. One cause for the relatively better understanding the Zionists had of American Jewry may have been that the Zionists were more oriented toward international Jewish ties and worked together with American Zionists (who were gaining great influence in the movement). The mainstream liberals, on the other hand, were oriented mainly toward Germany and issues directly affecting Jews there (especially antisemitism).[41] Neither group really considered American Jewry central to its concerns.

The Nazis' rise to power brought America back to the center stage of German-Jewish interest, but very slowly. In the first years of Nazi rule, most of the emigrants from Germany went to nearby countries from which they could return if Hitler fell. Only in the late 1930s did overseas emigration, especially to America, encompass the bulk of those leaving Germany. By then, according to an unconfirmed story, the item most frequently borrowed from the library by German Jews was the Manhattan telephone book (as an aid to finding relatives who might sponsor them).

In some ways the German Jews were unusually well prepared for their emigration. Not only had most read books and seen films with American themes but also the Jewish organizations published guides with detailed information on the proposed lands of immigration, including information on prices, wages, institutions, and general mores.[42] Yet the "preparation" the immigrants had received before coming to America was rarely helpful in making adjustment to the new land easier. As one writer wrote, they were "exceptionally well prepared and profoundly unequipped for life in America."[43]

We can get a fairly good idea of the image of America that

German Jews had while still in Germany by looking at their comments about what surprised them when they arrived in the United
States. Quite a few refugees admitted that they had derived false
impressions based on the movies or on writers like Upton Sinclair
(or, on a more vulgar level, the cowboy stories of Karl May). They
had expected to see Indians in full headdress and Chicago gangsters
everywhere, and had thought that all of America looked like lower
Manhattan. They had expected everything in America to be
ultramodern.

Others of their expectations sound very much like those of the
nineteenth century. They expected America to be driven by rugged
individualism, and they were impressed by the sense of freedom
here. A recurring theme is the relative lack of rigid social distinctions. Quite a few also remarked on the differences in family structure, with American families being less patriarchal and children
having much more freedom. Quite a few also repeated long-held
ideas about America being lacking in high culture, especially in
music and the visual arts. The view of Americans as practical rather
than theoretical minded was also similar to earlier beliefs about
America, as was the image of America as a country obsessed with
money. Related to this were frequent comments that American
friendliness and indeed America as a whole were often superficial.[44]

Many of these views did not have any specifically Jewish content. The more traditionally Jewish among the refugees had special
perceptions of their own. Like their nineteenth-century predecessors, they were surprised and disoriented at the lack of a compulsory
and centralized communal system.[45] Perhaps unlike their predecessors, they were impressed by what some of them referred to as the
"pulsating Jewish life" of America.[46] It took some adjustment before
they got accustomed to the broad social functions of American
congregations.

Just as in the previous century, refugees expecting America to
be a land of opportunity expressed shock at finding antisemitism
widespread in America. They were also unfavorably surprised by
the color line against Blacks and the rigid ethnic separation they
found in American social life.

The refugees of the 1930s were anything but a uniform group.
The most famous immigrants of the period—the intellectuals who

have received the most attention in print—were atypical in many ways. Although most of them, like other immigrants of the 1930s, expressed admiration for America, or at least paid lip service to such admiration, a group among them, especially as chronicled in Anthony Heilbut's *Exiled in Paradise*, was extremely critical. The most critical were radical sociologists and literary figures like Max Horkheimer, Theodor Adorno, Bertolt Brecht,[47] and Ludwig Marcuse. For the radicals, the image of America was that of a bastion of capitalism and imperialism built on economic exploitation. Its racism was exemplified by the Ku Klux Klan and its lynchings. Its religion was narrow minded and bigoted and far too pervasive. As for popular American culture, radical intellectuals saw its jazz as protofascist and its sentimental melodramas as antiprogressive.[48]

Although it is certainly true that some German refugee intellectuals held such views of America, the vast majority of German Jews expressed a very positive attitude toward America,[49] but with an element of reserve not usually expressed by other immigrants. This was because, unlike most immigrants, they had led middle-class lives in the Old Country and had had to accept a loss of status upon immigration. They were therefore less impressed by the material plenty of America than were earlier immigrants. Since many had received advanced educations in Germany, they also continued to respect the European intellectual tradition. Often in their comparisons between Europe and America they found much about Europe that they missed. Because of this nostalgia for what they had once been and had once had, the refugees were sometimes derisively known as "*bei unsers*" who always said "*bei uns*" ("back home"). The reputation of German Jews as arrogant was also due in part to the fact that they sometimes compared aspects of the Old Country favorably with America and thus did not seem properly grateful to the country that took them in.

In terms of images of America held by German Jews, we can see that some were fairly accurate and others were less so. For those German Jews who eventually came to the United States, the discrepancy between image and reality could cause difficulty. One scholar's description of this relationship could apply equally well to the nineteenth as to the twentieth century: "The individual struggle for adjustment overseas was different from the collective day-dreams which had provided the original impulse to emigrate."[50]

Jews in Germany—both those who eventually emigrated and those who did not—displayed interest in the American situation. America served as a model for many of those who desired a liberal and democratic Germany. It provided a haven for those who could no longer bear life in the Old Country. By the late nineteenth century, emigrants from Germany were showing their financial generosity to institutions in their former homeland. But in most things, especially intellectual and cultural, the influence was in the other direction. Though Jews in Germany might be interested in events in America, they were little influenced by them. American Jews hired rabbis from Germany and looked there for intellectual models, especially in the Reform movement. German Jews, on the other hand, did not look for leaders or platforms in America.[51] Even in the twentieth century, when American Jewish leaders did begin to make an impact on the world scene, the influence frequently continued to be from east to west. The impact of the immigration of the German-Jewish intellectuals of the 1930s on American intellectual life is a case in point. Only since World War II, with the destruction of the German and Eastern European Jewish centers, has the direction of influence been reversed.

Notes

1. Another source for knowledge about attitudes of German Jews toward America is the memoirs of immigrants to America who speak of their first impressions of the New Country and thereby reveal, at least in part, their expectations before coming. Unfortunately, most of the printed memoirs in Jacob Marcus's collection (*Memoirs of American Jews, 1775–1865*, 3 vols. [Philadelphia: Jewish Publications Society, 1955–1956]) contain only relatively short and sketchy mentions of the author's life in Europe or of first impressions upon arrival in America. Therefore, this article relies mainly on newspaper reports in the German-Jewish press.

2. Isaak Markus Jost, *Neuere Geschichte der Israeliten (in der ersten Hälfte des XIX. Jahrhunderts)* (Breslau: Wilhelm Jacobsohn, 1846–47). Heinrich Graetz, *Geschichte der Juden von den ältesten Zeiten bis auf*

die Gegenwart, 2d ed., Markus Brann, ed. (Leipzig: Oscar Leine, 1900), vol. 11 (which deals with the period 1750–1848) seems to contain only two short references to American Jewry. The first is a short mention of the legal status of American Jews as background to the controversy over the British Jew Bill of 1753, which made Jews eligible for naturalization. The second reference, which is somewhat longer (about fifteen lines), deals with the influence of radical German Reform Judaism on America (521).

3. A similar point is made by Lothar Kahn in his article "Early German-Jewish Writers and the Image of America (1820–1840)," *Yearbook of the Leo Baeck Institute* 31 (1986): 407–39, esp. 408.

4. Although this difference between Jews and non-Jewish Germans seems to hold for most German Jews, it is not completely valid for German-Jewish intellectuals. Heinrich Heine, for instance, sometimes indulges in anti-American satire based on a negative image of American commercialism (see Kahn, "Early German-Jewish Writers," 422, 429).

5. For discussion of the frequently negative image of America in German sources, especially in recent years, see Herbert A. Strauss, "The German Image of America as a Problem of Tradition and Prejudice," in Herbert A. Strauss, ed., *Jewish Immigrants of the Nazi Period in the U.S.A.*, vol. 6 (New York: Saur, 1987), 387–400; and Manfred Hennigsen, *Der Fall Amerika: Zur Sozial- und Bewusstseinsgeschichte einer Verdrängung: Das Amerika der Europäer* (Munich: List, 1974).

6. Because approximately ten times more Eastern European Jews came to the United States than German Jews, it is not generally recognized what a large proportion of German Jewry came to America.

The estimated population of Jews in Germany in 1816 (within the 1871 borders but excluding Alsace-Lorraine) was 257,000. If one adds the approximately 120,000 Jews from Bohemia and Moravia and the forty thousand from Alsace and Lorraine, this gives an approximate base population upon which to draw of some four hundred thousand. (By 1871 the number of Jews in Germany, including Alsace-Lorraine but excluding Bohemia and Moravia, had increased to 512,000.)

The four hundred thousand or so Jews in the Central European lands supplied over two hundred thousand immigrants to the United States in the years between 1820 (when the U.S. had about six thousand Jews) and 1880 (when it had about 280,000). Since the emigration was spread out over a long period (though concentrated between 1840 and 1860), it is impossible to say exactly what proportion of German-speaking Jewry emigrated. The order of magnitude seems to be that one Jew from the German-speaking lands emigrated to the United States for every two who remained at home.

This proportion is only marginally smaller than the proportion of East European Jews who emigrated. The approximate Jewish population of Eastern Europe around the middle of the nineteenth century (including the Russian Empire, Rumania, Galicia, and Hungary) was three million, a number that approximately doubled by the end of the nineteenth century. Approximately 2,378,000 Jews came to the United States between 1880 and 1925. This would indicate some two emigrants for every three who remained behind. Most of these approximate figures are based on the *Encyclopedia Judaica* (1973).

7. The poem was part of the series called *Zahme Xenien*. For the text of Goethe's poem in the original see Klaus Wust and Heinz Moos, eds., *Three Hundred Years of German Immigrants in North America, 1683–1983* (Munich, 1983), 55.

8. The full text of the letter by the society is published in Morris U. Schappes, *A Documentary History of the Jews in the United States, 1654–1875* (New York: Citadel, 1952), 159–60. A further discussion of the incident is found in Naomi W. Cohen, *Encounter with Emancipation: The German Jews in the United States, 1830–1914* (Philadelphia: Jewish Publications Society, 1984), 8–9. See also Hanns G. Reissner, "Rebellious Dilemma: The Case Histories of Eduard Gans and Some of His Partisans," *Yearbook of the Leo Baeck Institute* 2 (1957): 179–93.

9. Reissner, "Rebellious Dilemma," 182; Kahn, "Early German-Jewish Writers," 422. The statement ends with an even more negative tone in which the Jews in America recite their stock exchange dealings in pseudobiblical language.

10. The text of Kompert's "Up and to America" articles (in English translation) can be found in Rudolf Glanz, "Source Materials on the History of Jewish Immigration to the United States, 1800–1880," *YIVO Annual of Jewish Social Science* 6 (1952): 97–101 (items 20 and 21).

11. Glanz, ibid., 103–7 (item 23).

12. *Allgemeine Zeitung des Judentums* (hereafter *AZJ*) 10, no. 2. (hereafter 10/2).

13. It is unclear from the article whether Schulm Moses is a fictionalized character meant to symbolize the poor Jewish emigrant without proper papers, or whether Philippson is referring to an actual case.

14. *AZJ* 10/46 (1846).

15. Glanz, "Source Materials," 115 (item 47).

16. *Orient* 6, no. 46. This image of bringing America to Europe was also used by Ludwig Börne. See Kahn, "Early German-Jewish Writers," 412.

17. The prefatory expression of surprise or shock that the United States, too, was far from free of antisemitism and other blots on freedom can be found not only in many nineteenth-century reports but even in the twentieth century. Ismar Elbogen's article on antisemitism in America, published on August 9, 1923, in *C.V. Zeitung* 2/32:257–58, begins "Antisemitismus und Vereinigten Staaten scheinen unvereinbare Begriffe zu sein" ("Antisemitism and United States would seem to be irreconcilable concepts").

18. Among these incidents are the attempt to write an amendment to the United States Constitution declaring Jesus the Lord of America, the restrictions on Jewish rights in the consular treaty with Switzerland, the Sunday closing laws, General Grant's expulsion of all Jews from the military department of Tennessee, and anti-Jewish remarks by General Butler and Senator Sumner (*AZJ* 19/22, 28/13, 28/26, 28/19, 28/30, 29/13, 32/31, 32/53).

19. *AZJ* 19/22. Heine and the Hungarian-Jewish humorist Moritz Gottlieb Saphir (who lived in Germany and wrote in German) both severely criticized America for its acceptance of the institution of slavery (Kahn, "Early German-Jewish Writers," 428–29, 437).

20. *AZJ* 29/19.

21. *AZJ* 10/38, 11/2.

22. *AZJ* 11/2, 32/9.

23. See, for example, the warning by J. Bondi, editor of the *Hebrew Leader*, dated January 24, 1868, urging Jews, especially teachers, cantors, and ritual slaughterers, not to come to America because of the hard times (Panic of 1867), *AZJ* 32/9, 32/10. See also *AZJ* 38/27.

24. *AZJ* 19/21.

25. *AZJ* 28/4.

26. The oft-quoted but not necessarily typical memoirs of Abraham Kohn of Chicago are a particularly extreme example of the view that the fight for economic survival in America would cripple the Jewish tradition in America. In his early years, Kohn often regretted having left Germany to risk the economic hardships and religious compromises of America:

> This then is the vaunted luck of the immigrants from Bavaria! O misguided fools, led astray by avarice and cupidity! You have left your friends and acquaintances, your relatives and your parents, your home and your fatherland, your language and your customs, your faith and your religion—only to sell your wares in the wild places of America. . . . Is this the celebrated freedom of America's soil? Is it liberty of thought and action when, in order to do business in a single state, one has to buy a license for $100? When one must profane the holy Sabbath, observing Sunday instead? In such matters are life and thought more or less confined than in the fatherland. . . . O that I had never seen this land, but had remained in Germany, apprenticed to a humble country craftsman! (Marcus, *Memoirs of American Jews*, 2:5–6)

27. *AZJ* 19/25.

28. *AZJ* 28/9.

29. *AZJ* 38/34.

30. A passage within an article in *AZJ* 28/30 warning of the dangers to Jewish liberty in America from various religious groups states that the "jumping and noise" ("*springen und lärmen*") in Methodist churches was worse than among the Hasidim.

31. The term "humbug" was also used by American Jewish leaders who preferred the German to the American intellectual tradition, most notably David Einhorn. See Michael Meyer, *Response to Modernity: A History of the Reform Movement in Judaism* (New York and Oxford: Oxford University Press, 1988), 248. It is also to be found in *AZJ* 32/51, 38/52, etc.

 The warning about the exaggerations of the American press can be found in *AZJ* 38/16, 271, where it is assumed that the newspaper simply added an extra zero to the number of Jews in New York.

32. *AZJ* 28/28, 29/40.

33. *AZJ* 32/51.

34. *AZJ* 29/40, 32/45.

35. The best example of this attitude among Jews in America was that of Rabbi David Einhorn, who felt that the German language was a necessary vehicle for Reform Judaism in America and that the switch to English meant an irreversible cultural loss. Meyer (*Response to Modernity*, 248) quotes Einhorn's statement that "if you sever from Reform the German spirit or—what amounts to the same thing—the German language, you will have torn it from its native soil and the lovely flower will wilt."

36. A sampling of such advertisements in the *AZJ* (many of them repeated in several issues) are the following:

1855 seeking lecturer for Congregation Shearith Israel in New York (*AZJ* 19/8)

1855 seeking preacher for Temple Association of Philadelphia (*AZJ* 19/10)

1855 seeking assistant preacher for Temple Emanuel, New York (*AZJ* 19/33)

1864 seeking cantor and Torah reader for Temple Emanu El, San Francisco (*AZJ* 28/14)

1864 seeking rabbi for Congregation Anshe Chessed, New York (*AZJ* 28/23)

1864 seeking rabbi for Sinai Congregation, Chicago (*AZJ* 28/51)

1865 seeking rabbi and cantor for Congregation Beth Israel, Portland, Oregon (*AZJ* 29/13)

1865 seeking rabbi for Congregation Shaar Hashomajim, New York (*AZJ* 29/24)

1868 seeking cantor for Congregation Ansche Chessed, New York (*AZJ* 32/2)

1871 seeking cantor for Congregation Bnai Jeshurun, New York (*AZJ* 35/1)

1874 seeking rabbi and cantor for Congregation Anshe Chessed, Cleveland (*AZJ* 38/1)

1874 seeking cantor for Congregation Emanu El, San Francisco (*AZJ* 38/1)

1874   seeking preacher for Congregation Bnai Jeshurun, New York (*AZJ* 38/34)

The founding of Hebrew Union College in 1875 may partially explain why the importation of German-trained rabbis and cantors came to an end. By the 1880s advertisements for positions in America virtually disappeared from the *Allgemeine Zeitung des Judentums*.

37. *AZJ* 10/20, 335; 28/19.

38. Some of the many stories on building institutions or raising money in American Jewish communities reported in the *AZJ* are found in the following issues: 19/17, 19/28, 19/31, 28/8, 28/19, 28/53, 32/4, 32/24, 32/36, 32/39, 32/49, 32/50, 38/4, 38/12, 38/21.

39. A good example of a very negative view of American culture and life in Weimar Germany is Adolf Halfeld, *Amerika und der Amerikanismus: Kritische Betrachtungen eines Deutschen und Europäers* (Jena: Diederichs, 1927).

40. The *C.V. Zeitung*, for instance, includes a book review by Dr. Margarete Wiener of an autobiography of an American Jew (1926) that speaks of the failings of American culture. It uses standard anti-American language about *Amerikanische Ungeist* and speaks of the choice between "hypocritical religion and Prohibition on the one hand, and the raw vulgarity of the street and baseball mania on the other" (*C.V. Zeitung* 5:247–48). Another anti-American article is a humorous feuilleton called "Wie würde Amerika das machen?" (*C.V. Zeitung* 4/18 [March 1, 1925]) that describes in exaggerated fashion the lengths to which an American businessman would go to advertise his shoes.

41. *Jüdische Rundschau* gave far more space to international affairs in general than did the *C.V. Zeitung*, which was oriented mainly to issues of antisemitism in the early 1920s. Stories on America were rather uncommon in the *C.V. Zeitung* and often took the form of book reviews of American Jewish books, quotes from the American Jewish press, or discussions of American antisemitism (especially the Ku Klux Klan and the writings of Henry Ford). Sometimes they quoted anti-Zionist statements by leaders of American Reform Judaism. Except for a few articles by Ismar Elbogen (August 9, 1923, 1926: vol. 5, no. 51), who had spent time giving lectures in America, the *C.V. Zeitung* rarely carried reports from correspondents with direct knowledge of American Jewry. They often turned to interviews with visiting American Jews to get basic information on American Jewish life. This includes an interview with Dr. Julian Morgenstern, president of Hebrew Union College (July 2, 1926) and even with a visiting American subscriber, Mr. Bernstein of Chicago (August 2, 1923). This latter case especially shows how few sources of information the newspaper had even in the 1920s.

Occasionally the *C.V. Zeitung* showed hostility toward American Jewry, as in its article of July 27, 1922, "Die deutsch jüdische Wissenschaft in Gefahr," which reported with alarm that the Jewish Institute of Religion in New York was planning to hire leading Jewish scholars from America. "The currency-strong Americans had the hope to tear away our leading Jewish scholars from us." An article on Henry Ford's antisemitism on June 14, 1923, calls it "Bluff aus Amerika." See also the stories mentioned in the previous footnote.

By way of contrast, *Jüdische Rundschau* carried frequent short items on American conditions. Especially frequent were reports on Zionist activities in America as well as on the Joint Distribution Committee. Such figures as Louis Lipsky and Stephen Wise were mentioned fairly often.

42. See for instance Hilfsverein der Juden in Deutschland, *Jüdische Auswanderung: Korrespondenzblatt über Auswanderung und Siedlungswesen* (Berlin: Schmoller und Gordon, 1935 and 1936). The 1935 issue was dedicated to a survey of a large number of potential lands of emigration, including the United States (44–48). The 1936 issue was dedicated to South America.

43. Anthony Heilbut, *Exiled in Paradise: German Refugee Artists and Intellectuals in America from the 1930s to the Present* (New York: Viking, 1983), 48.

44. Maurice R. Davie, et al., *Refugees in America: Report of the Committee for the Study of Recent Immigration from Europe* (New York and London: Harper, 1947). See, for example, 48–69, which address the question of what the refugees thought of America.

45. See, for instance, the article in the first volume of *Jüdisches Gemeindeblatt* (November 12, 1938) as well as an article by Bert Lewkowitz in the *Jewish Way* entitled "Verweltlichung—die grosse Gefahr" (November 30, 1941), which refers to the strangeness of the lack of a centralized *kehilla* structure. Similarly the Orthodox bulletin *Moriah* wrote of "two million Jews without a *kehilla*."

46. This is the language used by Rabbi Hugo Stransky in the bulletin of his German immigrant synagogue (*Beth Hillel Bulletin* 143 [September–October 1957]).

47. Although Brecht was, of course, not Jewish, he had many ties to the Jewish refugees.

48. Heilbut, *Exiled in Paradise*, 49, 66, 102, 122–26, 127–28, 163, 166, 178. Adorno spoke of the "idiotic women's serial." Heilbut entitles a chapter dealing with the attitudes of some refugee intellectuals to American mass culture "New Opiates of the People."

49. Although apologetic publications about the refugees tended to exaggerate the degree of their love for America somewhat.

50. Hanns G. Reissner, "Ganstown USA—A German Jewish Dream," *American Jewish Archives* 14, no. 1 (April 1962): 31.

51. Perhaps the only major influence of American Jewry on German Jewry during the nineteenth century was the B'nai B'rith movement, founded

in the United States and introduced into Germany in the 1880s. In the first years of its existence, the German B'nai B'rith suffered from the fact that major decision-making powers remained with the American B'nai B'rith authorities. After some struggle, the German lodges obtained their independence (*Zum 50 jährigen Bestehen des Ordens Bne Briss in Deutschland. U.O.B.B.* [Frankfurt: Kauffmann, 1933], 21–23, 25–26, 31).

CHAPTER 3

The View from the Old World: East European Jewish Perspectives

Jacob Kabakoff

It has long been recognized that the bulk of the East European Jewish immigrants consisted of the masses of Jewish folk, rather than the elite. This immigration, which swelled from the relatively small influx of the late 1860s and 1870s to the gigantic proportions of the years immediately preceding World War I, was unparalleled in Jewish history in the scale and rapidity of resettlement.

It was increasing economic and legal pressures that made America appealing as a haven to the oppressed Jews of Eastern Europe, but there were additional factors as well that affected the decision of the Jewish masses to opt for the New World. To what extent did information about America in the press influence East European Jews? What impact did the discussions of Jewish intellectuals about the respective merits of America and Palestine have upon the public? To what extent did the opposition of the Orthodox rabbinate figure in dissuading Jews from emigrating? While much has been written to illuminate the immigrant experience, answers to these questions must be based on further research into such sources as the press, belles lettres, memoir literature, rabbinic writings, and folklore.[1] These works provide keys to a fuller understanding of the image of America in the eyes of nineteenth-century East European Jewry.

.   .   .

The Hebrew press served as one of the major instruments for shaping the East European Jewish image of America.[2] The influence of such periodicals as *Ha-Maggid*, established in 1956 in the Prussian border town of Lyck, of *Ha-Melitz*, established in 1860 in Odessa, and of *Ha-Zefirah*, established in 1862 in Warsaw, was considerable. The issues of these periodicals were widely read and often passed from hand to hand. Beginning with the 1860s, *Ha-Maggid* especially carried frequent reports concerning the new land.

A whole cadre of correspondents kept European readers informed about conditions in America and the problems of the immigrants. Even those correspondents who advocated emigration did not attempt to gloss over the materialism and laxity of religious observance in the New World. Nor did they mince words about the necessity of being ready for hard labor in order to survive.

The image of America in the Hebrew press is thus an ambivalent one. On the one hand, we find articles extolling the equality and freedom, the technological advances, and the natural wonders of the new land. On the other, there are recurring complaints about a lack of Jewishness and moving accounts of immigrant toil and suffering.

On various occasions, especially when editorial policy favored emigration to Palestine over America, *Ha-Maggid* and *Ha-Melitz* published dire warnings against going to the new land. *Ha-Maggid* characterized the immigrants as "the exiles in America." In its issue of 16 November 1881, for example, it reported that a group of immigrants had participated bareheaded in a Cincinnati synagogue service and declared that "the emigration to America will perhaps bring material benefit to some of the arrivals but they will be lost for Judaism." On another occasion, in the issue of 3 May 1882, a correspondent pleaded, "As a kindness to our oppressed brethren in Russia and for the good of all I beg of you . . . have mercy on the unfortunates and warn them with all your power of persuasion not to leave their native land to come to America."[3]

During the same year, in *Ha-Maggid* on 18 May 1882, Tuviah Pesach Shapiro, who had emigrated to America and after a few months returned to Russia, was critical of what he had found. He reported on the poor economic conditions and indicated that Russian-Polish Jews, except for the skilled, had not done well. He pointed also to the spiritual danger that faced Jews and to the specter of antisemitism. His findings led him to support *aliyah* to Palestine instead.

On 10 September 1886, *Ha-Melitz* published Hillel Malachowsky's impassioned plea from Pittsburgh to his overseas brethren. A *maskil* and Hebrew teacher, he wrote, "Those who consider America to be a Garden of Eden only lie." He cautioned them not to be misled by letters from abroad as he himself had been and urged them to stay home so that they would have no cause for later regrets.

One could continue to give examples of negative reactions in the press, but a number of correspondents chose to adopt a more positive approach. It was not that they were fully satisfied with conditions in the New World. Still, they felt that compared with their countries of origin, America was indeed a blessed land.

Rabbi Bernard Felsenthal of Chicago was one of the early correspondents who, as early as the end of the 1860s, advised Jews through *Ha-Maggid* to emigrate. In a report of 24 June 1868 he stressed that American Jews shared in the equality of their fellow citizens and indicated that anyone who could till the soil or engage in commerce or work hard would be able to support himself or herself. On 12 January 1869 he added that religious functionaries would find it difficult to eke out a living here. He suggested the formation of societies for emigration and urged that immigrants not limit themselves to New York and Philadelphia, but settle beyond the Mississippi River where they could still acquire land.

During the 1870s the question of support for the emigration of Rumanian Jews to America was raised by Leon (Aaron Judah Leib) Horowitz.[4] He had come to America in 1870 and soon became an enthusiastic advocate of settlement here. In his articles in the European Hebrew press he sang the praises of American tolerance and for some time was a regular contributor to the American Hebrew weekly *Ha-Zofeh ba-Aretz ha-Hadashah*. His views clashed, however, with those of Hayyim Zvi Schneurson, emissary of the Jewish community in Palestine, who was supported in his pro-Palestinism by the editor, Zvi Hirsch Bernstein. This difference of opinion regarding America and Palestine can be viewed as a prelude to the heated America-Palestine debate that developed later in Russia.

Horowitz continued his pro-American propaganda and in 1873

published a Hebrew book titled *Rumaniyah va-Amerikah* (Rumania and America), which offered information on American geography and civics to prospective emigrants. The final section presented a practical emigrant's guide to travel and jobs. In his public appearances back in Rumania Horowitz stressed the opportunities of America. Even following his final return to Europe, where he sided with the supporters of *aliyah* to Palestine, Horowitz still pointed to America as an important haven because of its material advantages.

The views of two early pioneers of Hebrew writing in America, Henry (Zvi) Gersoni and James (Yaakov Zvi) Soble, are noteworthy because of their comparatively optimistic outlook. Gersoni, who arrived here in 1869 and became active as a journalist and rabbi, soon began to send his reports to *Ha-Melitz*.[5] In the issues of 22–29 November 1869 he expressed his faith in the new land and stressed that the best prospects for the new immigrants were not in petty business but in labor and agriculture. Later, during the America-Palestine debate, he differed with Alexander Zvi Zederbaum, the editor of *Ha-Melitz*, who supported Palestine. Gersoni asserted that all who came here would eventually do well and that their children would grow up in freedom. He expressed a belief that Russian Jews would eventually assure the future of Judaism in America. In a postscript, Zederbaum based his differences with Gersoni on the fact that the new immigrants had already been forced to abandon their traditions.

Soble, who arrived in America in 1876, became convinced that the salvation of the immigrants lay in agriculture.[6] In 1877 he contributed an article to Peretz Smolenskin's *Ha-Shahar* entitled "Besorah Tovah" (Good Tidings), in which he pointed to the opportunities in farming. Like Gersoni he foresaw even prior to the pogroms that America was destined to become a haven for Russian Jews: "The Jews have come to America not on the basis of the advice of their leaders. Rather, each individual came here on his own because he had his fill with oppression and want while living under the rule of his tyrannical homeland."

Another active correspondent, Judah David Eisenstein, emigrated to this country from Miedzyrecz, Poland, in 1872 at the age of eighteen. In the letters he sent to members of his family at the end of the 1870s he still spoke of his desire to return to his birthplace.[7] He soon abandoned this plan and in his reports in the European Hebrew press expressed his conviction that America would become a haven for persecuted Jewry and a vital center of Jewish life. In his correspondence in *Ha-Zefirah* at the end of the 1870s he spoke favorably of the state of Judaism in the new land. He doubted, however, the success of Jewish agricultural efforts, which he felt were better suited to Palestine or Russia than to the American scene.

Following the Russian pogroms, Eisenstein penned a series of articles in *Ha-Zefirah* entitled "Ha-Yehudim ba-Aretz ha-Hadashah" (The Jews in the New Land) and mentioned that he was responding thereby to many letters of inquiry received from Russia. In the issue of 25 April 1882 he disagreed sharply with the anti-American policy of *Ha-Maggid* and declared that there were some twenty thousand observant Jews here. He played down the danger of antisemitism and asserted that the non-Jews favored immigration. While there were no opportunities for religious functionaries and *maskilim*, laborers and agricultural workers would find a place for themselves. As for trades- and businesspeople, success would depend on luck. In another correspondence, published in *Ha-Melitz* on 12 December 1882, Eisenstein was critical of the Hebrew press for its overwhelming emphasis on Palestine settlement. He upheld American Jewry's role in providing financial support for emigration and protested the emphasis in the press on the difficulties of the immigrants. All in all, his approach reflects a sober, balanced view.

The outbreak of the 1881 pogroms and the flight of refugees to Brody, Galicia, sharpened the debate regarding emigration and the choice of Palestine or America.[8] The Russian Jewish intellectuals argued the pros and cons of the emigration issue in the Russian Jewish press.[9] The periodical *Razsvet*, which had favored Russification, now published articles by such writers as Simon Dubnow and Mark Zamenhof in support of emigration to America. At the same time, Moshe Leib Lilienblum championed in its pages the cause of Palestine, arguing that only there could Jewish national aspirations be fulfilled. By the end of 1881, *Razsvet* supported emigration as part of its editorial policy. Another periodical, *Voskhod*, underwent various changes in policy and could not easily give up its opposition to emigration. Yet it, too, was led to recognize emigration as a fact and eventually supported Palestine *aliyah*.

The Hebrew press served as the battleground for the contesting views of the leading Hebrew writers. David Gordon, editor of *Ha-Maggid*, and Peretz Smolenskin, editor of *Ha-Shaḥar*, marshaled a host of arguments to demonstrate why Palestine was preferable to America. Judah Leib Gordon, however, expressed some doubts regarding the Palestine solution and in his essays and poetry advocated emigration to America.[10] An exponent of Haskalah, he argued that such emigration would not hurt the chances for the amelioration of the Jewish situation in Russia. His stand occasioned a sharp polemic in which both David Gordon and Lilienblum sought to refute his views.

Another Hebrew writer who supported America was Yehudah Leib Levine, known by his acronym Yehalel.[11] He outlined his views on the need for emigration to America and for Jewish territorial concentration there, dwelling on the economic advantages of the new land in a letter addressed to David Gordon in the *Ha-Maggid* issue of 6 October 1881. In his autobiography he wrote that he was attracted to the idea that if sixty thousand Jews were gathered in one place in America, they would be entitled to set up their own state in which they could enjoy their own enlightened form of government. The suggestion to establish a Jewish state in America was then current in various circles. It was voiced by Moses Schrenzel in his brochure *Die Lösung der Judenfrage* (The Solution of the Jewish Problem), published in Lodz in 1881, and also by Saul Pinhas Rabinowitz, who supported this idea in an article in *Ha-Zefirah* in the same year. It was not until the spring of 1882 that Yehalel retreated from his position and adopted the Palestine solution. Rabinowitz was likewise eventually won over to the Palestine cause.

No doubt the enormous economic opportunities of America, coupled with the promise of equality and freedom, led many intellectuals to support emigration there. These factors also gave rise to the establishment of the Am Olam movement, which attracted a diverse membership and adopted an idealistic program based on return to the soil and establishment of agricultural colonies in the

United States.[12] The members of the Vilna Am Olam group even dreamed of the establishment of a Jewish canton in the new land. During 1881–82 groups from various Russian cities and towns set out under the banner of the movement. In many places newly organized societies to promote emigration debated the merits of America and Palestine.

Valuable insight into the reaction of Russian Jewry during the crisis years of 1881–82 can be derived from the extensive memoir literature that reveals the feelings and hopes of the writers. The pages of *Voskhod* in 1889 contain serialized chapters of the diaries of Chaim Chissin, who was seventeen when the 1881 pogroms erupted.[13] He described an identity crisis engendered by the pogroms: until that time he considered himself a devoted son of Russia but then became interested in the Am Olam movement and looked to America. At the age of eighteen, however, he joined a Moscow group of Bilu students that decided to go to Palestine because fellow students Yehiel Tschlenow and Menahem Mendel Ussishkin countered his pro-American arguments and convinced him of the advantages of Palestine.

The memoirs of Abraham Cahan offer a vivid account of how the writer was led to join the ranks of Am Olam.[14] He related that, as a young man, he was swept up by the oppressive events and became convinced of the truth of Socialism. He met several times with Israel Belkind, who was recruiting students for the Bilu movement and then considered leaving Russia for Switzerland. Paradoxically, it was Belkind who steered the young Cahan toward America. Cahan, who joined the Balta group of the Am Olam, described the debates that took place in Brody between the supporters of America and Palestine and among the America-oriented emigrants. Cahan shared the Am Olam idealistic conception of the new land, writing that "they were motivated by a religious enthusiasm." He looked forward to America where he could help establish a Garden of Eden on earth and where people would become like angels: "I imagined a fantastic picture of a communist life in distant America, a land in which no man knew of 'mine' and 'thine,' where all are brothers and all are happy."

In the memoirs of Alexander Harkavy and Israel Isser Kasovich we find additional information on the emigration fever that gripped Russian Jewry. Harkavy told of the opposing America and Palestine factions and recounted how, in 1882, at the age of nineteen, he joined a group of Vilna intellectuals that was interested in farming in the new land. "We imagined to ourselves that we would easily be able to become farmers, especially on American soil, which we presumed a Garden of Eden."[15]

Kasovich also depicted the impact of the events that led to the formation of groups for emigration to America.[16] He related that he had received propaganda material from the Kiev Am Olam group regarding plans to settle overseas, describing the idealism of its members who arrived in Brody on the way to the New World. He recalled reading press reports that Russian Jewish immigrants had become farmers after having been granted land by the government. He wrote, "Our bitter lot in Russia created in me a strong desire to go to America." His memoirs record his disappointment with farming in America, which led him briefly to return home.

Many of the memoirs mention the role of letters from immigrant relatives in America as influencing the East European Jews to undertake the journey. Harris Rubin's memoir testifies to a "burning desire" to go to America that was strengthened by such letters.[17] According to Rubin, who was a Hebrew teacher, at the end of the summer of 1881 his brother-in-law came to his village of Kavarsk, Lithuania, bearing a letter from a relative "who gave a glowing description of the welcome he had received in America." Again, some years later, at the beginning of 1888, a letter came from a Mr. Silberman "who had been in New York for two years. In this letter he extolled the material benefits for Jewish immigrants in America to such an extent that the whole town was talking about it." Despite misgivings about his future religious observance in America, his mother-in-law urged him to go. Since he was leaving before the end of the term, there was a commotion in town. He managed to placate the townspeople by promising to write home about conditions in America so as to be of help to the many who were also thinking of making the journey. George Price, in *The Russian Jews in America* (St. Petersburg, 1893), which consists of articles that appeared originally in *Voskhod*, mentions that he was led to describe the life of the immigrants in their new abode because he had received more than one thousand letters of inquiry from abroad.

The memoir literature abounds in descriptions of the pain of parting from dear ones. Mordecai Zev Raisin related the circumstances of his father's leaving Nesvizh, province of Minsk, in 1889.[18] His father, who was a *maskil*, took this step even though he was fully cognizant of the popular opinion that only the poorer class of workers went to America, where little attention was paid to matters of the spirit. Raisin reported that his father kept his intention secret and that his mother felt shame because of his father's decision. In his first letter from America, Raisin's father listed the reasons that had motivated his act—poverty, the conditions in the Pale, the pogroms, his concern over the conscription of his sons, and, finally, his view of Russia as a *chazer land* (piggish land) that was unworthy of sacrifice. These factors were undoubtedly among the considerations that governed the decision of countless others to emigrate.

Because of their deep concern for the continued religious welfare of their children in America, parents occasionally wrote special letters admonishing them to remain faithful to the tradition. An example is the Hebrew missive of Meshulum Faitel Goldbaum of Kuznitzkah, Poland, written in 1875 to urge his American children to live a Jewish life.[19] The writer indicated that he was concerned about the state of religious observance in America and related that a returnee who had just arrived told him this was the reason for his return. Goldbaum adjured his children not to go astray and to be punctilious in their Sabbath observance.

Other forms of literature played a role in fashioning the image of America for East European Jews in the nineteenth century.[20] One of the early important works in that category was Joachim Heinrich Campe's *Die Entdeckung von Amerika*, the first part of which (dealing with Columbus) was translated into Hebrew by Moses Mendelsohn Frankfurt under the title *Metzi'at Eretz Hadashah* (The Discovery of a New Land) as early as 1817. In order to deal with his material, he had to find Hebrew equivalents for various technical terms, which he listed in a Hebrew-German glossary at the beginning of the book.

Other translations followed, attesting to the further popularity of Campe's book. Chaim Haykl Hurwitz reworked all three parts in 1817 in Yiddish translation and called his work *Tzofnat Pane'akh* (cf. Gen. 41:45).[21] In his introduction he pointed to the many benefits that had been derived by humanity from the discovery of the New World. The Hebrew writer Abraham Baer Gottlober recalled in his reminiscences in 1888 that Hurwitz's translation had a wide circulation and that almost all Jews, including women, read it.

In 1824 Mordecai Aaron Günzberg issued his translation of Campe's work, entitled *Gelot Eretz Hadashah* (The Discovery of a New Land).[22] He indicated that his aim was to depict America not only as a land that was discovered in the past but also as a social and economic reality in the present. Günzberg followed up his Hebrew translation with a Yiddish version the following year. Still another Hebrew translation and adaptation was *Metzi'at Amerikah* (The Discovery of America) by David Zamosc, also published in 1824. During the second half of the nineteenth century various geographical descriptions of America, including those by Issachar Baer Gordon and Kalman Shulman, made their appearance. All of these books served to whet the appetite of their readers for more information about the New World.

For Judah Leib Gordon, who had contributed greatly to the debate regarding emigration, America represented a symbol of enlightenment and liberalism, in contrast to the oppressive regime in Russia. Already in 1859 he had completed the first part of *Eretz Hadashah* (A New Land). (He saw fit to publish it in 1892, on the occasion of the four hundredth anniversary of the discovery of America.) In it a young couple who fall in love against the will of their parents flee to America, where they prosper and ultimately bring over their families. In the poem America is called "*eretz ha-tzevi*," "the land of beauty" whose fertility has made it a veritable Garden of Eden. The poet describes the motivation for the discovery and compares Columbus to Moses. America is praised as a refuge that receives new immigrants as brothers.

In 1882, Gordon published in a supplement of *Ha-Melitz* his poem "Ahoti Ruhamah" (My Sister Ruhama), in which he declared that redemption was possible only in the land of freedom, in America.[23] Moved by compassion, he called upon the persecuted Russian Jews to leave. Since there was no other safe haven, they would do well to seek refuge in America, where the light of freedom shines upon all. America could serve as a *melon orḥim* ("temporary resting-place") where they could stay and wait. This poem of Gordon's was severely criticized by Lilienblum and other adherents of Hibbat Tsiyyon, who accused the poet of disloyalty to the cause of Palestine.

In 1892 Gordon also published his poem *Tashlikh*, which he dedicated to a friend leaving for overseas. Earlier he had written an epic poem entitled *Bi-Metzulot Yam* (In the Depths of the Sea), in which he castigated Spain for expelling the Jews. But now, on the occasion of the anniversary of Columbus's discovery, he feels that he condemned Spain too harshly and expresses his gratitude for its role in establishing new havens of refuge. Gordon describes America as a good and bountiful land among whose people his friend would be able to enjoy in peace the fruit of his labors. Telling his friend to bless God for having prepared a refuge for the oppressed, he concludes, "When you traverse the ocean, cast my sin into the depths of the sea," referring thereby to his abovementioned epic poem in which he had been critical of Spain.

If Gordon was an eloquent supporter of emigration to America, his contemporary, Peretz Smolenskin, was equally persuasive in opposition. He made his opinion known not only in publicist essays but in belletristic writings as well.[24] Already in his early novel *Ha-To'eh be-Darkhe ha-Ḥayyim* (The Wanderer in the Paths of Life), America figures as a haven for individual Russian Jews, who, like the protagonist's father, have sought their fortune in the New World and have become wealthy.

In his novel *Gaon va-Shever* (Pride and Fall), Smolenskin strung together a number of loosely connected stories to indicate why some fugitives from the collapse of the Vienna stock exchange sought refuge in America.[25] The novel presents a gallery of unsavory characters whose conversations aboard ship serve as a clue to the author's views. An assimilationist, for example, declares that he looks forward in America to severing his ties with Jews, something he had been unable to do previously. When the fugitives land they are apprehended by the police and returned to Europe.

In another novel, *Ha-Yerushah* (The Inheritance), which Smolenskin completed shortly before his death in 1884, Zerachiah's mother is falsely informed that her son has left for America, the land to which one can apply the biblical verse "all who go to her cannot return." The woman is grief stricken, but she is consoled when told that many have returned after earning their fortune in the new land. Actually, Zerachiah is eventually reunited with his sweetheart and does not get to America.

As his contribution to the America-Palestine debate, A. B. Gottlober published a poem in *Ha-Maggid* (no. 6, 1882), which he entitled "Nes Tsiyyonah" (Signpost to Zion). He wrote,

> The new land is a blessed land.
> But you, my people, should not go there.
> For you will be a stranger there, a refugee.
> . . . .
> Not so the Holy Land, the land of Canaan.
> There every rafter shall proclaim:
> Your fathers have always dwelt here.

Typical of the Hebrew novels by lesser literary lights that reflect prevalent views of America are *Ester o le-Eretz Hadashah* (Esther; or, To a New Land) by Israel Joseph Sirkis and *Bein ha-Zemanim* (Between the Times) by Israel Weisbrem.[26] The novel *Ester*, published in Warsaw in 1887, describes a young woman who goes to America after being disowned by her family. Although the author informs us that she had been warned against America because many suffered hunger there, he remains a strong advocate of emigration to America and is publishing his novel to further this aim. The novel *Bein ha-Zemanim*, published in Warsaw in 1888,[27] depicts in melodramatic fashion the fortunes of Jonathan, the adopted son of the rabbi of a Lithuanian town, and of the shiftless Gershon. Both go to America, but whereas Jonathan becomes a rich manufacturer in Quebec, Gershon undergoes five years of hardship, first as a peddler and then as a miner.

After the two characters are reunited, they return to their hometown to establish a factory and to find happiness with their former lovers. The novel stresses a number of concepts that were then current regarding America. The new land was a place of opportunity, but at the same time immigrant life was no bed of roses. Also reflected is the hope that America need not be a land of no return and that it is possible for those who have left to take up the threads of their lives again in their hometowns.

Our survey of the belletristic treatment of America in Hebrew literature must also take account of the writings of two established authors—Reuben Asher Braudes and Mordecai David Brandstaetter. Braudes was the author of *Shirim Atikim* (Ancient Songs), a story that incorporates verse, diary entries, and letters and that first appeared in *Ha-Zeman*, the periodical that he edited in Cracow in 1890–91. As an exponent of the Palestine cause, Braudes chose to depict the sad fate of a *maskil* who had opted for America. We see the protagonist Naftali on his sick bed in a New York hospital, where he reflects on the path he chose. He muses on the many immigrants who were misled by unscrupulous people into sweatshop slavery and who were led to forsake their religious observance. His own life he characterizes as that of a lifeless and unfeeling machine similar to the machine over which he labored. How reminiscent of Morris Rosenfeld, who was later to compare the sweatshop worker to a machine and who became known as the Sweatshop Poet. In short, Naftali now rejects the American dream in favor of Palestine but his decision comes too late and he dies. In this graphic novel Braudes left no doubt as to where he stood in the Palestine-America debate.

Brandstaetter also expressed his disillusionment with the American dream in his story *Reb Lemel Tarvad* (Reb Lemel the Busybody), which was written at the beginning of the 1890s and was later included in his collected works. It deals with a Galician Jew whose two daughters are initiated into prostitution in America by connivers who had ostensibly come to seek brides. Brandstaetter made use of a sordid side of immigrant life to register his disapproval of emigration to the new land. The attempt of Reb Lemel and his son to bring the connivers to justice ends in failure.

Among Yiddish literary figures the strongest advocate of American emigration was Isaac Meir Dik.[28] In the Palestine-America debate he supported the views of Am Olam. He had incorporated favorable references to America in his popular writings as early as the 1850s. A prolific writer, Dik had a wide readership that was influenced by his repeated stress on America as a fabled land for Russian Jews, a utopia. He remained firmly convinced that only here was there opportunity for Lithuanian Jewish youth to develop into useful citizens.

Already in 1864 Dik published a story entitled *Reb Haykl Yentes fun Shtot Tsiyosk* (Reb Haykl, Yente's Son of the City of Tsiyosk), in which a poor *melamed* in the first half of the nineteenth century becomes the beneficiary of a large inheritance. His uncle had settled in Jamaica, where he owned a large plantation. Reb Haykl goes there to claim his inheritance and to his delight finds many Jews who maintain the tradition. A similar theme is the basis of Dik's story published in 1871 under the title *Di Yidn in Lite* (The Jews in Lithuania). Here, too, a Jew goes to America to claim an inheritance, this time in Louisiana. His prosperity does not cause him to forsake his religiosity.

In addition, Dik was the author of three specifically American tales. *Di Shklaferay* (Slavery), first published in 1868, was a reworking of *Uncle Tom's Cabin* in which the master is a Jew and in which other Jewish elements are introduced. A second tale, *Der Opekun* (The Guardian, 1872), is also set on a Louisiana plantation. The son of a purveyor of religious articles is brought up by a Jewish planter. He marries the planter's daughter and ultimately becomes a jurist who champions the abolitionist cause. Finally, Dik's *Di Amerikaner Geshikhte* (The American Story), which he began in the eighties and which was published in 1899 following his death, takes us this time to Guadeloupe, an island in the Caribbean. Here a Spanish-Portuguese Jew from Amsterdam settles and prospers. His assistant, who hails from Vilna, becomes his son-in-law. Thus, in all his tales Dik never missed an opportunity to romanticize America and to look to it as a source for the renewal of a more natural and patriarchal life.

Another central figure in early Yiddish letters was Shloyme Ettinger, who died in 1856. His collected works contain an unfinished play published by Max Weinreich and entitled *Der Feter fun Amerike* (The Uncle from America). Uncle Binyomin is described as a bankrupt merchant who is left so penniless in America that he does not have enough money for the return passage. This play may be taken to indicate that such occurrences were not infrequent.

Two popular accounts published in the nincties dealt with the unsuccessful returnees and their sad experiences. Ch. A. Yakhnuk of Bialystok had emigrated to New York and returned to Russia a disappointed man. He published his story, entitled *In Amerike oder fun Amerike* (In America or from America), in Warsaw in 1894. After describing the romantic notions of the immigrants he tells of their despair, which was occasioned by the economic crisis of 1893. There was simply no work to be had and many clamored to be sent home. The author himself relates that he was shipped back in a cattle ship. A similar tale of woe was related by Auser Blaustein in his *Der Pedler in Amerike* (The Peddler in America). The narrator regrets his trip to America and although he must return by cattle boat, he rejoices that he is headed for home. Blaustein was also the author of two humorous treatments of the immigrant experience, *Vikhne-Dvoshe Fort kayn Amerike* (Vikne-Dvoshe Goes to America) and *Vikhne-Dvoshe Fort Tsurik fun Amerike* (Vikhne-Dvoshe Returns from America). Both accounts were reprinted in New York.

Eliakum Zunser, who became known as the People's Bard, had long been a supporter of the Hibbat Tsiyyon movement and had planned to settle in Palestine. In 1899 he emigrated to America together with his eldest son, spurred on by his fear of arrest and encouraged by letters from Hibbat Tsiyyon activists in New York. Aboard ship he completed his "Columbus un Washington,"[29] an idealist paean of praise for the new land. Each of its stanzas presents a different person who has reason to bless America and its two heroes for the freedom to pursue his or her aims. He parades before us an artisan, an honest burgher, a bankrupt, a young woman, and a Yiddish actor who are liberated from their European shackles. In America Zunser went on to express the mood and feelings of the immigrant masses in such songs as "Die Goldene Land," "Der Griner," and "Tsum Pedler."

Undoubtedly, an important influence in shaping the image of America in the minds of East European Jews was the negative attitude of the Orthodox rabbinate. Leading Orthodox rabbis constantly complained of the lack of qualified religious leadership in America and the laxity of observance among the new immigrants. With the rise of the American Reform movement their opposition became even sharper. The reports by correspondents in the press regarding scandalous religious behavior in the so-called *treyfa medina* ("impure land") added fuel to the fire.[30]

In the Palestine-America debate that followed the outbreak of the 1881 pogroms, Rabbi Mordecai Gimpel Jaffe was among the rabbis who called for emigration to Palestine. In a letter published in *Ha-Levanon* (no. 13, 1882) he stressed that among the reasons why Palestine was preferable to America was that "most of those who go to America forsake their religion, either willingly or unwillingly." In 1882 three leading rabbis, Josef Baer Soloveitchik of Brisk, Shmuel Mohiliver of Radom, and Eliyahu Chaim Meisel of Lodz, issued a joint appeal to the fleeing Russian emigrants to choose Palestine over America because of the rampant irreligiosity in the new land.

Note should also be taken of the Hebrew book *Ha-Yehudim ve-ha-Yahadut be-New York* (Jews and Judaism in New York) by Moshe Weinberger, published in New York in 1887. The author intended his description of religious and spiritual Jewish life in America as a guide for European Jews who might be contemplating emigration to the new land. In one section of the book he addressed his honored readers, the Torah scholars in Russia, Poland, and Hungary, as follows:

> To you we have devoted this chapter: to the poor unfortunate man who in the midst of his sorrows may perhaps have considered coming here to seek a fortune. You have neither money nor tools, neither skills nor work. All you know is that you are a young scholar. So listen to us, and tough it out: stay home.[31]

Especially typical of the negative Orthodox approach to America were the writings of Rabbi Israel Meir Ha-Kohen, the Hafetz Hayyim. He saw fit to devote an entire tract entitled *Niddeḥei Yisrael* (The Dispersed of Israel, 1894) to the religious problems of those who were led to emigrate to far-off lands. He did his best to discourage such a step and urged those who had left to return. He warned especially against bringing up children in distant lands and being misled by economic success. The emigrant should make every effort to return home so as not to exchange an eternal world for a transient one.

Unquestionably, there were many who hesitated to leave for

America because of such exhortations. But the fact remains that the admonitions of the rabbis could not effectively stem the growing tide of emigration reaching these shores. Ultimately it was to be demonstrated that the New World could become a providential land of spiritual as well as physical well-being.

If literature is the reflection of life and its problems, then the Hebrew and Yiddish writings of the immigration era mirror not only the suffering and travail of East European Jewry but also their dreams and hopes and yes—even their misconceptions.

Notes

1. For a review of the literature on immigration see, for example, Lloyd P. Gartner, "Jewish Migrants en Route from Europe to North America: Traditions and Realities," in *The Jews of North America*, ed. Moses Rischin (Detroit: Wayne State University Press, 1987), 25–43; Eli Lederhandler, "Jewish Immigration to America and Revisionist Historiography: A Decade of New Perspectives," *Yivo Annual of Jewish Social Studies* 18 (1983): 391–408; Bernard D. Weinryb, "Jewish Immigration and Accommodation to America: Research, Facts, Problems," *Proceedings of the American Jewish Historical Society* 46, no. 3 (March 1957): 366–403.
2. See Harvey A. Richman, "The Image of America in the European Hebrew Periodicals of the Nineteenth Century (until 1880)" (Ph.D. diss., University of Texas at Austin, 1971). See also Joel S. Geffen, "America in the First European Hebrew Daily Newspaper, *Ha-Yom* (1886–1888)," *American Jewish Historical Quarterly* 11, no. 3 (March 1962): 149–67; "Whither: To Palestine or to America in the Pages of the Russian Hebrew Press *Ha-Melitz* and *Ha-Yom* (1880–1890)," *American Jewish Historical Quarterly* 59, no. 2 (December 1969): 179–200; and Sanford Ragins, "The Image of America in Two East European Hebrew Periodicals," *American Jewish Archives* 17, no. 2 (November 1965): 143–61.
3. Quoted in *Golden Door to America: The Jewish Immigrant Experience*, ed. Abraham Karp (New York: Viking, 1976), 83.
4. See Lloyd P. Gartner, "Rumania and America, 1873: Leon Horowitz's Rumanian Tour and Its Background," *Proceedings of the American Jewish Historical Society* 45, no. 2 (December 1955): 67–92; and E. R. Malachi, "Ayala—Ḥalutz ha-Ittonut ha-Ivrit ba-Amerikah," in *Sefer Hadoar* (New York: Histadrut Ivrit, 1957), 210–16.
5. See my monograph on Gersoni in my *Ḥalutzei ha-Sifrut ha-Ivrit ba-Amerikah* (Tel Aviv/Cleveland: Yavneh, 1966), 82–84, 92–95.
6. See my monograph on Soble in ibid., 49–50.

7. See Lloyd P. Gartner, "From New York to Miedzyrecz: Immigrant Letters of Judah David Eisenstein, 1878–1886," *American Jewish Historical Quarterly* 52, no. 3 (March 1963): 234–43.

8. For reviews of the America-Palestine debate see the following: Joseph Klausner, *Historiah shel ha-Sifrut ha-Ivrit ha-Hadashah*, vol. 6 (Jerusalem: Magnes, 1958), 133–34; and Israel Klausner, *Be-Hit'orer Am* (Jerusalem: Ha-Sifriyah Ha-Tsiyonit, 1962), 104–8, 135–55. For further discussions of the reaction to the pogroms see Steven M. Berk, *Year of Crisis, Year of Hope: Russian Jewry and the Pogroms of 1881–1882* (Westport, Conn.: Greenwood, 1987), chapters 5 and 6; and Jonathan Frankel, *Prophecy and Politics: Socialism, Nationalism, and the Russian Jews, 1862–1917* (Cambridge: Cambridge University Press, 1987), part 1, section 2.

9. For a detailed analysis of the attitude of the Russian-Jewish periodicals see Yehuda Slutzky, *Ha-Ittonut ha-Yehudit-Russit ba-Me'ah ha-Tesha-Esreh* (Jerusalem: Mosad Bialik, 1970). Slutsky noted that 273 articles on the Jews of America were published in *Voskhod* between 1881 and 1889, including fifty-two during 1882, the first year of mass migration. See his note 263 to chapter 11, on page 361.

10. See Michael Stanislawski, *For Whom Do I Toil? Judah Leib Gordon and the Crisis of Russian Jewry* (New York: Oxford University Press, 1988), especially chapters 9 and 10.

11. See my article "Bein Yehalel le-Sofrei Amerikah," in my *Shoharim ve-Ne'emanim* (Jerusalem: Rubin Mass, 1978), 70–77.

12. See Abraham Menes, "The Am Oylom Movement," *Yivo Annual of Jewish Social Studies* 4 (1949): 9–33.

13. See Chaim Chissin, *A Palestine Diary: Memoirs of a Bilu Pioneer, 1887–1889* (New York: Herzl, 1976), 31–32.

14. See Abraham Cahan, *Bletter fun Mayn Leben*, 2 vols. (New York: Forwerts, 1935), 1:50 ff. and 2:17–18.

15. See Alexander Harkavy, *Perakim me-Hayyai* (New York: Hebrew Publishing, 1935). The quotation is from "Chapters from My Life," by Harkavy, trans. Jonathan Sarna in Uri Herscher, ed., *The East European Jewish Experience in America (1881–1981)* (Cincinnati: American Jewish Archives, 1983), 59.

16. See his *Zekhtsik Yor Leben* (New York: Meisel, 1919), 210–12.

17. See "Harris Rubin: Worker on the Land," in Uri Herscher, ed., *East European Jewish Experience*, 17–51. The memoir is translated from the original Yiddish.

18. See Mordecai Zev Raisin, *Mi-Sefer Hayyai* (New York: Bitzaron, 1956), 30–31.

19. The Hebrew letter was published together with an English translation by Arthur A. Chiel in *American Jewish Historical Quarterly* 61, no. 3 (March 1972): 230–33. Another English translation of this letter is

found in Jacob Rader Marcus, *This I Believe: Documents of American Jewish Life* (Northvale, N.J.: Aronson, 1990), 115–17.

20. See the survey article by Ben-Ami Feingold, "Sifrut ha-Haskalah Megallah et Amerikah," in *Bein Historiyah le-Sifrut* (Tel-Aviv: Dyunon/Tel-Aviv University, 1983), 91–104.

21. On Chaim Haykl Hurwitz see Israel Zinberg, *A History of Jewish Literature*, vol. 9 (Cincinnati and New York: Hebrew Union College Press/Ktav, 1976), 225–31.

22. See Isaac Bartal, "Mordechai Aaron Günzberg: A Lithuanian Maskil Faces Modernity," in *From East and West: Jews in a Changing Europe, 1750–1870*, ed. Frances Malino and David Sorkin (Oxford/Cambridge, Mass.: Blackwell, 1991), 142–43.

23. See the discussion of this poem in Michael Stanislawski, *For Whom Do I Toil?*, 198–99.

24. See E. R. Malachi, "Amerikah be-Sippurei Smolenskin u've-*Ha-Sha-har*," *Bitzaron* 26, no. 5 (1963): 11–16, 44.

25. See, on this novel, David Patterson, *The Hebrew Novel in Czarist Russia* (Edinburgh: Edinburgh University Press, 1964), 13.

26. See David Patterson, ibid., on Sirkis, 30, and on Weisbrem, 31–32.

27. A translation of the novel appears in Alan David Crown, *Israel Weissbrem and His Work: Novels and Poems* (Tel-Aviv: Tcherikover, 1983).

28. See S. Niger, "Amerike in Dertseylungen fun A. M. Dik," *Yivo Bletter* 38 (1954): 106–15.

29. For the text of the poem see Mordkhe Schaechter, *The Works of Elyokum Zunser*, vol. 1 (New York: Yivo, 1962), 518–21. Zunser's autobiographical account appears in volume 2.

30. See Arthur Hertzberg, " 'Treifene Medina'—Learned Opposition to Emigration to the United States," *Proceedings of the Eighth World Congress of Jewish Studies: Jewish History* (Jerusalem: World Union of Jewish Studies, 1984), 1–30.

31. An English translation by Jonathan D. Sarna appeared under the title *People Walk on Their Heads: Moses Weinberger's Jews and Judaism in New York* (New York: Holmes and Meier, 1981). The quotation is found on 59.

CHAPTER 4

Jewish Writers on the New Diaspora

Ruth R. Wisse

"Twilight in Southern California," a 1953 short story by Daniel Fuchs, describes a small poolside gathering on a Saturday afternoon. The scene is typical California, but the characters don't sit comfortably in their setting:

> The novelty business was shot to pieces; the whole bottom had dropped out of the market. Mr. Honti, who manufactured the gadgets and gewgaws, was going through terrible financial troubles, dunned and driven on all sides, everything crashing down on his head, and Morley felt this was no time to run out on him. Morley Finch was a young physician who had opened a practice in Los Angeles just two or three years ago. He and his wife had been taken up by the Hontis, had gone up there to the swimming pool in Coldwater Canyon almost every Saturday, and Morley didn't see how they could stop going there now. The trouble was Barbara, his wife. She hated those visits. She said Mr. Honti was unbalanced.[1]

Alexander Honti is an excitable immigrant who a decade earlier had been chased "like an animal in the fields in Berlin, in Prague, in Paris" and is now, on the Saturday in question, trying to stave off bankruptcy in sunny California. His car having been repossessed, he is reduced to walking the canyon roads like his dog, Fidelio, who is out somewhere on the hot roads, searching vainly for his master. Honti is aware of his resemblance to his dog; not much about himself or his situation escapes his understanding.

The hostess, Lily Honti, had shared her husband's fate in Europe and continues to share it as his business associate. At the pool with them is a close family friend, Mr. Oleam, also a refugee, also in the novelty business, and like Honti in distressed circumstances. Oleam suffers the additional discomforts of a stiff neck and of having just lost his wife to another man. Honti's physician Morley Finch and his wife round out the guests. American-born Morley is almost as sensitive as his European hosts; because Honti's cheque to him had bounced the day before, he feels he has to show up at his home as usual lest his host assume there is some connection between the bounced cheque and his absence. Besides, he likes these intelligent people who have been so hospitable to him, and always know what he is thinking. "The trouble [as the story informs us in its opening paragraph] was Barbara, his wife. She hated those visits. She said Mr. Honti was unbalanced."

Honti knows that Barbara distrusts him, but he adores this lovely young woman, and despite his reminders to himself to be dignified and to leave her alone, he can't help paying her excessive compliments, also with his hands. Since his concern for his business is wrapped up with his desire to please her, he acts especially freakish this afternoon, and when he comes dripping out of the pool and grabs Barbara's wrist, actually just to peer at the time on her watch, she whacks him across the face, destroying three hundred dollars worth of bridgework. Being short-sighted, he had taken her hand to see whether it was already three-thirty, the hour at which he was expecting some good news. But Barbara, whom the Hontis refer to as a child—"She comes from New Hampshire"—misinterprets his gesture and shrieks at the touch of this "degenerate" man. She runs away from him, plunging poor Mr. Honti into despair and her husband into keenest embarrassment.

The word "Jew" is appropriately missing from the story, since none of its characters would have used it among themselves. The Hontis, Oleam, and Morley Finch are not really *Jews* in any way that suggests customs or affiliation, and Morley Finch is sufficiently assimilated to have married gentile Barbara. Certainly Barbara, being married to one, has nothing against a Jew as such. Yet the afternoon crumbles into catastrophe over what can only be understood as the explosion of the Jewish question. Suddenly, the depth of Barbara's fear and revulsion are revealed to her husband, to the Hontis, and to herself. Morley may have tried to negotiate the abyss between the Jewish refugees and his New England wife, but the revelation of her real feelings for these alien creatures will probably put an end to his efforts.

Daniel Fuchs offers a poignant image of American Jews at mid-century. The acculturated Jew was by then a full-fledged American; when he and his New England wife moved to L.A., fastest-growing city of the United States, he was likely to feel at least as much at home there as she did. The native New Englander, comfortably married to a Jewish husband, is ready to follow wherever he goes. Disturbing the gorgeous peace are only those haunted Jews who carry the mark—and who become the reminder—of sinister evil. By blessed American standards the Hontis and Oleam are "unbalanced"; their excessive history is inappropriate to the brilliant California sunshine. They realize that their attraction to America can never be reciprocated because to the same degree that they hope to be healed by American innocence, that innocence is in terror of being destroyed by them. Honti is oppressed by shame when he thinks back on his life:

> He loved that moment with the bricklayers and the light in Paris, and the rivers of France, the Hudson River Valley in this country, and the incredible California sunshine; the tragedy was that they did not love him back. Everywhere he was rejected, everywhere a trespasser. "Forgive me!" Honti suddenly said, pleading quietly but with all his heart and soul. "Forgive me! Forgive me!" Yes, it was his fault. He had trespassed, he had transgressed; he had committed abominations, stretched the truth and kited checks. He must have committed all the sins, for you weren't punished for nothing in this world, and God knew all Honti's lifetime had been a punishment.
>
> He humbly pleaded for forgiveness high on the mountaintop. To his left were the harbors, the beaches, the glinting Pacific Ocean. To the right lay the floor of the San Fernando Valley, and beyond that, the sullen ranges of the San Gabriels.

Daniel Fuchs does not flinch from exposing the comedy as well as the sorrow of this Zarathustra of suffering (who could have been played by Zero Mostel). Yet the story also awakens more respect and affection for Honti than he has for himself. This European novelty manufacturer, whose heart and intelligence were forcibly expanded during the war beyond what his fellow Americans ever had to feel or learn, appears to Fuchs as the reluctant prophet of the new California, and the standard of desperate knowledge to which Barbara Finch eventually may have to adjust.

Because of the extent to which America served the Jews as a *makom miklat*, a place of refuge, Jews have always had an especially keen interest in the capacity and willingness of America to absorb them. No one needed a new world as desperately as the Jews fleeing Europe, and their need sharpened their sensitivity to every shift in American policies and attitudes. Experience had taught them that in addition to the laws governing a polity, atmospheric conditions in society helped to determine how comfortably the Jews could bed down in any given place, and for how long. Part of the function of American Jewish writing, both in Yiddish and in English, has been to chart these atmospheric conditions, assessing whether "America" is warm or cool, and to what degree.

In the Tsarist empire, the home of most Jewish immigrants who fled at the turn of the century to come to America, authority imposed distinctions from above, and the cultural boundaries between Jews and their neighbours, while promising to crumble, still persisted as a result of centuries of enforced separation. Pogroms, anti-Jewish decrees, and the rise of antisemitism as a corollary of nationalism throughout much of Europe convinced millions of Jews to set out for the new world that advertised opportunity and equal rights. Accustomed to being at best a tolerated minority, Jews were enormously grateful for the benefits of America and became passionate lovers of its freedoms. But their acute dependency on America also made them wary and insecure. They did not know quite how to judge the fluid boundaries between themselves and other Americans. Furthermore, since their immigration coincided with the painful self-transformation from a tradition-bound people into a voluntary community, they had to weigh the advantages of acculturation against the dangers of national dissolution. To discover that a minority may penetrate all spheres of influence, blur its ethnic and religious distinctiveness, or even redefine the country in its own image could be frightening as well as liberating.

In many, perhaps in most respects, Jews resembled all other immigrant groups that had to adjust to America, each with its own set of problems. But the special complicating feature of antisemitism made the Jews something of a test case for America, and America a test case for the Jews. The persistence of Jew-hatred in Europe, diachronically the strongest force of continuity between Christian feudal Europe and secular nation-states, and synchronically the strongest common feature of nations that were otherwise separate and often in conflict, had been the most obvious sign of the failure of rational Enlightenment. Unless the new nation-states of Europe could successfully absorb their non-Christian minority, they could not pretend to have become fully fraternal, liberated, or just. Positively stated, the ideals of liberty, equality, and fraternity would have been confirmed by the single standard of toleration of the Jews. Europe's repeated failure to meet that standard, and its final collapse into barbarism, put steady pressure on America to demonstrate whether it was really a new world or merely a version of the old.

To the same degree that the Jews were a test case for America, America was a test case for the Jews. For if the new world lived up to its democratic promise, they would be solely responsible for their fate, without any more imposed restrictions to define their identity or to limit their reach. Through the centuries of exile, Jews had become a politically passive people compared with those among whom they lived in Europe and western Asia, but once they were no longer looking to God for their salvation, and no longer handicapped by punitive legislation, they would have to adopt an entirely new strategy for life. "Is America *golus?*"—a question often raised in the Yiddish press—was a matter of existential importance. If America was not exile, but home, then the Jewish posture of poised expectancy (of attendance on the messiah or on majority approval) was no longer appropriate, and American Jews were free to pursue their ambitions, to assume or to abdicate responsibility for their fellow Jews, to Judaize America or to evaporate. In other words, America and its Jews were mutually responsible for the disappearance of antisemitism and for the quality of Jewishness once it was gone.

There was also something else, in addition to antisemitism, that made Jews a little different from their fellow immigrants. Traditionally, through almost two millennia of exile, Jews had placed unparalleled emphasis on literacy and learning, on literary culture as the main civilizing agency. This emphasis of Jewish religious civilization on the study of Talmud as the supreme virtue and on mastery of Talmud as the supreme masculine attainment was bound to carry over to the secular way of life most Jews adopted in America, at least for one or two generations. Young modernizing Jews took up writing in great numbers, answering not simply their own need for creative self-expression but also a complementary need in their community for cultural leadership. Jewish writers were far more important to the Jews than were any other American writers to their constituency, in ways that were seldom fully understood or acknowledged by either the writers or their audiences. Jewish writers were both the agents and the observers of the mutual testing process that I have described.

The most popular Jewish view of America, certainly among the Jewish masses, was as moral alternative to corrupt Europe. Emma Lazarus's tribute to the Statue of Liberty as Mother of Exiles reinforced the country's image of itself as a haven of refuge, just as Rick Blaine's manly self-sacrifice for Victor Laszlo in the movie classic *Casablanca* reinforced Americans' idea of themselves as the noble saviors of a dying continent. Significantly, however, the Jews who forged these images did not single themselves out as special beneficiaries of American largesse because they may have recognized in the ecumenicism of the United States their best protection against discrimination. America gathered in people of all races and religions; whereas Hitler pursued the Jews, Americans went to war to help refugees of every nationality. The creators of these images felt a double security in being protected by America within the semantically undifferentiated category of "huddled masses yearning to breathe free."

The image of America as an alternative to corrupt Europe also figured in Yiddish literature at the beginning of the century. As the immigrants looked to the new land for material security, Yiddish literature discovered grandeur and release in the poetry of Walt Whitman. Some writers sought potency and rebirth in the new landscape of farmlands, cattle ranches, and skyscrapers. One bold story by Lamed Shapiro, written shortly after his arrival in America, tells of a Russian Jew who had been forced to witness the mutilation of his mother by pogromists, then to put her out of her misery with his own hands. In the aftermath of this degradation, he knows that he has to do more than seek revenge. He must transform himself from a humiliated Jew into an empowered man (who can also commit acts of violence of the kind that were committed against the Jews). The final phase of his self-empowerment takes place where else but in America, through confession of his past and symbolic baptism in American waters. Only then is he prepared to return to Europe where "a generation of iron men will arise and rebuild what we allowed to be destroyed." Shapiro credits the new world not only as a place of refuge but also as the redeemer of Europe's Jews.[2]

But the awareness of moral interdependency between the Jews and America also worked in the opposite direction to undermine the sense of mutual benefit and virtue. While no other group may have stood to gain as much as the Jews in coming to America, neither did any other group have as much to lose. Almost all other immigrants left behind a native territory and a language and a national culture that would remain intact, and to which they or their descendants might someday return. Jewish immigrants had no such assurance, especially not after the Russian pogroms of 1903–1905 and the mass destruction of Jewish communities in World War I. Even before World War I, and certainly after, a feeling developed on both sides of the ocean that America was rapidly replacing Europe as the guarantor of Jewish survival, including the survival of Jewish culture. American Jews would have to bear not only the burden of material assistance to those left behind but also responsibility for the Jewish future.

Yet these same Jews who were now expected to become the main repository of the Jewish heritage felt called upon to give up a good part of that heritage as the price of advancement in the new land. Jewishness being strictly neither a religion nor a nationality nor a culture but a way of life embedded in ancient history, the sacrifice of any part of Jewishness meant dulling a vibrant identity that had been developed through thousands of years. I have suggested that the legacy of antisemitism made it harder for Jews than for other immigrants to gauge just how much of themselves they would have to give up in order to be considered unexceptional, and the same communal experience of siege made it harder for those who left the fold to bear the guilt of betrayal. Being different from other perse-cuted minorities, such as Africans and Asians, whose physical char-acteristics imposed limits on their assimilation, individual Jews were able to choose how and to what degree they wished to assimi-late, and they had therefore to assume responsibility for their deci-sion and its consequences. All these elements—the contradictory pressures of antisemitism to adapt more quickly and to bear greater responsibility for the Jews, and the contradictory nature of Jew-ishness that made it such a powerful legacy yet one so easy to abandon—complicated the adaptation of the Jews to America. Those Jews who gave up everything at once, or too much too soon, often came to despise themselves and to resent the country that "made them do it."

Immigrant literature records the uneasy balance between gain and loss. Abraham Cahan's *The Rise of David Levinsky*, the first Jewish novel to become an American classic, records among many exceptional scenes an evening at a Jewish resort in the Catskills where the band is being drowned out by the conversation and laughter of the weekend guests.

> The conductor, who played the first violin, was a fiery little fellow with a high crown of black hair. He was working every muscle and nerve in his body. He played selections from "Aida," the favorite opera of the Ghetto; he played the popular American songs of the day; he played celebrated "hits" of the Yiddish stage. All to no pur-pose. Finally, he had recourse to what was apparently his last resort. He struck up the "Star-Spangled Banner." The effect was overwhelm-ing. The few hundred diners rose like one man, applauding. The children and many of the adults caught up the tune joyously, passion-ately. It was an interesting scene. Men and women were offering thanksgiving to the flag under which they were eating this good dinner, wearing these expensive clothes. There was the jingle of newly-acquired dollars in our applause. But there was something else in it as well. Many of those who were now paying tribute to the Stars and Stripes were listening to the tune with grave, solemn mien. It was as if they were saying: "We are not persecuted under this flag. At last we have found a home."[3]

Whereas the humbling gratitude in this scene momentarily sweeps up the author in an emotional tribute to America, the novel as a whole is a confession of betrayal and regret. David Levinsky, the narrator, feels that he became an American millionaire at the expense of what he ought to have remained, which is loyal to his mother, his deeper Jewishness, his poverty. "There are cases when success is a tragedy," says Levinsky at the conclusion of the book. However variously this sentence can be interpreted—as showing either that David's guilt subverted his achievement or that his crimes have not paid off or that America's promise had a false bottom or that Jewish yearning has become an end in itself—its judgment is conclusive: the success of the Jew in America was suspect because of the compromise of principle and sacrifice of identity that it required. Like many another hero of the anticapitalist *bildungsroman*, David experiences the failure of success, but with the added conscience of the Jew.

Yiddish writers had special reason to distrust their new-found freedom, since they were the first to pay its price. The same hospitality that benefited the Jews foretold the doom of their Jewish language. Peretz Hirshbein, recording his travels across America in 1917, was badly discouraged by the Jewish immigrant children who saw no value in Yiddish.[4] Writers have as much stake in their language as miners do in ore, and the closing of the mine (whether or not the air may improve as a result) means an end to their livelihood. As the Jewish masses took advantage of democracy to enter the cultural mainstream, Yiddish writers saw the shriveling of their own prospects. Yes, they could write whatever they pleased and publish whatever they wrote, but they could not compete with English on the open market.

Moishe Leib Halpern's lyric "Our Garden," which opened his 1919 book of poems *In New York*, became one of the most famous Yiddish images of the new world:

aza gortn, vu der boym
hot zikh zibn bletlekh koym,
un es dakht zikh, az er trakht:
—ver hot mikh aher gebrakht?
aza gortn, aza gortn,
vu mit a fargreser-gloz
kon men zen a bisl groz,
zol dos undzer gortn zayn

ot aza in morgnshayn?—
avade undzer gortn. vos den, nit undzer gortn?

(What a garden, where the tree is
Bare, but for its seven leaves
And it seems to be amazed,
Who has set me in this place?
What a garden, what a garden—
It takes a magnifying glass
Just to see a little grass.
Is this garden here our own
As it is in light of dawn?
Sure, it's our garden. What, not our garden?) [5]

Halpern's welcoming garden of Eden (read Hester Park on the Lower East Side) is less than glorious. Its watchman chases people off the grass, and the birds in its nests neglect their own young. This is the garden from which poets are now forced to draw their inspiration, immigrants their bit of pleasure. This is Halpern's America, materially and metaphysically. The poet affects a devil-may-care attitude to ease his disappointment, and with a shrug of "might as well face the music" he accepts the shrunken reality as his own. Implicating himself in the blight through the adoption of a coarse language and tone appropriate to his compromising new home, Halpern became the first Yiddish poet to find his voice in America by defining it as a reduced rather than expanded cultural landscape.

Between the two world wars, one might say, beginning with Abraham Cahan's *The Rise of David Levinsky* and Moishe Leib Halpern's *In New York*, American Jewish literature became more and more critical of the accommodation of Jews to their new surroundings. There are many reasons for the growing dissatisfaction, of which I will suggest only the most obvious. (1) The brutalities of World War I and the civil war in Russia were unprecedented. Immigrant Jews who lived by their newspapers had to face the daily reports of mass murders in their hometowns without being able to offer effective assistance. The effects of European antisemitism, particularly though not exclusively in the Ukraine, demoralized the new Americans and induced in some of them convulsions of guilt, rage, even madness. (2) The closing of the gates of America after World War I seemed all the crueler in the light of its reputation as a haven of refuge. Local debate over immigration quotas and over Communist influence stirred up nativist antisemitism and provoked in the Jews, if not the same adversarial relation to their country that they had been forced to feel in Russia, then at least a keener discomfort. Jews were forced to recognize that their agenda did not always coincide with that of their fellow Americans. (3) The steady social and economic progress of the Jews in America had mixed consequences. On one hand, it prompted restrictive quotas and discrimination to keep the Jews from advancing, but on the other, keener competition and bolder ambition among the Jews; in some immigrants it spurred defiant Jewish self-affirmation, including in the cause of Zionism, but in others, more resolve to leave Jewishness behind. The relatively firm "community" of the Lower East Side of New York began to disintegrate. (4) The Bolshevik revolution announced itself as the culmination of moral evolution. Of special interest to the Jews was its repeal of antisemitism and the boast of egalitarian justice. Suddenly it appeared as if the moral tables had been turned: promising America was just another flawed and sullied country while spartan Russia proved the fulfillment of human perfectibility on earth.

Lest we mistake this critical reappraisal as a Jewish point of view, let us recall that during the 1920s Hemingway, Faulkner, Dos Passos, e. e. cummings, and so many other writers of the postwar generation began to look at America *krum*—as the Jews would have said, sideways, ambivalently, askew. This was the great period of expatriation, when American writers sought out Gertrude Stein in Paris to learn from this non-Jewish Jew the secrets of art, or else settled in England where the debasement of democratic mass culture had been less severe. John Reed, not any Jewish journalist, was the great popularizer of Bolshevism in the United States, and the Anglican American T. S. Eliot defined the wasteland that secular Western civilization had become. So the Jewish views of America were part of the cultural mainstream, with the difference that most Jewish writers, being immigrants, could not join the expatriation and had to face the additional indignity of hatred directed against themselves.

These various trends and events triggered in American Jewish writers a powerful reaction against the so-called bourgeois capitalism of America, which was held responsible for the antisemitism, and against the so-called nationalist chauvinism of Jews, which was blamed for feeding it. The more antisemitism accused Jews of exploitation and subversion, the more Jewish writers and intellectuals tried to prove that they were against exploitation and that they were not loyal to the Jews. Antisemitism reached unprecedented heights during the 1930s; so, too, did the attempt of Jewish writers to dissociate themselves from what they assumed were the reprehensible aspects of their Jewishness.

In the 1925 novel *Bread Givers* Anzia Yezierska wrote of a Jewish immigrant girl who slips out of the clutches of her domineering old-world Jewish father to become an idealistic schoolteacher. As the story proceeds through the stages of her acculturation, the juicy vernacular of the Lower East Side that is heard in the early pages gives way to a prose as stilted and neutered as the heroine herself. The author presents the emptying out of Jewish family life and culture as a positive advancement that makes her heroine happier in America, and America happier with her.

Michael Gold's *Jews without Money* (1930) strikes a different kind of bargain. Gold's immigrant Jewish boyhood is valuable to him precisely because it was noisy, uncouth, overheated. His fictional memoir, which ends with the teenager's triumphant discovery of Communism, contains an implicit reproach of the prosperity and refinement that most American Jews were pursuing. Michael Gold was the most persistent, combative literary Communist of the interwar period, wielding great influence in New York, especially among the Jews. Using the moral authority of Communism as his badge, and a venomous critical stick, he charged all those who fell short of Party standards. Although his polemics were effective, they did not equal in influence the idea of this book, which is that Jewish poverty is something to be proud of. Poor Jews were good, and rich Jews were bad. Unempowered Jews were innocent, and powerful Jews were guilty. Whereas earlier writers like Sholem Aleichem had tried to defend the Jews in spite of their helplessness, American Jewish Socialists and Communists began to defend Jews because of their helplessness, and on that ground alone.

It is hard to exaggerate the hold of this equation on the imagination of Jewish writers as the Depression of the 1930s deepened. Lamed Shapiro, whose story of 1909 had cast the United States as the redeemer of European Jewry, spent the late 1930s writing a novel called *The American Demon*.[6] This book, never completed, was to be a panoramic study of the immigrant Jewish community, tracing its moral collapse. The devil of the title is Suzie Katz, a young factory worker who marries for money, then cheats on her husband with a former boyfriend. She also cheats on the working class by crossing a picket line to work in her husband's store when his employee is out on strike. Suzie's relatively minor crimes are inflated by Shapiro to demonic proportions because he recalls the idealized heights from which they are fallen. In this view, her concern for material security and creature satisfaction sapped the socialist idealism that might otherwise have reformed America as it reformed Russia and sustained the machinery of capitalism that Shapiro thinks is destroying the country. For the Yiddish writer Lamed Shapiro, Suzie's special failure is her adoption of English. For writers like Jerome Weidman in *I Can Get It for You Wholesale* or Budd Schulberg in *What Makes Sammy Run?* or, later, Mordecai Richler in *The Apprenticeship of Duddy Kravitz*, the paradigm of Jewish energy is the unprincipled hustler who would sacrifice his own mother or best friend or lover to advance his career.[7]

American Jewish literature of the 1930s and 1940s interpreted what some would consider the best qualities of the Jewish immigrants—their resilience, self-reliance, industry, talent, adaptiveness, worldliness, optimism, and love of freedom—as negative qualities of selfishness, greed, and opportunism. By "Waiting for Lefty" (title of the famous play by Clifford Odets),[8] most American Jewish writers of those decades tried to distinguish their own "working-class" principles from the debased values of their fellow Jews who were adjusting to a corrupt country. Not all American Jewish literature of this period throbs with these ideas to the same degree. But even the masterpieces of Henry Roth and Nathanael West are not entirely outside this framework. It is as though in drawing attention to their powerlessness, Jewish writers were absolving themselves from having to seek power on behalf of their endangered fellow Jews and claiming the sympathy of the world for themselves. The idealization of "Jews without Money" continued strong well into the 1950s, reaching its apogee in Bernard Malamud's American classic *The Assistant*, in which the grocer Morris Bober is the Jewish

Saint Francis of Assisi, with Christian suffering the criterion of his Jewish goodness. (Bober says to the Italian boy who held him up at gunpoint, then came to work for him, "I suffer for you.") Malamud also reinforced the same theme in later novels, notably in *The Fixer.*[9]

In effect, Yezierska's justification of Jews without accents and Gold's justification of Jews without money were two similar defenses against the humiliation of antisemitism. One demonstrated how the Jewish avidity for learning could become an American asset as the children of immigrant Jews became the purveyors of American culture. The other demonstrated how Jewish moral principles could be rechanneled into socialism, into a "disinterested" class consciousness and saintly asceticism. Both defenses concealed their resentment of America for having welched on its promises to the Jews behind complaints against its brutalizing vulgarity and protests against its social inequality.

At the end of the 1930s these same two principles of Jews without accents and Jews without money, raised to a much higher ideological level, became the twin pillars of the *Partisan Review* and its dominantly Jewish circle of New York intellectuals who were then coming of age. The group tried to bring about a reconciliation between two apparently contradictory commitments to modernism and Marxism, to the most complexly individuated expressions of contemporary culture and to the most egalitarian model of political economics. Whatever its theoretical merit, the pairing of these ideas produced remarkable results in the group that included Sidney Hook, Philip Rahv, Lionel Trilling, William Phillips, Mary McCarthy, William Barrett, Dwight Macdonald, Harold Rosenberg, Meyer Schapiro, Lionel Abel, Clement Greenberg, Robert Warshow, Delmore Schwartz, Isaac Rosenfeld, Daniel Bell, Alfred Kazin, Diana Trilling, Irving Howe, and the Nobel laureate Saul Bellow. It is enough to read off this partial list to make the point about just how great was their achievement and how important their contribution to American letters. Yet (as I've recently noted elsewhere) [10] from our privileged perspective of half a century later, it is equally clear that these twin ideas of modernism and Marxism had in common a determination to transcend the Jewish question, since modernism implicitly and Marxism explicitly rejected national preoccupations. The failure of this predominantly Jewish intellectual community to address the plight of the Jews was as pronounced as its successful advancement into the mainstream of American culture. Nor can one say about these writers, as one might say about some of their contemporaries, that they distanced themselves from politics. The New York intellectuals distinguished themselves precisely in their emphasis on politics as a feature of culture. Their definition of politics, however, did not include the political category of the Jew. The strenuous objection of antisemites to the Jewish people was a problem that the Jews would have to face as a people. Those few writers who did try to save Jews by promoting their right to settle in Palestine—Ludwig Lewisohn, Maurice Samuel, Meyer Levin, Ben Hecht, Judd Teller, A. M. Klein—were dubbed parochial and mediocre. And it must be admitted that the defense of the Jews rarely made for good literature.[11]

Until the waning of the 1930s it is still possible to speak of a single American Jewish literature in English, Yiddish, and, to a smaller degree, Hebrew. But the destruction of European Jewry *(khurbn)* changed that forever. The approach of the *khurbn* made Yiddish writers realize just how deeply their destiny was tied to European Jewry that had developed a European Jewish language, and to the surviving remnant that made its way to Palestine. When Yiddish writers sensed the impending tragedy overtaking their people, they felt themselves going under. Jacob Glatstein's lyric, "Wagons" (here translated by Chana Bloch), was written in 1938, after a trip back to his home city of Lublin:

> With quiet signs of faraway
> At dusk the mournful wagons come.
> Doors stand ajar,
> But no one waits to meet them.
> The town is peaceful, bells of silence toll . . .
> A few sickly Jews climb down from the wagons,
> And a clever word falters
> In every brooding head.
> God, on your scale of good and bad,
> Set a dish of warm porridge,
> Toss some oats, at least, for the skinny mules.

The deadness of the town grows dark.
A cruel silence afflicts the Jewish beards,
And each sees in the other's eyes
A prayer of fear:
When death comes,
Let me not remain the only one,
Do not pass over me with my thin bones.[12]

Once upon a time in Egypt, on the eve of leading them forth from slavery to freedom, God had spared his people by passing over the houses of the Jews. Expecting no such redemption, Glatstein's Jew chooses to drown among his people. Immediately after the war the American Yiddish poet H. Leivick wrote, "I was not in Treblinka or in Maidanek."[13] This was how the American Yiddish writers regarded themselves, even those like Glatstein, who had been graduated from Columbia University, and Leivick, who had been here since 1911.

American Jewish writers in English were experiencing quite the opposite sensation, a richer identification than ever before with "Our Country and Our Culture," meaning the United States and English.[14] They were the unwitting beneficiaries of the victimization of European Jewry and the rise of the State of Israel, since the combined guilt and admiration that Americans began to feel for the Jews gradually combined to eliminate lingering obstacles to their progress. For the next twenty-five years, until the ideological war against Zionism was launched by the Arabs in the early 1970s, Jews and Jewish writers were so popular they were actually chic. Cynthia Ozick's brilliant story, "Envy; or, Yiddish in America," captures with perfect pitch the voice of the Yiddish writer who realizes that he has been eclipsed from the future of the Jews in America at precisely the moment when Jewishness in English is becoming trendy. Comically deformed the Yiddish poet of her story may be, and slightly unbalanced like Mr. Honti by the unfairness of his fate, but when at the conclusion of the story he shouts into the telephone, "Amalekite! Titus! Nazi! The whole world is infected by you antisemites! On account of you children become corrupted! On account of you I lost everything, my whole life! On account of you I have no translator!" he is telling a complicated truth.[15] On one level, his rage has merely fixed on a convenient target in blaming the antisemite for all his troubles, but he happens to be right nonetheless: the antisemitism that destroyed the Jews in Europe did deform Jewish culture in America.

In their haste to leave Jew-hatred behind, many Jews were prepared to pretend that it did not exist, to underestimate its sincerity, or to redefine it as anything but what it was—hatred and opposition to the Jews as Jews. Regrettably, it could not be ignored or redefined without damage to the truth. It could not be erased through acculturation, nor through the substitution of socialism for capitalism, nor through proofs of Jewish liberalism, excellence, saintliness, or anything else. As long as political leaders and movements anywhere in the world singled out the Jews as the enemy of peace and of mankind, they would carry the message to America, reminding its citizens of the presence of evil *whether or not they believed the charges against the Jews* and making them uncomfortable on that account.

This brings us back to the story with which we began, Daniel Fuchs's "Twilight in Southern California," with its triangular rather than bilateral image of the Jews in America. All the Jews in the story adore America and want to be loved in return by the children of New Hampshire, who stand for decency, loveliness, unscarred innocence. In fact, the acute desire to bestow and receive affection is what they most have in common. What stands in the way of their complete "marriage" to America is the crippling damage of antisemitism. The acculturated Jew of Fuchs's story, raised in the security of this continent, is drawn in two directions at once: he is proud of his gentile wife and solicitous of her welfare, but the "experienced" Jews of Europe are more interesting to him, and he feels he owes them something. His American bride can't help being frightened by the intensity of these creatures from what seems to be an alien planet, and it remains to be seen whether the Jewish husband will mediate successfully between her and his fellow Jews, or leave them to fend for themselves. America, in Fuchs's story, gives the acculturated Jew the choice that the hunted Jew is never granted.

Notes

1. Daniel Fuchs, "Twilight in Southern California" (1953), in *The Apathetic Bookie Joint* (New York: Methuen, 1979), 270–86. The story was originally published in the *New Yorker*.

2. Lamed Shapiro, "Der tseylem," in *Di yidishe melukhe un andere zakhn*, 2d ed. (New York: Farlag yidish lebn, 1929), 139–61. Trans. by Curt Leviant as "The Cross," in Lamed Shapiro, *The Jewish Government and Other Stories* (New York: Twayne, 1971), 114–30; also trans. by Joachim Neugroschel in David G. Roskies, ed., *The Literature of Destruction: Jewish Responses to Catastrophe* (Philadelphia: Jewish Publication Society, 1988), 193–202.

3. Abraham Cahan, *The Rise of David Levinsky* (New York: Harper and Row, 1960), 423–24. The novel was first published by Harper and Brothers, 1917.

4. Peretz Hirshbeyn, *Iber amerike* (Across America) (New York: Literarisher farlag, 1918). Hirshbeyn comments also on the decline of native culture among Poles, Russians, and others he encounters on his travels through America.

5. Moyshe Leib Halpern, "Unzer gortn," in *In nyu york* (New York: Vinkel, 1919), 7–8. Trans. as "Our Garden," in Benjamin and Barbara Harshav, eds., *American Yiddish Poetry* (Berkeley: University of California Press, 1986), 395–96.

6. Lamed Shapiro, *Der amerikaner shed*, in *Ksovim* (Posthumous Writings) (Los Angeles: L. shapiro ksovim komitet, 1949), 204–317.

7. Jerome Weidman, *I Can Get It for You Wholesale* (New York: Simon & Schuster, 1937); Budd Schulberg, *What Makes Sammy Run?* (New York: Random House, 1941); Mordecai Richler, *The Apprenticeship of Duddy Kravitz* (Don Mills, Ontario: Andre Deutsch, 1959).

8. Clifford Odets, *Waiting for Lefty*, was first performed by the Group Theatre in New York, 1935.

9. Bernard Malamud, *The Assistant* (New York: Farrar, Straus & Cudahy, 1957); *The Fixer* (New York: Farrar, Straus & Giroux, 1966).

10. Ruth R. Wisse, "American Jewish Intellectuals and the Jews" (paper presented at the Association for Jewish Studies Annual Conference, December 1990).

11. The relation between aesthetic achievement, contemporary criteria of aesthetic achievement, and engaged effort on behalf of European Jewry remains to be explored in full. For the merest taste of the complexity of the subject, here is a passage by Edward Dahlberg, written at a time in the 1930s when he was still associated with the Left, though ever scrupulous in his defense of the supremacy of artistic criteria: "Dorothea Brande, an American writer with lean gifts, attacked Ludwig Lewisohn's recent critical work solely on racial grounds. This is not

very clever of Miss Brande; for she must have been intellectually hard
put, if she would attack Lewisohn as a Jew when it is so easy to destroy
him as a writer." "Fascism and Writers," in *Samuel Beckett's Wake
and Other Uncollected Prose*, ed. Steven Moore (Elmwood Park, Ill.:
Dahlberg Archive, 1989), 42. In another milieu, readers of the Jewish
Publication Society objected to the excessive bleakness of A. M. Klein's
poetry "in a day when nearly the only thing left to the Jew is hope."
Quoted by Jonathan D. Sarna, *JPS: The Americanization of Jewish
Culture, 1888–1988* (Philadelphia: Jewish Publication Society, 1989),
213. Meyer Levin traces his own decline into paranoia in *The Obsession*
(New York: Simon & Schuster, 1973).

12. Jacob Glatstein, "Vegener," in *Gedenklider* (Poems in Remembrance)
(New York: Farlag yidisher kemfer, 1943), 46. Trans. by Chana Bloch
as "Wagons," in *The Penguin Book of Modern Yiddish Verse*, ed. Irving
Howe, Ruth R. Wisse, and Khone Shmeruk (New York: Viking, 1987),
432.

13. H. Leivick, *In treblinke bin ikh nit geven* (I Was Not at Treblinka:
Lyrical and Dramatic Poems) (New York: CYCO, 1945).

14. "Our Country and Our Culture: A Symposium," *Partisan Review*
(May–June 1952).

15. Cynthia Ozick, "Envy; or, Yiddish in America," in *The Pagan Rabbi
and Other Stories* (New York: Knopf, 1971), 100.

CHAPTER 5

Movies in America as Paradigms of Accommodation

Stephen J. Whitfield

Let us begin, as a *Time* magazine cover story portraying the most successful director of all time begins, when "all is darkness—as dark as a minute to midnight on the first day of creation, as dark as a movie house just before the feature starts. Then the movement begins, a tracking shot down the birth canal of a hallway, toward the mystery. Suddenly, light! A bright room filled with old men in beards and black hats: sages, perhaps, from another world. At the far end of the room, on a raised platform, is a blazing red light. The senses are suffused, the mystery deepens. There is only one persuasive explanation for this scene. It *must* be from a Steven Spielberg movie. Well, no. And yes. It is Spielberg's earliest memory, from a day in 1948 [when he was about half a year old] when he was taken in a stroller to a[n Orthodox] Cincinnati synagogue."[1] That sense of wonder and strangeness is what gives even mediocre movies their transfiguring power, their dreamy magic; for films exude a special flair in seeming to reproduce the journey from darkness to light recounted in the first chapter of *Genesis*. This *Time* portrait (by Richard Corliss) also reminds us that the cinema is an expression of the memories, the visions, the talents of particular individuals; and perhaps nothing is stranger than the genesis of the American movie studios, which were built at the end of an exodus to southern California that started from a radius of a few hundred miles of Warsaw. When Henry James visited his native land in 1904, after an

79

absence of two decades, he toured the Lower East Side, noted its intensity and energy, and wondered "what the genius of Israel may, or may not, really be 'up to.'"[2] He did not guess the correct answer, which was movies. By 1926 the moguls had created the fifth-largest industry in the United States and were making 90 percent of the world's films.

No art form has ever seemed so compromised by the crassness of its origins. The sheer commercialism and lack of cultivation of the moguls make it all too easy to feel snobbish toward them. Harry Cohn, for example, could not correctly spell the name of his own studio (Columbia). The independent producer Schmuel Gelbfisz (aka Sam Goldfish, Samuel Goldwyn) was even more culturally adrift, referring to one of his most prestigious properties, Lillian Hellman's *The Little Foxes*, as *The Three Little Foxes*; even his most famous melodrama he labeled *Withering Heights*. He invited Sergei Eisenstein to repeat *Potemkin*, "but a little cheaper, for Ronald Colman." After the writer-director Preston Sturges (whom he called "Sturgeon") finished adapting Tolstoy's *Resurrection*, Goldwyn praised its "snappy nineteenth-century dialogue."[3] No wonder that the dapper Ivy Leaguer S. J. Perelman spoke for other disgruntled scenarists as well when he described writing screenplays as "an occupation which, like herding swine, makes the vocabulary pungent but contributes little to one's prose style."[4] Nor did the literary pyrotechnics of William Faulkner mean much to Jack Warner, who bragged, "I've got America's best writer for $300 a week." But to be fair, compare such coarseness to the failure of the future Nobel laureate's own publishing firm, by 1945, to keep any of his seventeen novels (except for *Sanctuary*) in print.[5] Warner Brothers appreciated "America's best writer"—and kept him alive—better than Random House did.

What distinguished the tycoons was their gaudy intensity. As sons of failed fathers, these first-generation Americans yearned to erase the hyphens and the humiliations and, through the ferocity of their own ambition, to extinguish the memories of family defeats. Only spectacular success might purge the shame of poverty, exclusion, and insecurity. In *Body and Soul* (1947) Charlie Davis (John Garfield) rejects the prospect of a life selling two cents' worth of candy to kids. His mobility will be upward: "I don't wanna end up like Pop." In Woody Allen's *Radio Days* (1987), set in the same era, the boy who plays the young Allen is humiliated by the occupation of his father (Michael Tucker), a mere cabby, which is also how the father (Jack Warden) of the itch-to-get-rich hustler Duddy Kravitz (Richard Dreyfuss) makes a living in the eponymous 1974 film. Even in the upscale world of *Goodbye, Columbus* (1969), the father of the groom wonders whether Neil Klugman (Richard Benjamin) disdains him—the president of Patimkin Sinks (Jack Klugman)— as "a *goniff*" in a grimy marketplace to which a Newark librarian can easily feel superior. Such patrimony could not be happily squared with the obligation to honor thy father.

Sometimes the shame to be exorcised is cultural. The stern cantor in *The Jazz Singer* (1927) embodies the paternalism of the Old World, the tradition of ascription; for Jakie Rabinowitz is intended to fulfill a destiny in the synagogue. But the son upholds instead the value of individual achievement, of liberation from the limitations of birth, reminding his father, "You're of the old world! If you were born here, you'd feel the same as I do." In Richard Benjamin's film, *My Favorite Year* (1982), its central character, the young gag writer Benjy Stone (Mark Linn-Baker), is as hungry for show biz success as the protagonist of *The Jazz Singer*. When asked what it is about his Brooklyn background that embarrasses him, he responds, "Everything." The theme of *The Chosen* (1981) is also the struggle for growth beyond the authority of the father, who "almost didn't recognize me," Danny Saunders (Robbie Benson) recalls after departing from the Chasidic section of Brooklyn and moving to uptown Manhattan, near secular Columbia University. The film is something of a rarity in its groping toward reconciliation, ending with the two generations again on speaking terms. For both cherish the meaning of the Talmudic tale of the king and his estranged son "who had gone astray," with the messenger bringing the royal assurance: "Return as far as you can, and I will come to you the rest of the way."

But for the early filmmakers themselves, Judaism itself was something from which to escape, a birth defect that the first moguls spent a lifetime struggling to correct. Harry Cohn enjoyed working on Yom Kippur. The refusal of Hollywood's most conspicuous Jew by choice, Sammy Davis, Jr., to work on the Day of Atonement on the set of *Porgy and Bess* astonished Sam Goldwyn. The first wives of Goldwyn, Cohn, Jack Warner, and Louis B. Mayer were Jewish; their second wives were not. But though the head of MGM was especially proud of his friendship with Francis Cardinal Spellman, the moguls stopped short of the foot of the cross, perhaps because of their immunity to the appeal of *any* faith. (Cohn once challenged his brother Jack to recite the Lord's Prayer. Equally truculent, Jack accepted the bet and began to intone: "Now I lay me down to sleep. . . ." Harry Cohn scowled as he pushed his money to his brother: "That's enough. I didn't think you knew it.")[6] In part the studio bosses remained within the fold because their rabbi was the soothing Edgar F. Magnin, who arrived in Los Angeles in 1915 and from the Wilshire Boulevard Temple dominated Hollywood's religious life for over six decades. Magnin disdained the resurgence of ethnicity and nostalgia for the *shtetl* and observed how the moguls "made idols out of *shiksa* goddesses. They worshipped those blue-eyed blondes they were forbidden to have."[7]

But Rabbi Magnin didn't get it: those goddesses were no longer forbidden. They became the mistresses, the wives, the daughters-in-law of these parvenus—a social transformation that Henry Ford recorded in his notorious *Dearborn Independent*. The "Jew-controlled" movie industry was sabotaging the stability of Protestant America because "it is the genius of that race to create problems of a moral character in whatever business they achieve a majority."[8] The religion of Hollywood Jews was not so much Reform as hedonism, and it was their worship of the golden calf that they encouraged a God-fearing nation to adopt. To the antisemitic imagination, Hollywood was dangerous because of its aura of moral dissolution, its promise of forbidden and subversive pleasure. But to the moviemakers themselves, Hollywood constituted a romance with America itself, a nation that would extinguish the primordial hatreds of the Old World.

That is in part why intermarriage is probably the most sustained theme in the cinematic images of Jews. Such nuptials would prove that America was different, and the rejection of one's father has meant above all the freedom to choose one's spouse. The ultimate sign of accommodation has been the opportunity to marry outside the faith in a nation that was so endearing because of its own hospitality to Jews, its receptivity to what they might offer, which is, finally, themselves. This is the lesson that Philip Roth's most famous character learns: "For every Eddie [Fisher] yearning for a Debbie [Reynolds], there is a Debbie yearning for an Eddie—a Marilyn Monroe yearning for her Arthur Miller—even an Alice Faye yearning for Phil Harris. Even Jayne Mansfield was about to marry one, remember, when she was suddenly killed in a car crash?" And as for Elizabeth Taylor, "who would have believed that this girl on the horse [in *National Velvet*] . . . was lusting for our kind no less than we for hers? Because you know what Mike Todd was—a cheap facsimile of my Uncle Hymie upstairs!"[9]

Alex Portnoy's list could easily be enlarged and updated, from Norma Shearer yearning for her Irving Thalberg to Janet Leigh yearning for her Tony Curtis to Pia Zadora longing for her Meshulam Riklis, from Christie Brinkley with her Billy Joel to Diane Sawyer and her Mike Nichols, plus Kathleen Turner (who is Mrs. Jay Weiss), not to mention Caroline Kennedy longing for her Edwin Schlossberg. The movies reflected, amplified, and exalted such bonds, which had their international versions as well, with Brigitte Bardot longing for her Sami Frey, and Lady Antonia Fraser her Harold Pinter. And how could Portnoy have ignored "sweater girl" Lana Turner, who was briefly married to Artie Shaw? The Hollywood happy ending is one that joins Jew and non-Jew in matrimony, or at least in love, triumphing over the narrowness of particularism. Movies are so addicted to this theme that even when Herman Wouk's bestseller concludes with Marjorie Morgenstern becoming Mrs. Milton Schwartz, her celluloid self manages to end up with the only gentile character in the picture, the blonde Wally Wronken. *Dirty Dancing* (1987), a second look at the summer camps of "the Jewish Alps," set a decade or so later than *Marjorie Morningstar*, features the romance between doctor's daughter Jennifer Grey and ethnic proletarian Patrick Swayze. Whenever Harry meets Sally, audiences expect differences to be transcended. Such expectations are fulfilled as recently as *White Palace* (1990), in which Max Baron (James Spader) renounces his family, his friends (mostly Jewish), his job (advertising), and his community (St. Louis) to live in New York with an ex-Catholic Hoosier waitress (Susan Sarandon) despite the barriers of class and sensibility that the film has—until the ending—underscored. From the perspective of Jewish destiny, however, these are fatal attractions; for they enfeeble a sense of separateness and endanger the continuity of peoplehood.

These impulses were fully revealed in *The Jazz Singer*, a film that, in memory and myth, has been so intertwined with the career of the star who initially inspired it that a consideration of Al Jolson's own career is relevant. Few entertainers have ever exuded his daemonic razzle-dazzle and kinetic force. Opening *Bombo* in New York in 1921, Jolson returned for thirty-seven curtain calls. At a U.S. Army benefit in 1918, it might have seemed malicious to bill him after Enrico Caruso; but when Jolson bolted onto the stage and assured the already dazed audience, "Folks, you ain't heard *nothin'* yet," a legend was born. Thrilling standing-room-only crowds, he lived up to the hype. But the ten films in which Jolson starred are, except for his first, forgotten; and even in *The Jazz Singer*, his acting is awkward and stilted. Because microphones and recording equipment were too primitive to capture the full timbre of his voice, the transition to radio was unsuccessful; and Decca has not rereleased his records. The electric charge that he emitted merely by strutting onto a stage, and dropping to one knee to worship "My Mammy," is dimmed. A headliner at the dawn of the century whose spectacular career was already fading by the Great Depression, Jolson can now be appreciated only by an act of faith.

Though no singer could more poignantly evoke the banks of the Swanee, waitin' for the *Robert E. Lee*, he had been born in Lithuania, probably in 1886, and came to the United States eight years later. His father Moshe Yoelson served as a rabbi in Washington, D.C., where his mother Naomi died soon after immigrating—a shock that may be the key to their fifth child's unappeasable appetite for the love of which he was so abruptly deprived. Where the relentless drive came from is less easily explained, but no one was more assertive of the right to renown that he believed his talent conferred. Success came quickly, bolstering an ego so huge that, by comparison, General Douglas MacArthur was downright self-effacing. At the age of thirty-five, Jolson had a Broadway theater named for him. He became enormously rich, the personification of all the glowing promises that the New World might bestow on so charismatic an adopted son. He reciprocated in part by a series of exhausting musical tours during the Second World War and the Korean War, enjoying something of a comeback before his death late in 1950.

"The World's Greatest Entertainer" was, however, a lousy role model for his fellow Jews. Neither the piety of his family background, nor his own fluency in Yiddish, nor the speed with which he reacted to antisemitic remarks with his fists exempted Jolson from the lures of assimilation. His four wives were gentiles—a record so perfect that it is no surprise to learn from his most recent biographer that Jolson was incapable of sexual relations with Jewish women. When Jolson once greeted his two-year-old son with the question, "Who am I, Sonny Boy?" the reply was humiliating: "You're the Jew."[10] Although *The Jazz Singer* ends with a return to the synagogue from which Jack Robin had fled as a youth, to substitute for his dying father by chanting "Kol Nidre," Jolson himself performed on Yom Kippur until, near the end of his life, the gossip columnist Walter Winchell shamed the star into altering such relentless work habits. Buried in a *tallis* (which he never wore) after a funeral service at Los Angeles's Temple Israel (which he never attended), Jolson was eulogized by comedian George Jessel (whom he detested) as a "great inspiration . . . to the Jewish people in the last forty years. . . . With a gaiety that was militant, uninhibited and unafraid, [Jolson] told the world that the Jew in America did not have to sing in sorrow. . . . Jolson is the happiest portrait that can be painted about an American of the Jewish faith."[11]

But that faith is precisely what Jolson was so eager to abandon; and his gaiety sprang from his American citizenship, not his Jewish origins—as *The Jazz Singer* itself makes clear. The enduring fascination of that first talkie, in which Jolson was lucky enough to play a version of himself, is the way the conflict of generations is adjudicated. Though loyal to the love of his mother, the heir to an unbroken cantorial tradition of "Rabinowitzes" betrays no remorse for having repudiated the world of our fathers. A factotum had to remind Jolson himself every winter to say *kaddish* for his mother. For his life mixed public acclaim and private emptiness, as though the transaction between the performer and the audience was too fulfilling to spill any love over outside of show business. Though often impulsively generous, Jolson was virtually friendless. Fanny Brice's reaction to the news of his death was rare only for its candor, not for its sentiment: "I never liked him."[12] The trajectory of the career of "The Sweet Singer of Israel"—the phrase inscribed at Jolson's grave site—was apt. Because silent movies had been popular in immigrant neighborhoods in part because no knowledge of English was required, the "talkies" with which he was so indelibly associated also accelerated the tempo of Americanization.

Among his successors in popular culture, the constraints of space permit consideration only of Woody Allen (b. 1935). He is ubiquitous, the subject of innumerable magazine cover stories and books; and French critics have paid him the ultimate accolade by placing him in the tradition of comic genius that stretches from Molière to Jerry Lewis. In the academy Woody Allen studies are as hot as a blast of geothermal steam; and in the pulpit, especially on Friday evenings when the Torah portion is remote or obscure, his films have become the topics of sermons. His comic persona has exploited a physical stature even less prepossessing than Jolson's. Allen's acting ability is equally modest, though put into the service of a fertile imagination as a writer and director. Both of Allen's wives have been Jewish, though his most publicized off-screen romances have been with gentiles. He seems to have understood the Hollywood tradition that cinematic romances across the gaps of religion and ethnicity are more combustible. When he plays a Jew, the involvement tends to be with gentile women (from *Sleeper* on, customarily with the characters played by Diane Keaton and Mia Farrow). In the earlier, wilder comedies, Allen's characters are apparently gentiles involved with characters played by manifestly Jewish actresses (Janet Margolin, Louise Lasser). Only in the "Oedipus Wrecks" segment of *New York Stories* (1988) does he turn to a Jewish woman, under the celestial influence of his mother.

As his characters have become more emphatically Jewish, they have synchronized with a more insistent moralism and a more pronounced social criticism in his films. The early parodies like *Take the Money and Run* (1969), *Bananas* (1971), and *Love and Death* (1975) did not bestow any noteworthy Jewish traits upon his protagonists. He had invented and played Jewish characters in *Play It Again Sam* (1972) and *Sleeper* (1973); but only with *Annie Hall*

(1977) did he begin to connect that ethnic identity with a sense of integrity. First the notion is aesthetic, such as his appreciation for foreign films and his opposition to the laugh tracks in television studios in Los Angeles, where "the only cultural advantage [over New York] is that you can make a right turn on a red light."[13] Then the notion is ethical in *Manhattan* (1979). Rebuked for his self-righteousness ("We're just human beings, you know. You think you're God!"), Isaac Davis (Woody Allen) replies, "I—I gotta model myself after someone!" Integrity means loyalty, commitment, faithfulness. "I think people should mate for life," he proclaims in the same film, "like pigeons or Catholics."[14] *Broadway Danny Rose* (1984) becomes even more explicit. As a talent agent on the shaggier fringes of show business, wearing a *chai* insignia around his neck, he is the impresario as *tsaddik*, yearning for *emes* as he provides Thanksgiving dinner for all the lonely people. Wearing a *yarmulke* near the end of *Crimes and Misdemeanors* (1989), Cliff Stern (Allen) makes integrity both aesthetic and moral: thou shalt not sell out like Lester (Alan Alda), for it is better to show documentaries in film festivals in Cincinnati; nor shalt thou kill, like Dr. Judah Rosenthal (Martin Landau), even though in this dreadful world it is possible to get away with murder. (In Allen's universe the violation of the Seventh Commandment is far more common; adultery is a major theme of many of his films, beginning with *Play It Again Sam*.) *Crimes and Misdemeanors* is a break-through because it even presents a rabbi as an object of sympathy rather than satire, gallantly dancing with his daughter at her wedding though he is afflicted with the curse of darkness. The equation, however fitful and preachy, of moral idealism with Jewishness represents an assurance that was previously beyond the reach of American films.

But the case for such ethnic confidence and even assertiveness should not be overstated. Take, for example, the pivotal issue of casting, which is more than a measure of the power of individual talent and stardom in Hollywood; it remains an interesting index of nervousness with Jewishness as well. The evidence is mixed. For even after the 1960s, when ethnicity became increasingly acknowledged and even celebrated, studio choices of particular actors and actresses have been peculiar. The movies written by Neil Simon (or adapted from his plays) often seem dislocated because they typically put gentile performers like Jack Lemmon and Blythe Danner in recognizably Jewish settings. In her novel *Heartburn*, Nora Ephron drew upon her marriage to crackerjack reporter Carl Bernstein, whom Dustin Hoffman had portrayed in *All the President's Men*. But the screen roles of Rachel Samstat and Mark Feldman in *Heartburn* (1986) were assigned to Meryl Streep and Jack Nicholson, making the film "so waspified," one critic observed, "you'd think Nora Ephron had married Woodward instead of Bernstein."[15] (It was perhaps the most bizarre piece of casting since Omar Shariff played Nicky Arnstein in *Funny Girl* [1968].) Eyebrows were further raised with Barry Levinson's *Avalon* (1990), in which Sam and Eva Krichinsky—the East European Jews who settle in Baltimore early in the century—are played by an East German and an Englishwoman, with Aidin Quinn playing their son Jules. Still speaking in the accents of universalism, Levinson justified his decision to make his dramatis personae immigrants rather than Jews with a Thanksgiving meal more important to such a family than what Marjorie Morgenstern's mother in the 1958 film calls "Passover dinner." (By contrast the *seder* is central to *Crimes and Misdemeanors* because it is the battleground of the quarrel with an absentee God.)

Indeed, several of these films suggest the importance of food consumption, which Jews tend to make into what comedian Jackie Mason calls "an emotional experience." For them eating well may indeed be confirmation of survival, proof of having prevailed against adversity. Noshing is sacred. In Alfred Kazin's Brownsville neighborhood, none of the kids could ever be considered overweight: "The word for a fat boy was *solid*."[16] Uncle Sampson compulsively gulps down grapes at the Morgensterns'; and the wedding in *Goodbye, Columbus* seems only to whet the guests' appetite, starting with the decapitation of the chopped liver dish sculpted in the shape of a chicken.

Dietary restrictions have also been among the biggest impediments dividing Jews from gentiles, which means that violation of *kashrut* has been a visible symbol of the hunger to join the larger society. The way barriers are broken between Jew and gentile is through food; for the cinematic Jewish men who mix with non-Jewish women have already mixed meat and dairy, already crossed over into *trefe*. Virtually the first sight that movie audiences had of Jolson himself is on the road, far from the influence of tradition and neighborhood that he fled a decade earlier, eating breakfast—ham and eggs—in the company of blonde showgirls. It is therefore not too precipitous to jump from *The Jazz Singer* to Alvy Singer, dining with the midwestern family of his girlfriend Annie Hall and politely praising the "dynamite ham."[17]

Across such dining tables, perhaps even more than across the tables of boardrooms, stereotypes are broken; and ignorance, superstition, and prejudice can be overcome in such movies. For the final accommodation to America is the falsification of stereotypes, dooming them to a joke and then to irrelevance and oblivion. The burden of stereotypes is among the complicating features of minority status, in which one is compelled to see one's self through the eyes of others. Such images may be positive or negative (or both— like the bumper sticker that is common on cars in Boston: "God created whiskey to keep the Irish from ruling the world"). But perhaps the strongest proof of the distinctiveness of a social group is the persistence of stereotypes about it. They may be unfair; they may be pernicious; they can be true or false as very loose generalizations (subject to shades of qualification). But they are unavoidable because, as Walter Lippmann argued in 1922, they simplify the complicating flux of experience, making it intelligible and predictable.

A change in stereotypes may signify the dramatic alteration in the condition of the group itself. The "Jewish American princess" can scarcely be found earlier than the 1950s, when the movement that began in the dream of escape from the East Side to the Bronx (in *The Jazz Singer*) was extended to the suburbs of Long Island and Westchester County and New Jersey. The stereotype emerges in two novels—Herman Wouk's *Marjorie Morningstar* (1955) and Roth's *Goodbye, Columbus* (1959)—adapted into films whose protagonists could have been played interchangeably by Natalie Wood and Ali MacGraw. Indeed, when newlyweds Ronald and Harriet Patimkin chat with Neil in Larry Peerce's film, Harriet envies the librarian's "first crack at all the best sellers" (a reading list that would surely have included *Marjorie Morningstar*, especially after *Time* put Wouk on its cover). However disagreeable the stereotype may be from the standpoint of both Judaism and feminism, it could have emerged only after affluence had been achieved.

As graduates of Hunter College and Radcliffe College, respectively, Marjorie and Brenda are finely attuned to the status of prospective husbands. Noel Airman, aged thirty-three, admits that he has "no head for business"; and having so spectacularly flunked out of Cornell Law School, he cannot aspire to the vocation of his father the judge. By changing his surname, Noel has ceased to be a man of honor (Ehrman) and has become a *Luftmensch* instead. Though living in Greenwich Village, he is hardly a bohemian; his target is Broadway. But the rebuke by Marjorie's mother—"A man has to be something"—applies equally to librarian Neil Klugman, who, referring to the philistinism of Brenda's family and friends, says he doesn't "want to spend the rest of [his] life grubbing around for money as though nothing else in the world existed." Not that bohemianism is an option either, for "grow[ing] a beard and sleep-[ing] in the park" also strike Neil as "so ridiculous." Such drifting is incompatible with the bourgeois ideals that have triumphed in America, including its Jews.

The depiction of materialism and the display of luxury beginning in the 1950s not only reflected social actuality but also suggested that the most ancient of all antisemitic stereotypes no longer intimidated Jewish moviemakers. Of all the crimes and misdemeanors charged to the Jews, the worst has been an uncanny or even supernatural capacity to make money, perverted into avarice. When the Reverend Jerry Falwell, for example, once addressed his followers on the steps of the Virginia state capitol a decade ago, he told them that Jews "can make more money accidentally than you can make on purpose."[18] This folk belief is articulated and addressed in *The Pawnbroker* (1965) when the Puerto Rican Jesus Ortiz asks the Holocaust survivor for whom he works, "How come you people come to business so naturally?" (In the novel the phrase is "you Jews.")[19] Sol Nazerman accepts the innocence of the question and replies, "You want to learn the secret of our success, is that right?" The reply is an acrid history lesson, an illustration of that "worldly asceticism," that deferral of the gratification of immediate comfort that Max Weber hypothesized was intrinsic to "the spirit of capitalism."[20] The sublime covenant of a chosen people, Nazerman explains, is reduced to "a piece of cloth" that facilitates the canny arts of millennial survival, and "a mercantile heritage" becomes twisted into the stereotype of "a sheeny, a mocky and a kike." The stereotype shows up again when Annie Hall realizes that Alvy Singer is what her "Grammy Hall would call a real Jew. . . . She hates Jews. She thinks that they just make money."[21] But then Annie herself quickly acknowledges her grandmother's hypocrisy and thus points to the paradox of such a stereotype in the United States, where the pursuit of riches is usually deemed worthy of admiration rather than a disgrace. "No stigma attaches to the love of money in America," Tocqueville observed a century and a half earlier, "and providing it does not exceed the bounds imposed by public order, it is held in honor. The American will describe as noble and estimable ambition what our medieval ancestors would have called base cupidity."[22]

Stereotypes can be ugly, but their emergence can signify the confidence that they are *only* stereotypes, not proof of the collective malevolence of the Jewish people. Perhaps it is only when they completely evaporate that Jewish survivalists should worry, for such disappearance might mean the end of historic distinctiveness. When images of Jews no longer need to be fulfilled or falsified, combated or ridiculed, the Jewish place in America will have been eroded, swept away by the riptides of assimilation. That possibility cannot be discounted in a society that does not honor the cohesive values that Judaism once sanctioned, a country that seems dedicated to fragmentation and discontinuity. The radical instability of American culture, its sanctioning of an aggressive individualism that exalts autonomy and independence, seems destined to contradict and defeat the verities of piety, family, and tradition. Accommodation is personified in the Charlie Davis of *Body and Soul*, a creature not of the Jewish past but of the American environment, a student not of the Torah for its own sake but of "the manly art" of bashing others for pay, a sportsman rather than a scholar, a believer in the superiority of winning over losing, a worshipper of what the philosopher William James called "the bitch-goddess Success." In Robert Rossen's emblematic film, Charlie Davis is a hero. In the light of the pre-American history of the *Galut*, however, he is an anomaly.

What the United States offered the children and grandchildren of immigrants was a vision of making it, an aspiration to climb to the top that was nowhere more powerful than within the precincts of show business itself. Jews have enriched American popular culture, from Jack Robin to Jolson, from the Warner Brothers (who were satirized in the 1930 Broadway comedy *Once in a Lifetime* as the Schlepkin Brothers) to Steven Spielberg (who is not shleppin' but Amblin—the name of his mini-studio), from Herman Wouk (who began by writing gags for Fred Allen) to Woody Allen (who began by writing gags for others), from Fanny Brice to Barbra Streisand— two distinctive entertainers who fit the definition of acting talent that director John Ford once applied to Barry Fitzgerald: "He could steal a scene from a dog." Such figures gave as well as received, even though this is also the place to record a certain regret that a definably Jewish subculture has often been left impoverished.

Because Jews in America were "born free" and did not need decrees or laws or military invasions to emancipate them from the ghetto, and because they are a minority in a nation that has never established a church nor even been officially Christian, the United States has been the locus classicus of accommodation. America has harbored the largest Jewish community in Diaspora history and, by any standard, the freest as well. The fate of American Jewry is therefore pivotal to any sense of the meaning of Exile (and to Israel as well). That destiny is the supreme test of how far acculturation can go without eroding the sense of distinctiveness, without subverting identity as an *am echad* (a singular people). Especially in our own time American Jewry is threatened by the unparalleled opportunities to disappear into the general population without guilts to be assuaged or penalties to be calibrated, and is challenged to summon its resources to legitimate the continuity of that history. So far American Jewry as a whole has not flunked this test of an open society. Sometimes they are in the dark, however, as this essay has suggested, bewitched by images of themselves.

The first human sounds in a feature film consisted of choruses of popular songs like "My Gal Sal," sung by Bobby Gordon as the young Jakie Rabinowitz. The second voice that audiences heard belonged to a Hungarian tenor singing "Kol Nidre," with lip synching by the actor Warner Oland (who became more famous as Charlie Chan). The order of appearance reflected the cultural priority, as all the vows were subordinated to the songs of Tin Pan Alley and Broadway—the Jewish music that impresarios like the Shubert brothers would make even more famous and beloved than Schubert *Lieder*, the melodies that Benny Goodman would transmit everywhere (except perhaps in the Williamsburg of *The Chosen*). Such talent for tapping and shaping popular feeling is also what the Jews who created Hollywood exhibited, and what the artists they employed have left us as a legacy to cherish and reconsider. That saga of creativity is still not over. The most ancient of peoples has not yet been diagnosed as suffering from chronic fatigue syndrome, even if the promise of a messianic age continues to seem so distantly over the horizon. Till then, as Henry James's dying novelist Dencombe reassures us, "We work in the dark, we do what we can—we give what we have. . . . The rest is the madness of art."[23]

Notes

1. Richard Corliss, "I Dream for a Living," *Time*, July 15, 1985, 54, reprinted in Arthur Asa Berger, ed., *Media USA: Process and Effect* (New York: Longman, 1988), 248.
2. Henry James, *The American Scene*, ed. Leon Edel (1907; Bloomington: Indiana University Press, 1968), 135.
3. A. Scott Berg, *Goldwyn: A Biography* (New York: Knopf, 1989), 193, 240–41, 322, 355.
4. S. J. Perelman, *The Most of S. J. Perelman* (New York: Simon & Schuster, 1958), 1.
5. Joseph Blotner, *Faulkner: A Biography*, vol. 2 (New York: Random House, 1974), 1187.
6. John Gregory Dunne, "Goldwynism," *New York Review of Books*, May 18, 1989, 28.
7. Magnin quoted in Berg, *Goldwyn*, 164.
8. Ford quoted in Neal Gabler, *An Empire of Their Own: How the Jews Invented Hollywood* (New York: Crown, 1988), 276.
9. Philip Roth, *Portnoy's Complaint* (New York: Random House, 1969), 151.
10. Herbert G. Goldman, *Jolson: The Legend Comes to Life* (New York: Oxford University Press, 1988), 229.

11. Jessel quoted in ibid., 301–2.
12. Brice quoted in ibid., 300.
13. Woody Allen, *Four Films of Woody Allen* (New York: Random House, 1982), 10.
14. Ibid., 197, 264.
15. Rita Kempley quoted in Paul Slansky, *The Clothes Have No Emperor: A Chronicle of the American Eighties* (New York: Simon & Schuster, 1989), 167.
16. Alfred Kazin, *A Walker in the City* (New York: Harcourt, Brace, 1951), 34.
17. Allen, *Four Films*, 55.
18. Falwell quoted in Frances FitzGerald, *Cities on a Hill: A Journey through Contemporary American Cultures* (New York: Simon & Schuster, 1986), 172.
19. Edward Lewis Wallant, *The Pawnbroker* (1961; New York: Manor, 1962), 42–43.
20. Max Weber, *The Protestant Ethic and the Spirit of Capitalism* (New York: Scribner's, 1958), 154, passim.
21. Allen, *Four Films*, 38–39.
22. Alexis de Tocqueville, *Democracy in America*, vol. 2, ed. Phillips Bradley (New York: Knopf, 1945), 248.
23. Henry James, "The Middle Years" (1893), in *The Short Stories of Henry James*, ed. Clifton Fadiman (New York: Random House, 1945), 315.

PART TWO

Jews and the American Liberal Tradition

CHAPTER 6

From Equality to Liberty:
The Changing Political Culture
of American Jews

Henry L. Feingold

Today, when the qualities that once differentiated Jews from other Americans have all but vanished, the distinctive political culture of Jews persists. They continue to be liberal, though no longer the most liberal group in the electorate. Today's brand of Jewish liberalism would hardly be recognizable to the immigrant generation. Liberalism is a dynamic, constantly evolving phenomenon. Survey research, which has become the preferred way of determining how liberal Jews are, merely presents a snapshot of its contemporary contours. Such research can tell us little of how Jewish liberalism evolved to become what it is today. Not only the persistence of Jewish liberalism but also the shape it has taken cry out for historical explanation. The thoughts that follow constitute an attempt to make sense of Jewish liberalism in its American historical context.

So disparate are the principles of liberalism that finding some internal logic is a daunting task. At the risk of oversimplification, we note that it is composed of the new relationship between the citizen and the secular state that grew out of the Enlightenment, as encompassed in the well-known slogan of the French Revolution: "Liberty, equality, fraternity." In the new civil society the citizen is as free to pursue happiness as the boundaries of the community allow. Whether that pursuit leads to some form of self-realization or the accumulation of estate does not matter. He is equal to every other citizen, at least before the law. Fraternity in its simplest form is related to the right of citizens to associate in religious, social, and political institutions, to form a civil society mediating between the state and citizenry.

In our country these rights are embodied in the Constitution and especially in its Bill of Rights. Liberty is also assured by what John Adams called "political architecture," which keeps the legislative, judicial, and executive functions separated and checking each other. It is designed, as Woodrow Wilson once noted, to handcuff government. That was no accident, since it was believed that a government that was prevented from governing assured the citizenry its sphere of liberty: "That government governs best which governs least." The form that liberalism took in the early National period was thus more libertarian than egalitarian.[1]

The perceptive reader will by now have noted what Marxist dialecticians like to call an "internal contradiction." Left to its own devices will liberty, which allows free rein for our unequal talents, not make a shambles of equality? That is what Tocqueville foresaw. The society of free and equal individuals envisaged by the French Revolution could exist only in theory. In reality a polis composed of free, private, individuated citizens had nothing to hold it together.[2] The disparities in wealth and station inevitable in the free society would surely erode the bonds of fraternity as well. How can justice prevail in such a society? A government that is so empowered might regulate such inequities, but in order to secure liberty we have by design underpowered government. How then can such a system work?

The answer might well be that it has worked more by dint of the ever-increasing size of the gross national product than by the internal logic of its founding principles. The defenders of the libertarian variety of liberalism, which today substitutes for a conservative politics in America, argue that this is no accident. Liberty in the economic sphere has released such enormous new productive energies that we have become the first society in history in which insufficiency of goods and services is not a perpetual plague. That makes the grinding problem of how to distribute wealth equitably far less stressful. If the economic pie is ever growing, less energy can be expended on the question of "who gets what."

From a historical point of view, all American politics is played out in the arena of liberalism. The American political dialogue has liberty at one end of its axis and equality at the other. That is why George Bush's use of the dreaded "L" word in the election of 1988 to put his opponent to rout is comical. From a historical perspective he qualifies as much for the liberal label as did Dukakis. There are no monarchists in America.

As the Enlightenment's favorite child, with very little of a feudal past, America could not legitimately produce a conservative ideology. Rather, in the liberal context, conservatives are those who try to get the government off the backs of the citizenry so that it can get on with the serious business of producing wealth. Conservatism in American politics is the tendency that, in the name of liberty, opposes expanding the government sector to furnish social welfare or even to regulate business. In contrast, the egalitarian-minded left wing of the Democratic party, to which most Jewish voters adhere, wants the wealth produced by private enterprise to be shared with those who have little to sustain themselves—the homeless, the unemployed, the handicapped, single parents, victims of AIDS, or whatever new group of unequals they can find. Predictably, liberals conceive of the government's taxing power as an instrument for the fairer distribution of wealth.

What liberalism does is what the Left has always done in parliamentary democracies. It seeks out the regnant inequity and places it on the political agenda. During the National period it sought to remove the remnants of feudalism, the payment of quitrent, and property qualifications for the franchise. During the Jacksonian period the franchise was further liberalized and the United State Bank was attacked as a citadel of privilege that ought not to be strengthened by government authority.[3] During the 1850s and the Civil War it sought to extend freedom and citizenship to the slaves. That was achieved through the civil rights amendments, especially the Fourteenth Amendment. The Progressives sensed that the trusts needed to be regulated because their power was not only corrupting the political process but also threatening to curtail liberty. It was a case of checking private power as government power was checked.

The New Deal is noteworthy because it tilted liberalism away from its libertarian pole toward its egalitarian-statist one. That was not precisely a new trend. There had been deep government intrusions during the Civil War and the Progressive period. For example, the Freedmen's Bureau specifically designed for the rehabilitation of the former slaves set a precedent for government-sponsored social engineering in the nineteenth century. But it was the Depression with its foreboding of revolution that set the stage for a broader, more sustained effort at restructuring through the agency of government.

During the Depression a much larger sector of the public required government nurture. Not only would the freewheeling capitalism that characterized post–Civil War industrial development have to be controlled but the citizenry would also have to be assured some kind of security from the vagaries of the business cycle: social security to protect the unemployed and the aged, the Civilian Conservation Corps (CCC) to protect the resource of youth, even an attempt at conservation on a regional basis to protect human and natural resources (the Tennessee Valley Authority). Government became a permanent fifth wheel in the economy. The legislation of the first New Deal marked the deepest government intrusion yet into the economy and through it into the lives of the citizenry. With it came a tilt to the egalitarian side of liberalism.

But the recurrence of economic collapse in 1937 cast serious doubts on the efficacy of a welfare program paid for through deficit financing rather than through wealth produced by the economy. There was a retreat from structural reform toward the more limited policy of providing a stable economic environment in which capitalism might thrive. By the second New Deal we note a steady retreat from the government intrusion and social engineering that characterized the early years of the New Deal. Aware that the early program was not producing desired results, Roosevelt abandoned the notion of working with "big business" (his NRA had in any case been declared unconstitutional) in favor of business regulation. The government would now attempt to stabilize the economy indirectly through its fiscal policy, including new banking laws and a strengthening of the existing Federal Reserve System. Under Thurmond Arnold, the antitrust division of the Justice Department was reactivated. The problems posed by the Depression were never fully resolved. The war started the economic machine pumping again. It pumped so well that, by the end of the war, managers were speaking of the "miracle of production" without which the Allied victory would not have been possible. The triumph of libertarianism, at least in the economic sphere, which can be noted in the "supply side" economics of the Reagan and Bush administrations, also grows out of the New Deal experience, especially the second New Deal and the wartime industrial mobilization.

Jewish liberals welcomed the New Deal's welfare state programs, especially its positive attitude toward organized labor. The "trickle up" twist of its economic policy, which pumped millions of dollars into the economy through "make work," placed the New Deal within ideological striking distance of Jewish political culture, which emphasized the just society in which the "forgotten man" would receive his due. (Rabbi Stephen Wise, the quintessential Jewish liberal of the first half of the twentieth century, took credit for the "forgotten man" phrase.) Jews, seeing the state as an instrument to help achieve a just society, were persistent in demanding that government do more. That tendency was buttressed by socialist ideology, which reinforced the statist aspect of Jewish political culture. American Jewry historically looked to government intercession for its brethren in the foreign policy arena. Now the second and third generation abandoned the pledge given to Peter Stuyvesant that Jews would always take care of their own. In 1933 hardpressed Jewish social-work agencies removed Jewish dependent families from their rolls so that they might qualify for government relief. For Jews, power was granted to government but its leaders are assigned a matching responsibility to "repair the world." Communalism is based on shared responsibility.[4]

That penchant for the egalitarian aspects of liberalism was not yet fully present in American Jewish political culture in the eighteenth and nineteenth centuries. Before the arrival of the East European Jews the Jewish political profile was kept low. The exposed position Jews assumed when they supported the Whigs in the American Revolution was exceptional although, considering the liberal bias of the Revolution and the relationship of its principles to the Enlightenment, the support it received in the small Jewish community seemed natural. Less easily explained is their support of the physiocrat, anti-urban Jefferson over Alexander Hamilton, whose financial program was designed to buttress the very commercial sector of the economy with which Jews had cast their lot. Apparently even during the National period Jews earned like Episcopalians but voted like the then equivalent of Puerto Ricans. In the liberal context such altruism is not so strange. "It is an ironic fact," observes George Will, "that we are a nation of people who talk like Jefferson, yet we live like Hamiltonians."[5]

Jews did not notably join in the struggle to abolish slavery, and with the exception of Louis Brandeis, who had not yet found his Jewish constituency, there was little interest in an ameliorative solution to the trust problem.[6] Socialist-oriented Jews preferred the totalistic solutions of socialism. The trust problem would be solved when government assumed ownership of the "means of production." There was a handful of acculturated Jews who involved themselves with progressive reform, especially its advocacy of municipal restructuring. But East European Jews, who were unfamiliar with the reform process, sought a total solution in the just society that socialism would bring.

Most first-generation East European Jews were not yet fully ready to enter the American political arena. In 1900 Jewish voting volume in New York City was low and socialist candidates ran poorly in Jewish districts, where the Republican was usually preferred.[7] Jews sought to solve their social, cultural, and economic problems by employing traditional instruments of communal organization that they believed could be recreated in the free environment of America. That was the thrust of the New York Kehillah, the American Jewish Committee, the Congress movement, and the Federation movement, all of which were established in the first two decades of the century.

Jewish liberalism became fully fashioned during the prosperous twenties and the Depression thirties. As the second generation became more involved with the problem of living in America, some of the European cast of Jewish political culture was abandoned. During the prewar period the thrust and energy of left-wing Jewish political culture was anchored in socialist ideology with its strong statist component. It was disseminated through the Jewish labor movement, a network of Yiddish schools and neighborhood social and fraternal clubs—the *landsmanshaftn*—and, above all, through the Yiddish press. These persisted in the twenties but would grow weaker as Yiddish-speaking culture declined.

The immigrant political culture was not alone in its concern for social justice. The Reform branch of Judaism had a strong social-action component active in everything from municipal reform to antilynching legislation.[8] Stephen Wise, a Reform rabbi, served as a bridge to the secular liberals who found their home in the reconstituted American Jewish Congress, which he led. It too had a social-action commission.[9] Rabbis Judah Magnes and Abba Hillel Silver were no less avid than Wise in their pursuit of liberal causes.

During the twenties the Jewish electorate shifted its allegiance to the Democratic party, which would become the home of egalitarian liberalism. In the 66th Congress (1919–1921) there were five Jewish Republican representatives and only one Democrat. By the 75th Congress (1937–1939) the situation was reversed. Of the ten Jewish representatives elected, nine were Democrats and only one was a Republican.[10] The number of Jews voting for Socialist candidates like Eugene Debs was disproportionately high, about 38 percent in the election of 1920. They also showed a maverick tendency to veer off to third-party candidates like the Progressive Robert M. LaFollette, Jr., who received 22 percent of their vote in the election of 1924. But the drawing power of socialist candidates in Jewish districts declined in the twenties. The Lower East Side district, which had sent Meyer London to Congress, was gerrymandered out of existence in 1922, and Jewish districts in Williamsburg and Brownsville, which had a sizeable socialist vote, were disrupted by the split in the Socialist party.[11]

The majority of Jewish voters were attracted to Al Smith, the Democrat reform governor of New York, who, although linked to the Tammany machine, displayed considerable political skill in creating the reform wing of the Democratic party. Smith, moreover, surrounded himself with a group of reform-minded Jewish advisors—Belle and Henry Moskowitz, Joseph Proskauer, Sam Rosenman, and Robert Moses—who were viewed with pride by Jewish voters. In the election of 1928, Jews gave Smith 72 percent of their vote. The liberal-urban-ethnic coalition, with its prominent role for Jewish advisors, which also would characterize Roosevelt's New Deal, actually found its roots in the Smith administration during his tenure as governor of New York.[12] The 82 percent of their ballots Jews awarded Roosevelt in the election of 1932, which rose to over 90 percent in the three subsequent presidential elections, was based squarely on the new constellation of forces that began in 1924 with second-generation Jewish voters. Even Jewish socialists felt compelled to vote for a high-born, reform-minded patrician, though we shall note that a third party had to be created so as not to compromise their socialist principles.

From the outset Jewish liberal political culture possessed both a statist and a libertarian/reformist wing, but the former outweighed the latter, especially when socialist-inclined Jewish voters are added to the scale. The acculturation process itself would, however, act to right the balance. Several developments in the twenties acted to weaken the socialist thrust while establishing the bases for a stronger libertarian one. While there was great concern about the restrictionism embodied in the immigration laws and the Harvard enrollment case and the virulent antisemitic rhetoric of Henry Ford's *Dearborn Independent*, it was clear that these forces were not sufficiently strong to halt the headlong drive by Jews to achieve middle-class station, which they achieved a generation before other ethnics of the "new" immigration. By 1923 they had wrung a satisfactory agreement from Harvard, which, on the surface at least, seemed to establish a precedent to give their children access to the nation's best universities.

By 1927 a humiliating public apology had also been wrung from Ford. The KKK and other nativist groups were much weakened by the end of the decade. Jewish students were flooding into law and medical schools in disproportionate numbers and professionalization was well underway. Jews, it became clear, were not the sons of workers nor would they produce sons who were workers. It seemed that even their sojourn in small business and manufacture would last only one generation. The prosperity of the twenties was fully shared by Jews. Under such circumstances, preaching the imminent collapse of the market economy sounded increasingly hollow and discordant. Not only was a growing number of Jews involved in the small business of the Jewish ethnic economy, which lent it a natural libertarian coloration, but their children were also moving toward the professions through formal education and certification. In the decades after World War II, the education and professional level of Jewish liberals matched that of the latter-day non-Jewish Progressive reformers.[13] Thousands of second- and third-generation Jews were exposed to the engine of American liberalism, the university. Once enrolled, Jewish students were far more prone to assume that there was a link between being educated and being liberal. Jewish liberalism, like its American counterpart, would be anchored in an educated middle class with pronounced elitist tendencies. A good part of the change in character of Jewish liberalism, its change from egalitarianism to libertarianism between 1920 and 1970, must be attributed to its changed class base.

The move to the center of the liberal spectrum was enhanced further by the collapse of the extreme Left in the Jewish political arena, where the most extreme egalitarianism and statism were anchored. The Russian Revolution had initially earned applause and support in the left wing of the Jewish community. It generated hope that a just society would finally be established in Russia in which Jews would share equally with other subject nationalities. Chaim Zhitlovsky, a well-known Jewish radical voice, for example, suggested that the newly established Communist International (Comintern) was "the only organization that seeks to realize the word of the prophets."[14] But even as the Joint Distribution Committee (JDC) appropriated millions of dollars in partnership with the Soviet government to resettle thousands of impoverished Jews in the Crimea, the benevolent aura cast by the revolution faded. The Soviet policy of reshaping the Russian Jewish class structure and its hostile attitude toward religion and Jewish communalism had led to the exile of thousands of rabbis, Hebrew teachers, and Zionist and Bundist leaders. Many were never heard from again. The Crimean venture, on which so much hope was staked, developed into a social engineering scheme to reshape Russian Jewry into something that might better fit the Communist mold. Clearly the Soviet government had little use for a separate Jewish ethnic culture, whether religious or secular.[15]

At the same time, the Communist party of the United States, following a strategy ordered by the Comintern, targeted the Jewish labor movement for penetration. It was viewed as a stepping stone to infiltrating the American labor movement. In 1926 that strategy led to a costly, mismanaged, 26-week strike that virtually destroyed the ILGWU. Communist organizers of the strike had not hesitated to use the union's security fund to keep their lost cause afloat.[16] The costly strike taught Jewish labor leaders a bitter lesson regarding the willingness of the Communist party to exploit the unions for their own grand design. By 1929 the Communist threat had peaked. Jews of the "socialist persuasion," like Lillian Wald, Horace Kallen, and David Dubinsky, distrusted the heirs of Lenin who ruled from the Kremlin. Baruch Vladeck, managing editor of the *Forwards*, and Morris Hillquit, chairman of the national committee of the Socialist party, adamantly opposed extending diplomatic recognition to the Soviet Union. The party underwent one of its many splits and the ILGWU again emerged in the thirties, under the leadership of David Dubinsky, firmly in the social-democratic fold and ready to accept ameliorative measures to improve the conditions of its rank and file. But by the midthirties the composition of the ILGWU, which more than any other Jewish agency pointed the way to the new liberalism, was paradoxically no longer predominantly Jewish.

That trend away from the statism of the totalitarian Left was disrupted by the Depression. The collapse of the economy after the crash of 1929 gave the failing Communist party another opportunity to root itself in the Jewish community. Many socialist-minded Jews became convinced that the long-awaited collapse of capitalism predicted by Marx had come to pass. The disaffection was especially strong among Jewish students whose career paths and hopes for attaining professional status had been disrupted. Some estimate that the Jewish membership of the Communist party may have reached 30 to 40 percent during the thirties.[17] That membership actually represented a minuscule proportion of the Jewish population, but it was sufficient to pin the "radical" label onto American Jewry again. In reality, the purges of the thirties and the signing of the Nazi-Soviet Nonaggression Pact in August 1939 caused a rapid decline of the Communist influence among Jews.

The most powerful influence on American Jewish liberalism was the overwhelming popularity of Roosevelt among average Jewish voters. It was said that Jews had *"dray velten—die velt, yene velt, un* Roosevelt" ("three worlds: this world, the next world, and Roosevelt"). The aura of the New Deal with its concern for the "forgotten man" and its social-welfare legislation fit neatly into Jewish political culture, which viewed government as an instrument to create the conditions for social justice. Indeed, the very term "New Deal" was thought to have been coined by Samuel Untermeyer.[18] The reformist, ameliorative New Deal program was within easy striking distance of the social-democratic principles to which many Jews were drawn.

American Jewish liberalism finally found a home and political address in the New Deal, but the first New Deal also reinforced the Jewish penchant for a liberalism with a strong statist component. The direct forging of that connection came through the ILGWU. Its leadership founded the American Labor party in 1935 in New York State. It called itself "the party of the permanent New Deal" and attracted thousands of Jewish voters to its banner. In the election of 1936, 40 percent of New York State's Jewish voters cast their ballots for the ALP ticket. It also broke the hold of the Socialist party on the Jewish Left. In that year Norman Thomas, the Socialist party candidate, received eighty-seven thousand Jewish votes, compared with 250,000 cast for the ALP. It served as a bridge for thousands of socialist-oriented Jewish voters to enter the mainstream of American politics. When the ALP was penetrated by the still-vigorous Communist party in 1938, it changed its name to the Liberal party, the only party in American political history actually to carry the term "liberal" into the political arena.

The fate of American liberalism in the postwar era need not occupy us very long. With the exception of the Eisenhower years (1952–1960), liberal Democrats—Roosevelt, Truman, Kennedy, and Johnson—occupied the White House between 1932 and 1968. Together with the Carter years (1976–1980), these Democratic administrations will probably go down in history as the liberal period, although Carter was an outsider whose administration may mark the final exhaustion of egalitarian liberalism. The willingness to absorb social democrats like Michael Harrington may have been the well-spring of Johnson's War on Poverty. The new university-educated liberals, who had a proclivity for making public policy but were anticommercial by career choice, may also account for the anti-business cast of these administrations. Their distaste for the acquisitive ethic led inevitably to the abandonment of the libertarian notion of equality of opportunity in favor of the egalitarian notion of equality of results, the high point of which was the imposition of affirmative action quotas. The new liberalism of the sixties challenged fundamental libertarian values like competition, equal opportunity, and free enterprise, values that the American electorate was not ready to give up. Prone to view itself as the protector of the oppressed, this "new class" was typical of intellectual elites in the West in its preference for public policy devoted to reshaping society. It was the inclination to social engineering manifest in the civil rights movement that took liberalism out of the mainstream of American politics.[19]

The counterthrust of the Reagan years was predictable. On the economic side we have already noted that the retreat from statism began during the second New Deal. During the prosperity of the postwar decades the swing to liberalism's libertarian pole was accelerated. While there was much hand wringing about government cost and the high taxes required to fund welfare programs (today called entitlement programs), there was little inclination among Republican libertarian liberals to remove the cushions that the New Deal had installed in the economy. Libertarians now talked of a social-service net that would let no one starve. Nevertheless, anti-government bias persisted.

The libertarian-liberal victory of the Reagan years was played out on a world stage. The Cold War was fought against a totalitarian power and tended to bring statism into more disrepute, even while its exigencies caused a growth in government power and expenditures at home. Ultimately, the collapse of the world Communist movement gave a powerful impetus to the idea of a market-economy mechanism and privatization. These economic resonances of libertarian liberalism were bandied about in Eastern Europe with the same fervor that "class struggle" once was. At home it was thought that even the public education system, once the stronghold of egalitarianism but now failing to develop the skilled work force requisite for an advanced industrial economy, would be improved by allowing the free market represented by the voucher system to work its wonders.

Unforeseen by libertarians was that, once the war was over and prosperity seemed assured, those hitherto neglected problems concerning race and social inequalities would be brought to the fore by liberalism playing its traditional role. As it turned out, whether such problems dealt with race or the destruction of the environment, they inevitably entailed increased government expenditures. Willy-nilly, American liberal politics became budget politics.

Unlike Europe, where the problem of class was uppermost, in America it was the unresolved problem of race that threatened, according to the Kerner Report of 1968, to split the nation into two contending parts. By the sixties the race problem had gained the highest priority on the liberal agenda. Accompanying the race question was a whole series of new problems: gender inequality, rights for the handicapped, gay rights, infants' rights, animal rights, and problems concerning the physical environment. Looming over all is the contentious question of abortion rights, which places the conundrum of the extent of human liberty in an entirely new context. It is a particularly vexing problem for conservatives, whose libertarian brand of liberalism would logically dictate a proabortion position. What greater liberty can there be than control over one's own body?

Now the best-informed and most activist constituency in the America electorate, Jews played an important role in the sundry "movements" that characterized the seventies and eighties. Survey research continued to find Jews "more liberal" than other groups.[20] But sociologists who seemed most preoccupied with the problem did not often understand that liberalism was an ever-changing phenomenon. Their surveys failed to pay adequate attention to the fact that on certain issues impinging directly on the Jewish interest, such as affirmative action quotas, Jewish opinion was actually undergoing a significant transformation that placed Jews outside the liberal consensus. This did not fully register since, on other issues such as support of welfare programs, the Jewish responses remained predictably liberal.

At the heart of that change was the long-range impact of the Holocaust on the Jewish *mentalité*. It undermined the optimistic assumption at the heart of liberalism, that there exists a "humanitarian spirit" or a "spirit of civilization" in the nation-state and the international order that could be mobilized to fill an ethical need. Most states had done little to rescue European Jewry during the Holocaust. Moreover, World War II and the postwar years contained some terrible lessons regarding the Soviet Union, a totalitarian state addicted to egalitarianism. For some it provided sufficient evidence that the American Founding Fathers had after all not been so far off the mark in their suspicion of state power. In both Nazi Germany and the Soviet Union, Jews had been subject to a special animus. The idea that the state itself might be malignant did not prevent most Jews from supporting the idea of a Jewish state. Many American Jews had come to believe that a state was a necessary step without which Jews would remain vulnerable. But there were some, like Hannah Arendt and Martin Buber and to some extent Judah Magnes, who saw even a Jewish state as retrogressive.

A second factor in transforming Jewish liberalism relates directly to the founding of that state in 1948. As early as 1940 the Zionist consensus had begun to change American Jewish political culture. After 1948 the care and support of the State of Israel became a major component of American Jewish identity. But support, as Brandeis had foreseen, did not mean that American Jews would have to settle there to build the new society. Rather, for American Zionists it meant political advocacy, the representation of Israel's case before the American seat of power. That, in turn, often required a partial abandoning of the universalism lying at the heart of Jewish liberalism. Increasingly Jewish liberals had to make difficult choices between the interests of Israel, the tenuous security of which required direct, sometimes preemptive use of military power, and such cherished universalist principles as the right of national self-determination, especially for Palestinians. The way Israel exercised power over its Palestinian population was particularly disturbing to those Jewish liberals who had come to view civil rights as the central principle of liberalism.[21]

Zionism particularized American Jewish political culture. It did something else as well. If with the creation of Israel Jewry reentered history, as Zionists were wont to claim, it seemed willy-nilly to draw American Jewry with it. American Jews came out from the behind-the-scenes role they traditionally played in politics as pundits, campaign managers, poll takers, the professionals, to become office holders and lobbyists. During the 1930s the number of Jews in Congress hovered around ten. The election of 1990 sent eight senators and thirty-three representatives to Congress. Today there are more PACs concerned with Israel and general Jewish causes than with the concerns of any other ethnic group. The result is a split in the Jewish electorate that is partly generational. Older Jewishly or Judaically committed Jews give the security of Israel the greatest priority and view the fulfillment of their liberal aspirations in terms of the welfare of the Jewish state. The younger group, strongly influenced by the war in Vietnam, is more concerned about traditional liberal values. Nurtured in America, many of these young liberals did not directly experience the bitter consequences that followed when Jews found themselves bereft of sovereign political power. Also, they were on a collision course with Israeli political culture, which was shaped by the power it exercised over an occupied people and by the need to assure its survival in a hostile region where it was often called upon to use its military power. Similarly, the separation of church and state, so central to the American Jewish sensibility, was less emphasized in Israel, where a Jewish state assured observant Jews the protected environment to live a religious life.

Another factor that altered the shape of Jewish liberalism in the sixties was the African American thrust finally to enter the mainstream of American life. The partnership between blacks and Jews on the civil rights issue had been well established before World War II. Jews had been instrumental in supporting black defense organizations like the NAACP, furnishing leadership training and legal resources, and supporting black colleges. During the twenties Louis Marshall, president of the American Jewish Committee, spon-

sored antilynching and anti–Ku Klux Klan legislation. Jewish impresarios played a major role in opening American popular culture
to black artists. The affinity between blacks and Jews, which may
have been based on a common feeling of victimization, was also
reflected in their voting behavior. Politically both groups had found
a niche in the left wing of the Democratic party during the New
Deal period. They became Roosevelt's staunchest supporters.

If during the thirties there were worrisome signs of disharmony
caused by the antisemitic oratory of black street-corner preachers
and the targeting of Jewish stores for looting during several riots, it
was underplayed in the Jewish press. That remained true even when
some black spokesmen, including W. E. B. Dubois, opposed the
admission of Jewish refugees, insisting that Germany had a legitimate grievance against Jews. One historian has suggested that Jewish support for black causes was a way for Jews to broaden their
own rights without becoming conspicuous by advocating their
group interest in creating a more open society.[22] Whatever the
motive, American Jews played an important role in advocating that
equality be fully extended to the nation's African American
citizens.

By the 1960s the black-Jewish linkage had begun to wear thin. A
new group of younger black leaders pushed Jews out of leadership
positions in the civil rights movement. The Ocean Hill–Brownsville
conflict serves as a historical marker for Jewish splitting off from a
liberalism now almost wholly dominated by the civil rights issue.
Preoccupied with the seeming intractability of the race problem,
the left wing of liberalism advocated special entitlement laws to
hasten the goal of black equality. Representative of such laws was
affirmative action, which required quotas. Most Jews opposed the
abandonment of the merit system that had smoothed their path to
achievement of middle-class status in prior decades and protected
their access to civil service employment.[23]

By 1990 the Jewish liberal profile showed a marked differentiation on other liberal issues requiring direct government intervention. Blacks replaced Jews as the most intensely liberal-minded
group in the electorate, especially on issues concerning government
programs to assist minority groups. The Jewish liberal often found
himself compelled to choose between the Jewish interest and the

liberal position. The polarization was widened by a growing sense that the black leadership was antisemitic. Leaders like Jesse Jackson reintroduced antisemitic currency, which had been all but ruled out in the political dialogue. Beneath it all was the question of resource allocation. Blacks, adopting the posture of an internal Third World nation, argued that monies given and lent to Israel would find better use in rehabilitating the people of the inner city. The argument then turned on the "who gets what" or spoils question, which has always been central in American politics.

Another reason for the Jewish swing to libertarian liberalism relates to what we may loosely identify as the American Jewish success story. It is no secret that by the 1960s Jews had achieved a numerically disproportionate position in the technocratic, cultural, governmental, and managerial elites who administer and shape American society. They are the ethnic group with the nation's highest per capita income and the highest professionalization. In the 1920s, when the foundations for that achievement were put in place, middle-class station was often achieved by aspiring Jews against considerable resistance and at great sacrifice by families living on the economic margin. There was an investment made in human capital. A son was sent to law school or medical school by the earnings of the entire family. Although there was some "suicidal altruism," that is, Jews who favored a public policy that automatically granted special advantage to victimized minorities as compensation, most Jews opposed policies that in the name of justice abandoned merit.[24] Their own achievement stemmed from an individual effort in a free society. They had adhered to the rules, which had now been abandoned. Government-sponsored programs to raise specific groups to a level that Jews had achieved on their own did not sit well. In entrance professions like teaching, long a favorite channel for aspiring young Jews, affirmative action translated into blocked mobility channels, the equivalent of employment discrimination.

Much that was statist and egalitarian was now bound up with the race question. Some Jewish thinkers undoubtedly were aware that it was the Communist party, following the dictates contained in Stalin's writing on the national question, that advocated a highly separatist policy to solve the race problem. When the party

fell further into disrepute among Jews because of its hostility toward Israel and the undeniable evidence of virulent antisemitism
in the Soviet Union and Poland, its stock declined even more. The
capture of the "Negro question" by the extreme Left made it anathema to many Jews.[25]

Reinforcing all these reasons was a historical change that went
almost unnoticed by social scientists. The institutions that supplied
the motor force of the Jewish liberal enterprise, the Jewish labor
movement, the *Forwards*, Workmen's Circle, and the dozens of
socialist-minded fraternities and summer camps, had by 1990 virtually vanished from the scene. Once the quintessential liberal agency
for secular Jews, the American Jewish Congress is but a bare shadow
of itself and has difficulty staying in business. Pressed by a trium-
phalist Orthodox branch, the Conservative and Reform movements
have grown far more concerned with their Jewishness, which, we
have seen, acts as a brake on highly universalistic liberal causes. By
1988 the Liberal party of New York State drew fewer voters than the
Conservative party and was virtually defunct. The agencies that
traditionally drew Jews to liberalism are much diminished in
influence.

This does not mean that Jewish liberalism has totally lost its
distinctive idealism. There is no scarcity of Jews who call on the
political process and the state to do more, to seek justice. The need
to search out the most pressing current inequity is insufficient to
explain why so many young Jews continue to be political activists
for causes as widely different as world peace and the welfare of
striped bass in the Hudson. They want to instill a humanitarian
conscience into the political process. Idealism is still a prized quality in American Jewish political culture.

On the surface, liberal politics is issue oriented, but beneath is
the politics of redemption. It is that characteristic of Jewish liberalism that makes it so difficult to carry forward transactional politics,
the kind preferred by American political culture. Dealing with
prophets whose politics are based on righteousness is never an easy
task. The issues of peace, the environment, or the homeless continue to draw a disproportionate number of liberal Jews, but they
do not easily lend themselves to the politics of the possible. There

has developed over the generations a distinctive Jewish political style that places a high premium on commitment, on giving oneself over to the cause. In the first generation it was called *ibergegebn-kayt*, which, translated from the Yiddish, means "devotedness." This phenomenon also needs to be taken into account in explaining the persistence of Jewish liberalism. Such liberals reject the contemporary solutions that place so much faith in the free market economy not because they favor socialism, as did an important segment of the first generation. One suspects that the new generation does not understand the difference between a market and a command economy, and the relationship this distinction bears to the two kinds of liberalism. They reject the market economy as a mechanism that cares little about those who cannot make it or about what is happening to the environment. For the liberal *mentalité*, life should be more than merely the providing of goods and services. It should have transcendence.

Taking leave from the left wing of the liberal movement did not mean that Jewish liberals became politically homeless. In some sense the Jewish electorate has moved closer to the American mainstream. The old ethnic and regional constituencies that buttressed the New Deal have gradually been homogenized out of existence. The defeat of McGovern in 1972 may have been the last hurrah of the old liberalism. The program of the statist liberals has been largely rejected by the American electorate. Jewish liberalism today is less committed to government-sponsored social engineering and more particularistic in coming to terms with the Jewish interest when it is in conflict with a universalistic one. But Jews remain well within the liberal camp of the Democratic party. Fifty percent of the campaign funds of that party is raised by Jews, and 68 percent of its vote in a recent election went to the liberal candidate (Dukakis), compared with 46 percent of the general electorate. But that is a far cry from the over 90 percent awarded to Roosevelt in 1940 and 1944. Being Jewish still remains a more powerful determinant of the Jewish vote than being rich. In California 65 percent of Jewish voters with an annual income of over seventy-five thousand dollars voted for the Democratic candidate Diane Feinstein, compared with 38 percent of non-Jews in the same income bracket. Seventy-three percent identify themselves as liberal, compared with 42.19 percent of non-Jews. Moreover, on liberal issues wealthy Jews differ hardly at all in their voting preference from less wealthy ones.[26] But Jewish liberalism has changed its orientation from an emphasis on egalitarianism to an emphasis on libertarianism. That has happened because it has undergone two processes since World War II, Judaization and Americanization, that make it different from what it once was.

In historical terms, the Jewish political posture corresponds roughly to the liberalism of the second New Deal, which abandoned social engineering in favor of indirect regulation of the economy. Jews continue to favor an active regulatory role for the state but they want it done through existing instruments, the taxing power, monetary policy, rather than through direct intrusions like affirmative action. It is in the area of taxation and spending that the sharpest differentiation occurs between Jewish liberalism and that of the general white liberal voter. Despite their considerable per capita income, Jews are more inclined to favor high taxes to fund entitlement programs. For example, they give much greater support to programs like Aid to Dependent Children, all forms of income maintenance programs, even support for AIDS research and care, but they overwhelmingly reject restructuring the economy to prevent great disparities of wealth, direct intrusion such as affirmative action quotas, censorship of pornography, and regulation of gay lifestyle, and they are more than twice as likely as their fellow Americans to support abortions without restriction.[27]

In a word, there has developed an antistatist libertarian component in Jewish liberalism. As Jews see it, job placement, sexual orientation, family planning, and religion are in the private realm and therefore by right ought to be free of government interference. It is not, however, a complete libertarianism. Like other Americans, Jews have come to favor capital punishment, but in lower percentages. Jews, therefore, are no longer so politically deviant, especially if one compares their political profile with that of other highly educated, high-income groups. Their liberalism has been open minded, tolerant, forward looking, peace oriented, and humanitarian, yet also aware of its own group interest. It has lost confidence that a just society can be created by government fiat. It is the liberalism of a secular, highly individuated, firmly middle-class yet ethnically conscious community. That should not surprise us. What else could it have been?

Notes

1. Woodrow Wilson, *Congressional Government: A Study in American Politics* (Boston: Houghton Mifflin, 1913); Michael Kammen, *Spheres of Liberty: Changing Perceptions of Liberty in American Culture* (Madison: University of Wisconsin Press, 1986). The problems posed by libertarianism for liberalism are most recently examined by James A. Monroe, *The Democratic Wish: Popular Participation and the Limits of American Government* (New York: Basic, 1990).
2. Francois Furet, "From 1789 to 1917 and 1989: Looking Back at Revolutionary Traditions," *Encounter* (September 1990): 3–7.
3. John M. McFaul, *The Politics of Jacksonian Finance* (Ithaca, N.Y.: Cornell University Press, 1985).
4. See Arthur Goren, "The Tradition of Community," in *New York Jews and the Quest for Community: The Kehillah Experiment (1908–1922)* (New York: Columbia University Press, 1970), 6–9.
5. George Will, "The Presidency in the American Political System," *Presidential Studies Quarterly* 14, no. 3 (1984): 324.
6. Melvin Urofsky, *Louis D. Brandeis and the Progressive Tradition* (Boston: Little, Brown, 1981), 71–86.
7. Moses Rischin, *Promised City* (Cambridge, Mass.: Harvard University Press, 1962), 221–35; Goren, *Kehillah*, 4, 24, 186; John D. Buenker, *Urban Liberalism and Progressive Reform* (New York: Scribner's, 1973).
8. Michael A. Meyer, *Response to Modernity: A History of the Reform Movement in Judaism* (New York: Oxford University Press, 1988), 286–89.
9. Morris Frommer, "The American Jewish Congress: A History" (Ph.D. diss., Ohio State University, 1978).
10. *American Jewish Year Book* 27 (1919–1920): 599; 39 (1939–1938): 735; 40 (1938–1939): 529.
11. Alan Fisher, "Continuity and Erosion of Jewish Liberalism," *American Jewish Historical Quarterly* 66, no. 2 (December 1976): 322–62.
12. See Samuel Lubell, *The Future of American Politics* (New York: Harper and Row, 1966), 35–43.
13. A portrait of the social-class background of the Progressive reformer is presented by George C. Mowry, *The California Progressives* (Berkeley: University of California Press, 1951).
14. Quoted in Arthur Liebman, "The Ties That Bind: The Jewish Support

of the Left in the U.S.," *American Jewish Historical Quarterly* 66, no. 2 (December 1976): 285–321.

15. Allen L. Kagedan, "The Formation of Soviet Jewish Territorial Units, 1924–1937" (Ph.D. diss., Columbia University, 1985).

16. Will Herberg, "The Jewish Labor Movement in the U.S.," *American Jewish Year Book* 53 (1952–1953): 5 ff.

17. Nathaniel Weyl, *The Jews in American Politics* (New Rochelle, N.Y.: Arlington House, 1968), 116–19.

18. Others attribute it to Samuel Rosenman. See Edward J. Flynn, *You're the Boss* (New York: Viking, 1948), 183.

19. Alonzo L. Hamby, *Liberalism and Its Challengers: FDR to Reagan* (New York: Oxford University Press, 1985), 220 ff.

20. Steven M. Cohen, *The Dimensions of American Jewish Liberalism*, Jewish Political Studies Series (New York: American Jewish Committee, 1989), 1–4.

21. For an elaboration of this dilemma see Edward Alexander, "Liberalism and Zionism," *Commentary*, February 1986.

22. Hasia Diner, "In the Almost Promised Land: Jewish Leaders and Blacks, 1915–1935" (Ph.D. diss., University of Illinois, Chicago Circle, 1975), xii–xvii, 237.

23. Cohen, *Dimensions*, 14.

24. The term "suicidal altruism" is used by Leonard J. Fein, "Liberalism and American Jews," *Midstream* 19, no. 8 (October 1973): 12.

25. For a recent elaboration of how the race question has been exploited to alter liberal assumptions from equality to preference, see Jim Sleeper, *The Closest of Strangers: Liberalism and the Politics of Race* (New York: Norton, 1990).

26. Alan Fisher, "Are We Changing?" *Comment and Analysis* 2, no. 1 (February 1991): 1–2.

27. Cohen, *Dimensions*, 14–20.

CHAPTER 7

Will Herberg's Path from Marxism to Judaism: A Case Study in the Transformation of Jewish Belief

David G. Dalin

The sociologist and theologian Will Herberg was an exemplary instance of the shift in Jewish ideological attitudes between the 1920s
and 1940s: the waning fervor of Jewish socialism and a concomitant
growth in political realism, a sharpened sense of the limitations of
radical change, a heightened desire to return to traditional spiritual
moorings. In his writings Herberg popularized the sociological
"law" that what the second generation (of an immigrant group)
wants to forget, the third generation wants to recover; the children
search for the ethnic and religious heritage that had been hastily
discarded in their parents' Americanization. Herberg himself was a
bridge between those two generations of Jews of East European
origin. He was also an early, outstanding, and influential illustration of the impact on American Jewish thought of a Protestant Neo-
Orthodoxy that combined a liberal political stance with a forthright return, albeit in a modern, sophisticated form, to theological
concepts shunted aside by religious modernists. Herberg was thus
a harbinger of a shift in Jewish religious thought toward greater
traditionalism and a concern with existential authenticity rather
than with rendering Judaism as compatible as possible with modern
science. In his own way, therefore, Herberg symbolizes the process
by which the American environment came to reshape Jewish politi-

cal and cultural attitudes by the middle decades of the twentieth century.

Will Herberg was born in the Russian village of Liachovitzi in 1901. His father, Hyman Louis Herberg, who had been born in the same *shtetl*, moved his family to the United States in 1904. When they arrived in America, his parents, whom he would later describe as "passionate atheists," were already committed to the faith that socialism would bring salvation to humankind and liberation from restraints that had bound Western society for centuries. His father died when Herberg was ten. His mother shared her husband's contempt for the American public school system; although Will attended Public School 72 and Boys High School in Brooklyn, his real education took place at the kitchen table of an apartment on Georgia Avenue in a lower-middle-class neighborhood of Brooklyn. A precocious and versatile student from his early youth, Herberg had learned Greek, Latin, French, German, and Russian by the time he was in his teens. Graduated from Boys High School in 1918, Herberg later attended City College and Columbia University, where he studied philosophy and history apparently without ever completing the coursework for an academic degree.

Herberg inherited his parents' "passionate atheism" and equally passionate commitment to the socialist faith. Entering the Communist movement while still a teenager, Herberg brought to radical politics an erudition that considerably elevated the intellectual level of American Marxism. Less prolific than writer Max Eastman or novelist John Dos Passos, Herberg was perhaps the broadest-ranging of Marxist polemicists during the 1920s and early 1930s. A regular contributor to Communist journals such as the *Working Monthly*, he was also a familiar ideologue in the *Modern Quarterly*, one of the chief theoretical journals of the Old Left.

Herberg wrote scores of articles and editorials on topics ranging from critiques of Edmund Wilson's views of proletariat literature to debates with Sidney Hook over Marx's ambivalent views on religion to the relationship between Freudian psychoanalysis and Communist thought. His attachment to communism reflected intellectual conviction as well as moral ardor. Perhaps his boldest contribution to the radical thought of the period was his effort to reconcile

Marxism to the cosmology of Einstein, the "second scientific revolution" that had gone virtually unnoticed among radical writers in America. While most Communists still condemned Einstein for rejecting "scientific materialism," Herberg insisted that both Marxism and the theory of relativity were scientifically correct. As a radical Jew, moreover, Herberg hailed Freud, as he did Marx and Einstein, as a modern prophet. "The world of socialism—to which nothing human is alien and which cherishes every genuine manifestation of the human spirit," he wrote during the 1930s, "lays a wreath of homage on the grave of Sigmund Freud."

First signs of Herberg's eventual disenchantment with orthodox Marxism came already in 1920, when he, Bertram Wolfe, and other young intellectuals and labor organizers joined a group, headed by Jay Lovestone, that split off from the main Communist party within the American party leadership. Lovestone, an American supporter of the Soviet theoretician Nicolai Bukharin, had, like Bukharin, advocated more autonomy for national Communist parties from control by the Communist party of the USSR. In 1929, Stalin struck back by demoting Bukharin and ousting Lovestone and his followers from leadership of the American movement. After breaking with the official party in 1929, Herberg became a staff member and then editor of the Lovestonite opposition paper, *Workers Age*, many of whose contributors would later become bitter anti-Stalinists.

As the 1930s proceeded, Herberg became disenchanted with his Marxist faith. The grotesque Stalinist purges, the Communist betrayal of the Popular Front on the battlefields of Spain during the Spanish Civil War, the Russian invasion of Finland, and the Stalin-Hitler Nonaggression Pact of 1939 all contributed to his growing disillusionment. The Moscow trials, Herberg maintained, indicated the barbarous measures to which Stalin would resort to suppress all resistance to his bureaucratic rule within Russia. For Herberg, as for so many ex-Marxists of his generation, the cynical, opportunistic Molotov-Ribbentrop agreement of 1939 dispelled any remaining belief that "only a socialist government can defeat totalitarianism." His final break with orthodox Marxism, which came in 1939, involved no mere change in political loyalties or repudiation of the political radicalism of his youth. As he would confess in recounting his journey from Marxism to Judaism on the pages of *Commentary* in 1947, Marxism had been, to him and to others like him, "a religion, an ethic and a theology; a vast all-embracing doctrine of man and the universe, a passionate faith endowing life with meaning."[1]

Put to the test, this Marxist faith had failed because, as Herberg would later express it, "reality could not be forever withstood." He had begun to recognize by the late 1930s that the all-encompassing system of Marxist thought could not sustain the values that had first attracted him to revolutionary activity. "Not that I felt myself any the less firmly committed to the great ideals of freedom and social justice," he reflected in 1947:

> My discovery was that I could no longer find basis and support for these ideals in the materialistic religion of Marxism. . . . This religion itself, it now became clear to me, was in part illusion, and in part idolatry; in part a delusive utopianism promising heaven on earth in our time, and in part a totalitarian worship of collective man; in part a naive faith in the finality of economics, material production; in part a sentimental optimism as to the goodness of human nature, and in part a hard-boiled amoral cult of power at any price. There could be no question to my mind that as religion, Marxism had proved itself bankrupt.[2]

Perceiving Marxism as a "god that failed" rather than as a "mere strategy of political action," Herberg was left with an inner spiritual void, "deprived of the commitment and understanding that alone made life liveable."

As the god of Marxism was failing him in the late 1930s, Herberg chanced to read Reinhold Niebuhr's *Moral Man and Immoral Society*. He later wrote,

> Humanly speaking, it converted me, for in some manner I cannot describe, I felt my whole being, and not merely my thinking, shifted to a new center. . . . What impressed me more profoundly was the paradoxical combination of realism and radicalism that Niebuhr's "prophetic" faith made possible. . . . Here was a faith that warned against all premature securities, yet called to responsible action. Here, in short, was a "social idealism" without illusions, in comparison with which even the most "advanced" Marxism appeared confused, inconsistent, and hopelessly illusion-ridden.[3]

More than any other American thinker of the 1930s and 1940s, Niebuhr related theology to politics through a realistic assessment of human nature that seemed inescapably relevant in a time of the breakdown of the Marxist (and liberal) faith in progress and enlightenment.

Some of Herberg's acquaintances would later liken his rejection of communism, and return to Judaism, to Paul's conversion on the road to Damascus. The comparison may have pleased him, for Herberg always felt that his return to Judaism was the product of events equally unanticipated and dramatic. His memorable road to *teshuvah*, inspired by his first encounter with Niebuhr, was unique in the annals of American Jewish intellectuals of that generation. In an autobiographical passage, Herberg said that even before he met Niebuhr personally, his encounter with Niebuhr's thought in 1939 was the "turning point."

Like Franz Rosenzweig, whose writings he began to read during the early 1940s, Herberg went through a wrenching inner struggle over whether to become a Christian. After several soul-searching meetings with Niebuhr, who was then teaching at Manhattan's Union Theological Seminary, Herberg declared his intention to embrace Christianity. Niebuhr counseled him, instead, to explore his Jewish religious tradition first and directed him across the street to the Jewish Theological Seminary. The professors and students at the Seminary undertook to instruct Herberg in Hebrew and Jewish thought.

Throughout much of the 1940s, while he was earning a living as the educational director and research analyst of the International Ladies Garment Workers Union, Herberg devoted much time and energy to the study of Jewish sources. Not having received a traditional Jewish education in his youth, Herberg was introduced to the classical sources of Judaism through the writings of Solomon Schechter and George Foot Moore and through the instruction of Judaic scholars who became his friends, such as Professors Gerson D. Cohen and Seymour Siegel and Rabbi Milton Steinberg. As Seymour Siegel has reminisced, Herberg was "extraordinarily moved" by the realistic appraisal of human nature in rabbinic literature, especially as expounded by Schechter.[4] He was impressed, also, by the writings of Martin Buber and Franz Rosenzweig who, together with Niebuhr, would shape his evolving views on religious existentialism and biblical faith.

Herberg found in Judaism, after years of searching, a faith that encouraged social action without falling into the trap of utopianism. Throughout the 1940s, he developed and explicated his emerging theology for journals such as *Commentary* and the *Jewish Frontier*. In demand as a speaker, he lectured on religious faith and the social philosophy of Judaism at synagogues and on college campuses, gaining the reputation of being "the Reinhold Niebuhr of Judaism." He met regularly at his home with JTS rabbinical students and others to discuss his theological ideas. "In those early days," one of these students remembered, "when the naturalistic theology so brilliantly expounded by Professor Mordecai Kaplan was the main intellectual influence in Jewish religious circles, we were fascinated by Herberg's espousal of the orthodox ideas of a supernatural God, messiah, and Torah, expounded with fervor and yet interpreted in a new way."[5]

Out of these intellectual encounters and out of several essays published in *Commentary* and elsewhere in the late 1940s came Herberg's book *Judaism and Modern Man*, which appeared in 1951. Acclaimed as a carefully reasoned and intensely written interpretation of Judaism in the light of an existentialist approach still new to America, *Judaism and Modern Man* was highly praised by Jewish scholars; Niebuhr himself said that the book "may well become a milestone in the religious thought of America."

Herberg's central concern, as he describes it in *Judaism and Modern Man*, is the spiritual frustration and despair of twentieth-century humanity. Herberg examines one by one the "substitute faiths" in which people have placed their hopes and aspirations—Marxism, liberalism, rationalism, science, and psychoanalysis, among others—and finds that each is a way of evading ultimate theological issues. "Man must worship something," Herberg wrote. "If he does not worship God, he will worship an idol made of wood, or of gold, or of ideas."[6] Moreover, intellectual affirmation is not enough. Essential to one's being is a "leap of faith": return and absolute commitment to the living God of Abraham, Isaac, and Jacob.[7]

In presenting his view of God and Judaism, Herberg criticized theologians of the 1930s and 1940s who espoused a rationalist approach and, in so doing, reduced God to an idea.[8] For a religious existentialist such as Herberg, deeply influenced by the dialogical I-Thou philosophy of Buber and Rosenzweig, God is important only if there is a personal relationship to him. Thus, for Herberg, Jewish faith cannot be predicated upon an abstract idea of God such as, for example, Kaplan's notion of "a power that makes for salvation." Rather, the God of *Judaism and Modern Man* is a God to whom we can pray with an expectation of a response, a God with whom we can enter into a genuine dialogue.[9]

As Seymour Siegel has noted, Herberg's theology was rather traditional, focusing on such beliefs as revelation, the covenant between God and the Jewish people, resurrection of the dead, and the coming of the messiah.[10] He also affirmed unequivocally a traditional conception of the chosen people: Jewish existence, argued Herberg, "is intrinsically religious and God-oriented. Jews may be led to deny, repudiate, and reject their 'chosenness' and its responsibilities, but their own Jewishness rises to confront them as refutation and condemnation."[11]

While believing in revelation, Herberg did not accept "the fundamentalist conception of revelation as the supernatural communication of information through a body of writings which are immune from error because they are quite literally the writings of God. . . . The Bible is obviously not simply a transcript from His dictation."[12] Rather, Herberg regarded revelation as "the self-disclosure of God in His dealings with the world" through active intervention in history, and the Torah as a "humanly mediated record of revelation."[13] In this and in other respects, his theology was at variance with Orthodoxy.

Above all, Herberg argued that a Jewish theology relevant to the postwar period would have to be predicated upon a less optimistic image of man, upon a sober recognition of human sinfulness and human limitations. The barbarities of Stalinism and especially the Nazi Holocaust seemed to Herberg to have destroyed the very foundations of the prevailing liberal faith in the natural goodness of man, shared by Reform and Reconstructionist Judaism. Liberal Jewish theology, he maintained, failed to answer the critical question of how evil regimes and institutions could have arisen if human beings are essentially good. The answer could be found in "Niebuhr's rediscovery of the classical doctrine of 'original sin,' which religious liberalism and secular idealism combined to deride and obscure." Sin, Herberg wrote, "is one of the great facts of human life. It lies at the root of man's existentialist plight." Without an understanding of the nature of sin, he concluded, "there is no understanding of human life . . . or man's relation to God."[14]

The approach of *Judaism and Modern Man* reflected the prevailing trend toward existentialism in American religious thought of the 1940s and 1950s. The post–World War II period saw an Americanization of Jewish theology in the United States as the religious thought of Rosenzweig and Buber, scarcely known in America prior to 1945, was translated for an English-reading American Jewish public.[15] In the late 1940s and 1950s, Herberg wrote a much-discussed interpretive essay on Rosenzweig for *Commentary* and edited a collection of Buber's essays.[16] In helping to popularize and reinterpret these men for the American Jewish laity, Herberg helped to lay the foundation for the creation and development of a new phase of Jewish thought on American soil. With its publication in 1951, *Judaism and Modern Man* became the first book-length English work of this new, postwar Jewish theology. The publication of *Judaism and Modern Man* was greeted with praise by several respected Jewish reviewers, such as Milton Konvitz and Milton Steinberg. Indeed, in a prepublication statement, Steinberg went so far as to say that Herberg "had written the book of the generation on the Jewish religion."

Herberg was one of the most American of Jewish religious thinkers. Much of his understanding of Jewish religious tradition derived from scholarship written in English and produced on American soil. Thus, his understanding of rabbinic thought was shaped almost completely by his reading of George Foot Moore and Solomon Schechter, rather than by the great works of traditional European rabbinic scholarship, medieval or modern.[17] As noted earlier, Herberg's encounter with the religious thought and personal example of Reinhold Niebuhr had been the decisive point in his spiritual journey.[18] Herberg carefully studied all of Niebuhr's writings, underlined them heavily, and "added little in the margins" by way of critical comment.[19] "Every work of Niebuhr's," he reflected in

1956, "almost every article he wrote, enlarged my understanding, deepened my insight, perhaps even confirmed my faith."[20] In Niebuhr's writings—especially *Moral Man and Immoral Society*, *Faith and History*, and *The Nature and Destiny of Man*—Herberg found a compelling theological realism from which to derive and affirm his post-Marxist faith. During the early 1940s, Herberg "had approached his understanding of Marxism from a Niebuhrian point of view"; his subsequent theological evolution proceeded from a conscious continuation of that perspective.[21]

As discussed above, the influence of Niebuhr's thinking is especially evident in Herberg's pessimism about human nature and in his understanding of the concept of sin.[22] Neither Herberg nor even Niebuhr posited man's "complete sinfulness." Nonetheless, Herberg's appropriation of the doctrine of original sin, a theological category neither inherent nor central to Jewish thought outside of America, has lent credence to the criticism that Herberg's theology was more Christian than Jewish.[23]

Niebuhr's influence on Herberg's thought can also be observed in Herberg's theological understanding of the nature of love and the self, including his approach to the problem of the human tendency toward self-deification.[24] Like Niebuhr, Herberg had rejected Marxism on the ground that it had overlooked the sinful nature of man and was utopian in perspective.[25] While the Marxist view of the state presupposed "the innate goodness of man," American constitutional democracy "acknowledged the sinfulness of man as well as his grandeur." Herberg wrote, "If it is man's capacity for justice and cooperation that makes society and the state possible, it is man's proneness to conflict and injustice that makes democracy necessary."[26] Reflected in Herberg's concern with the "biblical-realist" view of American constitutional democracy was the viewpoint that Arnold M. Eisen has persuasively attributed to several American rabbis and theologians of the 1930s and 1940s—that they argued for "the compatibility of Judaism with democracy, . . . the identity of American ideals with their own, . . . [and] that the nation's political system was based upon the Hebrew Bible."[27]

The American aspect of Herberg's thought is also expressed in his views on religion and the state, especially his critique of the long-standing liberal Jewish commitment to the principle of church-state separation.[28] As Franklin H. Littell has noted, the evolving "American pattern of 'separation' had its origin in the adjustments to the interaction of religion and politics that were unique to America."[29] The separationist principle was an American invention, as was the Jeffersonian metaphor of a "wall" between church and state, around which so much recent constitutional and Jewish public debate has revolved. The position Herberg espoused was predicated on the argument that the authors of the Constitution never intended to erect an impenetrable "wall of separation." Although the Founding Fathers did not want to favor any single religion, they were not against helping all religions, or all religion, equally. "Neither in the minds of the Founding Fathers nor in the thinking of the American people through the nineteenth and into the twentieth century," he wrote, "did the doctrine of the First Amendment ever imply an ironclad ban forbidding the government to take account of religion or to support its various activities." In the last years, this argument has been advanced with greater confidence than it was earlier; outside the legal community, Herberg was one of the first American intellectuals to articulate it.

Before most American Jewish intellectuals, Herberg called for a reassessment of the prevailing liberal Jewish consensus concerning the sharply delimited role that religion should play in American public life. In several articles published during the 1950s and 1960s, Herberg urged the Jewish establishment to reassess this position. "By and large," he wrote in 1952, those who speak for the American Jewish community

> seem to share the basic secularist presupposition that religion is a "private matter." . . . The American Jew must have sufficient confidence in the capacity of democracy to preserve its pluralistic . . . character without any *absolute* wall of separation between religion and public life. . . . The fear felt by Jewish leaders of the possible consequences of a restoration of religion to a vital place in public life is what throws them into an alliance with the secularists and helps make their own thinking so thoroughly secular.[30]

A decade or so later, frustrated by Jewish support for the 1963 Supreme Court decisions banning the Lord's Prayer and Bible reading in the public schools, he entered a plea for a restoration of religion to a place of honor in American life:

With the meaning of our political tradition and political practice, the promotion [of religion] has been, and continues to be, a part of the very legitimate "secular" purpose of the state. Whatever the "neutrality" of the state in matters of religion may be, it cannot be a neutrality between religion and no-religion, any more than . . . it could be neutrality between morality and non-morality, [both of which] are necessary to "good government" and "national prosperity."[31]

"The traditional symbols of the divine in our public life," he warned, "ought not to be tampered with."[32]

In developing a Jewish critique of the prevailing liberal American Jewish separationist position, Herberg articulated an American Jewish conservative perspective on the relationship between religion and the state and the growing secularization of American society. The liberal Jewish stance that religious freedom is least secure where government and religion are intertwined developed on American soil and was unique to the thought (and perspective) of American Jews.[33] So, too, the Jewish conservative critique of the "strict separationist" position, as espoused by Herberg during the 1950s and 1960s, was a position unique to American Jewish public thought, for which there was no precedent in the writings of European Jewish thinkers.

Herberg also was the first twentieth-century American Jewish theologian to write about judicial decisions in the area of religion and state, a subject that had not been systematically addressed by Jewish religious thinkers outside of Israel or America. His detailed analysis and critique of United States Supreme Court decisions on prayer in the schools and government aid to parochial education, relating Jewish religious values to American public policy, were distinctively American elements in his Jewish theology and mature political philosophy.[34]

When Will Herberg died in March 1977, American Judaism lost one of its most provocative thinkers. Having received no religious education or training in his youth, Herberg turned to the study of Judaism only after his romance with Marxism ended. A prolific and influential sociologist of religion, his spiritual journey from Marxism to Judaism was unique in the American Jewish intellectual history of this century. The only Jewish ex-Marxist to embrace Jewish theology and the study of religion as a vocation, Will Herberg had become the quintessential *baal teshuvah* of the post–World War II era.

Notes

1. Will Herberg, "From Marxism to Judaism: Jewish Belief as a Dynamic of Social Action," *Commentary* (January 1947): 25.
2. Ibid., 27.
3. Will Herberg, "Reinhold Niebuhr: Christian Apologist to the Secular World," *Union Seminary Quarterly Review* (May 1956): 12.
4. Seymour Siegel, "Will Herberg (1902–1977): A Ba'al Teshuvah Who Became Theologian, Sociologist, Teacher," *American Jewish Year Book* (1978): 532.
5. Ibid.
6. Janet M. Gnall, "Will Herberg, Jewish Theologian: A Bibliographical Existential Approach to Religion" (Ph.D. diss., Drew University, 1983), 51.
7. Will Herberg, *Judaism and Modern Man* (New York: Farrar, Straus, and Young, 1951), 25–43.
8. See Eugene Borowitz, "An Existentialist View of God," *Jewish Heritage* (Spring 1958).
9. Janet M. Gnall, "Will Herberg, Jewish Theologian," 54.
10. Seymour Siegel, "Will Herberg (1902–1977)," 533.
11. Will Herberg, "The Chosenness of Israel and the Jew of Today," *Midstream* (Autumn 1955): 88.
12. Herberg, *Judaism and Modern Man*, 244–45.
13. Ibid., 246.
14. Will Herberg, "The Theological Problems of the Hour," *Proceedings of the Rabbinical Assembly of America* (June 1949): 420.
15. Robert G. Goldy, *The Emergence of Jewish Theology in America* (Bloomington: Indiana University Press, 1990), 29–30.
16. Will Herberg, "Rosenzweig's 'Judaism of Personal Existence': A Third Way between Orthodoxy and Modernism," *Commentary* (December 1950); reprinted in David G. Dalin, ed., *From Marxism to Judaism: The Collected Essays of Will Herberg* (New York; Markus Wiener, 1989), 72–91; and Will Herberg, ed., *The Writings of Martin Buber* (New York: Meridian, 1956).
17. He cites Moore nineteen times in *Judaism and Modern Man*.
18. Most recently, Niebuhr's influence on Herberg and other post–World War II American Jewish theologians has been discussed in Robert G. Goldy, *The Emergence of Jewish Theology in America*, ch. 4.

19. Harry J. Ausmus, *Will Herberg: From Right to Right* (Chapel Hill: University of North Carolina Press, 1987), 112. See Will Herberg, "Reinhold Niebuhr: Christian Apologist to the Secular World," in Dalin, ed., *From Marxism to Judaism*, 39–40; and Will Herberg, "What I Owe to Reinhold Niebuhr as a Theologian," lecture notes on file at the Will Herberg Archives, Drew University, Madison, New Jersey. Herberg's analysis of Niebuhr's thought, in comparison with that of Paul Tillich, is found in his article "Reinhold Niebuhr and Paul Tillich: Two Ways in American Protestant Theology," *Chaplain* (October 1959): 3–9, 36.

20. Will Herberg, "Reinhold Niebuhr: Christian Apologist to the Secular World," in Dalin, ed., *From Marxism to Judaism*, 40.

21. Harry J. Ausmus, *Will Herberg: From Right to Right*, 113.

22. It is also evident in his understanding of the concept of salvation and its relationship to that of sin: "Salvation," wrote Herberg, "is salvation from sin because it is sin . . . which alienates us from God, disrupts society, and brings chaos to the world. . . . Salvation is by faith and grace alone. . . . From the pit of sin we can be saved only by God's grace" (Herberg, "The Theological Problems of the Hour," 424–25).

23. This criticism of Herberg is discussed in more detail in my article on Herberg in Steven T. Katz, ed., *Contemporary Jewish Thinkers* (Washington, D.C.: B'nai B'rith Books, 1991); and Robert G. Goldy, *The Emergence of Jewish Theology in America*, 32–34.

24. Harry J. Ausmus, *Will Herberg: From Right to Right*, 113; and Janet M. Gnall, "Will Herberg, Jewish Theologian," 72.

25. Harry J. Ausmus, *Will Herberg: From Right to Right*, 159.

26. Ibid., 169.

27. Arnold M. Eisen, *The Chosen People in America: A Study in Jewish Religious Ideology* (Bloomington: Indiana University Press, 1983), 36–41. On Herberg's identification of American democratic ideals with the religious values of Judaism, see Herberg, "The Biblical Basis of American Democracy," *Thought* (Spring 1955): 37–50; *Judaism and Modern Man*; as well as Janet M. Gnall, "Will Herberg, Jewish Theologian," 184–86.

28. This principle, first formulated by the New England religious reformer Roger Williams during the 1630s, is discussed in David Little, "Roger Williams and the Separation of Church and State," in James E. Wood, Jr., ed., *Religion and the State: Essays in Honor of Leo Pfeffer* (Waco, Texas: Baylor University Press, 1985), 3–23; Leonard W. Levy, *The Establishment Clause: Religion and the First Amendment* (New York: Macmillan, 1986), 183–84; and Robert L. Maddox, *Separation of Church and State: Guarantor of Religious Freedom* (New York: Crossroads, 1987), 53.

29. Franklin H. Littell, "Religious Liberty, the Free Churches, and Political Action," in Wood, Jr., ed., *Religion and the State*, 379.

30. Will Herberg, "The Sectarian Conflict over Church and State: A Divi-

sive Threat to our Democracy?" *Commentary* (November 1952): 459.

31. Will Herberg, "Religion and Public Life," *National Review*, August 13, 1963, 105.

32. Will Herberg, "Religious Symbols in Public Life," *National Review*, August 28, 1962, 162.

33. For a discussion and critique of the liberal Jewish separationist faith, see my review essay "Leo Pfeffer and the Separationist Faith," *This World* (Winter 1989): 136–40; and, more recently, my contribution to "Judaism and American Public Life: A Symposium," *First Things* (March 1991): 16–17.

34. On these issues, see the following works by Herberg: "The Sectarian Conflict over Church and State"; "Religion and Public Life," *National Review*, July 30, 1963, 61; "Religious Symbols in Public Life," 145, 162; "Justice for Religious Schools," *America*, November 16, 1957, 190–93; *Protestant-Catholic-Jew* (Chicago: University of Chicago Press, 1983), 232–34, 238–39.

CHAPTER 8

The Anomalous Liberalism of American Jews

Nathan Glazer

A recent study of religion in America tells us what we all know: that Jews are the most liberal religious group in the country. They have the smallest number of persons declaring themselves Republicans and the largest number declaring themselves Democrats. More detailed analysis would undoubtedly also reveal the great anomaly of Jewish liberalism, one that has been evident in studies for forty years: political allegiance in the United States is affected most strongly by economic status—but Jews break the pattern. The most prosperous of all religious groups, they are also the most liberal, by the use of the crude measure of how many vote Democratic and how many vote Republican, or indeed by any other measure one can think of. As Milton Himmelfarb once said, they are like Episcopalians in income, but vote as if they were Puerto Ricans. We are not surprised that when New York elected its first black mayor by a hair's-breadth majority, the only white group that gave him a substantial part of its vote was Jews.

This anomaly raises three questions: why does it exist, is it changing, and, as the complex of political and social attitudes that we know as liberalism breaks up, where will the Jews stand? I argue that this complex is breaking up, and it raises difficult questions as to the political orientation of Jews in the future.

American liberalism has been an odd mix based in part on political philosophy, in part on self-interest, in part on the particular and peculiar historical circumstances of the United States. Liberalism as a political philosophy defines itself in contrast to conservatism. While it had different elements in the various countries of Europe, it was uniformly a philosophy committed to a rational, indeed a scientific, approach to political questions. It was critical of established churches, of purely traditional and unthought-through commitments. Politics is of course more than philosophy: it is also interest. Liberalism was based on the business classes, which, in country after country in Europe, were opposed to the landed classes. It was based on new men making their money in new ways through industry and trade, as against those who inherited wealth and whose fortune was based on land. In England, the interest of those who employed their talents in industry and trade led them to support free trade in order to lower the cost of labor and to help the industrial and trading interests in a nation that was at the forefront of industry and trade. In countries that industrialized after England, the philosophy of free trade and a free market was often in competition with the interests of industrialists who wanted a protected market at home, but liberalism everywhere was associated predominantly with the philosophy of Adam Smith and classical economics: the narrow interests of those who called for protection would harm the larger national interest in trade and economic growth.

Whatever the fate of classic liberalism in Europe, in the United States liberalism was different, though there were continuities. As a political philosophy, liberalism continued to mean commitment to the rational rather than to the traditional; preference for experiments and new departures rather than cautious adherence to the established order; greater freedom in action for the individual rather than greater state restraint; rights for minority religions, minority political views, and minority social groups rather than acceptance of a traditional order that gave preference to a previously established religion or to charter social groups.

European liberalism was quite different from that American liberalism that we identify with Franklin D. Roosevelt's New Deal and its heirs: European liberalism opposed government direction and regulation of the economy. Indeed, Frederick Hayek and Milton

Friedman, who uphold these positions today, while called conservatives in the United States, would identify themselves as liberals in Europe. American liberalism became identified with activist government, protecting the workers, redistributing income to low-income groups, increasing regulation of business for the benefit of employees and consumers, guiding the economy through some kind of planning. To Hayek, this was the "road to serfdom": freedom in economic life was indissolubly linked to freedom in political and social life; to engage in restricting the first meant, in time, restricting the second. The Hayekian argument was that social democracy led to socialism, which led to communism. This aspect of liberalism was decisively rejected by American liberalism. It was rejected by American Jews, even though they are overwhelmingly in business and the professions—and as professionals in medicine, law, accounting, and a variety of other professions they are, for the most part, small businessmen. The anomaly of American Jewish liberalism was that American Jews were enthusiastic adherents to the American view of liberalism in the economic sphere, that is, they were for activist government and for regulation and redistribution as against the free play of economic forces, but their economic interests should have led them to become adherents of that other and earlier liberalism of Hayek and Friedman.

Yet Jewish interests did play a role in their adherence to American liberalism. I date the American liberal complex to the days of Franklin D. Roosevelt and the New Deal, now sixty years in the past. At that time, American Jews were for the most part workers. Progressive taxation, redistribution, and protection of organized labor were public policies that defended the interests of workers. As American Jews rapidly moved out of working-class status—and by the fifties this move was in large measure accomplished—they nevertheless stuck with the American liberal complex. Predictions heard as early as Eisenhower's victories in the 1950s that American Jews would bring their political attitudes into alignment with their economic interests remained unfulfilled. And they are still unfulfilled today.

Interest did play a role in their adherence to the Democratic party. In the North it was an immigrant party, a Catholic party, a big-city party, opposed to the native American and Protestant and small-town and rural party, the Republican. Like all American parties, the Democratic party has always been an amalgam of interests. The party of immigrants, it also included the fiercest opponents of immigrants: southern whites. But it stood to reason that Jews, as immigrant workers, would find it the most congenial party. For very many Jews, the Socialist party was even more congenial, but, with Roosevelt's victories, American socialism was reduced to a remnant. The Socialist Jewish workers and their children, one way or another, found their way to the Democratic party.

Aside from pure economic interest based on class, there is the interest of minorities in protecting their rights. As immigrants and the children of immigrants, Jews found the Democratic party comfortable. As a religious minority, they also found the Democratic party more congenial—the Republicans were too small-town, too Protestant, too distant from Jewish urban experience. Despite the strains of antisemitism among Catholic urban groups in the 1930s (the time of Father Coughlin) and despite anti-immigrant (and antisemitic) tendencies among southern whites, the Democratic party, in its northern big-city form, remained the preferred setting for them.

There is an anomaly in the continuing Jewish adherence to the immigrant party and the minority party, just as there is in their adherence to the working-class party. Jews are not immigrants anymore and do not have many relatives left abroad to bring into this country. To most Americans, they are no longer a "minority"— that is, an underprivileged group. Ninety percent of immigrants today are non-Europeans. It is the Asians, Hispanics, and Caribbeans whose interests are most affected by immigration policy. Yet immigrant issues still play a major role in the American Jewish political outlook. They were immigrants once; they were discriminated against once, not only as Jews. In the 1930s and 1940s the fate of the Jewish people was decisively shaped by restrictive American immigration legislation. For decades, Jews fought for the opening up of American immigration. In 1965, when this fight was finally won, it was clear that opening up American immigration was primarily for the benefit of others. As Jews and Jewish organizations supported freer immigration through the 1970s and 1980s, it became clearer that freer immigration was no longer a policy that primarily benefited Jews. Their commitment to these policies was more an act of sentiment, of honoring old commitments and old values, than of interest.

There is a third strand, perhaps the most distinctive, in American liberalism and one that one would think would weaken Jewish adherence to liberalism. This is the strand of race.

Liberalism meant equal rights for Blacks and the advancement of Black political and economic interests. Jews were happy to support that strand of liberalism too. (Other Democrats were not.) For a time, it was support out of common interest. Laws banning discrimination on grounds of race, color, and religion would help Jews as well as Blacks. By the 1960s these laws were clearly primarily designed for Blacks—Jews had already escaped most forms of damaging discrimination. By the 1970s, these laws had indeed shifted, in their implementation and administration, from being bulwarks of color blindness to being supports for color preference. Conflicts, including some grave ones, emerged between Jews and Blacks. Many Jews opposed the rise of a statistically based affirmative action on principle and on the basis of self-interest. They had always favored treatment of individuals strictly as individuals in order to escape from discrimination on the basis of religion. They did well themselves on tests of individual merit. I will not try to separate out the various strands of principle and self-interest that explained the Jewish reaction to affirmative action. Suffice it to say that the feelings that affirmative action aroused among Jews in the 1970s have become moderate in the 1990s. The strongest opponents of affirmative action today are to be found among policemen, firemen, and employees of some large corporations such as A T & T, who have been subjected to strict quota provisions in employment and promotion. There are not, however, many Jewish policemen and firemen, or telephone workers.

Self-interest, I would argue, no longer explains Jewish adherence to liberalism. The Jewish businessman and professional, if he were following his self-interest, would by now have become a Republican, as his Catholic and Protestant business and professional colleagues have become. The Jewish suburbanite, if she were following her self-interest, would have joined her Catholic neighbors in moving from the Democratic to the Republican party. There are a substantial number of Jewish neoconservative—and conservative—intellectuals who argue that the United States is not helped by the economic policies of liberalism (and business is certainly not helped by it), but they find few followers among American Jews. Jewish self-interest is no longer served by the civil rights agenda as it has moved from color blindness to color preference. But that too does not trouble Jews much. Their traditional commitment to liberalism is such that they are willing to go along with it. Jewish organizations supported the civil rights restoration act that sought to reverse recent Supreme Court decisions weakening the ability of lawyers to demonstrate discrimination on the basis of evidence from statistical disparity. As a markedly "overrepresented" group, one would think Jews would have a strong interest in reducing the weight of statistical arguments as a basis of finding discrimination, with a resultant imposition of quotas as restitution, and would favor greater weight on tests of individual merit.

Despite the lack of fit between Jewish interests and the three aspects of liberalism just discussed, Jewish attachment to liberalism has not declined much. Jews will side with a government active in the economic sphere in support of labor as against business, of consumers as against producers, of low-income groups as against upper-income groups. Jews are inclined to back an open immigration policy, even though there is now no urgent Jewish need to which it is responsive. Jews support the civil rights organizations in their push to make it more difficult for employers to use discretion in judging competence, to force them to take account of the representativeness of their labor force, and to consider race and sex in making promotions. In this case, shoring up relations with the civil rights organizations is more important to Jewish defense organizations than protecting the interests of individual Jews affected by these policies. Jewish organizations were more concerned when, in the 1970s, cases concerning quotas in law and medical schools came up. They are less interested in the rights of workers to opportunities for training and for promotions.

There is one element, however, in the complex of policies that make up liberalism that does agitate Jews and that has split many Jews away from liberalism. This is foreign and military policy. In foreign policy the issue of Israel arises, and attachment to Israel, for most Jews, is more important than defending their liberal credentials, allegiances, and alliances. It is an agonizing problem how to fit the defense of Israel into what they conceive of as a liberal foreign policy.

Just what a "liberal foreign policy" is, and whether the term "liberal" can be attached to foreign policy, is questionable. Fifty years ago, it was rather clear what a liberal foreign policy was: opposition to fascism. Less clear was whether this opposition should be military (many isolationists were liberal, or even farther to the left) or simply rhetorical. After the war, it was not quite so clear what a liberal foreign policy was, but there was general agreement that it meant creating a world safe for democracy by supporting the United Nations (half of whose founding members in those halcyon days were democracies) and by providing aid both to our democratic allies abroad and to the emerging Third World, which we hoped would become democratic through Western aid and influence. Liberalism had a more difficult problem with communism. Most liberals unhesitatingly opposed leftist totalitarian dictatorship; others, influenced by its historical origins in socialism and its rhetoric of defending the interests of workers and poor people, were more equivocal or even supportive of communism. But one could argue that the dominant strand of liberal foreign policy in the age of Truman and Kennedy was activist abroad in defense of democracy and in opposition to communism (which often meant supporting authoritarian but not Communist regimes). This strand of liberalism frayed badly during the Vietnam War, and has continued to unravel through the 1980s as a result of our policies in El Salvador, Nicaragua, Panama, and Grenada. One can see the division continuing in the background to the Iraqi war to the point where one would be hard put to say what is a "liberal" stance in foreign policy.

Eugene Rostow of the Committee on the Present Danger and Max Kampelman would call themselves liberal, I believe: they see themselves as in the line of Roosevelt, Truman, and Kennedy, as the heirs of senators Humphrey and Jackson. The problem of liberalism in foreign policy is best illuminated when we ask whether those who consider themselves liberals consider Rostow and Kampelman liberals. In large part, the split over what is liberal in foreign policy was determined by the attitude to communism. Should it be opposed militarily, and if so, with what kinds of arms and how big a buildup? Should one support nondemocratic states fighting communism? How suspicious should one be of movements using leftist and democratic rhetoric that are fighting for independence or autonomy or a change of regime? Should the democratic language of some of these groups be discounted as propaganda and disguise for Communist control or intentions? One might then think that the split would come to an end with the collapse of communism. But it has not been so. What is liberal in foreign policy still divides the Democratic party and liberals in general.

Should a "liberal" foreign policy be the policy of Jesse Jackson and the Democratic left wing, which holds the Third World, particularly in its more militant and anti-American manifestations, as worthy of support? Or should it be the by-now-old liberalism of Democratic Cold War warriors, the Eugene Rostows and the Max Kampelmans, the heirs of senators Jackson and Humphrey, who vigorously supported the buildup of American arms, the countering of Communist movements everywhere, a strong alliance of the wealthy developed nations? From their point of view, this alliance was the chief protector of democracy and freedom and the chief force for its expansion; from the perspective of the left wing of the party, it was an alliance of the rich against the poor, the white against the colored, the exploitative consumers of raw materials against the poor producers.

Underlying liberal opposition to the Gulf War was undoubtedly the scenario of rich, economically sophisticated nations overwhelming a poorer, economically more backward nation, of the power of modern Western technology brought overwhelmingly down on the heads of Third World people. Whatever the division caused in liberal ranks by the Gulf War, it was made even more painful among Jews. Jews have always, it seems, wanted it both ways: they wanted a weak military establishment but strong support of Israel. The contradiction came home most sharply in the conflict with Iraq when the arms whose development Jewish liberals had opposed, and the military force whose deployment they wanted to delay, served to protect Israel and to half-demolish its most dangerous military opponent. And it was the Democrats, the party in which the great majority of Jews feel most comfortable, that opposed military buildups and the early use of force.

If Jews become divided from the liberalism to which they have been attached for two-thirds of this century, it is because of the way Israel introduces complex cross-currents in liberal positions and in Jewish positions. When Israel was founded, these cross-currents were ignored. Israel was a country of refuge for survivors of Nazism; its founding was supported by the victorious powers in World War II; it was a democratic nation in a part of the world where democracy was rare or nonexistent and a social-democratic nation in a part of the world in which the rich and powerful dominated and exploited the poor. Why should not liberals have been supporters of Israel? And they were, pushing aside a fatal flaw—the dispossession of the Arabs of Palestine—a flaw that has grown to giant proportions, making almost impossible the effort to bridge the growing gap between the support of Israel and liberal positions on a host of issues.

I need not rehearse all the inconsistencies brought into classic American liberal positions by support of Israel. Liberals want to spend money on schools and housing rather than arms; but American sophisticated arms may defend Israel. They want to give aid to poor nations; but Israel, not a poor nation, engrosses a huge share of the American aid budget. They want to support democracies, and Israel is a democracy, but one in which the rights of a very large part of the population, Arabs within Israel and the occupied territories, are scarcely models of the rights people expect to have in a democratic society. Arabs in Israel have lesser rights than Jews, in the occupied territories even less rights. Liberals in this country support the strict separation of church and state and the equality of religions before the law, but they support a state in which one religion holds primacy and is backed by state power. They are against the conquest of territory by force but support a state that has doubled its size through force and over time has shown less and less inclination to give up its conquests. The measures Israel uses to put down the *intifada*, when resorted to by other democracies (for example, India), raise an outcry among liberals; in the Israeli case, the outcry is muted.

Each of the policies I have described, policies that liberals oppose, could be defended, to some extent even within a liberal framework. But whatever the justification, liberals are not comfortable
with the use of force to support state power and solve internal
problems. They believe there always should be an alternative.
Those alternatives are not evident in Israel, and Israeli liberals have
become weaker over time. Do American Jewish liberals weaken
year by year in the face of the imperatives set afoot by the very
decision to create a Jewish state in an Arab and Muslim world? I
believe they do. Jewish neoconservatives have in large measure
been created by the Israel issue: military power, force, the differen-
tial treatment of people of different ethnic origin, intrusive police
work, a ruthless intelligence agency, all seem to some degree justified in Israel, while the same policies would be, and have been,
denounced and opposed in the United States. Of course Israel's
situation is different, and one can reconcile justification of Israel's
necessitous resort to such measures with opposition to such measures in the United States. They needed to do it, we did not—
leading one, therefore, to support the military establishment and
tough measures in Israel on the one hand and to oppose the military
establishment and tough measures by the United States on the
other.

To some extent this works in the United States: liberals can
reconcile support of Israel with their general liberalism. It works
only because so many American Jews are liberals, so many American liberals are Jews, so much of the money and power that liberalism deploys in the United States is Jewish. Thus doubts and questions about Israel must be stilled. It works much less effectively in
Europe, where the Jewish component of liberalism is minuscule
compared with that in the United States; in Europe, the outcry in
favor of Arab national rights, of the maintenance of civil liberties
even during an insurrection, has been much stronger.

My discussion is analytical rather than prescriptive. The analysis
suggests that Israel introduces a fatal contradiction in the overall
liberal outlook of American Jews. The contradiction existed but
was scarcely evident when Israel had social-democratic governments, did not hold occupied territories inhabited by Arabs, did not
require huge quantities of military aid from the United States, did

not have extreme right-wing parties demanding the expulsion of the Arabs, was not enthusiastically greeting hundreds of thousands of Russian Jews who it hoped would replace Arabs in Israel and in the occupied territories. These are realities, and one does not see how the attachment to Israel, which affects almost all Jews, can be reconciled with a liberalism that is still the faith of a great majority of Jews. For many American Jews, there is no longer need for such a reconciliation. They see no alternative to a policy of blood, soil, arms, force; and they adopt more and more the political perspective in which such policies are at home.

One wonders how much longer American Jews can defend such policies in Israel and deny their justice anywhere else, how much longer they can defend the national rights of the Jewish people and the measures that defense makes necessary, without affecting their attitudes on a host of other issues that make up the complex of American liberalism. Israel and its needs may be the entering wedge that ends the anomaly of American Jewish liberalism, of a people supporting policies that reflect old sentiments and attachments but that hardly reflect current interests.

CHAPTER 9

Liberalism, Judaism, and American Jews: A Response

Jerold S. Auerbach

I am troubled by the reliance upon liberalism as a valid measure of the American Jewish experience or the broader currents of Jewish history. The identification of Jews with the American liberal tradition was not foreordained. It was, to be sure, one of the formative encounters in American Jewish history, but it is necessary to emphasize the contingent nature of this relationship. Before American Jews were political liberals—before, that is, World War I—they were political conservatives, without any sense that they were unfaithful to Jewish norms. Any assumption that "the distinctive political culture" of Jews is liberalism, traceable all the way back to the Hebrew prophets, is highly dubious.

Faithful to Professor Feingold's theme, "the Americanization of Jewish liberalism," I discern an altogether different historical process. It is the Americanization of Judaism, with liberalism as the connecting link. Liberalism, as we understand it, is two hundred years old, a phenomenon of Enlightenment ideology. Although Western Jews rushed to embrace its precepts and availed themselves of emancipation opportunities, they were a minority among Jews. The vast majority—by choice or necessity—remained securely within the norms of traditional Judaism, which was anything but liberal. Prior to the nineteenth century for virtually all Jews, and among the Orthodox thereafter, Judaism was thoroughly and profoundly conservative—although Jewish law contained mechanisms

144

for legitimate change, as long as it occurred within the bounds of rabbinic legal authority.

Not only was liberalism a relatively novel intruder upon Jewish history in the nineteenth century; it also remained largely foreign to the experience of the American Jewish community until well into the twentieth century. Until the 1920s the leaders of American Jewry were political conservatives, with the singular exception of Louis Brandeis, a latecomer and brief sojourner in American Jewish affairs. From abolitionism to populism, Jews had *not* been conspicuous on the liberal side of the great social issues of the nineteenth century. Even Reform, the prototypically liberal wing of religious Judaism, did not officially embrace progressive causes until the World War I era, and then only in the wake of the liberal Protestant denominations.

The American Jewish identification with liberalism, as Henry Feingold notes, was largely a second-generation Eastern European phenomenon. The children of Russian, Rumanian, and Polish immigrants wanted desperately to be good Americans. Caught in the economic collapse after 1929, they became New Deal liberals to achieve economic security and political integration. The fateful alliance of Jews with FDR has usually been explained as a reflection of the natural affinity of Jews for liberalism. On the contrary: the Roosevelt years culminated the struggle of American Jews for recognition as loyal Americans. Only this yearning can explain why American Jews bestowed such unbounded gratitude, then and since, upon a patrician gentile who gave them so little as Jews, and who was so indifferent to the plight of European Jewry. American Jews loved Roosevelt precisely because he recognized them as Americans only, denying Jewish particularity—either in the United States or, far more fatefully, as victims and refugees in Europe. The New Deal, that momentous turning point for American Jews, did *not* "fit neatly into Jewish political culture." Rather, it coaxed Jews into the American political mainstream, where they swam contentedly until the 1970s.

The political profile of American Jewry is growing more complex than it was when Jews led the New Deal chorus of "Happy Days Are Here Again." Was the Jewish turn toward neoconservatism an aberration, the abandonment of the "Jewish political culture"? Or did it represent a reasoned reading of Jewish values at a time when American Jews felt squeezed by affirmative action and political correctness, and while Israel remains a precarious island of Jewish nationality amid continuing Arab hostility? For better or worse, Israel has served as a Rorschach test for American Jewry. After 1977 the Jewish state pulled away from its Labor Zionist origins. As the Israeli political culture, responding to different themes and imperatives in Jewish history, became less liberal, American Jews felt acute tension between their liberal and Jewish commitments.

Between 1977 and 1992, Israel was subjected to constant criticism from American Jewish liberals. The issue varied—Likud dominance, settlements in the territories, "who is a Jew," the Lebanon war, the *intifada*—but lamentations about the lost soul of Israel persisted. Might it be, however, that Israelis knew something that American Jews had forgotten: that liberalism and Judaism form an odd couple indeed, the product of a shotgun marriage amid particular circumstances in the modern era? It even seemed to be time for a divorce, lest American Jews who identified Judaism with liberalism found it impossible to identify with the Jewish state. What is to be said for liberalism if it turned Jews in Israel and the United States into political adversaries?

Liberalism, after all, is a largely alien ideology, one that emerged from the Christian West two centuries ago with the demand, hardly friendly, that Jews relinquish their distinctiveness as the price for their entry into civil society. That was surely a fateful rendezvous, as momentous as the alliance, two millennia earlier, between Judaism and Hellenism. But once we adopt liberalism as the standard of measurement, as do Feingold and Glazer, we risk consigning Jews to the margins of our analysis. For the more that Jews are preoccupied with liberalism, the less concerned they seem with Judaism.

As transitory as the intersection of liberalism and Judaism may be in the larger currents of Jewish history, it has surely been fateful and formative for American Jews. That may even help to explain why the American Jewish community is obsessed with the question whether, through intermarriage or assimilation, it is self-destructing. Liberalism has served Jews well in their quest for a secure American identity, but that has less to do with Judaism than with the imperatives of Americanization. For the children and grandchildren of the Eastern European immigrants who fled to the very *goldene medina* that their rabbis cursed as *trefe*, liberalism has been the preeminent ideology of acculturation along with the momentous journey from *shtetl* to suburb.

Yet the anomaly identified by Glazer remains: in a country where political allegiance is molded by economic status, Jews, disproportionately prosperous, remain disproportionately liberal. But he suggests that the affinity between Jews and liberalism may now be dissolving, for reasons related to Israel. Attachment to Israel, he indicates, may be more important for American Jews than defending their liberal principles. If the Persian Gulf crisis is any indication, the foreign policy of the party of liberalism may now have diminished appeal to American Jews, at least when the interests of Israel are at stake. Israel, he notes, "introduces complex cross-currents in liberal positions," perhaps even a "fatal contradiction" in the liberalism of American Jews.

Glazer denies the possibility that American Jews can have their *ruggelach* and eat it too. If he is correct, and I believe that he is, American Jews will be able to have Israel or liberalism, but not both. I doubt, however, that most American Jews will be unduly troubled by this choice. They will, it seems evident, choose liberalism over Israel. Here I depart from the conventional wisdom that asserts a continuing intimacy of devotion between American Jews and Israel. Ever since 1948, American Jews have been far more ambivalent in their relationship to Israel than we might prefer to recall or acknowledge. "We Are One" is a wonderful slogan, but it is not good history. After the brief flurry of enthusiasm over independence, American Jews slipped into indifference—so much so that Glazer wrote, in his *American Judaism*, that Israel (like the Holocaust) had "remarkably slight" effect on American Jews of the fifties.

To be sure, that changed swiftly and dramatically in the spring of 1967. The passionate identification of American Jews with Israel that blossomed after the Six-Day War remained a potent factor in American Jewish life—for exactly a decade. After 1977, however, Israel was a constant thorn in the side of American Jewish liberals. If Glazer is predicting that when the moment of choice arrives,

Israel is likely to wean American Jews from liberalism, I strongly dissent. Indeed, I contemplate a far bleaker, even tragic, scenario: liberalism is likely to wean American Jews from Israel. The loss of Jewish support for liberalism would be bearable; liberalism can survive without Jews. But can Israel, and can the Diaspora, in turn, survive without a Jewish state? I am far more worried that American Jews will prefer liberalism to Israel than Israel to liberalism. What does it say about American Jewry that it might prefer a mess of Western liberal pottage to its national birthright in the Jewish state?

All of which returns us to our central theme: the place of Jews in American society—and, I would add, the place of American society in Jewish history. If Jews must choose between liberalism, the hallmark of our American identity, and Israel, the badge of our Jewish identity, what will we do? When liberalism no longer serves as the connecting bridge between Judaism and Americanism, how will Jews choose? Only time will tell how American Jews will confront the classic dilemma of divided loyalty that they have struggled so long, and so desperately, to elude.

PART THREE

Zionism in an American Setting

CHAPTER 10

Zionism and American Politics

Melvin I. Urofsky

"If I forget thee, O Zion" has been a pious incantation of the Jewish people for over two millennia. For most of that time, it has had a venerable religious meaning; Jews would continue to remember Zion, and their God would remember them, ultimately delivering them out of the bondage of exile and returning them to the land promised to their fathers. Human beings alone could do nothing to bring about this deliverance; God, at the chosen time, would accomplish the miracle.

In the nineteenth century many traditional Jewish assumptions were altered. The emancipation process initiated by the French National Assembly eventually freed Jews in various lands from discriminatory regulations under which they had lived for centuries. Departing the ghetto, many Jews also sought to leave behind what they considered anachronistic religious beliefs and practices. The Haskalah, the so-called Jewish enlightenment, led European Jews to seek cultural and political knowledge heretofore of secondary importance to them. For some, this in turn led to an abandonment of principles and rituals that had been part of Jewish life for centuries, including frequently expressed hopes for the ingathering of the exiled Jews to the Holy Land. Reform Judaism, for example, which sought a "modern" religion in a society where Jews would be French or German or English of the "Judaic persuasion," eliminated the prayers to return to Zion from its liturgy.

Exposure to nineteenth-century European secular thought, especially the waves of nationalism that swept over the continent, led other Jews to a different conclusion. They would seek to return to Zion not by divine intercession but by their own efforts. They would go to Palestine, they would build up the land, and they would create a new Zion themselves. The origins of modern Zionism, the tales of the Biluim and of the First Zionist Congress, are well known to us. We are also aware that from the beginning Zionism had different factions and was nearly torn apart by the resulting tensions. We can identify the factions and their leaders: religious Zionists, led by Isaac Jacob Reines, Abraham Isaac Kook, and Meyer Berlin (later Bar-Ilan); socialists, inspired by Ber Borochov and Nachman Syrkin; cultural or spiritual Zionists, who adhered to the teachings of Ahad Ha-am; and political Zionists, of whom Theodor Herzl was the towering figure in Europe.[1]

From the beginning, though, these strains overlapped, far more than many of their adherents admitted. Even the most fervent socialists often harbored strong religious and cultural ties to the land of Zion even if they refused to acknowledge them. Political Zionists, who concentrated on what they considered the chief task, that of securing the international arrangements that would allow the Jewish people to settle once again in its ancient homeland, shared these Jewish values. As time went on, these strains of Zionism developed their own agendas, not just religious, economic, and cultural, but political as well. Rather than acknowledging how much they had in common, they often seemed bent on emphasizing their differences. The old saw about the multiplicity of Jewish opinions seemed the hallmark of the Zionist movement in the first part of the twentieth century.

American Zionism from the start mirrored the European movement in its fragmentation. It also differed from it in many significant ways, and these differences would prove critical as the years went on.[2] Thus, American Jews did not face the rampant antisemitism that had long marked European society.[3] As a result, certain types of Zionism did not take root as strongly in this country as did others. Socialists, for example, found the United States so open a society and economy that, instead of attacking capitalism, they often ended up becoming capitalists themselves. Also, immigrants coming to the New World wanted to become "Amerikaners" and to shed as quickly as possible every cultural trait that marked them as different, be it the speech, dress, or religious practices of European Jews.

If being too religious or too socialist made recent Jewish immigrants uncomfortable, they found during the First World War that political Zionism was not only acceptable but highly effective. They learned, as Louis D. Brandeis constantly preached to them, that they could be both good Americans and good Jews by being good Zionists.[4]

I have argued elsewhere that, given the circumstances of American society in the first decades of the twentieth century, only the Brandeisian form of Zionism, with its emphasis on American values, could have succeeded.[5] It succeeded brilliantly, not only during the First World War but also after the Second, when American Zionists influenced the political situation that helped create the State of Israel. In certain ways, the very nature of American political Zionism was the cause of its great failure—the inability to save European Jews in the 1930s and 1940s—and the cause of its decline after 1949. I want briefly to limn the contours of American Zionism, both its triumphs and its failures, and to suggest why a political route may have been the only feasible one for Zionism in this country.

On the eve of World War I, Zionism in the United States seemed moribund. The umbrella organization, the Federation of American Zionists (FAZ), had about twelve thousand members, a large number of them recent immigrants, out of a total Jewish population that approached two million. The most dynamic figure in the movement, Rabbi Stephen S. Wise, had resigned from office, frustrated by the backstabbing and petty jealousies of European leaders who treated American Jewry as a provincial backwater good for nothing else but monetary support (which, they complained, never met their expectations).

The problems of the American Zionists went beyond the animosities between the world organization and the American one. Immigrant Jews looked not to the Zionists, most of whom were themselves also newcomers, but to the German Jews, the Yahudim, who had immigrated a generation earlier and were now well established economically and socially. The Yahudim emphasized the need for rapid Americanization; they urged those who had recently arrived to shed their old language, their old clothes, and their old religious practices. Nothing less fit their notion of true American values than Zionism, which they derided as fostering dual loyalties. It was one thing to pray, in the abstract, for a return to Zion (although most of them as Reform Jews did not do that); it was quite another to embark on a harebrained scheme to bring it about.[6]

The leaders of the FAZ could do little to galvanize the members; most paid the *shekel* but did little else to further the Zionist cause. After all, they had made *aliyah*, not to Eretz Yisrael, but to the *goldine medine*, America. Here they faced daily problems of making a living, of keeping a roof over their heads and food on their family tables. The American capitalist system offered enough of a challenge; socialists did not have time to worry about the utopia they hoped to build in Palestine. Religious Jews discovered that a land of freedom could be just as destructive of tradition as a land of pogroms, while those who read Ahad Ha-am had a better idea of what a cultural center might resemble in some future Jewish homeland than how to foster that Jewish culture in America. Aside from raising some money for the Jewish National Fund and the Zionist Bank, the FAZ did not offer much by way of a program.

All this changed when war broke out in August 1914. Zionists now had a specific task, that of saving the fledgling Jewish settlements in Palestine. It soon became clear that the American Jewish Committee, the organization of the Yahudim, dominated overseas charity work. The Zionists would have to figure out not only how to raise money but also how to deliver that money to Palestine, and at the same time how to gain a voice in American Jewish affairs. These tasks called not for religious zeal, socialist idealism, or cultural sensitivity but for political pragmatism—the strength that Louis D. Brandeis and his lieutenants brought to American Zionism when they took over the leadership in the summer of 1914.

Brandeis and men like Felix Frankfurter, Julian Mack, Bernard Flexner, and Stephen Wise had honed their political skills in the arena of progressive reform. If, as some critics claimed, they made redeeming the Holy Land sound like enacting a factory safety law, they proved adept at both. Within a short period the invigorated Zionist movement became a major player not only in American

Jewish affairs but also in American political life. It played an effective role in raising relief funds, and, through the American Jewish Congress movement, it challenged the Yahudim for leadership of the community. When Great Britain expressed a willingness to sponsor a Jewish homeland in Palestine after the war, Brandeis and Wise played a critical role in securing approval of the Balfour Declaration from the Wilson administration. By 1919, the Zionist Organization of America (ZOA), as it was now called, had over 170,000 members, operated medical and relief facilities in Palestine, and had access to the world's leaders at the Paris Peace Conference.

Why this sudden success, and why the collapse of this power within two years? Success came because the war presented tangible objectives that the Zionists could address through methods acceptable to the general populace. Relief work for the settlements in Palestine could be seen as part of a larger effort by many Americans to help war-torn communities in Europe, such as the program headed by Herbert Hoover to aid Belgium. Just as immigrants and their children assisted relatives and friends in the old country, in the Zionist case Jews were helping other Jews.

For quite different reasons, the Zionists also found widespread public support for the Balfour Declaration. Although some Christian groups opposed granting Jews hegemony over Palestine, many more believed that both divine and secular reasons justified a Jewish return. For some sects, Jewish return to the Holy Land would precede the second coming of Christ and should therefore be encouraged, a belief that still undergirds fundamentalist Christian support of Israel. Also, the Zionist campaign made support of the Balfour Declaration appear very American, an endorsement of Jewish pioneers settling and reclaiming a wilderness, just as Americans had done.

One can speculate that antisemitism and xenophobia also played a role. Immigration restriction had been gaining ground even before the war and even won its first major victory in the passing of a literacy test for immigrants over Wilson's veto in 1917. The war slowed down migration but the pace picked up immediately after the end of hostilities, triggering renewed efforts to limit or cut off the flood of newcomers entering the country. Many of the prewar immigrants had been Jews from Eastern Europe, and Zionists recognized that there would be no place for them to go if the anti-immigration forces had their way. By calling for a home in Palestine, the Zionists played this card to their advantage.

Relief work and lobbying for the Balfour Declaration involved little that could be described as overtly Jewish. American Zionists, then and later, would have their greatest success when they could clothe their efforts in nonreligious garb. They could utilize as justification for their movement the age-old yearning for redemption, but that was an idealization that Christian Americans could easily accept without identifying it as peculiarly Jewish. Moreover, for American Zionists, return was indeed an abstraction; they wanted a homeland not for themselves but for Jews fleeing persecution in Europe. In short, the Zionists would be most effective, as Brandeis predicted, when they acted primarily as Americans and not as Jews.

This proved anathema to Chaim Weizmann and the leadership of European Zionism. For them redemption had not only religious connotations but also an immediate relevance for their own lives—they did plan to make *aliyah*, they did plan to participate personally in rebuilding the land, and, regardless of their party affiliation, they did wholeheartedly believe that the rebuilt homeland in Palestine, whatever its political or economic configuration, would be Jewish. To them, the Brandeisian approach robbed Zionism of its Jewish core, reducing it to little more than a philanthropic endeavor.

Soon after the war, Weizmann and his coterie decided to wrest the momentum back from the American leadership. On one level, this amounted to little more than a power play to determine who would govern the invigorated Zionist enterprise. On another level, however, it involved a struggle for the Jewish soul of Zionism.[7]

The Eastern European immigrants who made up the bulk of ZOA membership had applauded the Brandeis leadership and reveled in the idea that Zionism—to them an overwhelmingly *Jewish* activity—could be made respectably American. But they never understood or accepted the nuances that Brandeis used to make Zionism divisible from Judaism. When Weizmann came to America in 1921, they saw a Jewish leader who was recognizably Jewish, a *mentsh*, a man who spoke Yiddish as well as English and who emphasized the Jewishness of the return. Given this situation and the attitudes of

American Jewry at the time, Weizmann won his victory at the ZOA convention in Cleveland in 1921.[8]

Weizmann installed his supporters, all of whom shared his views, as the leadership of the movement. American Zionism practically disappeared in the 1920s; membership dropped from 180,000 in 1919 to eighteen thousand in 1929. In the Roaring Twenties, a movement that emphasized ethnic or religious particularism seemed out of step in a nation that closed its gates to further immigration, a nation in which the Ku Klux Klan and other groups preached a doctrine of conformity to white, Christian values.[9] The decline could not, of course, be blamed entirely on the incompetence of Louis Lipsky and his clique. Even had the Brandeisians retained power there would have been a drop in membership and influence. But one segment of American Zionism did not abandon the earlier model: Hadassah, which continued to follow the Brandeisian ethos, alone of all American Zionist groups retained its strength and influence during this decade.

The Brandeisians, now led by Stephen Wise and Robert Szold, returned to power in the early thirties and began the slow process of rebuilding the movement. Unfortunately, at the same time they had to deal with the greatest threat ever faced by the Jewish people. Some writers have placed particular blame on American Zionists for American Jewry's failure to rescue European Jews from the Nazis. They charge the Zionists with refusing to cooperate with other groups and with ignoring possibilities for rescue in a calculating, cold-blooded drive to secure a Jewish state after the war.[10] Other scholars have argued that, given conditions during the Depression and in wartime America, American Jews did all they could have done; nothing would have deterred Hitler from his monomaniacal quest to exterminate the Jewish people.[11]

My views coincide with those of the latter group.[12] Let me suggest that, in the 1930s and 1940s, rescue in the sense of bringing Jews to America went against what could be considered "American values."[13] Placing rescue first would have appeared to be special pleading for a particular group at a cost that all Americans would have to pay. As long as millions of Americans remained out of work, and as long as American boys faced death at the hands of the

Axis, special pleading for Jews—or for any other ethnic or religious group—would have triggered opposition and not support from the American people.[14]

Stephen Wise recognized this and so did Abba Hillel Silver. It was Silver who made the decision that, if the Zionists could not effect a rescue during the war, they should get on with the task of securing an independent Jewish homeland so that the survivors would have a place to go after the war.[15] This decision should be placed in the context of Zionist political activity as described earlier. The numbers of American Zionists increased; their influence expanded; they won widespread support from all segments of American society as they focused their energies on the task of securing an independent Jewish state in Palestine.

Part of their success derived from their skillful exploitation of the guilt the Holocaust had engendered in Christian America. Other Jewish groups that wanted to bring Jews to America did not succeed because their appeals struck Congress as special pleading, pleading at the expense of other groups also wounded by the war and of Americans in general.[16] The Zionists put forward a plan that did not threaten American jobs or resources. They called on Americans to help the Yishuv stand on its own feet, to allow Palestine to be a haven for the oppressed—in short, to do the "American thing." Probably no more successful lobby effort can be found in American history than that undertaken by the American Zionists after the war, and it succeeded in large part because an Americanized leadership, schooled in American political practice, utilized traditional American devices to win support for what they depicted as a prototypically American enterprise. There was little if any religious content to the Zionist effort. They reminded the American people that Jews had been the major victims of the Nazis; for millions of Americans, as well as for American Jews, to be good Americans in the late 1940s meant being good Zionists, defined as supporting the creation of a Jewish state.

Then, once again, a movement that bestrode the American political scene like a colossus collapsed and practically disappeared from view. Forty years after the establishment of Israel, American Zionism is a hollow shell without purpose or influence. The only exception is still Hadassah, and even that group does not command the power it enjoyed in past years. There are several reasons for this development. One of them might be described as becoming the victim of success.[17]

Traditionally the Zionist movement outside of the Holy Land had three major programs—fundraising, education, and political activity. Hadassah raised money to support medical and educational work in the Yishuv; the Jewish National Fund sought funds to reclaim land and plant trees. Other Zionist agencies supported educational work, such as teaching Hebrew as a modern language or running summer camps to prepare people to live in Palestine. Political activity involved lobbying Congress, garnering public support, and making presentations to the Congress, the League of Nations, royal commissions, and the United Nations.

The crises of the Holocaust and the establishment of Israel had meant that the Zionists had to put nearly all of their energy and resources into political activity in the decade ending with Israeli independence. Now, the sovereign Jewish state—not the Zionist Organization of America—would speak for the Yishuv to the United States, the United Nations, and other world bodies. Even before 1948, the locus of fundraising had shifted from Zionist agencies to the United Jewish Appeal, which had access to a larger constituency and to wealthy Jews who might be friendly to Israel but did not consider themselves Zionists. Moreover, the largest single source of outside funds for Israel in the past four decades has not been the Jewish communities of the Diaspora, but the government of the United States, to which Israeli officials spoke. The ZOA had never done well in its educational efforts (nor, for that matter, had any other Zionist body outside a very limited periphery). What would Zionists do?

They could do little. In part this resulted from a decision by the Israeli government and its prime minister, David Ben-Gurion, to cut down the power of American Zionism and especially the influence of Abba Hillel Silver, whom Ben-Gurion saw as a rival.[18] But even if Ben-Gurion had wanted to maintain a strong Zionist force in the Diaspora, it is unlikely that he would have succeeded. Given the American polity, it would have been impossible for an American organization to be a strong and continuing advocate of a foreign nation and its policies. Moreover, the contradictions between the Israeli and European Zionist agenda and the philosophy of the American Jewish community would have led at some point to a split.

Even had there been no divergence between American Zionism and the Israeli government, hard times would have befallen American Zionism after 1949. Membership in the movement dropped after the establishment of Israel, just as it had plummeted after the success of World War I. Many Jews joined the Zionist movement because it was the only outlet through which they could express support for the Yishuv. After 1949, American Jewry became Zionized in the sense that nearly all American Jews support the continued existence of the State of Israel. But they do so not through Zionist organizations (with the exception of Hadassah) but through local community federations and the United Jewish Appeal.[19]

Zionism in the United States today is the legacy of the Brandeis era in that it is widespread, does not hold *aliyah* to be a central tenet, and supports the Jewish community in the Holy Land. It is far more philanthropic than ideological. While Israel occupies a central place in the minds and hearts of American Jews,[20] it does so as a cultural and emotional symbol rather than a religious one.

American Jews express their support of Israel through donations to the UJA and specific programs such as the Hadassah hospital, the American Friends of Israeli Universities, and so forth. They travel to Israel and may even send their children there for summer or semester programs. When Israel is endangered, they are vocal in its support. But Zionist organizations such as the ZOA, Mizrachi, and even Hadassah are notable by their absence from any central place in this scheme. The chief organ for the expression of American Jewish views is the Council of Presidents of Major Jewish Organizations. While a Zionist will occasionally be elected as the spokeperson, he or she will not bring any overtly "Zionist" message to that task, other than generalized support of Israel. The most effective Israel lobby is the American-Israel Public Affairs Committee (AIPAC), a registered agent of a foreign government.[21]

Does this mean that American Zionists no longer play a political role in the nation's life? In comparison to the work of the Zionist Organization of America from 1917 to 1919 under Brandeis, or the

American Zionist Emergency Council under Silver and Wise from 1942 to 1949, there is no organized Zionist presence on the American political scene today. If we define Zionism as support of Israel, then the federations, the Council of Presidents, and others work long, hard, and effectively to maintain public support for the Jewish state. Their success is limited by variations of the same constraints that limited Zionists during the 1930s and 1940s—support of Israel must be cast in terms of American interests and American principles.

During most of the past forty years this has not been difficult. Americans had little love for the Arab states, which have nondemocratic governments. The rise of Islamic fundamentalism, with hatred of Israel as a rallying cry, has not set well with Americans, who, no matter how strong their own religious convictions, believe in separation of church and state. Until 1980, Israel seemed to be David battling Goliath, and its impressive military victories, especially in 1967, won the hearts of many Americans. From 1949 to 1980 one could be pro-Israel and call for American support of Israel on the grounds that it would be good for America.

Since 1980, this has not been easy. Israel's invasion of Lebanon, its rule of Arabs in the occupied territories, its intransigence regarding discussions with the PLO, and the rise of a Jewish fundamentalism as narrow minded as its Islamic counterparts have led to significant decline in support of Israel, not only among Americans in general but also among American Jews. It is, after all, difficult to talk about "endangered Israel" when the evening news features film clips of Israeli soldiers beating Arab children. The principle that held true in 1917, in 1941, and in 1991 remains constant: American Jews lobby effectively to support the Jews in the Holy Land only if such support is perceived as not running counter to American ideals or interests.[22] The Gulf War, in which Israel showed remarkable constraint, has made the backing of Israel once again compatible with the overall scheme of American interests; pictures of Israeli children in gas masks huddling in shelters during SCUD attacks did much to cancel, at least temporarily, the earlier pictures of Israel as a brutal occupational force.

In sum, the success of American Zionists, either in earlier organizational manifestations or in a generalized contemporary form, has been directly tied to how well they acted within acceptable *American* norms. So long as the Zionists remained dominated by European ideological thinking, they were ineffective. The American people would only side with the Zionist dream, and later the Jewish state, if they could see it in terms of American ideals and principles; in a similar fashion the American government has been most supportive of Israel when it has appeared to be in America's interests to be so.

In the debate over the alleged failure of American Jewry during the Holocaust years, critics have accused American Jews in general and the Zionists in particular of not using their immense political power. The error here is to assume that the successes of the Zionists in rallying support for Israel, such as in the late 1940s and then in the midsixties, represents the normative level of Zionist political power. Although the so-called Jewish lobby is well organized, its power is far less than meets the eye. The best study of this subject concludes that although the pro-Israel lobby does have political muscle, its story "is a very American story, . . . a tale of how the American system works, for better or for worse, and how one group has exploited it on behalf of its own interests."[23]

What Zionist leaders with any understanding of the American political process learned long ago is that their achievements were directly related to their ability to channel their efforts within mainstream American politics. When they could argue that the Zionist cause complemented American interests and ideals, they flourished; when they could not, no matter how great the need, they failed. The politicization of American Zionists is, therefore, in many ways their Americanization as well.

Notes

1. For the beginning years of the Zionist movement and the early settlement in Palestine, see Howard Morley Sachar, *A History of Israel: From the Rise of Zionism to Our Time* (New York: Knopf, 1976), chs. 1–4. An older but still useful source that reflects the attitudes of the early years is Nahum Sokolow, *History of Zionism, 1600–1918* (New York, 1919; repr. New York: KTAV, 1969).

2. I have explored these themes in greater detail in *American Zionism from Herzl to the Holocaust* (Garden City, N.Y.: Anchor/Doubleday,

1975) and *We Are One! American Jewry and Israel* (Garden City, N.Y.: Anchor/Doubleday, 1978).

3. I am not saying that there was no antisemitism in the United States but rather that compared with European society, prejudice against Jews was functionally nonexistent. While there had been restraints against Jews in colonial days, by the late nineteenth century no state barred Jews from voting or holding office or from engaging in any trade or profession. Although some upper-class German-American Jews faced social discrimination toward the end of the century, the mass of Eastern Europeans who came here after 1880 marveled at the freedom they found in this country. For a good survey, see John Higham, *Strangers in the Land: Patterns of American Nativism, 1860–1925* (New Brunswick, N.J.: Rutgers University Press, 1955).

4. Louis D. Brandeis, *The Jewish Problem, and How to Solve It* (New York: Federation of American Zionists, 1915).

5. *American Zionism*, especially ch. 4.

6. See Naomi W. Cohen, *Encounter with Emancipation: The German Jews in the United States, 1830–1914* (Philadelphia: Jewish Publication Society, 1984); and Moses Rischin, "The American Jewish Committee and Zionism, 1906–1922," *Herzl Year Book* 5 (1963): 65–81.

7. A good exploration of the beliefs and tensions of the two men (although I do not agree with some of his conclusions) is Ben Halpern, *A Clash of Heroes: Brandeis, Weizmann, and American Zionism* (New York: Oxford University Press, 1987).

8. *American Zionism*, ch. 7.

9. Higham, *Strangers in the Land*, ch. 10.

10. The best-known exposition of this view is David S. Wyman, *The Abandonment of the Jews: America and the Holocaust, 1941–1945* (New York: Pantheon, 1984).

11. Here the most lucid explanation is that of Henry L. Feingold, *The Politics of Rescue: The Roosevelt Administration and the Holocaust, 1938–1945* (New Brunswick, N.J.: Rutgers University Press, 1970).

12. See Melvin I. Urofsky, *A Voice That Spoke for Justice: The Life and Times of Stephen S. Wise* (Albany: State University of New York Press, 1982), ch. 22.

13. None of the other options that defenders of the Bergson group and other "rescue efforts" acclaim would have been viable, and no one really took any of them seriously. The only real option would have been Palestine, but the gates to the Yishuv had been closed by the British with the 1939 White Paper.

14. See the exchange between Ben-Gurion and unidentified American Jews early in World War II, when Ben-Gurion sought increased aid for the Yishuv, reported in Robert Silverberg, *If I Forget Thee, O Jerusalem* (New York: Morrow, 1970), 183–84.

15. Marc Lee Raphael, *Abba Hillel Silver: A Profile in American Judaism*

(New York: Holmes & Meier, 1989), ch. 6. No one, not Silver nor Wise nor even Weizmann, knew the full extent of the massacres until after the war.

16. See Leonard Dinnerstein, *America and the Survivors of the Holocaust* (New York: Columbia University Press, 1982). The American Council for Judaism, an anti-Zionist body, did work assiduously to get Congress to allow more Jews to enter the United States after the war, but had no success at all. See Thomas A. Kolsky, *Jews against Zionism: The American Council for Judaism, 1942–1948* (Philadelphia: Temple University Press, 1990), 160–61.

17. Here again, I rely upon but do not wish to repeat arguments made earlier; see *We Are One!*, esp. ch. 11. More optimistic views can be found in the discussions in Moshe Davis, ed., *Zionism in Transition* (New York: Arno, 1980), particularly 45–78 and 275–372.

18. *We Are One!*, ch. 11.

19. Marc Lee Raphael, *A History of the United Jewish Appeal, 1939–1982* (Chico, Calif.: Scholars Press, 1982).

20. The importance of Israel has, however, slipped recently. See Steven M. Cohen, *Content or Continuity? The 1989 National Survey of American Jews* (New York: American Jewish Committee, 1991), 33–35.

21. See David Howard Goldberg, *Foreign Policy and Ethnic Interest Groups: American and Canadian Jews Lobby for Israel* (Westport, Conn.: Greenwood, 1990); and especially Edward Tivnan, *The Lobby: Jewish Political Power and American Foreign Policy* (New York: Simon & Schuster, 1987).

22. A suggestive parallel is that of American Irish support of a unified Ireland. The more violently the Irish Republican Army acts, the less politically feasible it is to support its political goals in the United States. Similarly, Americans support the idea of a secure Israel but cannot condone the tactics adopted by the Jewish state in the last decade to achieve that goal.

23. Tivnan, *The Lobby*, 12.

CHAPTER II

Spiritual Zionists and Jewish Sovereignty

Arthur A. Goren

In a seminal essay, "The Americanization of Zionism, 1880–1930," Ben Halpern compared two strands of Zionism.[1] One, secular and political, associated with Louis Brandeis, came to dominate the American Zionist scene. But in fact, the other, cultural and spiritual, Halpern claimed, was the more "thoroughly American variant of Zionism." It "succeeded most fully in impressing its stamp upon American Jewry at large." It was led by a group of "rabbinical Zionists around the Jewish Theological Seminary, beginning with their ally Judah Magnes and culminating in the fully developed theories of Mordecai Kaplan. Their religious revision of the ideas of Ahad Ha-am and Dubnow fitted well into the place alloted to the Jews as a religious community in the American scheme of things."[2] The discussion that follows examines one facet of this cultural-spiritual strand of American Zionism. It probes the response of four influential figures who defined themselves as cultural or spiritual Zionists to the two penultimate, decisive political events in Zionist history: the Balfour Declaration's expression of support for a Jewish national home in Palestine and the final struggle for the establishment of the Jewish state. Following the British cabinet's issuance of the Balfour Declaration in November 1917 and for several years thereafter, Israel Friedlaender, professor of Bible at the Jewish Theological Seminary, and Judah Magnes, an ordained Reform rabbi close to Seminary circles and chairman of the New York Kehillah, were the most important spiritual Zionists to contribute to the public debate that ensued. Nearly two and a half decades later, in May 1942, an extraordinary conference of American Zionists adopted the Biltmore program calling for the establishment of a Jewish commonwealth in Palestine. From that moment until the Jewish state was proclaimed six years later, the question preoccupied the organized Jewish community. Once again, two spiritual Zionists—this time Mordecai Kaplan, long associated with the Seminary, and Louis Finkelstein, the Seminary's president—grappled with the meaning of Jewish sovereignty. For these Zionists, Jewish political sovereignty was problematic. The reason for this brings into focus some of the dilemmas inherent in spiritual Zionism and explains in part the political reticence of its ideologists, except for a short period during the early years of the American Zionist movement.

During that short but revealing period, spiritual Zionists, in fact, directed the affairs of the movement. From 1905 to 1911, Magnes and Friedlaender held high office in the Federation of American Zionists and were its most prominent spokesmen. In 1905, Solomon Schechter, the esteemed president of the Seminary, officially joined the Federation and soon after issued his influential statement on Zionism that stressed its religious-national character. "The rebirth of Israel's national consciousness and the revival of Israel's religion," he declared, "are inseparable."[3] Although Magnes, Friedlaender, and their coworkers among the leaders of the movement subscribed to Schechter's pronouncement, their conception of what Zionism should be in America was more inclusive than his. Their beliefs are best understood through a brief consideration of the Zionist program they formulated.

The hallmark of their program was their calculated attempt to integrate the needs of American Jews with Zionism's goals. These pragmatic spiritual Zionists emphasized those phases of the world Zionist platform that they believed best enabled the American movement to appeal to the masses of American Jews, and they sidestepped ideological positions that appeared inappropriate in the American context. One example, their shunning of the preeminence that the world movement assigned to political action, will suffice. In June 1906, in a plaintive letter to David Wolffsohn, the president of the World Zionist Organization, Magnes, the newly elected secretary of the Federation, begged for a presidential message of encouragement for the Federation's annual convention. While not questioning the "thorough political character" of the world movement, Magnes asked Wolffsohn, "if not officially, at least morally," to sanction the support of "active work in Palestine." The world organization's preoccupation with political work, Magnes complained, important as it was "from the point of view of the development of politics in Europe," was of no interest to American Jews.[4]

In fashioning an indigenous American Zionism that would speak to American Jewry as a whole, the spiritual Zionists confronted, as their predecessors had, the dilemma posed by the fundamental premise of classical Zionism: Jewish homelessness, a problem that was to be solved only through geographic concentration in Eretz Yisrael, did not apply to American Jews. Indeed, on first sight, the mass migration to America disproved the central thesis of Zionism's solution of the Jewish problem. In coping with the paradox, the spiritual Zionists expanded upon the formulations they inherited from such early leaders of the movement as Richard Gottheil. In the first place, the basic tenet of Zionism was declared valid for the *other* Jewish diasporas—not for the American diaspora, which was exceptional. *To keep it exceptional*, immigration was best deflected to Palestine, which would advance the cause and avert the creation of a "Jewish problem" in America. In the second place, the spiritual Zionists explicitly accepted the permanency and desirability of Jewish life in America. Although never stated so baldly, self-interest demanded a strong Zionist movement in America, both to channel immigration elsewhere and to enrich culturally and direct spiritually a community made up of growing numbers of new immigrants adrift in a sea of social and personal turmoil. The programmatic side of the dual strategy the spiritual Zionists adopted consisted, on the one hand, of organizational innovations such as establishing a Zionist fraternal order to better mobilize communal and financial support for the cause. But the leadership failed dismally in these undertakings. On the other hand, the leaders formulated a doctrine that located American Zionism firmly within the Jewish community. The demand for the democratization of Jewish communal life, a cardinal precept of Zionism in Europe, was adapted to American circumstances. The examples par excellence of this strategy were the early attempts to launch a national representative body of American Jewry, the *kehillah* movement, and support of all collaborative communal enterprises such as education and overseas relief.[5]

The other component of the program the spiritual Zionists espoused—its cultural and spiritual dimension—was its most important legacy. Israel Friedlaender, Judah Magnes, and Mordecai Kaplan—and, hovering in the background, Solomon Schechter—placed great stress on the benefits Zionism would bring to American Jews. Simply put, they presented Zionism as a cultural and spiritual movement that would become, in the words of Schechter, "the mighty bulwark against the incessantly assailing forces of assimilation." At the core of their Zionism was Judaism, as Schechter had formulated it, which Friedlaender defined as "a national religion, its bearer a national community." The national religion had preserved the memory of a national life in the land of Israel and the hope for the return to Zion. The rebirth Zionism promised would bring about a rapprochement between the contending definitions of the Jewish people that had marked its entry into modern life: a religious faith or a national entity. Fulfilling Zionism would go hand in hand with a religious revival anchored in historic Judaism.[6] However, in contrast with Schechter, who rejected any compromise with Jewish secularism, the Magnes-Friedlaender group posited a different priority.[7] Magnes aphorized, "Zionism means battle on behalf of Jews and Judaism. There can be no Judaism without the Jews. Zionism is the battle to save Judaism by saving the Jews." For the Jews of Eastern Europe it meant fighting "for their equal political rights, for their economic betterment, for an eventual place of refuge for thousands in our ancient home, the land of Israel." Borrowing from Ahad Ha-am, he continued, "If in the lands of oppression, the Jews be held in bodily bondage, in the lands of freedom all too many are spiritual slaves." Zionism's task was "to make Jews free . . . in body and spirit."[8]

The spiritual Zionism of Friedlaender and Magnes was, consequently, all inclusive. As nationalists, they considered the preservation of the Jewish people, wherever it might be, as a value transcending all particularistic conceptions of Judaism and Zionism. Each saw himself primarily as an educator of American Jewry. On the lecture circuit, in articles and books, and not infrequently from the pulpit or university podium, they addressed the contemporary problems of American Jews: Jewish group survival, cultural and spiritual continuity and revival, and the place of Zionism and Judaism in the life of American Jews. They rejected with vehemence the negation-of-*galut* concept. If they despaired at times about the cultural and spiritual state of the new Jewish center in America, the Zionist revival in Eretz Yisrael promised to radiate spiritual and cultural sustenance. Here was the importance of Zionism for American Jews. In a word, for these Zionists, education, rather than politics, was the decisive Zionist act.[9]

This spiritual conception of an Americanized Zionism coexisted with a secular version that rather quickly became the prevailing one with the advent of Brandeis to leadership in 1914. The reasons are known: the increasing secularization of Jewish life, the political cast of the new Zionism, and the "nonsectarian" emphasis of a movement seeking the broadest common denominator. But surely the most powerful and immediate factor was the cataclysm of war. With all of European Jewry caught up in the conflagration and the tiny Zionist settlement in Palestine facing annihilation, forceful leaders were required more than devoted educators. It was this sense of extreme peril that explains Brandeis's astonishing acceptance of the leadership of American Zionism. "Organize," "mobilize," "numbers," "fundraising," and "efficiency" became the watchwords.

In accounting for the enormous growth of the movement under Brandeis's leadership, we must recognize that more was involved than his eminence, political acumen, and organizational ability. At a time when a militant nativism increasingly demanded unconditional assimilation, and the compact masses of Yiddish-speaking immigrants loomed so large and threatening in their alienism in the eyes of the acculturated Jewish establishment, Zionism's ultimate goal of national sovereignty for the Jewish people raised the specter of dual loyalties. Spokesmen for Reform Judaism aggravated these fears by intensifying their ideological war against Zionism, which they considered not only historically and theologically false but also politically perilous. Brandeis addressed these issues. Melvin Urofsky, in his studies of American Zionism, has ascribed the movement's success to Brandeis's seminal role in formulating an ideology of an American Zionism that legitimized it in American terms. By defining Zionism as the highest ideal of the Jewish people—the quest for social justice—and equating that ideal as America's highest as well, Brandeis identified Zionism with Americanism. A typical Brandeis remark pointed to the "self-governing" Zionist colonies being built by "our Jewish Pilgrim Fathers." These models of progressive democracy were proof of the compatibility of American and Zionist values. "The descendants of the Pilgrim Fathers," he commented on another occasion, "should not find it hard to understand and sympathize with it [Zionism]."[10]

However, the Brandeisian formula failed to lay to rest an inner disquiet. Whenever Jewish sovereignty in Palestine became an international issue, it distressed American Jews, including some Zionists. In fact, when the Balfour Declaration was issued, Brandeis wrote privately that he neither advised nor desired an independent state. He considered statehood "a most serious menace."[11] At such times, the spiritual Zionists could be eloquent defenders of the Zionist cause. Religious figures occupied a respected place in American public life. When the spiritual Zionists invoked scripture and theology, they effectively refuted the attacks of classical Reform Judaism and Christian anti-Zionism. By placing Zionism in the prophetic tradition, one stole the thunder of the Reformers and spoke to Christian America in terms it understood. "The Jewish prophets," Friedlaender chided a gentile American journalist who had asked why a distinct nationhood for the Jew, "were both universalists and nationalists, believing in the realization of the universal ideal through the channel of national existence." But "nationhood" (or, later, "peoplehood") was not sovereignty. Once the sovereignty issue arose, the spiritual Zionists had to grapple with politics.[12]

When the British issued the Balfour Declaration, neither Magnes nor Friedlaender held Zionist office. Magnes had resigned his office in 1915; Friedlaender had followed a year later. Both men were casualties of the Zionist challenge to the hegemony the American

Jewish Committee had maintained in national Jewish affairs. They had belonged to both groups. Magnes remained with the Committee while Friedlaender withdrew from both bodies. Where Magnes moved into the broader sphere of American politics, becoming a leading spokesman of the antiwar movement and an advocate of civil liberties and other radical causes, Friedlaender continued to maintain close ties with the Zionist leadership. In fact, until his departure for Europe in January 1920 on a relief mission that ended tragically with his murder in the Ukraine, he served as one of the movement's best public advocates.[13]

Friedlaender's first published response to the Balfour Declaration came only weeks after it was issued. The article, entitled "Zionism and Religious Judaism," appeared in the *New York Evening Post*, at that time New York's most liberal newspaper, in December 1917. It was reprinted shortly thereafter in pamphlet form by the Zionist Organization of America. The article, addressed to a wide public, expounded the significance of the Balfour Declaration on the high ground of religious ideals.[14]

It was an effective apologia. Clearly, Friedlaender wrote, the importance of Palestine as the connecting link between three continents and three religions was incalculable, whether considered from the political, economic, or religious point of view. Friedlaender chose to deal with Jewish resettlement from the religious perspective. For those Jews who believe that Judaism "has a religious message to the world and to those Christians who share or appreciate these sentiments," the religious aspect was of "paramount consideration."

In a succinct exposition, Friedlaender explained that the "religion of Judaism" was indissolubly bound up with the homeland of the Jewish people. Only in the middle of the nineteenth century had some modern rabbis, catering to the desire for civil and political emancipation, begun preaching the dispersion of the Jews as divine providence. In a phrase that surely challenged the Reformers and his Christian readers, Friedlaender asserted that the "restoration of Israel to its ancient soil was an indispensable condition for the realization of the religious mission of Judaism." Judaism was embodied in "concrete human institutions, in a nation, a commonwealth, a state. . . . The ideal of Jewish prophecy, Justice and Righteousness, presupposed a definite social order, such as can only be realized in a body politic." No conflict existed between renewed nationhood and universalism. "Zion is conceived as the place where in an ideal future the 'Word of the Lord' will proceed to the rest of the world."[15]

Six months later, in June 1918, in an address delivered at Carnegie Hall at the opening of the annual convention of the New York Kehillah, Friedlaender dwelt on the historic significance of the Balfour Declaration. He acclaimed Britain's role. "A great Government has recognized the right of the Jewish people to be a people, and the claim of Palestine to be Eretz Yisrael, the Land of Israel." It was not political expediency that had prompted Britain to act, but the manifestation of "that large-hearted policy which modern England has always pursued toward our people." The declaration had also vindicated Wilson's leading the American people into war. Victory would assure the rights of the smaller nationalities. "Palestine represents [to us] the same ideals for which our country, for which the United States, is fighting, . . . ideals of justice and righteousness, the ideals that right stands above might, that spirituality stands above materialism."[16]

In his peroration, Friedlaender mentioned "commonwealth," with its implied notion of Jewish political sovereignty. The passage reads,

> Upon the gates of the Third Jewish Commonwealth will be inscribed the same prophetic words which greeted the establishment of the Second Jewish commonwealth:
>
> "Not by might, nor by power,
> But by My spirit, saith the Lord of Hosts."[17]

The optimistic and congratulatory tone of the address is understandable given the time and place. A wartime America was in the grips of a patriotic fever that few (Magnes being one of them) dared resist. Britain was about to complete the conquest of Palestine, and Wilson's pronouncements on the postwar peace were clothed in prophetic visions. Friedlaender's assignment was to call for Jewish unity, to inspire and encourage, and to stimulate material support for Zionist work. He used "commonwealth" not as a political term—it aroused no controversy—but as an inspirational text, a rallying cry of the spirit.

Much as the Zionists played down the question of Jewish political sovereignty, indeed, evaded it when they could, opponents of Zionism focused on it. One line of attack faulted a policy that led to a Jewish state when Arabs outnumbered Jews six to one. How could one ignore "the Arab problem"? In an internal memorandum addressed to the Zionist Organization of America, "A Few Suggestions concerning the Relations between the Jews and the Arabs," Friedlaender defined the importance of the issue. (Undated, the memorandum was most likely written in early 1919 at the time when the Middle East was a center of intense diplomatic maneuvering at the Peace Conference.) Among the American Zionists none but Magnes had given the matter any serious thought until then. Friedlaender brought to bear the authority of the expert, an Arabist and scholar of medieval Arab-Jewish history.

The realization of the Zionist claims, Friedlaender explained, would undoubtedly stimulate Arab national aspirations. The "Arab problem" would surely affect *"the future Jewish Commonwealth in Palestine* [emphasis mine]. Whatever may prove to be its geographic extension, it is bound to appear as a tiny Hebrew island in the midst of an Arabic ocean." Not only will the Jews in Palestine be surrounded by a "politically rejuventated Arabic-speaking population" from the Atlantic in the West to Persia in the East but also, within "the future Jewish Commonwealth itself, the Arabic element will, for a considerable time at least, form the majority, and for a much longer time, a substantial minority of the Palestinian population." Rather than ask how a Jewish commonwealth would govern under such circumstances (which Magnes did), Friedlaender proposed a program of education and public relations. Jews would learn about Arabic life and culture. The Arab world would be informed about the vast Jewish literature in the Arabic language created during the "Golden Age."[18]

In April 1919, Friedlaender published his most notable defense of Zionism, a rejoinder to a sweeping indictment of Zionism by Herbert Adams Gibbons, author of *The New Map of Europe* and Paris correspondent of *The Century*. Friedlaender dismissed the objections Gibbons had based on geopolitics, religion, and moral law. He was especially irked by Gibbons's argument that "a Zionist state in Palestine" flouted the Wilsonian vision of a just peace because of the enormous Arab majority. It was "the only objection that is apt to command the serious attention of the Zionists," Friedlaender wrote, "because in their desire to establish a commonwealth on the foundations of the ancient Jewish ideals of justice and righteousness, they are anxious to avert anything that might in the slightest degree conflict with these ideals." Friedlaender cited Emir Feisal's public assurance of his readiness to cooperate with the Zionists, and he rejected the claim that the Palestinian Arabs were in fact opposed to Zionism. Arab opposition came almost entirely from Syrian Arabs and Egyptians, Friedlander claimed. The country had room for large population growth, and the rights of the "non-Jewish communities" were safeguarded. However, the thrust of his argument was that Palestine was "neither historically nor emotionally" an Arabic country. "When the Arabs dream of their ancient glory . . . they think of Nejd and Hedjaz, the cradle of their race and religion; they think of the splendor of the Ommiads at Damascus, of the magnificence of the Abbassides at Bagdad, of the power of the Fatimites at Cairo; but they do not think of Jerusalem." During the twelve hundred years the Arabs had lived in Palestine, they "had never developed an Arabic culture worth speaking of." The handful of Zionists who had come to Palestine and been willing "to brave the dangers and hardships, which can be paralleled only by the similiar experiences of the early colonists of New England, have succeeded in setting up . . . the beginnings of a civilization which . . . is the greatest cultural factor in Palestine today."[19] It was a brilliant exposition for the general public, weaving the religious and political imperatives into a tight design, and then embellishing them with biblical and American motifs. But clearly Friedlaender was at his most eloquent pleading the religious and moral case. The Zionist Organization promptly reprinted his statement for mass circulation.[20]

Of the four spiritual Zionists we are considering, Magnes was the most political and the most fearless. Under enormous pressure to cease speaking on behalf of pacifism and radicalism lest it stir up antisemitism ("you are giving aid and comfort to the enemy," Louis

Marshall, his brother-in-law, told him), Magnes rejected the demand. For Magnes, higher principles, Jewish and American, compelled him to follow his conscience. "This is not the first time that the Jews have been threatened with, or have had to suffer from antisemitism because of their convictions," he explained in a letter to a friend. Zionism and Jewish sovereignty were no exceptions to the moral compulsion to speak the truth.[21]

In December 1917, soon after the Balfour Declaration was issued, Magnes addressed a fundraising meeting sponsored by the People's Relief Committee. The talk masked a philosophic rejection of Jewish political sovereignty. Under the title "The Jewish People—A Spiritual Force," Magnes offered the familiar notions of a "Jewish national spirituality" with its "international" commitment to the universality of humankind. Jewish nationalism was not arrogant, he declared. It "stood for the eternal right of every minority to be true to its innermost convictions." It did not "desire the territories of other men, it is not a material, an economic, a political imperialism." It sought "an empire of the spirit, that is, the recognition by all men of the Fatherhood of God and the Brotherhood of Man."[22]

Lest his universalism be equated with what he considered to be the vapid, passive rhetoric of Reform Judaism, he lashed out at the war patriotism of "the Reformed Jewish Church." It had made a sham of its doctrine of Israel's mission to bring the prophetic message of brotherhood to the world. Not a single Reform leader had spoken out on "behalf of the revolutionary Jewish idea of the Fatherhood of God and the Brotherhood of Man" and the Jewish people's "inherent repugnance to the spilling of blood."[23] (Privately, Magnes put the matter even more explicitly: he praised "the antimilitarist outburst on the part of the Jewish masses and their elemental passion for peace." That "the Jewish masses have expressed themselves as they have" was one of the glories of Jewish life. It distinguished *Jewish prophetic nationalism* [emphasis mine] from the heathen nationalism of the Christian nations.")[24] In concluding his address, Magnes gave Palestine its due. The land was offering "this ancient people a renewal of youth." Perhaps, he mused, "new thoughts, new ideas, radical and revolutionary action will come from the Jewish Center."[25] But neither at this time nor in speeches that followed did Magnes criticize the Balfour Declaration directly.

Clearly, he was curbing his impulse to lash out at the declaration, as he later did, as the misbegotten offspring of British imperialism.

Finally, in August 1921, Magnes published a letter on the political significance of the declaration in the London *Jewish Chronicle*. Years later he explained the circumstances that led him to break his silence on the subject. His manifesto—for it was more a manifesto than a letter to the editor—was composed immediately after the Jaffa riots of May 1921 when forty-seven Jews were killed. The letter was also "an answer to a question of some of my friends in America as to why I could not reenter Zionist life." Obviously the timing of the letter was Magnes's way of reentering Zionist life. It appeared a week before the first World Zionist Congress convened following the war.[26]

"Wartime Zionism," Magnes began his piece, "aroused swollen expectations among the Jews, just as the war did among other peoples. Palestine was to be presented to the Jews as a political gift, and the Jewish people was to be delivered, bag and baggage, to a single Imperialistic Government in return for a political declaration." The Jews should have learned long ago that "Jewish politics must be independent politics and skeptical of all political favors."[27] Palestine could be won, not through war or political privilege or the oppression of one's neighbors, but on equal political terms with others. All the Zionists required were the "rights of free people anywhere in the world," certainly the rights of Jews in Palestine, "of free immigration, free land purchase, and free cultural development." This was not political favoritism. It did not "compel good men to interpret 'self-determination' as meaning one thing throughout the world and another thing for Palestine." Referring to the rejoicing that followed the San Remo conference, which had incorporated the Balfour Declaration in the League of Nations mandate and conferred it upon the British, Magnes wrote,

> Almost every principle of democracy, of self-determination is denied. The fact is that Palestine has five or six times as many Arabs as Jews. You speak of "historic rights" of the Jews to offset the claims of the present-day Arab majority. I am aware of the way in which historic rights and strategic rights and economic rights have been manipulated whenever it suited the needs of the conquerors. Yet, I, too, believe in the "historic right" of the Jewish people to the Land of

Israel. . . . the free and unhindered opportunity to come into the land
. . . and to become, in the course of time, if they can, the preponder-
ant element of the population.[28]

A remarkable dualism marks Magnes's political philosophy. Realism led him to admit that the mandate offered the Jews opportunities for developing the country. Yet it was folly not to recognize the
harsh truth that "economic imperialism" was not to be relied upon.
This was all the more reason to remember the old adage, "Put not
your trust in princes." What remained? "The one kind of *realpolitik*
with any chance," Magnes concluded, "must be based upon simple
justice, because this is the Jewish tradition." It was just, for example, for the Zionists "to be inexorable and unyielding" in the struggle for free Jewish immigration.[29]

Soon after the publication of the manifesto-letter, Magnes settled
in Jerusalem. In 1930, when he had become chancellor of the Hebrew University, he published a small booklet, *Like All the Nations?*
It was prompted by the Arab riots of August 1929 in which more
than four hundred Jews were killed or wounded. Magnes included
the 1921 letter in the booklet "in order to show that my present
attitude is not new, and that it is the result of a view of life and a
conception of the ethical function of Judaism, and does not just
spring from tactical or strategic motives."[30]

Neither Louis Finkelstein nor Mordecai Kaplan is associated with
the great debate that rose over the question of Jewish sovereignty in
the early 1940s and that culminated in the declaration of the State
of Israel in 1948. However, like Friedlaender and Magnes, Finkelstein and Kaplan were authentic voices in the tradition of spiritual Zionism. Peripheral as their positions were to the political
struggle for statehood, their thoughts on sovereignty are important
for understanding that strand of thought among the spiritual Zionists that I have discussed thus far.

Kaplan, in his sixties during the period we are considering, was
at the height of his influence in his dual capacity as a member of
the faculty of the Jewish Theological Seminary and leader of the
Reconstructionist movement. Finkelstein had recently become president of the Seminary. A prolific scholar, he became an innovative
administrator. He not only broadened the Seminary's influence in

the Jewish community at large, but he also created a center where scholars and clergy of all faiths examined the moral and social issues that appeared so acute in the dark years of the war.

Kaplan and Finkelstein shared a similar Zionist outlook. They supported a Jewish national home in Palestine, saw it as an asylum for persecuted Jews, acclaimed the accomplishments of Zionist pioneering, were inspired by the revival of Hebrew culture, and assigned the national home a major place in building a creative Jewish life in America. They insisted that Jewish nationalism and religion were inextricably linked. In these sentiments, they faithfully reflected the views of a large segment of American Zionists, and in time, of most of American Jewry.

However, in the critical years leading to the establishment of the state, they entertained serious reservations about statehood as the immediately attainable or desirable goal. In maintaining their position they were moved by several political considerations: belief in liberal internationalism as expressed in America's war aims and dread that the struggle for statehood would bring war and destruction to the Yishuv. Finkelstein also feared that a secularized state would compromise Judaism's moral and spiritual values. Kaplan weighed the effect of a sovereign Jewish state on the unity of the Jewish people.

Today, nearly fifty years after the Second World War ended, it is difficult to comprehend the depth of faith many Americans had in the new international order that they hoped would assure peace and guarantee human rights. Harry Truman captured this sentiment when he told the founding conference of the United Nations in June 1945, "Before us is the supreme chance to establish a world-rule of reason—to create an enduring peace under the guidance of God."[31]

However, during the interwar years, only a small band of internationalists—keepers of the faith—lobbied and preached for that supreme chance. It included pacifists, champions of disarmament, and supporters of a stronger League of Nations and world court. Liberal church organizations and leading Protestant ministers and theologians were prominent advocates of one or another of the programs. For Christian liberals, internationalism was an integral part of a religious commitment to social justice.[32] So it was with the Central Conference of American Rabbis. From the early 1920s to the mid-1930s, the Conference adopted strong antiwar positions and resolutions, calling on America to join the League and the World Court. In 1932, the Rabbinical Assembly followed suit. It formed a Committee on Social Justice that established ties with the National Council for the Prevention of War and the Committee of International Justice of the Federal Council of Churches, among other groups. The Committee's first public statement, addressed to the Geneva Disarmament Conference, was a resolution favoring universal disarmament and expressing the need for "instruments and agencies" to resolve international disputes.[33]

The cumulative effect of the failures to contain aggression in the 1930s, the outbreak of world war, and finally America's entry into the war fomented a national debate on organizing the postwar world. Civic agencies appointed planning commissions and recruited experts to prepare proposals. The Federal Council of Churches, for example, established a Commission to Study the Bases of a Just and Durable Peace in December 1940. Almost simultaneously the American Jewish Committee created the Research Institute on Peace and Post-War Problems, and the American Jewish Congress and World Jewish Congress established the Institute for Jewish Affairs. After Pearl Harbor, pressure mounted on the State Department to begin designing an international organization to keep the peace.[34]

Of particular signifiance for the debate over the wisdom of pressing for a Jewish commonwealth, which was about to begin, was an early notion of the direction the organization of peace should go. John Foster Dulles articulated the sentiment well in an address before a Methodist conference in May 1941. The moving spirit behind the formation of the Federal Council's Commission on a Just Peace and its chairman, he undoubtedly reflected in his remarks several months of commission deliberation. "The sovereignty system," Dulles stated, "is no longer consonant either with peace or justice. It is imperative that there be a transition to a new order."[35] That such thoughts were current in liberal internationalist circles is corroborated by a letter Judah Magnes sent to Felix Frankfurter from Jerusalem in November 1941. Magnes, whose views on international affairs were deeply influenced by these circles, wrote, "I come more and more to the conclusion that there should be the smallest possible number of small states with independent armies and independent foreign policies. Armies and foreign relations should be in the hands of unions or federations. Of course to work out 'the national genius,' a state ought to be absolutely and completely sovereign and independent. But the ills resulting from this are so massive that it is better that the 'national' genius suffer than that these states and peoples plunge the world into misery through their exaggerated national egos."[36]

Finkelstein, as we shall see, shared these views in common with the group of Protestant theologians at the Union Theological Seminary who were among the most influential activists in the cause of internationalism. He also shared with them a broader concern: mobilizing the spiritual and moral resources of the nation, no less than its material resources, in a total war against the forces of darkness. The ecumenical notion of a Judeo-Christian tradition answered the nation's need for unity and amity. It also enjoined Christians to repudiate the central thesis of Nazi ideology—the demonic, depraved nature of Jews and Judaism—and to link the war against Nazism and antisemitism with the defense of democratic values. At the annual Conference on Science, Philosophy, and Religion and Their Relation to the Democratic Way, which Finkelstein was instrumental in organizing, Christian theologians portrayed the Judeo-Christian tradition as the "spiritual underpinning of democracy" and the antithesis of fascism. The Hebrew prophets served as the hyphen that united the tradition. On a more profound level, Reinhold Niebuhr reflected in 1944 on how, as a Christian theologian, he had "sought to strengthen the Hebraic-prophetic content of the Christian tradition." Thus much of the rhetoric explaining America's war aims carried the universal message of the prophetic ethic.[37]

Finkelstein brought this world view of a Judeo-Christian universalism to bear on specific Jewish questions. Two of Finkelstein's essays on Zionism illustrate this milieu. Both were published in the *New Palestine*, the journal of the Zionist Organization of America, the first in May 1943 and the second in September 1944. Their titles are illuminating: "Judaism, Zionism, and an Enduring Peace" and

"Zionism and World Culture." The core idea of these essays is the universal significance of the Jewish experience.

As one would expect from Finkelstein, his argument was historical and theological. His 1943 essay began by expounding the place of Palestine in Judaism. "For the Jewish religion," Finkelstein explained, "Palestine is the land of the Lord, set aside from the beginning as a unique sanctuary for distinctive forms of communion with God." Although "especial merit attaches to those who dwell in the Holy Land . . . the Jew regards his native land, wherever that may be, as his hearth and home." Palestine was the spiritual home for all Israel. How then was Palestine linked to world peace? The prophetic vision of redemption, of the brotherhood of man, and of a world of enduring peace included the reestablishment of a Jewish homeland in Palestine. In the world struggle between pagan chauvinism and the prophetic doctrine, "the prophetic and rabbinic form for world peace" mandated the "restoration of Judaism to Palestine." As Palestine, the "home of the prophetic tradition," distilled the "moral basis for medieval and modern civilization, so the Holy Land potentially could unify all mankind."[38]

In discussing Judaism and world peace, Finkelstein echoed Reform Judaism's classic formulation. Providentially, history had prepared Israel for its unique role. Scattered across the earth, the Jews had become conversant with different civilizations. "Parent to Christianity and Islam, Judaism bears certain similarities with the Oriental faiths." The reestablishment of a Jewish homeland in Palestine would be the means of developing better mutual appreciation between East and West. Finkelstein failed to mention "exile," so central to the Judaic tradition. The Jews had been prepared by their bondage in Egypt to proclaim freedom to the world and by medieval persecution to defend their right to be different, and their dispersion among the nations was fortuitous. With its nucleus in the Holy Land, Judaism was prepared to serve mankind.[39]

Finally, Finkelstein considered the political history of the Jewish national home, which he infused with transcendent significance. Echoing his generation's dashed hopes in the aftermath of the last war, he wrote, "At the end of the First World War, mankind was on the threshold of prophetic fulfillment. A world association of nations all but emerged; and with it a recreated Jewish homeland in Palestine. But mankind faltered. The League of Nations became an instrument of power-politics, and the resettlement of Palestine was caught in calculations of empire." Only if mankind proved capable of rising to "prophetic spiritual levels would a world association of nations emerge and under its aegis a Jewish homeland in Palestine."

Finkelstein acknowledged the encouraging signs of a spiritual rebirth in Jewish Palestine. Without parallel in modern times, the Yishuv was attempting to implement the prophetic and Talmudic ideals of justice, and alone among the peoples of the world it opened its arms to the stricken. But, he warned, Jewish national secularism would subvert the promise. Indeed, in his 1944 article, Finkelstein complained that the basic concept of Judaism as a ministry and a service, and of the Jewish people as a Kingdom of Priests, had all but disappeared. "We have failed to make the world understand that we Zionists consider the establishment of a Jewish Palestine indispensable to a reformation of world culture as well as one of the major expressions of that reformation itself."[40]

Dominant though the religious motif was in his interpretation of Zionism, with its implicit rejection of a secular state, Finkelstein objected to a Jewish state on other grounds. "The creation of an enduring peace," he wrote in his 1943 essay, "presupposes an active cooperative relationship among nations and peoples, which makes the question of statehood less and less relevant; while emphasis on national sovereignty anywhere must be fatal to civilization."[41]

The influence of internationalist thought is apparent in Finkelstein's remarks before an executive committee meeting of the American Jewish Committee in October 1944. The meeting was called to decide whether to withdraw from the American Jewish Conference after it had gone on record in favor of a Jewish commonwealth in Palestine. Finkelstein opposed a commonwealth and favored withdrawal. Morris Waldman, the executive secretary of the Committee, describing the meeting in his memoirs, noted how influential Finkelstein's remarks were. Among other reasons, Finkelstein opposed a Jewish commonwealth because "by saying we want the Jewish commonwealth in Palestine . . . we are helping to defeat that which is the salvation of the Jews, as of all other people, namely, the creation of states on political and economic and geographical bases and without regard to ethnic religious and other divisions." In the mind of many liberal thinkers the national state had fostered the chauvinism, intolerance, and extremism that had culminated in the satanic power now threatening to subjugate the free world. Surely other political arrangements were possible that would further the Zionist undertaking in Palestine. In fact, abandoning the unrealistic demand for a Jewish commonwealth would place the Zionists and their confederates in a far stronger position to gain concessions from Britain, above all the abrogation of the White Paper.[42]

If liberal internationalism, rooted as it was in religious and humanistic visions of a better world, shaped Finkelstein's understanding of Zionism, Kaplan, the pragmatist, approached Zionism as a resource for maintaining Jewish life in the Diaspora. Living in two civilizations, the American Jew, in Kaplan's celebrated analysis, subordinated the Jewish to the American. "Judaism is unlikely to survive, either as an ancillary or as a coordinate civilization, unless it thrive as a primary civilization in Palestine."[43] Only in the environmental conditions of a Jewish national home could Judaism become a modern, creative civilization. Writing these words in 1934, Kaplan contended that the Yishuv was, in fact, fulfilling this mission. "Palestine has become to the Jews everywhere 'a symbol of corporate existence.' All Jewish activity throughout the Diaspora which bears a constructive character and has in it the promise of permanence, derives from the inspiration of Palestine." Palestine's present influence upon the Diaspora was "but a dim forecast of the incalculable spiritual impetus that Jewish life will acquire when Palestine civilization shall have grown to its full stature."[44]

Although Kaplan assigned a less transcendent, more temporal role to Palestine than Finkelstein had, it did not follow that sovereignty was a prerequisite for fulfilling its obligations. Ironically, Kaplan's rejection of the doctrine of the Chosen People, his religious naturalism, and his concept of Judaism as an evolving religious civilization gave Jewish Palestine even greater weight in his scheme for Jewish survival. In a human-centered universe, surely the power of sovereignty offered the potential strength to achieve this end. Moreover, a state promised to alleviate the most pressing problem of all, the saving of the remnant of European Jewry. Nevertheless, in the years when the debate raged over statehood, Kaplan's main concern remained the spiritual and cultural condition of the Jews.

Power and politics, however, could not be ignored. As a theologian and an American democrat, Kaplan remained wary of state power. In 1934, he asserted in *Judaism as a Civilization* that nationhood did not confer the right to absolute self-determination. If democratic nationalism was true to itself, "it would have to concede the right of the Jews throughout the world to retain their status as a nation, though the retention of such status involves their becoming a new type of nation—an international nation with a national home to give them cultural and spiritual unity." In conceding this right to the Jews, "democratic nationalism would be living up to its own ethical conception, the conception which sees in internationalism the only hope of civilization."[45]

Twelve years later, as the final stage of the campaign for a Jewish state began, Kaplan addressed the issue once more. What Zionism required, he declared, was not "the sort of irresponsible and obsolete national sovereignty that modern nations claim for themselves. This doctrine of 'absolute national sovereignty' with its assumption that the interests of one's own nation must always override those of other nations, is responsible for the international anarchy of the modern world, and is liable to bring about a catastrophe that will destroy the very foundation of human civilization."[46]

In *The Future of the American Jew*, which he completed in February 1947, he redefined commonwealth in typically Kaplanian fashion so that it no longer meant sovereignty but acquired a spiritual and ethical resonance. "A Jewish commonwealth in Eretz Yisrael has become indispensable to us, individually and as an indivisible people," he announced early in the book. But commonwealth status, he explained later, merely implied the occupation of a definite territory and self-government. "The Jewish commonwealth in Eretz Yisrael," he added in italics, "need not and should not be a sovereign nation." Indeed, the term "nation" should be avoided, for "it connotes first and foremost an organization of power, in a combative sense. Religion is altogether precluded, and culture or civilization is decidedly secondary."[47]

Kaplan's understanding of the term "commonwealth" reveals how he was influenced by American political culture. "Four States of the United States are officially designated 'Commonwealth.' They are Massachusetts, Pennsylvania, Virginia, and Kentucky." Kaplan then offered this analogy: the Jewish commonwealth, like Pennsylvania, would command the loyalty and interests of its own citizens; just as Pennsylvania had no political control over citizens of the remaining states of the federal union, neither would the Jewish commonwealth have sovereign power over the diaspora communities. Most striking of all in the analogy are Kaplan's American perceptions of the Jewish Diaspora as a federalist polity and the limited sovereignty assigned to a commonwealth.[48]

Despite his notion of limited sovereignty, Kaplan began to edge toward support of a fully sovereign Jewish state in the spring and summer of 1947. Viewing the question of power instrumentally, as the means of reaching a larger end—the survival of the Jewish people—he was able to abandon on pragmatic grounds the ideological stance he had adopted earlier. On the evening of November 29, 1947, following the announcement of the UN General Assembly vote approving the partition plan, Kaplan wrote in his diary, "Considering the dreadful finality that an adverse vote might have had in that it would have put an end to all our hopes of resuming life as a nation in our homeland and would have rendered futile all efforts to keep Judaism alive in the diaspora, we should thank God with the benediction *Gomel*."[49]

Nevertheless, the considerations that had led to his reservations continued to preoccupy Kaplan after the state came into being. Ideologue of American Jewish survival, he called on Israel to reconstruct its inner life to aid diaspora survival more effectively, even if that meant subordinating its sovereignty to a higher one, that of the Jewish people.

In the months following the UN partition decision, the Haganah, the Yishuv's main underground fighting arm, suffered severe defeats. Finkelstein recalls how active Zionists felt that the plan to go ahead with establishing a state could lead to a second Holocaust. In March 1948, Secretary of State George Marshall warned Moshe Sharett, head of the political department of the Jewish Agency, that he saw little chance that the Haganah could stand up to an invasion by the regular Arab armies. For a time in late March and April, it appeared to some as though America's abandonment of partition in favor of a temporary trusteeship offered a last-minute reprieve from disaster. Postponing the declaration of a Jewish state, scheduled for May 15, would end the fighting and provide a second chance for a political settlement. Eager to win support for trusteeship among American Jews, State Department officials considered inviting Judah Magnes to the United States. Convinced that Magnes's views now accorded with official American policy, the State Department encouraged an ad hoc committee headed by Alan Stroock, who was also the chairman of the board of trustees of the Jewish Theological Seminary, to sponsor Magnes's visit. Finkelstein participated in the early deliberations of the committee.[50]

When the ad hoc committee met with Magnes on April 26, Finkelstein failed to appear, at the very moment when the attempt to strengthen the hands of the trusteeship forces promised to gather some momentum. The rapidly changing political and military situation may explain Finkelstein's withdrawal from this last-chance peace effort. The UN Security Council had repeatedly shown its inability to mediate a ceasefire, and the trusteeship plan was caught in the mesh of the UN General Assembly. But perhaps most of all, the surge of public support for the embattled Yishuv had reached its peak. Opposing a Jewish state now would have placed him beyond the consensus that had built up so quickly and with such passion. Writing in 1985, in his ninetieth year, Finkelstein recalled his opposition to a Jewish state. He admitted that he had believed the odds were too great. "It did turn out that the people who had faith and were willing to risk everything for the sake of a Jewish state were right."

Surely there were institutional considerations. On the one hand, wealthy and influential supporters, like Alan Stroock and *New York Times* publisher Arthur Hays Sulzberger, adamantly opposed a state. On the other hand, Finkelstein was well aware that his faculty, but even more so the Conservative rabbinate, were bastions of pro-Zionist and pro-state sentiment. Kaplan caught Finkelstein's dilemma in a diary entry dated February 28, 1948. At the previous meeting of the faculty the granting of an honorary degree was on the agenda. Finkelstein had recommended replacing Moshe Sharett with Paul Baerwald, the banker and honorary chairman of the American Jewish Joint Distribution Committee. When partition was carried out, Finkelstein suggested, those responsible would be honored with honorary degrees in a special convocation. Hillel Bavli protested: the Yishuv had to be encouraged now. "At one point Finkelstein screamed at Bavli, and Bavli paled with anger. Bavli charged the Seminary with being among the sha'ananim [the complacent], and Finkelstein yelled back at him that individually, the men on the faculty, singling out [Simon] Greenberg and me, have worked for Zionism, and that the R.A. [Rabbinical Assembly] both individually and as a group have done more for Zionism than any other group in this country."[51]

There were different faces to spiritual Zionism. If I have here limited it to those who were in the mainstream of the Conservative movement and have used the dilemma over Jewish sovereignty as a lens for examining it, then one must also account for Solomon Goldman, Israel Goldstein, Israel Levinthal, and others who were willing, to use Finkelstein's words, to "risk everything for the sake of a Jewish state." Granting this, I can only say that Kaplan and Finkelstein were authoritative leaders of American Judaism and master builders of the Conservative movement who correctly saw themselves as authentic Zionists. However, they saw their chief mission as nurturing and sustaining a meaningful Jewish life in America. It was an all-consuming task, with success uncertain. Eretz Yisrael was of pivotal importance, a needed cultural and spiritual resource. Until 1945, the issue of Jewish sovereignty appeared to some to be an academic issue, or at most a questionable bargaining point. Pursuing it diverted energy from other matters. Defining "commonwealth" and "state" as their supreme and immediate goal of Zionism ran against their spiritual grain. Indeed, it diminished the merit of the Spiritual Center. Finkelstein and Kaplan were in good company. Besides Magnes there was Martin Buber, who had repeatedly expressed his fear that the single-minded pursuit of political sovereignty would subvert the true goals of Zionism. However, the reality of Jewish need was greater. Nevertheless, the questions the spiritual Zionists posed did not vanish with the creation of the State of Israel. Today, much of American Jewish thought is concerned with reconciling a belief in the centrality of Israel in its transcendent importance for the Jewish people with the reality of the State, the commitment to a creative Jewish life in America, and the ways of fulfilling the obligations imposed by both.

Notes

1. A grant from the Lucius N. Littauer Foundation enabled me to pursue the research for this article.
2. Ben Halpern, "The Americanization of Zionism, 1880–1930," *American Jewish History* 69 (September 1979): 32–33.
3. Solomon Schechter, *Seminary Addresses and Other Papers* (New York: Burning Bush, 1961), 97.
4. Judah L. Magnes to David Wolffsohn, June 19, 1906, in Arthur A. Goren, *Dissenter in Zion: From the Writings of Judah L. Magnes* (Cambridge, Mass.: Harvard University Press, 1982), 82–83; Evyatar Friesel, "Magnes: Zionism in Judaism," in *Like All the Nations? The Life and Legacy of Judah L. Magnes*, ed. William M. Brinner and Moses Rischin (Albany: State University of New York Press, 1987), 72–73; idem, *The Zionist Movement in the United States, 1897–1914* (in Hebrew) (Tel Aviv: Hakibutz Hameuchad, 1970), 77–108.
5. Friesel, *The Zionist Movement*, 109–24, 160–70; Yonathan Shapiro, *Leadership of the American Zionist Organization* (Urbana: University of Illinois Press, 1971), 37–46.
6. Schechter, *Seminary Addresses*, xxiv; Israel Friedlaender, *Past and Present* (Cincinnati: Ark, 1919), 159–84.
7. In a letter to Magnes dated March 31, 1908, Schechter wrote,

   I had hoped to find peace in Zionism, but my hopes are shattered. When I see men like Ben Jehudah, who forbade his son to read the Bible because he wanted him to be a Jew in the same manner as a Frenchman is a Frenchman (that is, anti-clerical and anti-religious); when I see the prominence given to the productions of the Gordons and other men of the same style; when I see the idol made of the Yiddish language at the expense of the Hebrew, I gain the conviction that Zionism will not fulfill its mission without a thorough cleansing of its anti-religious and anti-Judaism elements. We cannot afford any new destructive forces no matter under what disguises they may appear, be it even under the disguise of Nationalism.

   Elsewhere in the letter Schechter attacked the Socialist-Zionists "who are outspoken enemies of Judaism, if not of the Jews, are traitors of their God and of their nation." Judah Magnes Papers, Central Archives for the History of the Jewish People, Jerusalem (hereafter, Magnes Papers), File 115.
8. Judah L. Magnes to Mass Meeting of Federation of American Zionists, July 3, 1910, Magnes Papers, File 534.

9. Baila Round Shargel, *Practical Dreamer: Israel Friedlaender and the Shaping of American Judaism* (New York: Jewish Theological Seminary, 1985), 8–20, 103–82; Arthur A. Goren, "The Wider Pulpit: Judah L. Magnes and the Politics of Morality," *Studies in American Civilization*, ed. E. Miller Budick, et al. (Jerusalem: Magnes, 1987), 106–14.

10. Melvin Urofsky, *American Zionism from Herzl to the Holocaust* (New York: Doubleday, 1975), 116–63, 427–29; idem., "Zionism, an American Experience," *American Jewish Historical Quarterly* 63 (March 1979): 215–30; Jerold S. Auerbach, *Rabbis and Lawyers: The Journey from Torah to Constitution* (Bloomington: Indiana University Press, 1990), 133–46; *Brandeis on Zionism: A Collection of Addresses and Statements by Louis D. Brandeis* (Washington, D.C.: Zionist Organization of America, 1942), 28, quoted in Allon Gal, *Brandeis of Boston* (Cambridge, Mass.: Harvard University Press, 1980), 181–82.

11. Stuart E. Knee, *The Concept of Zionist Dissent in the American Mind, 1917–1941* (New York: Speller, Sons, 1979), passim; Naomi Cohen, *The Year after the Riots* (Detroit: Wayne University Press, 1988), passim; Auerbach, *Rabbis and Lawyers*, 141.

12. Quoted in Shargel, *Practical Dreamer*, 171–72, 180.

13. Shargel, *Practical Dreamer*, 15–40; Norman Bentwich, *For Zion's Sake: A Biography of Judah L. Magnes* (Philadelphia: Jewish Publication Society, 1954), 68–75, 97–127.

14. Reprinted in Friedlaender, *Past and Present*, 445–50.

15. Friedlaender, *Past and Present*, 446, 447.

16. *American Hebrew*, June 7, 1918, 114–15. See different version in Friedlaender, *Past and Present*, 488.

17. Friedlaender, *Past and Present*, 488.

18. Israel Friedlaender, "A Few Suggestions concerning the Relations between the Jews and the Arabs," n.d., Magnes Papers, File 1704.

19. Shargel, *Practical Dreamer*, 180.

20. Herbert Adams Gibbons, "Zionism and the World Peace," *Century Magazine* (January 1919): 369–72; Israel Friedlaender, "Zionism and the World Peace: A Rejoinder," *Century Magazine* (April 1919): 807–9. For a perceptive discussion of the Gibbons-Friedlaender exchange, see Shargel, *Practical Dreamer*, 171–80. One is left wondering how Friedlaender would have responded to the Arab extremism that exploded in the Jaffa riots in May 1921. See idem, pp. 36–37, for Friedlaender's forebodings.

21. Arthur A. Goren, *New York Jews and the Quest for Community: The Kehillah Experiment, 1908–1922* (New York: Columbia University Press, 1970), 232–34; Goren, *Studies*, 114–15.

22. J. L. Magnes, *War-Time Addresses, 1917–1921* (New York: Seltzer, 1923), 99–102.

23. Ibid., 96–97.

24. Judah Magnes to Mayer Sulzberger, October 10, 1917, Magnes Papers, File 1348.
25. Magnes, *War-time Addresses*, 105.
26. J. L. Magnes, *Like All the Nations?* (Jerusalem: privately printed, 1930), 5.
27. Ibid., 45–46.
28. Ibid., 53–56.
29. Ibid., 56–57.
30. Ibid., 5.
31. Harry S. Truman, *Memoirs*, vol. 1 (New York: New American Library, 1965), 326.
32. *Peace Movements in America*, ed. Charles Chatfield (New York: Schocken, 1973), 171–91; idem, *For Peace and Justice: Pacifism in America, 1914–1941* (Knoxville: University of Tennessee Press, 1971), 91–328; Robert A. Divine, *Second Chance: The Triumph of Internationalism in America during World War II* (New York: Atheneum, 1971), 7–28.
33. Roland B. Gittelsohn, "The Conference Stance on Social Justice and Civil Rights," *Retrospect and Prospect: Essays in Commemoration of the Seventy-Fifth Anniversary of the Founding of the Central Conference of American Rabbis, 1889–1964*, ed. Bertram Wallace Korn (New York: Central Conference of American Rabbis, 1965), 89–94, 103–5; *Proceedings of the Thirty-second Convention of the Rabbinical Assembly of the Jewish Theological Seminary of America* (New York, N.Y.: 1932), 358–64; *Proceedings of the Thirty-fourth Annual Convention of the Rabbinical Assembly of America* (Tannersville, N.Y.: 1934), 156–64; *Proceedings of the Forty-first Convention of the Rabbinical Assembly of America* (Philadelphia: 1941), 39–50.
34. Divine, *Second Chance*, 36–39, 57–58; Morris R. Cohen, "Jewish Studies of Peace and Post-War Problems," *Contemporary Jewish Record* 4 (1941): 123–25; Salo W. Baron, "What War Has Meant to Community Life," *Contemporary Jewish Record* 5 (1932): 504–5; *Unity in Dispersion: A History of the World Jewish Congress* (New York: World Jewish Congress, 1948), 134–47.
35. Quoted in Divine, *Second Chance*, 37.
36. *Dissenter in Zion: From the Writings of Judah L. Magnes*, ed. Arthur A. Goren (Cambridge, Mass.: Harvard University Press, 1982), 378.
37. Mark Silk, "Notes on the Judeo-Christian Tradition in America," *American Quarterly* 36 (Spring 1984): 65–72.
38. Louis Finkelstein, "Reflections on Judaism, Zionism, and an Enduring Peace," *New Palestine*, May 21, 1943, 2–3.
39. Ibid., 4–5.
40. Ibid., 5–6; "Zionism and World Culture," *New Palestine*, September 15, 1944, 505.

41. *New Palestine*, May 21, 1943, 8.
42. Morris Waldman, *Nor by Power* (New York: International, 1953), 258–61. It is interesting to compare Finkelstein's thoughts about a Jewish commonwealth soon after the establishment of the state with his perception of his own views in the 1930s. Writing in 1950, Finkelstein declared, "At the Zionist Convention in 1935, I recall suggesting that to one accustomed to read Scripture, and to read the newspaper headlines in the light of Scripture and the writings of the talmudic sages, it seemed probably that just as Sennacherib is remembered today primarily as the emperor whose activities were the subject of the prophecies of Isaiah . . . so the future historian of civilization will think of Nazism primarily as the evil which made the third Jewish commonwealth indispensable and inevitable" (*Conservative Judaism* 4 [May 1950]: 2).
43. Mordecai M. Kaplan, *Judaism as a Civilization* (New York: Macmillan, 1934), 273.
44. Ibid., 251, 278–79.
45. Ibid., 232–33.
46. Mordecai M. Kaplan, *The Future of the American Jew* (New York: Macmillan, 1948), 125.
47. Ibid., 37, 66–67.
48. Bernard A. Rosenblatt formulated this interpretation of "commonwealth" as a limited sovereign state. In his *Federated Palestine and the Jewish Commonwealth* (New York: Scopus, 1941), 39–40, he wrote, "It is necessary to offer *full opportunity for the Jewish National Home to develop as 'The Jewish Commonwealth'*—as free as Pennsylvania or Massachusetts now operate, with full control over their domestic affairs." Such a commonwealth would be joined to a Middle Eastern federation. *Federated Palestine* was reviewed favorably in the *Reconstructionist* of November 28, 1941. "State" and "commonwealth" were often used interchangeably by Zionist leaders. But note David Ben-Gurion's studious evasion of "state" and his use of "commonwealth" in the early 1940s as discussed by Allon Gal, *David Ben-Gurion: Toward a Jewish State* (in Hebrew), (Beersheva, Israel: Ben-Gurion University Press, 1985), 116–17.
49. *Reconstructionist*, March 21, 1947, 3–4; April 18, 1947, 3–4; April 29, 1948, 3–4. Mordecai M. Kaplan Journals, Jewish Theological Seminary, New York.
50. Goren, *Dissenter*, 53–56, 462–63, 482–88.
51. Zvi Ganin, *Truman, American Jewry, and Israel, 1945–1948* (New York: Holmes and Meier, 1979), 175–76; Louis Finkelstein to Abraham J. Peck, February 25, 1985 (copy in the possession of the author); Goren, *Dissenter*, 462–63, 482–88. Mordecai M. Kaplan Journals, February 28, 1948, Jewish Theological Seminary, New York. In an interview with Simon Greenberg (April 18, 1991), he stressed Finkelstein's perpetual

anxiety over the financial condition of the Seminary. While the Seminary's alumni were immersed in Zionist political activity and fundraising, he felt that they neglected the institution that had nurtured them. The observation reminds one of Schechter's similar concerns over Seminary finances and his resentment when faculty members assisted other institutions.

CHAPTER 12

Zion in the Mind of the American Rabbinate during the 1940s

David Ellenson

Jews often say that America is different: conditions and contexts that have marked Jewish life in other times and places have been absent here or have been reconfigured in unique ways. Thus, the American Jewish experience is singular because a strong commitment to Enlightenment, liberal ideals, the relative weakness of antisemitism, the absence of a medieval corporate past, and the high degree of separation between religion and the state have all combined to make this country an extraordinary locus for Jewish life.[1]

In the early twentieth century, this distinctiveness manifested itself among American Jews in the rapid diminution of the ethnic-national components of their Jewishness. Systematic accommodation to the realities of American life meant that, with the advancing Americanization of the descendants of Eastern European immigrants, American Jewry transformed itself, according to Will Herberg, "into an American religious community."[2] Oscar Handlin concurred that "Jewish identification remained most meaningful in the [only] area of diversity America most clearly recognized—that of religion."[3] Certainly by the 1940s public self-identification in religious, not ethnic or national terms, was the dominant, albeit not exclusive, tendency among American Jews.

For American Zionism, the American conceptualization of Judaism as essentially a religion in the American sense had far-reaching consequences. Like American Jewry in Jewish history, American Zionism has been distinctive in the modern Zionist movement. Evyatar Friesel maintained that American Zionism "exercised very little leadership in the development of Zionism either ideologically or organizationally. . . . It had no influence on the growth of the Zionist party system, . . . a system which ran against the political patterns of American general society."[4] Eliezer Livneh in *State and Diaspora*, published by the Jewish Agency in 1953, concluded, "The truth is that there never existed in America a Zionist movement in the accepted [European] sense of that term."[5]

Unlike Europe, then, Zionism in America was to be spoken of primarily in religious, not nationalistic, terms. Melvin Urofsky, in his comprehensive study of the Zionist movement in America during the period prior to the creation of the State of Israel, observed that as early as Brandeis, who established the contours of American Zionism, the American movement constantly "downplayed the nationalistic ideology upon which European Zionism thrived." Given the nature of American society, there was, in effect, no choice. "To have done otherwise," Urofsky wrote, "would have condemned Zionism in America to the perpetual status of an ethnic fringe group, which immigrants in the process of acculturation would have shed."[6] Evyatar Friesel concurred that American Zionism "integrated religion and Zionism in a workable way that was never reached in European-based or European-inspired Zionism." Friesel continued, "It is justified to speak about a Zionized American Jewry represented in large measure by its religious movements."[7] A link between religion and Zionism was forged in the United States that was unique in the history of the Zionist movement.[8]

The principal architects of this link were rabbis, chief among them Conservative rabbis trained at the Jewish Theological Seminary of America.[9] "A veritable bastion of Zionism" at the turn of the century, JTSA, under the leadership of Solomon Schechter, affirmed a notion of cultural Zionism that, as Naomi W. Cohen has observed, would promote "a strongly religious national life for diaspora Jewry."[10] Schechter and Conservative rabbis such as Mordecai Kaplan and Solomon Goldman, who were informed by the moralism that has dominated American religious life, portrayed "Jewish nationalism and American values" as fully compatible.[11]

The goals and activities of America's Puritan forefathers and Israel's twentieth-century pioneers were seen as essentially the same.

As the twentieth century has progressed, demographic differences between Jews of Eastern European and Germanic descent have become less striking. As a result, all the religious movements of American Jewish life came to be "more and more like each other."[12] Changes within Reform were particularly striking. Children of Eastern European immigrants began to join Reform temples, bringing with them sympathetic attitudes toward Zionism. The leadership of Stephen S. Wise and Abba Hillel Silver, the establishment of the Jewish Institute of Religion in 1922, and the Columbus Platform formally approved by the Central Conference of American Rabbis in 1937 meant that the inroads of Zionism among the Reform elite were considerable. Reform and modern Orthodox rabbis increasingly came to parallel their Conservative peers in fashioning a uniquely American form of the Zionist dream.

In short, Zionism in America evolved into a movement whose messages and meanings were congenial to the terms dictated by American society. It is not surprising that rabbis came to occupy a central role in the transmission of the Zionist vision to American Jews and gentiles alike. As Ben Halpern has argued, these men not only produced "the most thoroughly American variant of Zionism," but they also succeed "in impressing [their] stamp upon American Jewry at large" because their brand of "cultural-spiritual" Zionism "filled the place allotted to the Jews as a religious community in the American scheme of things."[13]

This essay will examine a crucial decade in American Zionism: the years immediately prior to and after the establishment of the state. The portrait of American Zionist ideology that emerged in the 1940s will be drawn from an analysis of representative sermons and pamphlets delivered and written by both prominent and lesser-known rabbis. These genres are ideally suited for such a study, inasmuch as sermons and popular pamphlets, written and delivered by a religious leadership accorded a great deal of ascribed status by the American setting, were a major conduit for transmitting Zionist visions and values. We can assume that, in turn, these sources reflect the needs, values, and aspirations of the people to whom the rabbis preached. Since the rabbis, as well as the congregants whom they addressed, were part of a common American universe of discourse, these sources will provide a picture of the Zionist beliefs and values that marked American Jewish society during this period. They reflect the Zionist idea in America as the broad majority of American Jews would have then understood it, an image of American Zionism that is still dominant in many American Jewish circles today.

Baruch Treiger, a 1933 ordinand of the Jewish Theological Seminary and rabbi of Agudath Achim Congregation in Orange, New Jersey, is representative of a Conservative rabbinate passionately devoted to transmitting the American Zionist message. In an address delivered on October 25, 1943, Treiger maintained that a commitment to Palestine lay at the heart of Judaism. Mindful of the genocide of European Jewry occurring while he spoke, Treiger recalled the positions put forth by Herzl, Nordau, and their successors among the political Zionists. No one could deny the legitimacy of their claims that Israel was absolutely essential to the Jew as a "land of refuge." Yet he took exception to Nordau's assertion that "Zionism is the result of . . . antisemitism."[14] Instead, claimed Treiger, "Zionism . . . has its roots in Jewish idealism even more than in Jewish suffering."[15]

In a tone akin to that of Schechter and Brandeis, Treiger proclaimed that the Jewish passion for justice was inextricably linked to the Zionist dream. Jewish idealism asserted "that the survival of the Jew as a fighter against injustice was bound up with the survival of his creative facilities," which could be nourished only in the Land of Israel, "the national homeland for the Jewish people where the great Hebrew prophets preached the Unity of God and the brotherhood of man."[16] Zionism was not primarily a nationalistic movement but "part and parcel . . . of the ethical substance" that marks Judaism as a "religious civilization."

Based upon a divine promise that God made to Abraham, a promise "animated by the highest ideas of justice," this commitment to Zion as the land where the ethical genius of the Jewish people discovers its ultimate and most complete expression is found in every genre of Jewish literature. The purpose of Zionism, Treiger contended, was to return the Jewish people "unto the Land of Israel

to serve God as it befits a people of God." Treiger approvingly
quoted Rav Abraham Isaac Kook in his assertion that the work of
the secular pioneers in Palestine must be understood in religious
terms, thus wedding the moralism of American religious life to the
particularity of Jewish attachment to the Land according to biblical
and traditional rabbinic warrant.

Treiger went on to cite a midrash in Genesis Rabbah 1:21, where
the academies of Shammai and Hillel are reported as having debated whether the heavens or the earth had been the first to be
created. Ultimately, Rabbi Shimon bar Yochai settled the debate by
contending that "*Sheneihem nivre'u yaḥdav*—both were created at
the same time." This, Treiger said, is "the underlying philosophy of
Zionism": the Land of Israel is the place where the Jew will continue "to contribute [so much to] the religious life of all the
world."[17] A notion of Jewish mission similar to that articulated by
classical Reform rabbis of the nineteenth century was linked here
to Jewish nationalism. In a series of talks and sermons delivered a
few months later in January 1944, Treiger concluded a presentation
entitled "This Is the Land," "For from Zion will go forth the Torah,
and the word of the Lord from Jerusalem," interpreting the verses
from Isaiah in his prayer in the following manner: "May we hope
that in our day Palestine will become the Jewish Commonwealth
from whence justice and righteousness may once more radiate for
mankind at large."[18] The quest for normalization and the desire to
be "like all the other nations" characteristic of large segments of
political Zionism is here absent. Instead, the religious thrust and
universalistic hopes attached to Zionism and the Jewish national
idea are preeminent.

Rabbi Louis Levitsky, spiritual leader of Congregation Oheb Shalom in Newark, New Jersey, and president in 1943 of the Conservative Rabbinical Assembly, uttered sentiments akin to those of
Treiger in "The Religious Spirit," a pamphlet issued that same
year.[19] At the outset, Levitsky wrote, "no Jew who calls himself
religious can fail to be a Zionist. Conversely, no Jew who claims to
be an intelligent Zionist can be truly understanding in his profession of the cause unless he comprehends the primacy of the religious
factor in Zionism." Herzl notwithstanding, "Zionism is older than
1896. . . . We must not . . . forget that the rebuilding of *Eretz Yis-*

rael is not dependent upon bigger and better pogroms." It is not sufficient "to be satisfied with Palestine as a haven of refuge for our persecuted people who have at present no other visible land to which they can apply for admission." A political Zionism of completely secular dimensions is to be absolutely rejected. "Such secular Zionism," Levitsky charged, "fails to realize the religious idealism upon which the whole structure of Jewish life, of which Palestine is an integral part, has been built."

Levitsky pleaded, "We want Palestine as a place where Israel's soul can be free and expand, and we can expect God's help only when we can say to Him today, as our ancestors pleaded with Him anciently, 'Return, O Lord, unto the tens of thousands of families of Israel.'" A "Godless Zionism" is oxymoronic, for the love of Zion "did not spring from the despair aroused by pogroms and the pains of the Cossack's knout. It arose in the soul of a people expressed by its prophets, spread by its teachers who associated Palestine with the word redemption." Once more, a purely cultural or political Zionism is rejected in favor of a religious vision imbued with the universal ethical and religious message of redemption for all humanity.

To make explicit the principle that "God can only be understood by and through the lives and deeds of men," Levitsky addressed the "religious Jew":

> *Eretz Yisrael* is bound up with the eternity of God himself, and His reality is made manifest only as the Jew is able to realize, economically and socially, God's Kingdom on earth. While these values must be extended to include the whole world, they emanate from one central point—the Holy Land. There is a "Jerusalem on high" which a religious Jew is obligated to duplicate on earth. The reality of a life in Palestine is one of the historical dogmas of the Jew, a Palestine made holy because of the lives of Jews and non-Jews who will people it.

Levitsky's hopes for a rebuilt Jewish homeland, and his explicit inclusion of non-Jews within it, like Treiger's, expresses the sense that the religious and ethical ideals of America and Judaism are thoroughly compatible.

Israel Levinthal, another prominent Conservative rabbi who served the Brooklyn Jewish Center for the greater part of his career, presented a talk entitled "The Religion of Israel and the Land of Israel" on May 31, 1943. Like Treiger and Levitsky, Rabbi Levinthal produced numerous prooftexts to affirm the centrality of the Land in Jewish tradition. "Jewish religion," he declared, cannot be separated "from the rebirth of *Eretz Yisrael*."[20] This unity between religion and land in Judaism meant that "there can be no conflict . . . between the spiritual values of religion and those of the Land of Israel. . . . We want the Jewish religion, we want to further the old Jewish prophetic ideas." To do that "we need the land, the land that gave birth to . . . and saw the flowering of that prophetic religion, the land that has so much yet to contribute to the religious life of the entire world." The prophets, visionaries who were seen as proclaiming the universal moral ideals and tasks for the Jewish people and all humanity, are placed at the heart of Levinthal's description of a Judaism that incorporates Zion as a central component. The land is the conduit that will permit Israel to fulfill its universal messianic task to bring the "blessing of the heavens to fruition, realization, here on earth."

Levinthal asserted that these universal themes, in keeping with the contours of American religiosity, are also "harmonious with the Four Freedoms" advanced by President Roosevelt. In the final part of his preachment, Levinthal undertook to speak directly to the "conscience of Christendom." Not only would devout Christians support the rebirth of the Jewish state so that "the historic justice due to the Jewish people will be realized," but they would do so because the Bible supplies the Jewish people with a divinely mandated right to the Land. When believing Jews and Christians "hear that the [British government's anti-Zionist] White Paper has not yet been rescinded, we hear the command of God, *kene lekha ha-sadeh*, 'buy the field' (Jeremiah 32), *ki lekha mishpat hage'ulah liknot*, 'for you have the right of redemption,' the moral right . . . to redeem the land." While philosophers routinely distinguish between religious and ethical warrants for an action, Levinthal here collapsed the two. The Jewish claim to the land is mandated by a commanding and ethical deity whom Jews and Christians alike recognize. Levinthal points to a Zionism he believed was enshrined as well in the mythology of a Christian America that recognized that Holy Scriptures granted the Jewish people a right to their ancient homeland. His sermon reflects a dovetailing of the belief system of a Christian America and an American Zionism in the minds of Zionism's American adherents.

In the Midwest, Conservative rabbis such as Abraham Halpern of B'nai Amoona in St. Louis preached a similar vision. Speaking on April 24, 1948, the eve of the establishment of the State of Israel, Rabbi Halpern delivered a sermon the title of which employed Patrick Henry's words, "Give Me Liberty or Give Me Death."[21] Exhilarated by the happiness caused by the United Nations decision of November 29, 1947, to establish a Jewish state in Palestine, Halpern was distressed by what he saw as the lack of American resolve to support the yet-to-be-born Jewish state. Drawing upon the themes of Passover, Halpern queried his congregation, "Are we to shut out the light that appeared in the darkness of our day and bring the makas hoshech—the plague of darkness, on us and the rest of the world? This is what happened in ancient Egypt when a whole people was enslaved." Is America, like the new Pharaoh of old "who knew not Joseph," about to abandon and betray the Jews?

Halpern indicated to his listeners that Zionism embodies the lesson of Passover. "The world needs to learn continually the meaning of the Festival of Freedom, and it is the task of the Jew to teach the world that freedom is the basic idea for human happiness. . . . We lose sight of the fact that the whole Pesach festival is to keep alive this essential social ideal for man, namely liberty and freedom and the right of self-expression by all the children of God." The progressive and humanistic political agenda associated with the liberal ideal is seen by Halpern, as by his colleagues cited above, as being embodied in the building of a Jewish state. "We began our march throughout the ages speaking in the name of our God that we must proclaim liberty in all the land to all the inhabitants thereof." In performing this divinely commanded mission, the Jew causes all humanity, Jew and gentile alike, "to reach upward and take hold of the hand of God." The Jewish ideal of "justice and righteousness, of equality and freedom" is manifest in "the courage of the Jew of Palestine." It is an ideal found in the Magna Carta, at Concord and Valley Forge, and in the speeches of Patrick Henry. It is contained in the work of those who fought to free the slaves during the Civil War, those who gave their lives in World War I to make the world safe for democracy, and the American and Allied soldiers who fought and died to thwart Hitler in World War II.

Halpern's sermon not only cloaked Zionism in the robes of American democracy and equality but also provided religious warrants for both. The rebuilding of the Jewish state represented "a great hope for the realization of our ideals and through which the Jew might again bring light to the world, so that it be said of him as it was in the days of Pharaoh, 'And to all the children there was light in their dwellings.' . . . The celebration of Pesach was to stir within us the urge to demand freedom not only for ourselves, but for all the children of God." The Jewish state is a particularistic manifestation of the mission mandated by God for Israel and, through Israel, all humanity. Israel does not contest universalistic religious teachings; it is religious expression of a universal divine ideal. Zionist identity coincides with the religious and moral heritage of America and reinforces both. Halpern's sermon reflected the contours the United States created for Judaism and also expressed the high degree to which Jewish religious leaders had internalized its strictures in defining their Zionism.

While Conservatism perhaps played the most prominent role in the transmission and depiction of Zionism to a majority of Americans, prominent Orthodox rabbis sympathetic to the Zionist cause drew similar portraits. David de Sola Pool, for example, the eminent rabbi of Sephardic Congregation Shearith Israel in New York and a former president of the Synagogue Council of America, in a 1943 essay entitled "Substance and Spirit," criticized those "Zionists who would live solely as a racial relic, as a national remnant, ignoring the Judaism which alone gave them birth and made it possible for them to be Jews. . . . The Zionist who could cut himself away from his religious roots is trying to preserve a container emptied of the precious contents which gave it value."[22] As an Orthodox Jew committed to the Zionist enterprise, it was impossible for Rabbi de Sola Pool to envision Zionism apart from its religious roots. His vision of the religious character of Zionism, however, also bore a strong affinity to America's view of Judaism and the Zionist enterprise. When he asserted that only Zion could permit Judaism "to enrich universal religion with its own unique values," there is a moralism as evident here as in the writings of the Conservative rabbis.

Joseph Lookstein, a leader of the Mizrachi (Orthodox Zionist) movement and rabbi of Kehilath Jeshurun on the Upper East Side of Manhattan, evidenced the same perceptions even more strongly, perhaps, also in a 1943 essay, "The Religious Character of Jewish Nationalism."[23] Lookstein maintained at the outset of his paper that Herzl, the arch-secularist, had held the view implicitly "that a return to Zion must be preceded by a return to Judaism." Lookstein took the well-known aphorism of David Ben-Gurion, "The Balfour Declaration is not our Torah; the Torah is our Balfour Declaration," to imply that Ben-Gurion saw the Bible as giving a divine, not a secular nationalist sanction to the Jewish yearning for return to Eretz Yisrael. The creation of a religious Ben-Gurion out of the secularist, like that of a religious Herzl, is as much the result of an American vision of Zionism as of Lookstein's own Orthodox background and beliefs. Like the non-Orthodox rabbis, he defended Zionism as part of the Jewish mission. Zionists, he wrote, "are accused of loving humanity less because we love Judaism more. We are indicted on the count that our nationalism contradicts the essential universalism of our religion. Even our prophets are summoned to testify against us." Such a reading of Jewish tradition, Lookstein averred, is a distortion. As the prophet Isaiah recognized, in Judaism there is "no contradiction between universalism and nationalism. Isaiah, the prophet of universal peace and brotherhood, might be considered the forerunner of the ideal toward which our generation is striving: . . . the integration of the peoples of the world into a family of nations under the fatherhood of God."

Modern Orthodox rabbinic proponents of American Zionism did insist on the role of *halakhah* in the Zionist enterprise, which distinguished their Zionism from that of their more liberal colleagues. Paradigmatic of the tenor of these sermons is "Sinai Speaks to Israel," delivered by Rabbi Morris Max, executive vice-president of the Rabbinical Council of America, on the festival of Shavuot, in 1949, one year after the State was born.[24] Max began by proclaiming that "the principal source of strength" for the Jewish people, even in their darkest hours of Egyptian slavery, was their hope and desire that they could establish and dwell in a homeland. Yet, even then, the people understood that this national life was contingent upon their acceptance of Torah "as the basis of the new life they were about to create." A committed Zionist, Max applauded the creation of the new Jewish state and the reestablishment of Jewish national life in Israel's ancient land, but, as an Orthodox rabbi, he insisted that "the Torah [should serve] as the basis of the new Jewish State."[25]

Max cited a well-known talmudic passage (*Kiddushin* 68) that stated that when God revealed the Torah to the people Israel, the Divine held the mountain over the people's heads and told them, "If you accept the Torah, it shall be well with you, and if not, your burial place shall be there." This midrash is often seen as embodying a heteronomous ethic, inasmuch as God coerced Israel into accepting the Law. Max contended that in these "words of our sages," God, as it were, was saying to the people Israel, "If you will accept the Torah and create a divine culture of your own—your own unique standards of justice and righteousness as set down by God, then you will fare well in the Promised Land. . . . Nationhood alone will not give you the strength to create a new way of life and a new ideal that will withstand all the vicissitudes of national life." Max recognized a secular Zionism distinct from the religiosity of his own vision, but he affirmed that the Torah was the embodiment of the American democratic values of "justice and righteousness." Inasmuch as "the foundations of American democracy," Max observed, "were 'cemented with Hebraic mortar,' surely we should not hesitate to establish the first true Democracy in the Near East— our own State of Israel—on the foundations of the Torah, . . . 'the most democratic book in the world.'" He concluded, "Blaze a new trail in the field of democratic society and government by making Israel a dynamic living state enriched by the living waters of our divine Torah." While the sentiment possessed a tenor distinct from that of other rabbis surveyed, Max's identification of Torah and religious law with American democracy revealed once more the power of American culture to shape the Zionist vision even of the Orthodox rabbinate in America. Like his rabbinic peers, Max championed a traditionally religious Zionism in terms congenial to American spiritual-democratic values.

Max's close friend and colleague, Rabbi Israel Tabak of Shaarei

Zion Congregation in Baltimore, delivered a sermon in defense and support of Israel on April 10, 1949, on the "Church of the Air of the Columbia Broadcasting System."[26] Entitled "Liberty versus Security" and intended for a gentile as well as Jewish audience, it reflected the transdenominational as well as religious democratic vision of Zionism that had emerged at this time. Like Halpern one year earlier, in this Passover sermon Tabak drew upon the history of the American struggle for freedom to interpret the meaning of Zionism for his audience. "The American system teaches that liberty is the greatest human good and is to be cherished and treasured above all other human wants." There is a confluence, Tabak maintained, between American and Jewish values, for the teaching of Passover is that "the lessons of liberty must remain fresh in mankind's memory."

Tabak went on to assert that the liberation of Israel from Egyptian bondage portrays two types of men. One type, like Patrick Henry, who proclaimed "Give me liberty or give me death," consisted of those who "risked their lives and invited the wrath of Egyptian taskmasters by fearlessly insisting upon their liberty." The other consisted of those who "constantly reproached Moses for having liberated them, looking back with longing to the life in Egypt 'when we sat by the fleshpots, and when we did eat bread to the full.'" Tabak asserted that genuine servants of "the living God" could not "wear the chains of slavery. God-intoxicated men of all creeds possess the same passion for freedom. Abraham Lincoln, the great Emancipator, once said, 'As I would not be a slave—so I would not be a master.'" Drawing upon parallels between the American experience and the Jewish heritage, Tabak favorably compared this sentiment to the story told in the Book of Judges about Gideon, who would only select troops for his "army of liberation" from those who drank water from the brook standing upright—like free people. "This is the ideal of free men in a free society. This is the true spirit of America." Tabak then applied this to the State of Israel:

> The people of Israel will forever be grateful to the United States, for the friendship and sense of righteousness with which [Americans] have supported them in the hour of their greatest need. But the establishment of the Jewish state would never have been possible

without the superhuman courage and the endless sacrifices they themselves offered for their independence. Had they placed material security ahead of liberty, there would have been no problem. The British and the Arabs were ready to grant them anything short of independence, but the modern Israelites, like their ancient ancestors and like the American revolutionaries two centuries earlier, cherish their liberty above all worldly goods, and prefer "the bread of affliction" . . . to the "flesh pots" of Egypt. . . . It is no wonder . . . that the founding fathers of this country looked to the story of the Exodus for inspiration in their struggle for independence.

Tabak's sermon, like Halpern's, cloaks the Jewish state and its founders in the robes of American freedom. It provides Jewish sources for American ideals and makes Zionism the incarnation of the highest spiritual values of American civilization. Modern Israel, like ancient Israel, will be a wellspring of inspiration for freedom-loving peoples everywhere, a democratic model for nations through-out the world. His sermon, like the others examined in this essay, demonstrates how the United States had created a framework for the interpretation of Judaism, and how rabbis such as Tabak em-ployed that framework to explain Zionism both to themselves and to an American audience composed of Jews and gentiles.

Rabbis such as Louis I. Newman of New York, Felix Levy of Chi-cago, and Max Nussbaum of Los Angeles are representative of the ever-increasing inroads Zionism was beginning to make among Re-form rabbis at this time. These men shared a vision of Zionism that made them virtually indistinguishable from their more traditional rabbinic colleagues, though they were aware of an active anti-Zionist party within the Reform camp. Newman, the scholarly and powerful spiritual leader of Congregation Rodeph Sholom in Man-hattan, delivered a brief for Zionism entitled "Palestine plus the Diaspora" on November 18, 1947, less than two weeks before the United Nations voted for the partition of Palestine.[27] In this speech, he affirmed the religious-cultural brand of Zionism that had marked the American movement throughout its history. "Our relationship to the 'medinah Yehudit,'" he proclaimed, "will be a cultural, spiritual, communal, philanthropic, and brotherly relationship." Israel, he was certain, was "destined to exert an enriching and vitalizing influence upon American Judaism, and upon Judaism throughout the nations," because "great spiritual truths are being formulated and enunciated [there]."

Like the rabbis cited above, Newman refused to concede that there was a nonreligious Zionism, calling the pioneer builders of the land "so-called secularists" who were, in fact, "laboring for a revival of Prophetic Judaism." By viewing them in this way, Newman, like other American rabbis, was defining the Zionist enterprise in light of his own beliefs as an American Jew. Furthermore, as a Reform rabbi, he was conscious of the Reform critique of the movement's nonreligious character. Thus, he asserted, "Regarding the Mission of Israel—a theme so dear to the heart of Reform Jews—the Hebrew writers of Palestine have written with grandeur and insight." Religious and cultural creativity would "flow" from the Jewish state so that the voice of "the spiritual ideals" of the Jewish people would find expression for all humanity. In this way, the "lessons of the Hebraic legacy" could be applied "to the events of the hour." The Jewish people outside the Land would receive "religious nurture," Newman confidently predicted, "from the new Hebraism of Zion."

The genocidal fury unleashed by Hitler in his war against the Jews made political Zionism and the establishment of the Jewish state a moral imperative. Eleven days earlier, on November 7, 1947, Newman had delivered a sermon at Rodeph Sholom on "Our American Citizenship and the New Jewish State."[28] He began with a strong attack on those who opposed the creation of the Third Jewish Commonwealth on the grounds that "the creation of a Jewish State in Zion will imperil the status of Jews in countries outside of Palestine." Such people "fought Herzl . . . fifty years ago . . . [and many] have died in Hitler's Extermination Camps—they or their descendants who have echoed their fears. It is unnecessary to pay any . . . attention to the contemporary heirs of this preachment." The need for Israel as a Jewish "land of refuge" was undeniable. While "most American Jewish youth will remain in the United States," the State would alleviate the deep distress of a majority of the Jewish people who were unable to experience the privileged prosperity of American Jews.

Newman was confident that Israel "will be a democracy in the best sense of that term. . . . The civil and religious rights of all individuals . . . will be . . . safeguarded." Newman labeled those Jews who opposed the creation of the State "anti-Zionist assimilationists." Israel would be the vehicle that would permit the Jews, "an international people," to "cement the ties of brotherhood between all nations." In the State of Israel, the spiritual talents of the people of Israel would be liberated. "The artists, the poet, the religious leader and teacher, the sage and the prophet can once again influence the world for blessing and for light." Israel, he concluded, represents "the harbinger of the Messianic days in our own time." The depth of feeling evidenced in Newman's preachments is palpable.

Max Nussbaum had been an active Zionist while serving as rabbi in Berlin, Germany; he was called to the pulpit of Temple Israel of Hollywood, California, in 1942. The active role he played in the Zionist movement in the United States reflects the urgency and concern of his own personal experience as well as a Zionist vision nurtured and informed by the cultural Zionism of Ahad Ha-Am. In an article written for the *Congress Weekly* in 1942 entitled "Under Hitler," Nussbaum praised Zionist leaders in Germany for their foresight.[29] Unlike other German Jewish leaders, "the assimilationists" who "still believed in a very brief existence of the Hitler government," the Zionists "recognized the danger" and promoted a program of "cultural autonomy" that fortified the morale of German Jewry during its darkest hour. Through active encouragement of immigration to Palestine, the German Zionist movement managed to save over sixty thousand Jewish souls. "More than that," Nussbaum concluded, "it touched into flame the concealed spark of Jewish national dignity within the hearts of thousands of German Jews who are now scattered all over the world. As always in Jewish history, one remnant finds its way home, physically or spiritually. This is what Zionism achieved in that period of agony: the *She'ar Jashuv*."

Almost a decade later, in a sermon entitled "Israel—The Career of a Name," Rabbi Nussbaum takes as his starting point the word "Israel," which, hallowed by thousands of years of tradition, "came to mean excellency of character, religious devotion, and the quality of spiritual values."[30] "Israel" bespeaks the "spiritual aristocracy" and mission of the Jewish people, "which denotes both the spiritual, religious, and ethical values for which Judaism stands, as well as the idea of noblesse oblige" that compels the Jewish people "to give an ethical example to the whole of mankind." The term reflects the Jewish people's obligation to "serve as a means by which other people may be led to the light."

Expressing the humane qualities that characterize the Jewish people, as well as the people's special relationship with God, the name *Israel* cannot be divested of "religious significance." According to Nussbaum, the founders of the Jewish state appropriately selected this name when they established a political homeland for the Jews in the contemporary world. "When Herzl wrote his famous book on Zionism," Nussbaum observed, "he called it *Judenstaat* and the Hebrew translator rendered it *Medinat Hayehudim*, 'State of Jews.'" Herzl's aim was to restore the name "Jew" to a place of dignity.

> However, the founders of the new Jewish State, after much consideration . . . on the selection of a proper name, came up unanimously with the choice of *Israel*, thus again emphasizing the spiritual quality of our people, its conception of humanity, and its relationship with God. . . . The young Jewish State of today is not only an aggregation of *Yehudim* defending themselves against their enemies, . . . but the Land of Israel from which will again come forth the Torah and the word of God, a new conception of humanity, and a new message to a troubled world.

Hitler and the plague of modern antisemitism made the political dimension of Zionism an imperative, but Hitler could not deflect Israel and Zion from the fulfillment of their universal task. Once again, the Western and American vision of the meaning and significance of the Jewish state is apparent.

In a 1943 article, "Zionism: A Religious Duty," Felix Levy, rabbi of Emanuel Congregation in Chicago and president of the Central Conference of American Rabbis, began, "We are a religious nation. . . . The Jew never thought of religion apart from his people, as the doctrines of election, mission, and messianism attest."[31] While other classical Reform rabbis would undoubtedly have disputed this assessment, Levy, as a leader of the Reform rabbinate, was expressing views shared by most of his Reform colleagues at this point. Levy maintained that "we liberal Jews. . . . see in Zion the opportunity for the grandest kind of [universal] Jewish self-expression." In an ironic twist, Levy even cited Kaufmann Kohler to rebut the claim of the anti-Zionists remaining in the Reform camp. (Kohler's antipathy to Zionism was so great that, as president of the Hebrew Union College, he purged the HUC faculty of all persons sympathetic to the Zionist cause and had forbidden the teaching of modern Hebrew literature in the curriculum of the College.) Levy's citation of Kohler in support of the Zionist idea, whatever its historical accuracy, was meant to be an effective rhetorical device.

Levy insisted that "Zionism, let it be repeated again, is not an exclusively political movement. It is from one point of view an end; from a larger and truer survey it is the means for Jewish survival, not as a nation in the accepted sense of the term, but as God's people who through and in Zion can better perform a great task." Levy stated in conclusion, "There is far more universalism among the Jews in Palestine than there is anywhere else in the world." Once more, the claim is put forth that the particularity of Jewish nationalism and the demands of a prophetic universalism do not clash. The former becomes the means whereby the ideals of the latter can be best realized.

Like Newman and some of his Orthodox and Conservative colleagues, Levy was sensitive to accusations of "irreligiosity" hurled against the Zionist movement and acknowledged their partial truth. "Unfortunately," he wrote, "some Zionists and some leaders of Zionism have been anti-religious and this charge, in so far as it is true, is deserved. We have, however, another instance in the development of what in its Herzlian phase was perhaps an exclusively secular interpretation of Judaism, *metoch shelo lishma ba lishma*."[32] Unlike Lookstein or Newman, Levy had no need to convert Herzl or the secular Zionists to religion, but he had the same desire to view Zionism as a distinctly religious expression of Judaism. "Anyone who reads the contemporary literature of the homeland realizes that the spirit of God is hovering over *Eretz Yisrael*." Zionism is a movement, Levy proclaimed in conclusion, "imbued by the highest religious, yes universalistic ideal."

This survey of representative rabbinic writings on Zionism during the 1940s bears out Friesel's and Ben Halpern's contention that a strong link between religion and Zionism has been a hallmark of the American movement. Indeed, there was virtually an identity of postures toward Zionism adopted by rabbis in each of the movements. Each viewed Zionism in religious and moralistic terms and sought to downplay the exclusively ethnic or secular nationalist elements that characterized the movement in Europe. The key role these rabbis played in transmitting the Zionist message to Jews and non-Jews alike distinguished the American branch of the movement. This desire, as well as the content of this rabbinic message, aptly reflected the American environment that led Jew and gentile to define Judaism in essentially religious terms by the 1940s. The force of the Zionist model these men held was so attuned to the pulse of America that, over forty years later, its visions still resonate among many American Jews. It is this linkage between religion, morality, and Zionism, in large measure, that leads to the criticisms significant numbers of American Jews hurl at some contemporary Israeli policies. That, however, is another topic. The reader should simply note the potency of the cultural and spiritual model of Zionism these rabbis framed, as well as the American context that contributed so substantively to its creation.

Notes

1. I would like to thank my colleagues Steve Zipperstein and Stanley Chyet for their help in conceptualizing this paper. I also acknowledge the support of Kevin Proffitt of the American Jewish Archives in locating many of the sources employed in this study.
2. Will Herberg, *Protestant, Catholic, Jew* (Garden City, N.Y.: Anchor, 1960), 173, 187, 190, citing the work of Marshall Sklare.
3. Ibid., 203.
4. Evyatar Friesel, "American Jewry as Bearer of Contemporary Jewish Tasks," *American Jewish History* 78 (1989): 492.
5. As quoted in Herberg, *Protestant, Catholic, Jew*, 205.
6. Melvin Urofsky, *American Zionism from Herzl to the Holocaust* (Garden City, N.Y.: Anchor, 1975), 427.
7. Friesel, "American Jewry as Bearer of Contemporary Jewish Tasks," 491.
8. Ibid., 492–93.
9. Urofsky, *American Zionism from Herzl to the Holocaust*, 102.

10. Naomi W. Cohen, *American Jews and the Zionist Idea* (New York: Ktav, 1975), 11.

11. For an excellent discussion of the term "moralism" and the role this plays in American religious life, see Joseph Blau, *Judaism in America* (Chicago: University of Chicago Press, 1976), 9–10.

12. Herberg, *Protestant, Catholic, Jew*, 193.

13. Ben Halpern, "The Americanization of Zionism, 1880–1930," *American Jewish History* 69 (1979): 32–33. I thank Professor Arthur Goren for bringing this article to my attention.

14. See Nordau's 1902 essay, "Zionism," in Arthur Hertzberg, *The Zionist Idea* (New York: Harper Torchbooks, 1959), 242.

15. Taken from Baruch I. Treiger Papers, American Jewish Archives, Manuscript Collection No. 244; Box 2, Folder 6, "The Religious Aspects of Zionism." All quotations taken from Treiger are found in this manuscript collection.

16. This particular sentence is taken from Treiger's "The Romance of Zionism." Other quotations in this paragraph are taken from his "The Religious Aspects of Zionism."

17. See Israel Levinthal, "The Religion of Israel and the Land of Israel," in Israel Levinthal, *Judaism Speaks to the Modern World* (London: Abelard-Schuman, 1963), 144.

18. Treiger, "The Romance of Zionism."

19. All quotations from Rabbi Levitsky are found in Louis M. Levitsky, "The Religious Spirit," in *Zionism and Judaism: A Symposium* (Washington, D.C.: Zionist Organization of America, 1943), 31–40.

20. Levinthal, 143–49. All Levinthal's quotations are taken from this address.

21. Abraham E. Halpern, "Give Me Liberty or Give Me Death," in Bernard S. Raskas, ed., *A Son of Faith: From the Sermons of Abraham E. Halpern* (New York: Bloch, 1962), 222–27. All the Halpern citations in this article are taken from this sermon.

22. David de Sola Pool, "Substance and Spirit," in *Zionism and Judaism*, 7–13.

23. Joseph H. Lookstein, "The Religious Character of Jewish Nationalism," in *Zionism and Judaism*, 26–30.

24. Morris Max, "Sinai Speaks to the State of Israel," in Asher Siev and Theodore L. Adams, eds., *The Rabbinical Council Manual of Holiday Sermons, 5710–1949* (New York: Rabbinical Council Press, 1949), 175–82.

25. Leo Jung, the famed rabbi of the Jewish Center of Manhattan and professor of ethics at Yeshiva University, offered a similar and representative Orthodox viewpoint concerning the contemporary State of Israel in his "The Creative Impulse of the Mitzvoth," in Leo Jung, *The Rhythm of Life: Sermons, Studies, Addresses* (New York: Pardes, 1950), 165–78.

26. Israel Tabak, "Liberty versus Security," in Siev and Adams, eds., *The Rabbinical Council Manual of Holiday Sermons*, 148–55.
27. Louis I. Newman, "Palestine plus the Diaspora," in Louis I. Newman, *Sermons and Addresses*. Vol. 6, *Becoming a New Person* (New York: Bloch, 1950), 120–25.
28. Louis I. Newman, "Our American Citizenship and the New Jewish State," in ibid., 126–33.
29. Max Nussbaum, "Zionism under Hitler," in Max Nussbaum and William Kramer, eds., *Temple Israel Pulpit: A Selection of Published Sermons, Speeches, and Articles* (Los Angeles: Union of American Hebrew Congregations, 1957), 38–44.
30. Max Nussbaum, "Israel—The Career of a Name," in ibid., 45–49.
31. Felix A. Levy, "Zionism—A Religious Duty," in *Zionism and Judaism*, 14–25.
32. The Hebrew phrase literally means, "That which did not spring originally from a selfless motive ultimately comes to embody one." Levy's point is that while Zionism, particularly in its political dimensions, was originally informed by secular concerns, it eventually came to embrace religious motives.

PART FOUR

Traditional Religion in an American Setting

CHAPTER 13

The Evolution of the American Synagogue

Jonathan D. Sarna

The idea that ours is an "evolving" American Jewish community seems, at first glance, self-evident. A closer look, however, discloses that the word "evolving" is cognate to "evolution," a controversial term in modern culture that most of the time is used all too loosely. "Evolution" has meant different things to different people, and each meaning is ideologically freighted.

According to Raymond Williams, the word "evolution" derives from a Latin forerunner meaning "to unroll," as in "unrolling a book." Used in this sense, "evolution" implies *inherent* development, the unrolling of something that already exists. In the nineteenth century, particularly under the influence of Darwinism, "evolution" took on a different meaning. The new definition, according to Williams, involved "a process of natural *historical* development," a nonteleological process, unplanned and without any sense of inherent design, such as in the common understanding of the phrase "the evolution of humankind." Over the course of the past century, "evolution" has taken on an additional meaning: slow change that is "controlled by what already exists." In this sense evolution is juxtaposed to revolution, which involves "faster changes designed to alter much of what exists." Evolution is unhurried and conditioned; revolution is sudden and violent. (This leads to an implicit value judgment: slow, measured change—evolution—is seen as in step with nature and good; sudden, radical change—revolution—is seen as out of step with nature and bad.)[1]

All three definitions of "evolution" have their counterparts within the American Jewish community, resulting in three interpretations of the phrase "the evolving American Jewish community." Following the first definition the community's history is viewed as unfolding (or "unrolling") along a predetermined course, usually one leading inexorably to assimilation and decay. According to this interpretation, the question is how far American Jewry has already come along the road to its inexorable end. Are we close to our inevitable fate, approaching the midway point, or still back at the beginning of the journey, with miles to go before we weep?

By contrast, the second definition looks upon the American Jewish community as an object of history, shaped and reshaped by forces external to itself. Like an evolving humanity, the community is constantly evolving and will continue to do so. It may be transformed, but it will not necessarily disappear.

According to the third definition, the Jews have control of their own communal destiny: they can promote evolution by pursuing modest changes, or they can promote revolution through more radical ones. "The evolving American Jewish community" is a prescriptive rather than a descriptive title and, by implication, usually favors an evolutionary strategy for American Jews as against a revolutionary one.

With these definitions in mind, I should like to focus on one aspect of American Jewish communal evolution: the development of the American synagogue. "The evolution of the Synagogue as the basic institution in Jewish group life is *central* to the history of the Jewish community in America," according to Moshe Davis,[2] so one could scarcely hope for a better case study. In the concluding section, I will attempt to delineate those elements that shed light on broader questions of religious and institutional change within the American Jewish context and to explain why the ambiguity concealed in the definition of the word "evolution" is appropriate.

The first American synagogue was founded in the late seventeenth century in New York City. Jews had settled in New Amsterdam back in 1654, but by law they could not worship publicly, only privately. After the surrender to the British in 1664, this changed; by 1700 a rented piece of real estate on Mill Street (now South William Street) had become known as the "Jews' Synagogue." Appropriately, the congregation's official name would be Shearith Israel ("remnant of Israel," see Micah 2:12); it is today popularly known as "the Spanish and Portuguese Synagogue."[3]

In 1728, the members of Shearith Israel purchased a small parcel of land on Mill Street for a new synagogue. Consecrated on the seventh day of Passover, April 8, 1730, "it was the first structure designed and built to be a synagogue in continental North America" and is known historically as "the First Mill Street Synagogue."[4]

Like all early American synagogues, and indeed most synagogues in Europe, Shearith Israel saw itself as a *kahal kadosh*, a holy congregation, an all-embracing synagogue-community. It was lay dominated—no ordained rabbis graced American pulpits until the 1840s. It followed Sephardic ritual, even though by 1720 the majority of American Jews were already of Ashkenazic descent.

The synagogue-community had no legal standing in the colonies. Jews were not required to join it. In practice, therefore, on many issues, the congregation could only act on the basis of consensus— a pattern that holds true for many American synagogues today. Unlike the contemporary synagogue, the early American synagogue-community held a virtual monopoly on most aspects of Jewish religious life, including circumcisions, marriages, and burials, making it easier to enforce its authority. (The standard punishments meted out by synagogues throughout the Western world were fines and threats of excommunication.) "In this phase of Jewish history," Martin Cohen writes, "the synagogue reinforced the basic values . . . which traditionally have shaped Jewish life. Socially it was the place where Jews met, commented on events, communicated their needs, planned their charities, adjudicated their disputes, and held their life-cycle events. In the synagogue, bridegrooms were given recognition, mourners comforted, strangers fed and housed, and the *herem* or ban of excommunication, pronounced against recalcitrants."[5]

The American Revolution brought about great changes in the American synagogue. By that time America's Jewish population had grown to over one thousand. There were five synagogues operating in the former colonies, one in each of the major communities where Jews lived. Buffeted by contemporary ideological currents, Jews widely approved of the new values: democracy, liberty of conscience, church-state separation, voluntarism. If synagogues wanted to maintain their members, they had to adapt.[6] This was not just another case of Jews blindly following the supposed rule that "as go the gentiles so go the Jews." Instead, Jews and Christians alike were influenced by similar communal and cultural developments, ones to which all religions needed to respond. In studying "the evolving American Jewish community," we should be wary of dismissing as assimilation what might more appropriately be understood in terms of challenge and response.

How did synagogues respond? For one thing, they composed new constitutions. The very term "constitution" was an innovation; formerly, synagogues had called their governing regulations by the more traditional Jewish term of "Hascamoth." The new documents contained large dollops of republican rhetoric and permitted more democracy within the synagogue than before. One constitution began, "We the members of K. K. Shearith Israel . . ." Another opened, "We, the subscribers of the Israelite religion resident in this place desirous of promoting divine worship, . . ." and then proceeded to justify synagogue laws in staunchly American terms.

Several synagogues introduced into their laws what they called a "bill of rights": provisions that set forth members' "rights and privileges" and made it easier for all members to attain synagogue office. Formerly synagogues had been run by a self-perpetuating elite that paid the bills and made the rules. In the post-Revolution era, particularly in Shearith Israel of New York and Mikveh Israel of Philadelphia, younger leaders emerged, among them men of comparatively modest means. Several synagogues now used a new term, "president," to describe their leader, replacing the traditional Hebrew term "parnas." At an early stage, then, the American synagogue sought to harmonize itself with the values, traditions, and even the standard vocabulary of the larger society.[7]

The next critical juncture in the history of the American synagogue—perhaps the most important change from the beginning until now—was the shift in the first half of the nineteenth century from synagogue-community to community of synagogues. For over a century each community had one synagogue and no more, a practice that unified Jews but stifled dissent; from then on communities would be divided among many different and competing synagogues. Philadelphia is the first city to have had two synagogues: a Sephardic synagogue, Mikveh Israel, was founded in 1771; an Ashkenazic synagogue, Rodeph Sholom, was established in 1802 (possibly earlier). Why this second synagogue was founded is unclear, but the name, meaning "pursuer of peace," hints at the absence of communal peace; *shalom*, in most such cases, was more hope than reality.[8]

In 1824–25, in Charleston and New York, the power of the synagogue-community was effectively broken through secession. In both cities the challenge came largely from young Jews dissatisfied with synagogue life and concerned that Judaism would not survive unless changes were introduced—a perennial theme in modern Jewish movements. In both cases, the young Jews petitioned for changes: the Charleston Jews sought rather radical reforms, the New York Jews more moderate ones. In both cases their petitions were denied. The dissenters then did what religious dissenters usually do in America: they formed their own congregations, B'nai Jeshurun in New York and the Reformed Society of Israelites in Charleston.[9] Henceforward, in larger communities, dissenters no longer needed to compromise principles for the sake of consensus: they could withdraw and start their own synagogue—which they did time and again. In New York, there were two synagogues in 1825, four in 1835, ten in 1845, over twenty in 1855. Some synagogues split several times over.[10] Five corollaries about American Jewish religious history can be derived from this development:

1. *De facto pluralism*. Although throughout the nineteenth century American Jewish leaders continually sought to unify Jews around a single ritual—what Rabbi Isaac M. Wise liked to call "Minhag Amerika"—religious pluralism became the reality for American Jews, like Protestants before them. Nineteenth-century Jews (and their Christian counterparts) considered this to be a misfortune. In the twentieth century, as American Jews embraced

cultural pluralism as an alternative to the melting pot, many came to see the development as a good, even as a key factor in preserving American Judaism from one generation to the next.

2. *Competition.* The existence of multiple synagogues within one community fostered competition for members. Synagogues thus had a new interest in minimizing dissent and keeping members satisfied. They emulated one another's successes, exploited failures, and instituted changes to stave off membership losses. Synagogues that refused to compete disappeared.

3. *The end of synagogue coercion.* Pluralism changed the balance of power between the synagogue and its members. Before, when there was but one synagogue in every community, it could take members for granted and discipline them, for they had no option but to obey. Now, Jews did have an option; in a sense, synagogues now needed them more than they needed any particular synagogue. As a result, by the midnineteenth century, synagogue bylaws listed punishments (fines) only for a small number of infractions—unexcused absences from meetings or funerals, unwillingness to accept proffered synagogue honors, or gross breaches of discipline—and most fines were later remitted. The once feared *herem* (excommunication) virtually disappeared. Where competition was sharpest, synagogues became more concerned with attracting members than with keeping them in line.

4. *Ashkenazic predominance.* Sephardic synagogues suffered most from the breakdown of the synagogue-communities because the conditions that had maintained Sephardic hegemony for more than a century after the Sephardim themselves had become a minority now disappeared. Practically all the new synagogues were in one way or another Ashkenazic in ritual and custom (German rite, Polish rite, English rite, and so forth) because, with the growing democratization of American Jewish life, the majority ruled.

5. *Communal reorganization.* Increasingly, American synagogues—autonomous congregations based upon ritualistic, ideological, and region-of-birth differences—came to represent diversity in American Jewish life; they symbolized and promoted fragmentation. To bind the community together and carry out functions that the now privatized and functionally delimited synagogues could no longer handle required new organizations capable of transcending

these differences. Beginning in the 1840s, philanthropic and fraternal organizations—B'nai B'rith, the Hebrew Benevolent Society, and other associations—moved into the void. Henceforward, the community's structure mirrored the federalist pattern of the nation at large, balanced precariously in a tension between unity and diversity.

Within congregations themselves, the breakdown of the synagogue-community set off a period of enormous change. Pent-up dissatisfaction, fear for the future of Judaism, the need to attract new members, the influence of European Reform Judaism and American Protestantism, a desire to win the respect of Americans for Judaism, and a feeling that the synagogue had to come to terms with the realities of American life all resulted in a series of reforms that completely revolutionized synagogue life and worship. Throughout the country, synagogues moved more into line with Protestant-American religious norms in the hope that this would make them more appealing to the younger generation.[11]

What kinds of changes were introduced?

1. *Rules concerning decorum and etiquette.* "The chaotic, self-governing congregation," in the words of Leon Jick, now became "a training school in propriety." Explicit rules, welcomed by most congregants, banned talking, spitting, loud kissing of *tzitzit*, walking around, standing together, conversing with neighbors, and cracking jokes or "making fun."[12]

2. *English-language Bibles, prayerbooks, and prayers.* Most American Jews did not understand Hebrew; many could not even read the language. As a result, and probably influenced by the vernacular prayers of American Protestants, some expressed deep dissatisfaction with the traditional liturgy that contained no English whatsoever. Translations that individuals could read while the traditional Hebrew was intoned solved the problem in part. Many congregations admitted selected English prayers into the worship service.

3. *Regular vernacular sermons.* Sermons, the centerpiece of Protestant worship, were no more than occasional features of the traditional Sephardic liturgy, delivered only on special occasions or when emissaries came from the Holy Land. The move to a regular weekly sermon in the vernacular was inaugurated in 1830 by Isaac

Leeser, the foremost traditionalist American Jewish leader of the early nineteenth century and at the time the minister at Congregation Mikveh Israel in Philadelphia. His example was widely emulated.[13]

4. *Aesthetic improvements to the synagogue.* In an effort to make the synagogue more appealing so that it might attract new members and proudly be displayed before Jews and gentiles alike, architectural and aesthetic reforms were introduced, aimed at transforming the synagogue from a simple house of prayer into a showpiece. The new focus on aesthetics affected not only the physical appearance of the synagogue but also the worship itself, which became more formal and performance oriented.

In addition to these reforms, which could be justified on the basis of Jewish law, an increasing number of synagogues by midcentury initiated more radical changes. They feared that cosmetic alterations alone would be insufficient to preserve American Judaism for subsequent generations. Hoisting the banner of Reform, these synagogues introduced bolder innovations than had hitherto been sanctioned. The pace and extent of reform differed from synagogue to synagogue, but generally the changes included liturgical and theological innovations, increasing use of the vernacular, the introduction of an organ and a mixed choir, a shift from separate to mixed seating, and abandonment of headcoverings, prayer shawls, and the second ("extra") day of Jewish holidays.[14]

For many Jews in the nineteenth century, the synagogue now became the locus of religion, replacing the home, where fewer and fewer ceremonies were observed. Indeed, traditional home ceremonies like candlelighting, *kiddush*, and *sukkah* were increasingly shifted into the synagogue. This had important implications for women, whose domain formerly had been the home. In the nineteenth century they flocked to the synagogue, just as Protestant women flocked to church, and synagogues had to find ways of meeting their needs. Suddenly, and perhaps for the first time in history, some synagogues had more women in attendance on Saturday morning than men. The significance of this phenomenon has only begun to be studied, but on the basis of what we know already, we can conclude that the impact of these women on the life of the synagogue was enormous.[15]

East European Jewish immigrants, in the period of mass immigration (1881–1924), found the American synagogue alien, different from anything that they had experienced before. They therefore created *landsmanshaft* synagogues that at once linked them to the Old World, replicated many of the broad functions of the traditional synagogue-community (burial, sick care, etc.), and aided them in the process of Americanization. In other words, the synagogue served as a "mediating structure," easing immigrants' transition from Old World to New. In time, these synagogues underwent many of the transformations experienced by the Sephardic and Ashkenazic synagogues of the previous century. Showpiece synagogues, performance-oriented Judaism, an emphasis on decorum, and a liturgy spiced with English and highlighted by a weekly sermon all came to characterize the congregational life of East European Jews too, with further changes introduced later for the sake of their children.[16]

By the end of the nineteenth century a spectrum of synagogues dotted the American landscape, from traditionalist Orthodox to middle-of-the-road Conservative to innovative Reform. Synagogues proliferated, competing with one another and catering to different tastes and needs. Despite talk of unity, diversity had become institutionalized through different movements, and individual synagogues still preserved their own autonomy. What did unite synagogues—and what continues to unite them—was the determination to preserve Judaism, to keep it alive for the next generation. There was, of course, no agreement as to how to do this. Instead, different synagogues pursued different strategies directed toward this aim.

This brings me to twentieth-century developments, which, given constraints of space, I can do no more than outline. Many of the following themes in recent synagogue history have nineteenth-century roots.

1. *Professionalization.* Rabbis, cantors, and synagogue administrators have become professionals over the past century, complete with their own professional training schools and their own professional organizations. This has improved their status and pay but has tended to create a "professional distance" between them and those they serve. It has also tended to make the atmosphere of the

synagogue more businesslike—so much so that many contemporary synagogues are run on a corporate basis, with charters, board rooms, and a chairman of the board.

2. *Synagogue involvement in social action.* Influenced by the Protestant Social Gospel and the challenge posed by Felix Adler's Society for Ethical Culture, this movement in synagogue life has attempted to prove that Judaism is no less concerned than Christianity about the ills of our society, and that one need not abandon Judaism in order to become active in social reform. It also offers those who find regular worship unappealing a way of involving themselves "Jewishly" in a religiously sanctioned manner.

3. *The synagogue-center movement.* The effort to broaden the reach of the synagogue by turning it into a full-fledged community center, or *bet am*—a place where organizations can meet, recreation and education take place, and Jews socialize—has deep roots in Jewish tradition, including, as we have seen, in American synagogue history itself. It also was influenced by the Protestant institutional church movement, by a perceived need to involve the synagogue in the effort to solve urban problems, and, most of all, by the desire to find a way of luring the disaffected children of Jewish immigrants back to the synagogue. Championed (but not originated) by Mordecai Kaplan, this idea has had an enormous influence on all American synagogues by encouraging them to broaden their activities into areas that they had neglected.

4. *Pastoral care.* The allure of Christian Science and the popularity of such books as Joshua Loth Liebman's *Peace of Mind* demonstrated a demand by American Jews for psychological guidance from their religious leaders. In response, seminaries introduced into their curricula courses in pastoral psychology, and synagogues encouraged their rabbis to set aside time for pastoral counseling. This further broadening of the synagogue's role illustrates the process by which the twentieth-century synagogue confronted new challenges and met them successfully.

5. *Child-centeredness.* One of the major objectives of the twentieth-century synagogue has been to instill Jewish consciousness into school-age youngsters. More adults join a synagogue when their children reach school age than at any other time, and they do so in the hope that the synagogue can inspire their youngsters to main-

tain Judaism when they grow up. To meet this challenge, synagogues have become increasingly child centered. Activities, rituals,
and even the worship service itself are frequently arranged with
children in mind.

6. *Feminism.* The feminist movement has affected American synagogues in a variety of ways. Women now serve as rabbis, cantors,
officers, and in other important capacities, and more women expect
to be treated equally in all aspects of Jewish law and practice.
Synagogues have become more conscious of women's issues, sensitive to "sexist language," and innovative in their approach to
women's rituals and spirituality. Indeed, feminism may well prove
to be the most far reaching of all the challenges that the twentieth-
century synagogue has encountered.

7. *Privatization.* While less noticed than the other themes I have
touched upon, privatization has had a major impact on contemporary synagogue life by emphasizing family at the expense of community and by elevating intimacy into a spiritual goal. This development is particularly apparent in architecture; "intimate
settings," back from the street and nestled among the trees, have
become favorite locales for new synagogue buildings. Within the
synagogue, joyous family celebrations, including bar and bat mitzvah, are now more often private events, shared with family and
friends, not with the full community of worshippers. The *havurah*
movement and the proliferation of Orthodox *shtiblekh* reflect, in
part, a similar search for intimacy. Indeed, Harold Schulweis, who
views "the primary task on the agenda of the synagogue" as "the
humanization and personalization of the temple," once described
the *havurah* as a "surrogate for the eroded extended family." [17] This
is a far cry from the idea of the synagogue as community that was
for so many years widely articulated.

What do all of these changes teach us about the evolving American Jewish community? First, that change has historically come
about in the American Jewish community through a process of
challenge and response. In the eighteenth century, religious liberty
introduced free-market competition into American religion; dissatisfied Jews now had the option of looking elsewhere. The fear
that Jews might trade in old loyalties for more accommodating new
ones acted as a major spur to communal change. Prevented by

American law and tradition from either locking out external challengers or banishing internal ones, the community, in order to survive, has had to keep its constituents reasonably contented. That goal has frequently entailed sanctioning modifications ("reforms") of one kind or another to prevent defections and to hold challengers at bay. The paradoxical result is that those who have sought to weaken the community have often been the catalyst for changes that made it stronger.

Second, communal challenges have usually been met in ways that reflect different strategic analyses of how best to promote communal survival. Historically, some sectors of American Jewish leadership have emphasized the importance of educating Jews to ward off challenges, others have insisted that Judaism itself must bend to survive, and most have called for some combination of these strategies. Diversity of religious options within the American Jewish community mirrors the diversity of the community itself. Changes in American Judaism have proceeded along a multitude of paths, some of which have ultimately led to dead ends while others have broadened into spiritual thoroughfares.

Third, young Jews have played a disproportionate role in promoting communal change. In 1825, the movement for religious change in New York was led by "young gentlemen," while the average age of those involved in the Charleston Reform movement around the same time was thirty-two. Subsequent movements for Jewish "reform," "revitalization," "advancement," and "reconstruction" have displayed a similar tendency to attract young people (or "Young Israel") for understandable psychological reasons. Where such movements have likewise attracted older Jews, their justification usually lies in concern for communal survival—the fear that unless Judaism changes, the next generation will abandon it.

Fourth, changes in the American Jewish community have in many cases run parallel to changes taking place in other American faith communities and within the nation at large. Religious liberalism, the social justice movement, pastoral psychology, neo-Orthodoxy, religious revivalism, feminism—all are examples of movements that have left a broad impact on American religion, transforming Christianity and Judaism alike. Mutual influences, important as they are, are not the critical factors here, nor can these phenomena be explained on the basis of "mere" assimilation or independent parallel development. Instead, both Christianity and Judaism have been influenced by developments affecting the nation as a whole, developments to which all American faiths have been challenged to respond.

Finally, although nobody doubts that the American Jewish community has evolved through the decades and continues to evolve, disputes over the meaning of these changes and their long-term implications for Jewish life have flared repeatedly for almost two centuries. From one direction have come warnings that changes of all kinds only hasten American Jewry's inevitable demise— whether through assimilation, antisemitism, or communal division. From another direction, assurances have been heard that celebrate many of these same transformations as signs of communal vitality and ongoing creativity. From a third direction have come voices of compromise, championing modest changes as a brake against radical and dangerous ones.

Each of these arguments can be defended, and as we have seen, each may be inferred from the word "evolution" itself, as it has been variously defined. Indeed, the three approaches stand in vigorous tension to one another: each corrects the other's excesses. This "evolution debate" is more than just a problem of definition and interpretation. At a deeper level, the ambiguity of meaning bespeaks a cultural ambiguity: the dynamic struggle between tradition and change that lies at the heart of the American Jewish experience as a whole.[18]

Notes

1. Raymond Williams, *Keywords: A Vocabulary of Culture and Society* (New York: Oxford, 1976), 103–5.
2. Moshe Davis, "The Synagogue in American Judaism," in *Two Centuries in Perspective: Notable Events and Trends, 1896–1956*, ed. Harry Schneiderman (New York: Monde, 1957), 210 (emphasis added).
3. David and Tamar de Sola Pool, *An Old Faith in the New World: Portrait of Shearith Israel, 1654–1954* (New York: Columbia University Press, 1955).
4. Ibid, 44.
5. Martin A. Cohen, "Synagogue: History and Tradition," in *The Encyclo-*

pedia of Religion, vol. 14, ed. Mircea Eliade (New York: Macmillan, 1987), 212.

6. Jonathan D. Sarna, "The Impact of the American Revolution on American Jews," *Modern Judaism* 1 (1981): 149–60.

7. Many of these constitutions are reprinted in Jacob R. Marcus, *American Jewry Documents: Eighteenth Century* (Cincinnati: Hebrew Union College Press, 1959). See also Sarna, "The Impact of the American Revolution," 155–56; and Jonathan D. Sarna, "What Is American about the Constitutional Documents of American Jewry?" in *A Double Bond: The Constitutional Documents of American Jewry*, ed. Daniel J. Elazar, Jonathan D. Sarna, and Rela Geffen Monson (Lanham, Md.: University Press of America, 1992).

8. Edwin Wolf II and Maxwell Whiteman, *The History of the Jews of Philadelphia* (Philadelphia: Jewish Publication Society, 1956, 1975), 222–33; Jacob R. Marcus, *United States Jewry, 1776–1985*, vol. 1 (Detroit: Wayne State University Press, 1989), 221–23.

9. The history of the Charleston Reform Movement has been frequently recounted. The most complete and up-to-date account is in Gary P. Zola, "Isaac Harby of Charleston: The Life and Works of an Enlightened Jew during the Early National Period" (Ph.D. diss., Hebrew Union College–Jewish Institute of Religion, Cincinnati), 336–463; see also Marcus, *United States Jewry*, 1:622–37; Michael A. Meyer, *Response to Modernity: A History of the Reform Movement in Judaism* (New York: Oxford University Press, 1988), 228–35; and Robert Liberles, "Conflict over Reform: The Case of Congregation Beth Elohim, Charleston, South Carolina," in *The American Synagogue: A Sanctuary Transformed*, ed. Jack Wertheimer (New York: Cambridge University Press, 1987), 274–96. For B'nai Jeshurun, see Israel Goldstein, *A Century of Judaism in New York: B'nai Jeshurun, 1825–1925* (New York: Congregation B'nai Jeshurun, 1930), 51–56; Hyman B. Grinstein, *The Rise of the Jewish Community of New York* (Philadelphia: Jewish Publication Society, 1945), 40–49; Marcus, *United States Jewry*, 1:224–26; and the documents in Joseph L. Blau and Salo W. Baron, eds., *The Jews of the United States, 1790–1840*, vol. 2 (New York: Columbia University Press, 1963), 533–45.

10. Grinstein, *Rise of the Jewish Community of New York*, 472–74; Gerard R. Wolfe, *The Synagogues of New York's Lower East Side* (New York: New York University Press, 1978), 37.

11. Lance J. Sussman, "Isaac Leeser and the Protestantization of American Judaism," *American Jewish Archives* 38 (April 1986): 1–21; Leon A. Jick, *The Americanization of the Synagogue, 1820–1870* (Hanover, N.H.: Brandeis University Press, 1976).

12. Jick, *Americanization of the Synagogue*, 115–16.

13. Lance J. Sussman, "The Life and Career of Isaac Leeser (1806–1868): A

Study of American Judaism in Its Formative Period" (Ph.D. diss., Hebrew Union College-Jewish Institute of Religion, Cincinnati), 84–96.

14. Jick, *Americanization of the Synagogue*, 76–194; Naomi W. Cohen, *Encounter with Emancipation: The German Jews in the United States, 1830–1914* (Philadelphia: Jewish Publication Society, 1984), 159–202; Meyer, *Response to Modernity*, 225–63.

15. Karla Goldman, "The Ambivalence of Reform Judaism: Kaufmann Kohler and the Ideal Jewish Woman," *American Jewish History* 79, no. 4 (Summer 1990): 477–99.

16. Jonathan D. Sarna, ed., *People Walk on Their Heads: Moses Weinberger's Jews and Judaism in New York* (New York: Holmes & Meier, 1982), 4–29.

17. Harold M. Schulweis, "Restructuring the Synagogue," *Conservative Judaism* 27 (Summer 1973): 18–19.

18. Portions of this essay have appeared previously, in different form, in my introduction to *American Synagogue History: A Bibliography and State-of-the-Field Survey* (New York: Markus Wiener, 1988), 1–22; and in my "The American Synagogue Responds to Change," *Envisioning the Congregation of the Near Future* (typescript, Benjamin S. Hornstein Program in Jewish Communal Service, 1990), reprinted in *Cincinnati Judaica Review* 2 (1991).

CHAPTER 14

Consensus Building and Conflict over Creating the Young People's Synagogue of the Lower East Side

Jeffrey S. Gurock

It was a moment of both satisfaction and expectation for Elias L. Solomon when, on February 3, 1904, he rose at a public meeting of the New York Board of Jewish Ministers to report on the activities of the Jewish Endeavor Society (JES). Just two days earlier, "the movement for the erection of a Young People's synagogue on the lower East Side" had taken a major stride forward when a conference that he had chaired, organized by the Endeavorers, had unanimously resolved "that the service they desired was an orthodox one, with the sermon and some prayers in English, and with the Singer Prayer Book."

This had been no mean feat for the twenty-five-year-old, Vilna-born, CCNY-educated Jewish Theological Seminary student and the coterie of classmates he led. Many individuals and organizations downtown were concerned that second-generation Jews, born in this country, were rapidly drifting away from synagogue life and basic Jewish commitments. He and his friends had convinced the seemingly disparate and often competitive thirty-five organizations in attendance, including the immigrant Congregation Agudath Achim Cracow, the Zionist Council of Greater New York, the New Era Club of the Educational Alliance, the Young People's Auxiliary of the Machzikei Talmud Torah, and the Reform Emanu-El Brotherhood, that JES's approach to synagogue life had the best chance of attracting back to Judaism "the well-intentioned young man and woman reared in this city with American ideas and American views [repelled by] the various existing *shules* . . . suitable only for the old generation." Solomon was now advancing one step further his cause of "recall[ing] . . . indifferent Jewry to their ancestral faith." He was seeking interdenominational approbation from New York's most prestigious Americanized Jewish clergy. These respected leaders were, not incidentally, the rabbis of uptown's best-known philanthropists, the Jews most capable of granting Endeavorer efforts the consistent financial support they required.[1]

As Solomon, wary of opponents, surveyed the room in search of allies, he might have caught the eye of Seminary president Solomon Schechter and JTS executive committee member Simon M. Roeder. Concerned that he present himself well before these eminences, he was confident of their support because the Jewish Endeavor Society had the deepest of ties to the Seminary. Bernard Drachman, professor of Bible, Hebrew grammar, and codes, would later assert that the JES was "the fruit of my efforts . . . to influence the students of the Seminary and other youths and maidens in the same period of life, to organize a movement for the winning of adolescents for Traditional Judaism." Whatever Drachman's input, it is clear that Seminary students, both men and women, had been the backbone of the Society since its founding in 1900.[2]

Solomon could count among his closest male associates JES founders and board members rabbis Charles Kauvar, Phineas Israeli, Herman Abramowitz, and Mordecai Kaplan, all recent graduates of the Seminary rabbinical school. Also, Solomon was not unmindful of the contributions of Seminary Teacher's Course students Ida Mearson, Irene Stern, and Frances D. Lunevsky to Endeavorer educational programs. Mearson, chairman in 1904 of the JES Religious Schools Committee, had been principal for two years of Endeavorer Religious School for Children #1 on Chrystie Street. Likewise, Stern was principal of School #4 on Lexington Avenue in Harlem, while Lunevsky was JES secretary to the board. Seminary linkage to the Endeavorers was further confirmed when one or another Seminary leader—Drachman, Louis Ginzberg, Israel Friedlander, or Schechter himself—lectured to their group. Just two days earlier,

Joseph Mayer Asher, the Seminary professor of homiletics, had given Solomon's JES conferees heartening "words of encouragement" when their proceedings had come to an end.[3]

Confident that Schechter and Roeder would be proud of his manner and diction (the Russian-born, Jerusalem-reared Solomon had worked hard under JTS tutor of elocution Grenville Kleiser to speak an unaccented English), Solomon shifted his gaze to senior rabbis of whose support he was far less assured. Samuel Schulman and Maurice H. Harris were spiritual leaders of Temple Beth-El of Fifth Avenue and Temple Israel of Harlem, respectively, both staunch advocates of classical Reform Judaism. Would they acquiesce to the Board of Ministers projecting an American Orthodox service as the way to reach the next generation of Jews?[4]

Solomon did more than merely hope that they would. In a nuanced letter to the editor of the *American Hebrew*, published just before the February 3 meeting, he had taken pains to reach out to potential supporters in formulating a definition of JES activities that would suggest the commonalities between Orthodoxy and Reform. In arguing the merits of an "orderly, dignified [Orthodox] service, accompanied by congregational singing and an English sermon," he had said that "the *Orthodox* young people represented by the Jewish Endeavor Society have for the last four years been clamoring for *a properly reformed service*" (emphasis mine). He had suggested that "given a service, orderly, dignified, accompanied by congregational singing and an English sermon, what objections can even the Reformers raise against it?"[5]

Looking further around the room on February 3, 1904, Solomon would have seen two of New York's most renowned Jewish communal workers, Lillian Wald of the Henry Street Settlement and Henry Moskowitz of the downtown branch of the Ethical Culture Society. Though Solomon may have mused that these two old hands at social-work practice should have been impressed with the acumen and perspicacity of a young man able to bring together thirty-five disparate groups, he had to have wondered what interest and support these secularized Jews would manifest for a traditional Jewish initiative.

Solomon's eyes narrowed as his stare met that of his certain opponent in the room, Rabbi Joseph Silverman of Temple Emanu-

El. Just six weeks earlier, Silverman had begun offering a decidedly Reform religious alternative to "the young men and women of the East Side [who are] . . . repelled rather than attracted by the antiquated mode of life led by their orthodox parents." His English-language services, held at his newly established Emanu-El Brotherhood on East Fifth Street, had featured an organ and a choir and utilized the Union Prayer Book. Although soon Silverman had substituted the Singer (English-Hebrew) *siddur* for the Union Prayer Book and had eliminated the organ and choir, reportedly in response to downtown criticism, Solomon perceived those modifications as merely tactical retreats. He was also not impressed that a lay leader of the Emanu-El Brotherhood, a Mr. J. Levinson, had signed Monday's conference memorandum. Solomon suspected that a push for Reform hegemony in youth religious work was still in the offing, and he was unconvinced that Emanu-El's rabbi would countenance an established Orthodox ritual for this neighborhood-wide intiative.[6]

To Solomon's great pleasure, his remarks were well received by the Board of Ministers meeting. Speaker after speaker, from Schechter to Wald to Moskowitz, "with a single exception," rose to support Solomon's point of view. Wald even brought words of support for the effort from "Christian ministers [who] had told her of the need of a religious center to which they might direct persons who come under their observation." That unsolicited source of backing probably surprised the representatives in attendance from the Union of Orthodox Jewish Congregations. These Orthodox Jews, who wanted backing for their antimissionary efforts against downtown Christian social groups that did not refer Jewish clients to Jewish organizations, would be looking for disingenuous ulterior motives in that statement. Despite JES's high profile against Christian activities in the ghetto, Solomon was undoubtedly gratified that Wald's remarks only raised a few eyebrows and did not divert discussion from the announced topic. At evening's close it was resolved that because the need for "religious centers or settlements" was a real one, "one or more should be started under the Board of Ministers and that therein the Jewish Endeavor Society and other bodies should find fields for their activities." Rabbi Silverman was the sole dissenting voice. As anticipated, he rose to offer a motion in "favor of a Reform Synagogue." His move, seconded only "as a matter of courtesy," was voted down unanimously.[7]

Although none of the assembled identified this meeting as the landmark it was, a consensus was reached in outline on an approach to worship acceptable to almost all Americanized religious elements for answering the needs of second-generation East European Jews; the dissenting voices in a seemingly unified opinion on how to address a basic religious problem came from the newly arrived East European Orthodox rabbinate identified with the Agudath ha-Rabbanim (Union of Orthodox Rabbis of the United States and Canada) and one lone voice in the Reform camp.

Emerging from that meeting, Solomon had good reason to trust that the imprimatur of this alliance would afford the Endeavorers critically necessary financial support. Simultaneously he had to have wondered if this interdenominational agreement would help or hinder the efforts of the JES to sell its modern synagogue concept to suspicious immigrant elements downtown. Truth be told, in JES's four years of existence, its services had been received with mixed reviews on the streets of the Lower East Side.

There were, to be sure, synagogues like Congregation Shaarei Zedek of Henry Street and "the Norfolk Street" Synagogue (possibly Beth Hamidrash Ha-Gadol, but more likely Congregation Ohab Zedek) that periodically opened their doors to JES services and classes. In every instance, these relationships had not long endured. To that date, the JES had been turned away, not because downtowners questioned or rejected its religious philosophy, but rather because of its inability to compete with the *magiddim* (itinerant preachers) who rented the limited meeting space available in downtown synagogues. Arnold Eisemen, Endeavorer board member and Solomon's JTS classmate, explained his group's dilemma: "The services were successful but, unfortunately, . . . a 'maggid' usually appeared on the scene followed by his hosts and naturally the services had to . . . make room for the Yiddish preacher."

At the Monday conference, a trustee of the Pitt Street Congregation Agudath Achim Cracow, a Mr. Leinkram, offered that synagogue's Beth Midrash to the JES. The offer might have reassured Solomon that now the community would be more supportive, but he also had to have known that with the Reformers on board, it was essential for the JES to project fidelity to Orthodoxy if it was to gain the confidence of downtown. Potential critics were certainly watching.[8]

One immigrant Yiddish press editorialist may have been giving vent to this wariness when he wrote that "the public will want to know the character of the service [and] the tendency of the resident minister who is to conduct the services and preside over the activities." While this moderate writer was not a priori about to withhold "support for the People's Synagogue Association," he did assert that "it will have to refrain from giving offense to the Orthodox tastes and susceptibilities on the East Side and refrain also from any attempt to substitute old forms for new."[9]

Accordingly, the Endeavorers took care in addressing the knotty question of how much English could be used in the service without violating Orthodox strictures (and, at the same time, without undermining their interdenominational coalition). While Solomon and his group advocated the need for an English-language sermon and a Hebrew-English *siddur*, they also emphasized that they did not "care to put the stamp of approval on the ignorance of the Hebrew language . . . by conducting services in English." While that statement did not fully close off the possibility that some of the service might be in the vernacular, at least the core of the *tefillah* would be in Hebrew. Responding to doubts concerning the intelligibility of the service to those with minimal Jewish or Hebraic backgrounds, the Endeavorers offered to hold classes to help "young people acquire sufficient knowledge . . . to follow the services." "One need not be a profound Hebrew scholar," they averred, "to participate in the Orthodox service."[10]

Not incidentally, this stance did not sit well with the editors of the *American Hebrew*, a publication read by many of the JES's uptown coalition partners. The *American Hebrew* openly feared that the Endeavorers' approach "of retaining Hebrew as the backbone of the service" would fail to serve the religious needs of their second-generation constituency. "The great multitude of young people downtown never enter a synagogue because . . . they know nothing of it." On a more philosophical tack, the editors of the *American Hebrew* entered the long-standing debate over the place of the vernacular in services by arguing that "sufficient Hebrew to enable a person to *follow* [emphasis theirs] the service does not appeal to us; some of the service must reach the heart and that is only possible when the language of prayer is understandable to the person."[11]

The Endeavorers were soon to find that their position was actually more traditional than that of at least one outspoken lay leader of the Orthodox Union. (Like the Seminary, the Orthodox Union had long-standing ties with the JES.) Lewis N. Dembitz, Orthodox Union vice-president, entered the fray with the remark that "on the language question . . . both of you [the *American Hebrew* and the Endeavorers] are wrong." But as he developed his rambling thoughts, it became clear that he was less sympathetic to the JES than to their interlocutors. Dembitz dismissed the objection that "putting any of the *obligatory parts* [emphasis mine] of the ritual in English . . . would drive off the parents of the young folks entirely." He evoked as his prooftext for a minimal use of English in the service "the express words of the Mishna (Sota, vii:1) that the Prayer and the 'Shema' is lawful in any language." But he was not opposed to a possible alternative direction more akin to JES's. "Perhaps," he wrote, with the needs of the older generation in mind, "the matter might be compromised by only having a Methurgeman [translator] for the prophetic lessons and some parts of the Sedrah and by singing some English hymns." Dembitz's advice was to let "the matter take shape according to the tastes and desires of those who attend the services." If all could not agree on every detail for a single Orthodox service, he concluded, "downtown is big enough for two or three such synagogues."[12]

The JES's intention to adhere to a strict version of Orthodoxy— stricter than Dembitz's—was often lost on downtown's older generation and its rabbis, who did not appreciate the delicacy of the JES stance. Years after his involvement with the JES, Mordecai Kaplan would remember the unhappiness of an immigrant father who chastised his son for attending Endeavorer Saturday afternoon services in the Henry Street Synagogue. "You are a *shaigetz* [for attending]," the father apparently said, "and Kaplan is a bigger *shaigetz* for conducting the prayers." The "orderly fashion" of the prayers, Kaplan allowed, had in itself rendered the JES "treif."[13]

Rabbi Jacob David Willowski must have seen Endeavorer sensitivities on the use of English as a meaningless gesture, in no way protective of the sanctity of Orthodox tradition. This well-known and outspoken East European *rov*, the Agudath ha-Rabbanim's *zekan ha-rabbanim* (senior rabbi), remonstrated against the use of English even in sermons, not to mention in the prayers. In his *She'elot u-Teshubot Bet Ridbaz*, he derided such homiletics as containing "no guidance for the Jewish people, . . . mak[ing] them like the rest of the nations . . . [and] open[ing] the gates leading to . . . Reform Judaism."[14]

The Agudath ha-Rabbanim, according to at least one reputable source, may have been in less than full concurrence with the senior rabbi's perspective. Later in 1904, the *Yiddishes Tageblatt* pilloried the European rabbis for "declaring as blasphemous the use of English in the Jewish pulpit"; the *American Hebrew* damned them for "resolv[ing] to boycott any of their colleagues who dared to preach in English." Orthodox immigrant *literatus* Judah David Eisenstein was quick to clarify and amplify the Agudath ha-Rabbanim's position: "The Union of American Orthodox Rabbis," he averred, never condemned "preaching and teaching in English." In fact, he continued, "several of their own members often preach in English." Eisenstein explained that the real problem exercising local religious Jewry and necessitating unequivocal rabbinical condemnation was the arrogation of the term "orthodox" by Seminary figures, who, of course, were involved with Jewish immigrants and their children.[15]

Reading the denigration of professors Schechter and Ginzberg, JES leaders surely had cause for concern about the impact of such denunciations upon their own efforts downtown. While the Agudath ha-Rabbanim had never publicly questioned the personal religious reliability of Solomon and his fellow Seminary men and women, Solomon had to know that it would be a large step for the European rabbis to approve Endeavorer activities. English-language sermons might be deemed halakhically appropriate on principle but not when they were given by so-called expounders of the Higher Criticism, men who were "*kofer ba-Torah* [heretics] [who] would not have a share in the World to Come."[16]

For all these real and potential encumbrances, Solomon and the Endeavorers had to have believed that credit earned among the large, youthful constituency downtown would ultimately carry them to success. They were admired for their record in battling missionaries. Their services constituted an effective way to combat those scandalously entrepreneurial "temporary synagogues" that brought "shame to every self-respecting man and woman" every High Holyday season. The JES exemplified the pride of an emerging body of young Jews who attended "our universities, acquiring the universal knowledge which their fathers seldom possessed," and who were eager to better themselves. Everything considered, they had to believe that if they could keep their coalition together, with its promise of ongoing support and financial encouragement, their long-awaited, permanent religious center would become a reality.[17]

To the Endeavorers' certain dismay, the consensus developed with the help of the Board of Ministers did not long endure. Rabbi Joseph Silverman seems to have been the major undermining force. He continued to work for an Emanu-El and Reform role, if not hegemony, in religious youth work. Soon after being voted down at the Board's public meeting, Silverman went on the offensive, claiming that his initiative was "the first attempt to meet the religious needs of the younger generation which is not attracted to the services of the older generation." Predictably, Elias Solomon was quick to upbraid the seeming disingenuousness of the Reform leader. The Endeavorer reminded his listeners that the JES started young people's services four years before the Emanu-El Brotherhood and he asked rhetorically, "Is this the standard of ethics which the great adopt unto themselves, to be different from that which they set up for the lower level to follow?"[18]

One downtowner, identifying himself only as "an East Sider," could not have been more direct. "Dr. Silverman," he contended, "has come downtown to compete with the Jewish Endeavor Society." It is "hardly a dignified proceeding on the part of the rabbi of Emanu-El . . . now when success is in sight . . . to step in to reap the glory."[19]

Silverman had, apparently, more than bluster. Possibly behind the scenes, Emanu-El's rabbi was working to get the Ministers to grant equal recognition to his efforts. The success of his infighting became noticeable at an April 8, 1904, meeting of the Board of Jewish Ministers, when a committee of seven reported on final plans for the Young People's Synagogue. Among the recommendations

were that the "number of *synagogues* [note the plural] be determined by the desire of the neighborhood and according to the state
of funds [and that] as experimental places of worship the Jewish
Endeavor Society Synagogues and Emanu-El Brotherhood be
approved."[20]

To be sure, the suggestion that the Ministers authorize two very
different initiatives was reported out of committee only after great
debate. A newspaper account of the in camera deliberations stated
that "the voting for one synagogue instead of two or more, had been
3 against 3, and that the chairman (Mr. Isaac S. Isaacs) had given
the casting vote against one synagogue." It is unknown what
motivated the president of the West End (Reform) synagogue to
break the tie. But at least one influential member of the committee of seven, a Mr. Bullowa, was an Emanu-El Brotherhood
representative.[21]

The adoption of this report did not preclude additional interdenominational cooperation in support of a permanent Endeavorer
synagogue downtown. In fact, a substantive enabling resolution
was appended to the report, which referred to an ongoing "People's
Synagogue Association," a central council, and so forth, to coordinate future efforts. In practice, the designation of both the JES
and the Brotherhood as "experimental places of worship" meant
competition between them and denied the aspiring downtown
youngsters their requisite financial support. When all was said and
done, the Emanu-El Brotherhood was legitimized to project its
"model" Reform services as an answer to second-generation religious disaffection and to the "lures . . . of the music halls and
gambling dens where vice . . . beckons to destruction."[22]

Over the next months and years, the Emanu-El Brotherhood proceeded with "delicate caution" in addressing its downtown constituency: it offered a predominately English-language service but required men to keep their heads covered during prayers and
prohibited smoking in its meeting rooms on the Sabbath day. Rabbi
Silverman was seemingly less concerned with downtown sensitivities than were his board members. He even contemplated passing a
collection plate around during Friday-night services. A remonstra-
tion from the first East European Jew on his board in line with
the Brotherhood's publicly announced intention to "be strongly

conservative so as not to repel the elders" seems to have stopped him.[23]

These policies and efforts achieved an early modicum of success for the Brotherhood as it grew from "an experimental place of worship" to being a recognized fixture on the Lower East Side. By 1910, the *American Hebrew* printed without comment or critique a report on the fifth annual meeting of the Brotherhood, replete with the hyperbole that they are "doing excellent pioneer work in a direction not hitherto attempted and in a section of the city not covered by similar organizations."[24]

As the Emanu-El Brotherhood proceeded on its own, the Board of Ministers' plans "for a permanent building [for an umbrella Young People's Synagogue] after a year's work of experimental synagogues" lost momentum and ultimately any chance of coming to fruition. Regardless of whatever deliberations were held, initiatives toward a Board of Minsters–sponsored synagogue were dropped after 1905.[25]

Left to their own devices, JES leaders and members still continued to struggle to make their synagogue activities and classes a permanent reality in the downtown neighborhood. Despite this disappointment, Endeavorers displayed no loss in enthusiasm for their labor in the succeeding months. In April 1905, for example, an unnamed author, signing his letter to the *American Hebrew* only as "Endeavorer," announced with "a feeling of happiness" that "after an interval of two long years" an organization "that is quietly but surely teaching the tenets of the Jewish religion to the younger generation" would be resuming Sabbath afternoon services. The Endeavorers' friend, Mr. Leinkram, and "the broad-minded trustees and members" of the Pitt Street Synagogue seemed to have worked out a way for the synagogue to be the site for a "service that would be as severely Orthodox as the rest, and at the same time, to exclude those features that are objectionable to the younger people."[26]

As it turned out, "Endeavorer" spoke too quickly. In the few days between the receipt of his letter and its publication, the congregation changed its mind, necessitating the *American Hebrew* to place an asterisk next to "Endeavorer's" missive calling attention to a footnote referring to a "change of program due to the bigoted refusal of said Congregation to fulfil its promises to the Society." Elsewhere in the weekly, they explained that

> notwithstanding the hearty endorsement of the society and its workers . . . by Rabbis Henry Pereira Mendes and Bernard Drachman [of the Orthodox Union], . . . a number of the members of the congregation, including the President, and many of the younger element tried very hard but in vain to obtain use of the synagogue. At a meeting of the congregation held last week, a committee from the society was in attendance but not allowed to speak.[27]

Although there are no extant records to ascertain why the Endeavorers were silenced at the meeting and again were turned down, it is not unreasonable to surmise that they had fallen victim once more to what an angry *Yiddishes Tageblatt* editorialist had earlier described as "the petty politicians and blind fanatics [who] cannot be brought to their senses."[28]

Though rebuffed, the JES perservered as late as 1908, in its semimonthly Sunday-evening lecture series. That year, Endeavorer alumni Mordecai Kaplan and Elias L. Solomon (now ordained rabbis) were among the invited speakers. Bible and Hebrew classes for young adults conducted by Jewish Theological Seminary student Louis I. Egleson also met twice a month. Meanwhile, Egleson's classmate Joseph L. Schwartz served as principal of a Sunday School for girls. Through it all, JES continued its "appeals to the Jewish public for a home of its own." But the dream of "a Synagogue, particularly for young people, where regular services will be held on Sabbath and Holidays, with a sermon in English," was never realized.[29]

The demise of the Jewish Endeavor Society (circa 1910) may have resulted primarily from the graduation from the Seminary of Elias L. Solomon's generation of JTS students, who moved on to more substantial Jewish leadership careers. Such was the view of Endeavorer mentor Bernard Drachman, who would later write that the "Jewish Endeavorer Society ceased to exist [because] . . . so many of its leading spirits and chief workers found their life work in other fields and other places and were unable to devote their efforts to its service." In fact, Endeavorer alumni, drawing in part upon the invaluable "field experience" gained on the Lower East

Side, were destined, over the next fifty years, to make significant contributions to the maintenance of Jewish identification among second- and third-generation Jews.[30]

After graduation from the Seminary in 1904, Elias L. Solomon assumed the pulpit of Congregation Beth Mordecai in Perth Amboy, New Jersey. A year later, he moved to the Bronx's Congregation Kehilath Israel, which was to be a founding member of the (Conservative) United Synagogue of America in 1913. In 1919, Solomon became English-speaking rabbi of a Manhattan Orthodox synagogue, Yorkville's Kehilath Jeshurun. He was called to the pulpit of Congregation Shaare Zedek on New York's West Side in 1922, a position he would hold for the next thirty-four years. He had sunk enduring roots in the emerging Conservative movement.[31]

To be sure, the second-generation Jewish community on the Lower East Side was not left bereft of those endeavoring to effect "a revival of Judaism among the thousands of Jews and Jewesses . . . whose Judaism is at present dormant." There was Rabbi Silverman and his Brotherhood. And by 1910, as if compelled by the idea of multiple synagogues and the spirit of competition engendered by the Board of Ministers' actions, Stephen S. Wise of the Free Synagogue offered his version of a model Reform to downtown masses. For Wise, too, the Lower East Side was an open field for approaching those who "had not forsaken their Orthodox Jewish moorings and yet were eager . . . to hear the word and message of an intensely loyal Jewish liberal." His implicit message was that existing Reform initiatives had not hit their mark.[32]

Wise's religious efforts—he used a hand organ and passed the plate around on the Sabbath and prayed and preached with his head uncovered—may have sparked new Orthodox efforts to reach the unaffiliated. According to one account, the "sons of . . . pious Jews" founded the Young Israel Synagogue in 1912 because "they feared Wise's invasion," even as "they were a trifle drawn to his eloquence and sophistication." Another view has it that these worthy successors to the Endeavorers, as Rabbi Drachman characterized them, simply emerged, like the Kaplans and Solomon before them, out of JTS classes "to awaken young Jewish men and women to their responsibilities as Jews in whatever form these responsibilities are conceived." This appeal soon translated itself into a complex of classes, forums, lectures, and, of course, Americanized Orthodox services.[33]

As the Young Israel and the Lower East Side efforts of the Free Synagogue took shape and as the Emanu-El Brotherhood continued its work in the years before 1920, no consensus developed on the type of services to be offered to young downtown Jews. The February 1904 Board of Ministers concordat would remain a unique, never-repeated moment. Nonetheless, even as they consistently differed in their approach and policies, all these Young People's Synagogues were united in a common goal and fate. Theirs was the challenge to motivate second-generation Jews to look beyond the road to assimilation toward an American Jewish religious identity with which they could be comfortably at home.

Notes

The following abbreviations are used in these notes: *AH* = *American Hebrew*, *AJHQ* = *American Jewish Historical Quarterly*, *AJYB* = *American Jewish Year Book*, *HS* = *Hebrew Standard*.

1. "Religious Centers Downtown," *AH*, February 5, 1904, 391; "Young People's Synagogue," *AH*, April 5, 1901, 596; "The Problem of the Ghetto," *HS*, May 9, 1902, 6. For a biographical sketch of Solomon, see *AJYB* (5665/1904–1905): 224.
2. Bernard Drachman, *The Unfailing Light: Memoirs of an American Rabbi* (New York: Rabbinical Council of America, 1948), 225.
3. For listings of JES board members, chairmen, and enumerations of those who spoke before the group, see *Prospectus of Lectures Offered to the Public by the Jewish Endeavor Society* (1900–1901), (1902–1903), (1904–1905), (1905–1906), (1907–1908) (Library of the American Jewish Historical Society). An examination of the *Register of the Jewish Theological Seminary of America* (1903–1904), (1904–1905), (1907–1908), (1909–1910) indicates that at least twenty-one of the forty-six identifiable leaders of the JES between 1900 and 1910 were Seminary students. Most of the men were rabbinical students. A few of the men and all of the women were students around 1902 of a Seminary Teacher's Course, which seems to have been an early coeducational incarnation of the Seminary's Teachers Institute.
4. Kleiser's teaching position is noted in *AJYB* (5664/1903–1904): 145. For a short biography of Harris and a description of the stance of his

congregation, see Jeffrey S. Gurock, *When Harlem Was Jewish, 1870–1930* (New York: Columbia University Press, 1979), 19–20, 94, 96; see *AJYB* (5664/1903–1904): 93, for a biographical sketch of Schulman.

5. Elias L. Solomon, "To the American Hebrew," *AH*, January 29, 1904, 349.

6. For the Emanu-El Brotherhood's initial statement of purpose, see its "Circular: Emanu-El Brotherhood, Its Aims and Purpose Taken from the Emanu-El Brotherhood Minute Book Board of Trustees Minutes, November 15, 1903," as published in Myron Berman, "A New Spirit on the East Side: The Early History of the Emanu-El Brotherhood, 1903–1920," *AJHQ* (September 1964): appendix 1, 78. For reports on Silverman's quick change in plans, see *AH*, February 5, 1904, 378. The Singer prayerbook to which reference has been made was *The Standard Prayer Book [with] Authorized English Translation* by the Reverend S. Singer, first published in England in 1890 and authorized by the Chief Rabbi, Dr. Nathan Marcus Adler. It offers the complete Orthodox rendering of the prayers with a page-by-page English translation. For a brief history of the Singer prayerbook, see Vivian Silverman, "The Centenary of the Singer Siddur," *Journal of Jewish Music and Liturgy* (5751–5752/1990–1991): 43–45.

7. "Religious Centers Downtown," *AH*, February 5, 1904, 391. On downtown, and particularly Orthodox Union, opposition to Christian influence among immigrants and their children, see Jeffrey S. Gurock, "The Americanization Continuum and Jewish Responses to Christian Influences on the Lower East Side, 1900–1910," in Todd Endelman, ed., *Christian Missionaries and Jewish Apostates* (New York, 1987), 255–71.

8. "Jewish Endeavor Society," *AH*, November 11, 1901, 660; "Jewish Endeavor Society," *AH*, January 24, 1902, 313; "Jewish Endeavor Society," *AH*, February 7, 1902, 375; Arnold Eiseman, "Letter to the Editor," *AH*, November 16, 1903, 298.

9. "Should Act Wisely," *Yiddishes Tageblatt*, April 22, 1904, 8.

10. Elias L. Solomon, "Letter to the Editor," *AH*, January 29, 1904, 349.

11. "Who Are the Unchurched," *AH*, January 29, 1904, 346. For a discussion of Orthodox Jewish difficulties in Europe with the use of vernacular in the prayers, see Jakob J. Petuchowski, *Prayerbook Reform in Europe* (New York: World Union for Progressive Judaism, 1968), 92–94.

12. "Religious Work Downtown," *AH*, February 5, 1904, 384.

13. Mordecai Kaplan, "Journal," vol. 15 (unpublished diaries, Jewish Theological Seminary of America), September 17, 1950.

14. Jenna Weissman Joselit has pointed out that the often-combative Willowski not only wrote about the evil of English-language sermons, an opinion that was finally published in his *She'elot* in 1908, but also, at the very time of Endeavorer activities (circa 1904), when "invited to attend High Holiday services . . . he insisted on delivering the sermon himself" (in Yiddish). See Joselit, "What Happened to New York's

'Jewish Jews': Moses Rischin's *The Promised City* Revisited," *American Jewish History* (December 1983): 168. On Willowski's activities and statements, see Jacob David Willowski, *She'elot u-Teshubot Bet Ridbaz* (Jerusalem, 1908), 11, as quoted and discussed in Aaron Rothkoff, "The American Sojourns of Ridbaz: Religious Problems with the Immigrant Community," *American Jewish Historical Quarterly* (June 1968): 561–62.

15. "Fanaticism Run Wild," *Yiddishes Tageblatt*, April 29, 1903, 8; "A Word of Caution," *AH*, May 13, 1904, 794; Judah David Eisenstein, "The Orthodox Rabbis and the Seminary," *AH*, July 1, 1904, 180.

16. Judah David Eisenstein, "The Orthodox Rabbis and the Seminary," *AH*, July 1, 1904, 180. For specific criticism of the JES earlier on for inviting "Reform ministers" to their meetings, see Yehudi, "Our Duty to Our Faith," *HS*, November 1, 1901, 11.

17. "Jewish Endeavor Society," *Yiddishes Tageblatt*, November 2, 1903, 8; "Interaction of Uptown and Downtown," *AH*, March 21, 1902, 840; "A Remedy for Disgraceful Synagogues," *AH*, October 17, 1902, 608.

18. Joseph Silverman, "Religious Work of the Emanu-El Brotherhood," *AH*, February 5, 1904, 384; Elias L. Solomon, "The Endeavorers and the Brotherhood," *AH*, February 12, 1904, 416.

19. An East Sider, "Endeavorers and the Brotherhood," *AH*, March 19, 1904, 443.

20. "Young People's Synagogue," *AH*, April 8, 1904, 683.

21. "Young People's Synagogue," *AH*, April 8, 1904, 663. For a background sketch on Isaac S. Isaac's personal and institutional relationship to Reform Judaism, see *AJYB* (5665/1904–1905): 122. The importance of Mr. Bullowa on the committee may have indicated that it was he who ultimately reported the committee decision to the floor of the meeting.

22. "Young People's Synagogue," *AH*, April 8, 1904, 663; Berman, "A New Spirit on the East Side," 79.

23. See "Circular," in Berman, "A New Spirit on the East Side," 79. See also the interview with Louis Rosensweig summarized in Berman, 67.

24. "The Emanuel Brotherhood," *AH*, January 7, 1910, 265.

25. "Young People's Synagogue," *AH*, April 8, 1904, 663.

26. "Jewish Endeavor Society," *AH*, April 4, 1905, 645.

27. "Jewish Endeavor Society," *AH*, April 14, 1905, 645, 648.

28. "Do Something Quickly," *Yiddishes Tageblatt*, October 20, 1903, 8.

29. Jewish Endeavor Society, *Prospectus of Lectures* (1907–1908), 1–4.

30. Drachman, *The Unfailing Light*, 226.

31. For biographical data on Solomon, see *Register* (1904–1905), (1913–1914), *AJYB* (5665/1904–1905): 224; *Universal Jewish Encyclopedia*, vol. 9 (New York: Universal Jewish Encyclopedia, 1943), 640. Other important Endeavorers, most of whom became leaders of the United Synagogue, the Rabbinical Assembly, and, ultimately, the Conservative movement, include rabbis Herman Abramowitz, Charles Kauvar,

Phineas Israeli, Aaron Drucker, Aaron Abelson, Israel Goldfarb, Jacob Dolgenas, Louis Egleson, Aaron Eiseman, and, of course, Mordecai M. Kaplan. Another well-known Endeavorer was Gabriel Davidson, who became executive director of the Jewish Agricultural Society. Biographical information on these important men's later careers is noted in Drachman's memoir and is available in the Seminary's frequent *Registers*, with the 1931–1932 (5692) register being particularly useful. Unfortunately, to date I have been unable to track the later post-Endeavorer activities of the some fourteen women listed as leaders between 1900 and 1910. Most likely, if they pursued Jewish careers, they did so in the field of Jewish education, but there is no comparable listing of teachers from which information may be gleaned.

32. "For a Jewish Revival," *AH*, January 10, 1913, 303. Quoted from Shulamith Berger, "Youth Synagogues in New York, 1910–1913" (seminar paper, YIVO Institute, 1981); Stephen S. Wise, *Challenging Years: The Autobiography of Stephen Wise* (New York, Putnam, 1949), 102.

33. On the type of service held at the Free Synagogue, see Wise, *Challenging Years*, 103; and Melvin I. Urofsky, *A Voice That Spoke for Justice: The Life and Times of Stephen S. Wise* (Albany: State University of New York Press, 1982), 63. It should be noted that ephemeral youth-oriented Orthodox synagogues appeared during the hiatus between the JES and the Young Israel. Modern Talmud Torahs conducted youth services and the New York Kehillah toyed with the idea of "model synagogue" programs. See Gurock, "The Orthodox Synagogue," in Jack Wertheimer, ed., *The American Synagogue: A Sanctuary Transformed* (New York: Cambridge University Press, 1987), 79 n. 74. The origins of the version that the rise of Young Israel is linked to Rabbi Wise's activities is based on two relatively late sources, *Young Israel Synagogue Reporter*, Fiftieth Anniversary Edition (New York: Young Israel, 1962); and David Stein, "East Side Chronicle," *Jewish Life* (January–February 1966): 31. This version was later repeated in Irving Howe, *World of Our Fathers: the Journey of the East European Jews to America and the Life They Found and Made* (New York: Harcourt, Brace, Jovanovich, 1976), 197; Howe added the suggestion that the young people were drawn to Wise's eloquence. Urofsky, 64, tells the same story, relying on Howe. An earlier source on the Young Israel's origins is Hyman Goldstein, "History of the Young Israel Movement," *Jewish Forum* (December 1926): 529–30; Goldstein indicates that the primary sources make no reference to Wise's activities.

CHAPTER 15

Jewish in Dishes:
Kashrut in the New World

Jenna Weissman Joselit

Recently, the front page of a well-regarded metropolitan newspaper, the *New York Observer*, carried a headline that read, "Many Jews in the City Forgo Temple; Rabbi Says Zabar's Does the Job." Explaining that Jewish New Yorkers do not feel they have to go to synagogue to express their Jewishness, the article acknowledged that "in New York City, Zabar's [the renowned Upper West Side food emporium] does that job for you." Nominally about synagogue attendance, the article underscored the relationship between food and identity characteristic of American Jews.[1]

Whether reference is made to "kitchen," "culinary," or "gastronomic Judaism," the notion that food is a powerful vehicle by which Jews (or, for that matter, any group) express a religious, cultural, or ethnic identity has a long and popular history in both the Old World and the New. Heinrich Heine, in fact, was among the first to popularize the concept of *fressfrömmigkeit*, the expression of piety through the eating of holiday foods. The popularity of that concept, loosely rendered in English as "kitchen Judaism," was especially marked in the New World, where the American Jewish laity excelled in creating all sorts of inventive gastronomic alternatives to more traditional modes of Jewish identification. One Conservative rabbi in the mid-1940s even went so far as to propose a brand-new denominational model of American Jewry in which he substituted such new categories of affiliation as "A" Jews, or "Jews

247

by Accident," "B" Jews, or "Bar Mitzvah Jews," and "G" Jews, or "Gastronomic Jews," for the standard typology of Reform, Conservative, and Orthodox. Not surprisingly, the "gastronomic Jewish" community boasted the greatest number of adherents. "Gastronomically considered, we do have 100% a religious community," he concluded wryly.[2] Delmore Schwartz's aunt put it even more revealingly when asked about the extent of ritual attentiveness within her own second-generation American Jewish family. Searching about for a concise and accurate definition, she instinctively drew on the vocabulary of food to make her point: the family is proudly Jewish, she reported, "but not Jewish in dishes or anything."[3]

When it comes to being "Jewish in dishes," the centrality of kashrut, the dietary laws, to Jewish cuisine complicates the relationship between food and culture still further. The Jewish case is a particularly complex one because of the way ritual restrictions define and shape both the preparation and the consumption of food. "The simple act of eating has become for us a complicated ceremony, from the preparatory phases of ritual slaughter through *milchigs* and *fleishigs*, *kosher* and *treif* . . . what Sacred Communion is to Catholics, the everyday meal is to Orthodox Jews."[4] What is more, as the history of "kosher-style" cooking and dining suggests, American Jews could successfully detach from and disregard the ritual of kashrut while actively maintaining an affinity for and a commitment to Jewish cuisine. Improvising on tradition, American Jews fashioned a unique culinary phenomenon, remarkable for its blend of innovation and nostalgia. "'Delicious home-cooked meals, kosher style, like mother used to make' is a sign featured in most delicatessens today," observed Ruth Glazer in 1946, noting the growing popularity of the distinction between "Jewish" and "kosher." "Uncertain, in a precarious world, of the articles of their faith, the Jews of the neighborhood," she continued, "could make one affirmation unhesitatingly. Jewish food was good."[5]

By and large, the extant memoir and scholarly literature has tended to look at those "uncertain" Jews who jettisoned tradition, not at those who maintained it. This article presents the perspective of those who, to one degree or another, held tight, affirming the possibilities of tradition in the modern era, whether it be in the realm of food, prayer, or education. As this account suggests, religious culture is itself a fluid social construct, shaped actively by the exigencies of class, acculturation, and urbanization. Viewing the maintenance of kashrut as a case study of adaptation, one sees how modernity, economic mobility, consumerism, and the marketplace affected virtually everything associated with the dietary laws, from the ideology of or rationale for such behavior to its observance.

The study of kashrut in America touches on a wide range of issues: the relationship between domesticity, gender roles, and ethnicity; the Americanization of diet; the cultural improvisation of religious tradition; and distinctions between public and private realms of behavior.[6] The focus here is on the *ideology* of kashrut or, to put it differently, on how American Jewish cultural authorities— which I define broadly to include rabbis, sisterhood presidents, cookbook authors, as well as commercial manufacturers of kosher food—understood and promoted the Jewish dietary laws in the years between the first and second world wars.

Harnessing such trappings of modernity as advertising, cookbooks, and commercial food products, they promoted an ancient ritual. Advocates of the dietary laws drew on a wide range of arguments and artifacts in their campaign for kashrut. Science, reason, emotion, domesticity, gender, aesthetics—each was pressed into the service of the sacred, as were recipes, manuals, advertisements, scientific experiments, and iconography. "It is indeed desirable," wrote one kashrut adherent, "to inoculate the appreciation of the [dietary] laws through every means possible," through "historical, physiological, hygienic, scientific, or any channel of investigation."[7] From the pulpit and the printed page, in sermons and in pamphlets like "Yes, I Keep Kosher," the affinity of kashrut with the modern world was repeatedly and imaginatively emphasized. Theological imperatives or, for that matter, such touchstones as God, the Bible, or the Talmud were conspicuously absent.

What united these disparate interpretations, apart from any mention of the divine, was the fact that in the America of the interwar years kashrut was no longer a given, a cultural assumption, or an intrinsic part of the modern Jewish experience. What earlier generations took for granted had now to be explained, interpreted, actively championed, and, to succeed, thoroughly modernized as well. American Judaism, observed a leading Conservative rabbi, has become an "optional Judaism. *Everything* has now become optional," he noted, pointing to the abandonment of Hebrew, Sabbath observance, and especially the dietary laws. American Jewry, he concluded, is "rapidly becoming denuded of all Jewish religious practices."[8] Another rabbi observed that the "philosophy which prevails [among American Jews] is convenience. If there be no inconvenience involved in the observance of religious custom, good and well. The American Jew will relish the knadlach, homentashen, gefilte fish but would strenuously object if you will interfere with his gastronomic inclinations."[9]

Statistical evidence, though admittedly slight, bears out these observations. Between 1914 and 1924, the consumption of kosher meat in the New York area fell by 25 to 30 percent.[10] Elsewhere throughout the nation, the decline was equally pronounced. A Minneapolis rabbi in 1948 estimated that less than 15 percent of the Jews in his city kept kosher; including those Jews who kept kosher at home but not outside, he wrote, "brings the number to less than half of this number."[11] Meanwhile, sociological studies of ritual behavior in the postwar era revealed an even more precipitous falling-off in the observance of kashrut: where an estimated 46 percent of second-generation American Jews followed the dietary laws, less than 10 percent of their children maintained the practice in its fullest, traditional sense.[12] "During the war I decided not to buy kosher meat any more because it was very difficult with the ration points. So we gave up keeping a kosher house," a suburban informant told sociologist Marshall Sklare. "But in many ways we do keep the Jewish customs nevertheless," she continued, "and I could never buy pork or serve butter with meat at meals."[13]

It is against this background of a growing optional or selective American Judaism during the interwar years that active propagandizing on behalf of kashrut became more pronounced. As the number of adherents fell off, explanations multiplied: kashrut was variously sanitized, domesticated, aestheticized, commodified, and reinterpreted. In most instances, these interpretations were designed expressly to inspire and encourage the continued practice of kashrut by emphasizing its consonance with modernity. "Kashruth need not be a burdensome affair," explained the editor of the *Jewish*

Examiner Prize Kosher Recipe Book in 1937. "The substance of kashruth needs only to be made available in terms that are *understandable* to the young American Jewish housewife, to gain for the Biblical dietary laws the allegiance to which they are entitled."[14] Latently, though, these latter-day interpretations served an altogether different function: to challenge and undermine the critique of kosher food as poorly prepared, inadequate, tasteless, and at once socially and gastronomically inferior, a critique rooted in a mix of theological, cultural, and nutritional concerns. As Mrs. Levy's *Jewish Cookery Book*, the first American Jewish cookbook ever published, insisted as far back as 1871, "without violating the precepts of our religion, a table *can be* spread, which will satisfy the appetites of the most fastidious. Some have, from ignorance, been led to believe that a repast, to be sumptuous, must unavoidably admit of forbidden food. We do not venture too much when we assert that our writing clearly refutes that false notion."[15]

Modern-day champions of kashrut frequently drew on science for legitimation, hoping to endow the ancient practice with a rational, dispassionate "stamp of approval."[16] Hailing the dietary laws as among the "first public health rulings," a wide range of voices, including those of cookbook authors, rabbis, anthropologists, and pharmacologists, insisted that when subjected to the "searchlight of science," kashrut made sense empirically, medically, and nutritionally.[17] "Whoever made the Jewish dietary laws, whether given by Hammurabi in his code, or by Moses in the Thora, or by Joseph Karo in the Shulchan Aruch, . . . each and every one of them was, as you might say, a bacteriologist, a pathologist," commented one doctor in 1903, interjecting a rare note of comparative religion into the discussion.[18] Still other texts affirmed that "medical science reveals, after exhaustive research, that the Dietary Laws have sound, practical knowledge behind their religious significance."[19]

In many instances, this "sound, practical knowledge" was based on insights derived from the increasingly popular fields of nutrition and medical anthropology. "In short, 'kosher' means wholesome and sanitary," one writer on the topic observed categorically in 1912, "while '*treife*' conveys the idea of anything that is either directly unhealthy, malign, poisonous, or inefficient for the needs of the human body."[20] Although quite a few experts, among them renowned anthropologist Maurice Fishberg, found the Jewish diet deficient in a number of areas—an abundance of salt, not enough vegetables—they tended to find the kosher palate as a whole inherently sound. "The food of the Russian Jews," Fishberg observed in his much-read 1903 treatise, *The Health and Sanitation of the Immigrant Jewish Population of New York*, "is considered to be above reproach even by those who are prejudiced."[21] Repeatedly, Fishberg and others following his lead equated kashrut with freshness, noting that meat more than three days old was not considered kosher and that kosher poultry was "fresh and comes from healthy animals."[22] By their lights, kosher meat and poultry were intrinsically pure, "more fit for human consumption than that in the average non-Jewish butcher shop."[23] While Fishberg focused his scientific attentions on kosher meat and poultry, his colleagues studied the effects of the kosher diet on the digestive tract. "By many experiments in this line made by myself," wrote one medical authority in an article entitled "The Dietary Laws and Health," "it is well-founded that meat and milk do not readily mix for a good digestible food."[24]

Nutrition and anthropology were by no means the only sciences to which kashrut champions looked for support. Contemporary findings derived from zoology, chemistry, toxicology, biochemistry, and pharmacology were also enlisted and then widely popularized in monographs such as *The Jewish Dietary Laws: From a Scientific Standpoint* and "The Scientific Aspects of the Jewish Dietary Laws."[25] The first text, published in 1912 by Bloch Publishers, was based on the research conducted by a Detroit physician, N. E. Aronstam, and presented at the International Exhibition of Hygiene a year earlier in Dresden.[26] Drawing on Darwinian theories of evolution, he sought to validate and ratify the biblically mandated choice of ritually permissible foods in contemporary scientific terms. Forbidden foods like reptiles, mollusks, and crustaceans, Aronstam argued, were less complex anatomically and hence "insufficient as articles of diet"; they also contained various poisonous microorganisms. Fish with scales, he added, "stand higher on the ladder of evolution," and as a result are more digestible and "of greater nutritive value" than piscatory creatures without them.[27]

After placing each category of forbidden food within a comparative evolutionary context, the good doctor concluded forcefully that the precepts of kashrut "are in accordance with the doctrines of modern sanitation and its regulations compatible with the dictates of hygiene. The Bible is the pioneer of the sanitary sciences of to-day." [28]

"The Scientific Aspects of the Jewish Dietary Laws," published approximately two decades after the Aronstam monograph, was another much-publicized and frequently quoted scientific validation of kashrut. Written by David I. Macht, a Johns Hopkins pharmacologist and the author of nine hundred scientific articles, it presented a sophisticated, measured, and empirical argument on behalf of kashrut.[29] The latest advances in medicine, toxicology, and biochemistry do not discredit but rather enhance the value of kashrut, Macht stated, describing at some length recent pathology experiments that detected the presence of deadly germs in oysters, shellfish, and pork products; toxicology experiments that uncovered poisonous substances in a wide range of forbidden foods; and assorted nutrition-related investigations that demonstrated a physiological basis for the distinction between forbidden and permissible fats. "Another dietary injunction which was puzzling and unexplainable until recent years is the distinction made by the Jewish law between various kinds of fats," he noted, pointing out that permissible fats were fat soluble and digestible while forbidden fats were not.[30]

Commercial purveyors of kosher food products also championed the notion that kosher food was healthy food by emphasizing the sanitary, controlled conditions under which it was manufactured. During the interwar years, the number of available mass-produced kosher foodstuffs grew enormously: by 1945, more than thirty-seven companies, including national companies like Heinz and Procter & Gamble and smaller Jewish concerns like Rokeach, Horowitz Bros. & Margareten, and Goodman & Sons, produced close to two hundred kosher food products, skillfully integrating kashrut into their mass-marketing strategies. "The Hebrew Race had been waiting 4000 years for Crisco," the maker of vegetable shortening exuberantly proclaimed in 1912 when it first introduced the product to the kosher market.[31] Crisco's imaginatively designed marketing campaign, which invoked both tradition and modernity, stressed that its newfangled product carried not only a traditional rabbinic imprimatur but also a laboratory seal of approval.

Elaborating on the kashrut-as-health motif, commercial manufacturers pointedly associated kosher food with the streamlined factory and the rigorously sanitary laboratory kitchen. Rokeach Foods, manufacturers of gefilte fish, borscht, and Nyafat (its answer to Crisco), boasted in words and pictures of its "sunflooded, modern plant" while Horowitz Bros. & Margareten, the matzoh manufacturers, publicly extolled the virtues of its "scientific baking." "We have raised the kneading and baking of Matzoh from haphazard, careless hit-or-miss to a science. . . . We bake by carefully computed formulae," a full-page advertisement in the *Hebrew Standard* carefully explained.[32] Meanwhile, an abundance of references to the sanitary packaging of kosher products reflected the debt owed to the success of Uneeda Biscuit's In-Er-Seal, a moisture-proof package constructed of waxed paper and cardboard that debuted at the turn of the century. As moisture-proof packaging became de rigueur, Jewish food manufacturers were quick to follow suit. An advertisement for Manischewitz matzoh depicting a block-long, one-million-square-foot, smoke-stacked factory, allegedly the "largest institution of its kind in the world," bore the following copy: "Here's Where They Come From—Clean and Wholesome—Matzos under the Most Sanitary and Modern Methods."[33] Several years later, a competitor made a point of stressing that its products "all come packed in dust proof cartons, clean and handy, according to the best modern sanitary practice. Thus we leave nothing to be desired in quality or cleanliness."[34] Not to be outdone, the B. Manischewitz Company also maintained the "Manischewitz Experimental Kitchens," where recipes using Manischewitz products were tested by the company's very own "Domestic Science Expert and Graduate in Institutional Management."[35]

Implicit in the scientific approach to Jewish dietary behavior was the notion that kashrut was not simply a peculiar, antiquated rite but rather a rational, sensible regimen. Booklets designed to familiarize non-Jewish manufacturers with the intricacies of Jewish law (and, in turn, to encourage them to submit to ritual supervision) were most explicit on this point. Downplaying the exoticness of the dietary laws, they transformed kashrut into a phenomenon that was rational and comprehensible. "Some of the customs described here," stated a 1934 General Foods publication entitled *Customs and Traditions of Israel*, "may appear bizarre, some even fantastic, but one fact must be stressed: they are universally premised upon sound reason and rooted in beautiful sentiment. Superstition, irrational belief, and narrow-mindedness have no place in Jewish observance."[36]

More forthright still was the publication in 1941 of a pamphlet entitled *The Jewish Culture—and What It Means to the American Manufacturer in the Marketing of His Products*.[37] Prompted by the "friendly questioning" of food manufacturers about Judaism, this 29-page text diligently explained Jewish ritual behavior, providing capsule summaries of the Jewish holidays, mourning and wedding customs, synagogue practices, including bar mitzvah celebrations, and the nature of Yiddish. A kind of abbreviated *shulkhan arukh*, it attempted to make Judaism accessible and less daunting to a non-Jewish audience. The richest and most detailed section by far of *The Jewish Culture* related to food and the subtleties of kashrut. "Many people who did not adhere to other phases of the religion are careful to abide by the Dietary Laws," related the pamphlet, adding that "practically all of the Jewish people have a natural, inherited repugnance towards certain distinctly *non-kosher* items."[38] It then went on to explain the function of rabbinical endorsement and "the importance of kashruth" before concluding with a few select passages on the Talmud.

In the course of rationalizing and de-exoticizing the Jewish dietary laws, this pamphlet also offered up a portrait of the kosher consumer, de-exoticizing him or her as much as the distinctive cuisine each (allegedly) consumed. The text forcefully made the point that the kosher consumer—especially the Orthodox consumer—was average, a regular Joe. "Due to mis-statements presented in the guise of truth, many non-Jews believe that the 'orthodox' Jew has peculiar idiosyncracies; that he is definitely set in his ways, requiring none of the necessities of life or its luxuries; that his mode of living and psychological reactions are entirely different from those of the average human being. Nothing could be further from the truth." In the interests of demystifying the kosher consumer, the pamphlet then concluded on a dramatic note: if kosher consumers were "mingled with a group of non-Jews, you could not pick out those who are Jewish and those who are non-Jewish. . . . The average American of the Jewish faith—whether 'orthodox' or not—talks, walks, dresses like the average American of other faiths."[39] As the text implied, the kosher consumer was an "average American" who just ate funny.

Actually, though, the kosher consumer ate (or could eat) exactly the same foods as those consumed by America's white population more generally. Thanks to the wholesale kasherization of basic American food products in the years between the wars, the constraints of kashrut were more a matter of *process* than of cuisine or taste; they affected only the way the food was made, not the food itself. By the early 1930s, kosher pantries could be abundantly stocked with the likes of Aunt Jemima buckwheat pancakes, Hershey's chocolate kisses, Durkee's mayonnaise and salad dressings, Ovaltine, Loft's chocolates and ice creams, and more than twenty-six of Heinz's 57 Varieties of pickles, condiments, creamed soups, and baked beans, that all-American gustatory sensation. If the availability of these products is any indication, the observance of kashrut posed no barrier to participation in the wider world, at least culinarily.

Cookbooks, especially that genre known as "product cookbooks" for their explicit use of brand-name items, also normalized and Americanized the kosher palate. Gold Medal Flour's 1921 Yiddish cookbook is a wonderful case in point. While lamenting the limits of the Jewish diet, this text suggested that Jewish cooks familiarize themselves with parmesan cheese, anchovies, and rose water as well as the "modern dishes"—Swedish fish soup, caramel ice cream—described throughout the cookbook.[40] Procter & Gamble's bilingual edition of *Crisco Recipes for the Jewish Housewife*, published in the early 1930s, encouraged Yiddish-speaking mothers and their English-speaking daughters to use Crisco, a "modern" cooking fat, in making both traditional and new American dishes such as *chremsel* and apple pie.[41] Similarly, Mildred Bellin's popular 1930s cookbook, *Modern Jewish Meals*, and its successor, *The Jewish Cookbook according to the Jewish Dietary Laws*, brought together "modern American cooking" with the "old Jewish dishes" in a well-conceived and ambitious attempt to demonstrate the inherent adaptability of kashrut to modern eating. Offering "first aid" in the preparation of "modern, economical, palatable, scientifically prepared Kosher food," Bellin's cookbooks provided a wealth of recipes, from fish croquettes to devil's food cake, that balanced nutrition, variety, and flavor with kashrut.[42]

Despite the allure of science, kashrut advocates liked to sentimentalize the dietary laws and to leaven their arguments on its behalf with emotion. As more than one kosher cookbook reminded its readers, "But kashruth is more than a matter of health and sanitation. It is a state of mind."[43] As much an emotional as a social phenomenon, the consumption of kosher foods became a way of affirming and celebrating tradition, Jewish identity, and cultural continuity. Family recipes, handed down over the years, evoked the past while serving as a tangible link with Jewish history. "Will we be wise enough to recognize the importance of these traditions and to hand them down intact to future generations?" asked a popular interwar Jewish cookbook rhetorically. "All we need to remember is that by the beautiful expedient of surrounding certain foods with the halo of religious associations and with the magic charm of 'once in a while,' our mothers were able to preserve these traditions for us down through the ages."[44] As physical connections with the Old World and its cultural heritage dimmed, food became an increasingly important way to recapture and revivify that sense of connection. "To permit that link to be weakened by modern cynicism is to undermine the whole chain of Jewish tradition at its most strategic point, the home," explained the editor of the *Jewish Examiner Prize Kosher Recipe Book*, who was also known as "Balabusta." "To rehabilitate that link through a wider and more devoted acceptance of kashruth is to add dignity to the Jewish home and contribute something constructive to Jewish life today."[45]

Mordecai M. Kaplan was perhaps the keenest exponent of the "constructive" view of kashrut. Pronouncing the scientific approach to kashrut as "gratuitous," he urged his followers not to overstate the practical importance of the dietary laws.[46] "By giving them a utilitarian purpose, their function as a means of turning the mind to God is bound to be obscured," he wrote in his seminal *Judaism as a Civilization*.[47] Instead, Kaplan preferred to think of kashrut as a

"Jewish folkway" that enhanced the quality of modern Jewish life. "But if Jews are not to exaggerate the importance of the dietary practices," he cautioned, "neither should they underestimate the effect those practices can have in making a home Jewish. If the dietary folkways are capable of striking a spiritual note in the home atmosphere, Jews cannot afford to disregard them."[48] By turns instrumental and emotional in his views on kashrut, Kaplan squarely situated its observance within a contemporary framework: by his lights, kosher food, along with Jewish artwork and Jewish bric-a-brac, infused the middle-class Jewish home with an appropriately Jewish sensibility. Inasmuch as the preparation and consumption of kosher food added Jewish atmosphere to the home, the practice was to be encouraged but by no means was it obligatory.

Interestingly enough, the founder of Reconstructionism also localized the practice of kashrut, restricting its observance to the home. "Moreoever, since the main purpose of these practices is to add Jewish atmosphere to the home, there is no reason for suffering the inconvenience and self-deprivation which result from a rigid adherence outside the home. . . . By this means," he continued, "dietary practices would no longer foster the aloofness of the Jew, which, however justified in the past, is totally unwarranted in our day."[49] As much a reflection of the times as its creation, Kaplan's geography of kashrut highlighted the extent to which "eating *out*" developed into a normative American Jewish practice. Comments on the order of "well, I keep a kosher home as far as possible . . . but when I go out I eat all sorts of things I don't have at home," emerged, in due course, as a standard refrain.[50]

The constructive approach, with its heavily affective, sentimental overtones, fed most directly into the ceremonializing or occasional consumption of kosher food at holiday time. For many American Jews, the "once in a while" adoption of kashrut became the most widely practiced form of dietary adherence. "While dietary observance per se is highly exceptional," writes Sklare, "when a dietary observance is connected with a holiday or festival . . . it is observed more widely than the daily dietary laws."[51] By transforming Jewish cuisine in general and kosher foods in particular into an inextricable, vital part of holiday observance, American Jews heightened their cultural significance: foods associated with the holidays (and, less frequently, the Sabbath) were increasingly described, often in lavish, emotional prose, as distinctive and unusual. Humble items like *haroset* and *russel,* a popular kosher cookbook observed characteristically, "acquire a dignity, bordering upon sanctity, which elevate them to the status of religious traditions."[52] "The foods mentioned here," Bellin related in her exhaustive survey of Jewish cuisine, referring to roast chicken, brisket, and kashe and noodles, "are those which, through generations of use, have acquired either general festive connotation, or a specific connection with a certain holiday."[53]

Of all the Jewish holidays, Passover, with its array of built-in culinary restrictions, most clearly dramatized the complex relationship between kashrut, cuisine, and American Jewish identity. Many households, otherwise lax in their attention to kashrut, became punctilious during the week of Passover. Others, generally unaccustomed to eating typical Jewish foods, delighted in serving up kosher meals at the seder table. "This generation," observed the daughter of a second-generation New York Jewish family, "brought a certain playful solemnity to the preparation of certain festive dishes."[54] Cookbooks capitalized on the holiday-induced attractiveness of kashrut, helping to diffuse a highly ceremonialized interest in Jewish cuisine. "Much of the spirit of the holiday would be lost without our traditional dishes," explained the 1936 *Passover Cook Book: Traditional and Modern Recipes in Keeping with Jewish Dietary Laws* in a classic formulation of that position.[55]

Manufacturers and advertisers were equally as sensitive as consumers to seasonal adjustments in American Jewish culinary behavior. "The home and its inhabitants acquire a festive atmosphere, and every member of the family is 'rehabilitated' in preparation therefor," related *Jewish Culture,* the 1941 food manufacturers' guide to Jewish consumer matters. "Festive meals are the order of the day for all of the aforementioned holidays," the text advised, referring to Passover, Purim, Hanukkah, and other moments on the Jewish calendar. "The week preceding them, in each instance, is a *big buying period,* when the sale of commodities increases tremendously."[56] To stimulate the consumer, manufacturers evoked notions of domesticity, nostalgia, and camaraderie in connection with their kosher-for-Passover products. Drawing on both words and pictures, they hailed cans of ritually approved chicken soup or assortments of chocolates as a "holiday tradition" and decorated wine bottles, candy tins, and matzoh boxes with warmly hued images of a multigenerational Jewish family seated around a seder table resplendent with family heirlooms and a surfeit of food.

In what was perhaps the most far-reaching reinterpretation of the so-called dietary inhibitions and the one most consciously aimed at women, kashrut was likened to a "fine art" and aesthetic canons applied to its performance.[57] "Living as a Jewess, is more than a matter of faith, knowledge, or observance," stated one popular ritual text. "To live as a Jewess, a woman must have something of the artist in her."[58] Kashrut, then, was the implied medium and Jewish cuisine the vehicle by which the talent and artistry of the modern committed Jewish woman could be demonstrated. *The Jewish Home Beautiful*, a compendium of recipes, decorating hints, and thoughts on Jewish home life, represented the fullest, most comprehensive, expression of the aesthetic approach to kashrut. First published in the early 1930s as a series of articles, *Jewish Home Beautiful* went through several different avatars, among them a cantata and pageant at the 1939 World's Fair, before becoming codified in book form; in that capacity, *Jewish Home Beautiful* enjoyed immense popularity among all segments of the American Jewish population and was released in twelve editions.

Frank in its evaluation of the needs of the upwardly mobile American Jewish woman, *Jewish Home Beautiful* acknowledged, and then sought to remedy, what many modern Jewish women perceived to be the aesthetically unsatisfying, lackluster quality of Jewish life. "Jewish mothers of today," it observed, "have not lost their desire to introduce beautiful pageantry into the home. But they have turned to strange sources for their inspiration. The attractive settings offered by our large department stores and women's magazines for Valentine's Day, Hallowe'en, Christmas, and other non-Jewish festive days have won the hearts of many of our women."[59] In an effort to win back the hearts of contemporary American Jewish women, the architects of the *Jewish Home Beautiful* approach to modern Jewish life appropriated the "attractive settings" and secular, middle-class notions of taste and decor—

dinner parties with themes, color-coordinated table appointments, formal floral arrangements—and applied them inventively to a broad Jewish domestic context of which food was only a part, albeit an important one. The Sabbath, for example, was seen as a special culinary and aesthetic opportunity. "In the *Jewish Home Beautiful*, the elaborate preparations on Friday, the extra cooking, the special dishes, the more than usual cleanliness of the home, and the beauty of the table appointments, leave no doubt in anyone's mind that a great day is approaching," the text observed.[60] In preparation for Shavuot, *Jewish Home Beautiful* recommended that the house be "fragrant with blossoms and flowers" and that dairy foods be served, a custom both "sensible and beautiful; sensible because of the warm season of the year and beautiful because of the association with the Torah."[61]

Through its recipes, suggestions for floral displays, and photographs of various "set tables," *Jewish Home Beautiful* cultivated an American Jewish aesthetic while attempting to overturn the powerful stereotype of an impoverished Judaism. Aestheticizing the practice of kashrut and the celebration of Jewish holidays, *Jewish Home Beautiful* held out the possibility that Judaism could more than hold its own in complexity, interest, color, taste, and variety with secular consumer society. The volume per se and the movement it inspired tried hard and imaginatively to "urge every mother in Israel to assume her role as artist and on every festival, Sabbath, and holiday, to make her home and her family table a thing of beauty as precious and as elevating as anything painted on canvas or chiseled in stone."[62]

Attempts to reconcile the constraints of kashrut with the freedoms of contemporary America gave rise to a modern ideology of Jewish food practice, some of whose interpretations were rational and hard hitting, others fanciful and frivolous. Though differing from one another in detail and focus, each of the three distinct approaches to kashrut surveyed in this paper internalized—and then turned on its head—an existing critique of Judaism. Recasting the "dietary injunctions" in alternately scientific, affective, and aesthetic terms, kashrut advocates sought a contemporary, modern imperative for continuing and sustaining the practice. "In a Jewish home, a perfectly prepared meal, daintily served is not enough," they insisted, in what might be seen as a kind of apotheosis of the modern-day approach to kashrut. "It may satisfy the physical desires and the esthetic sense but *to be perfect*, it must be kosher."[63]

Notes

1. *New York Observer*, January 21, 1991.
2. Quoted in Response of Rabbi Hyman Rabinowitz to "The Future of the American Jewish Community," *Proceedings: The Rabbinical Assembly* 12 (1948): 215.
3. Quoted in James Atlas, *Delmore Schwartz: The Life of an American Poet* (New York: Farrar, Straus & Giroux, 1977).
4. Isaac Rosenfeld, "Adam and Eve on Delancey Street," *Commentary* (October 1949): 386. See also "Letters from Readers," *Commentary* (November 1949): 501.
5. Ruth Glazer, "The Jewish Delicatessen: The Evolution of an Institution," *Commentary* (March 1946): 61, 63. See also Jack Kugelmass, "Green Bagels: An Essay on Food, Nostalgia, and the Carnivalesque," *YIVO Annual* 19 (1990): 57–80.
6. These topics will be treated at some length in my forthcoming book on American Jewish domestic culture, *The Wonders of America: Reinventing Jewish Culture, 1880–1950*.
7. David I. Macht, "Scientific Aspects of the Jewish Dietary Laws," in Leo Jung, ed., *The Jewish Library*, 2d series (New York: Bloch, 1930), 214.
8. Max J. Routtenberg, "Report of the Vice-President," *Proceedings: The Rabbinical Assembly* 15 (1951): 34–35.
9. Rabinowitz, *Proceedings: The Rabbinical Assembly* 12 (1948): 215.
10. Harold Gastwirt, *Fraud, Corruption, and Holiness* (New York: Kennikat, 1974), 7.
11. Albert Gordon, "Towards a Philosophy of Conservative Judaism," *Proceedings: The Rabbinical Assembly* 12 (1948): 158.
12. Marshall Sklare and Joseph Greenbaum, *Jewish Identity on the Suburban Frontier: A Study of Group Survival in the Open Society* (New York: Basic, 1967), 50–55, especially 52.
13. Marshall Sklare, *Conservative Judaism: An American Religious Movement* (New York: Schocken, 1972), 204.
14. "Why the Kosher Cookbook?" *The Jewish Examiner Prize Kosher Recipe Book*, ed. "Balabusta" (New York: Jewish Examiner, 1937), iv.
15. Esther Levy, *Jewish Cookery Book on Principles of Economy, Adapted for Jewish Housekeepers* (Philadelphia, 1871), 3 (my emphasis).
16. N. E. Aronstam, *Jewish Dietary Laws from a Scientific Standpoint* (New York: Bloch, 1912), 4.

17. Mildred Grosberg Bellin, *The Jewish Cook Book* (New York: Bloch, 1958), xiii; Aronstam, *Jewish Dietary Laws*, 5.
18. Dr. B. Bernheim, "The Dietary Laws and Health," *American Hebrew*, July 31, 1903, 337.
19. Joseph Jacobs, *The Jewish Culture—and What It Means to the American Manufacturer in the Marketing of His Products* (New York, 1941), 19.
20. Aronstam, *Jewish Dietary Laws*, 4.
21. Maurice Fishberg, *Health and Sanitation of the Immigrant Jewish Population of New York* (New York: Philip Cowen, 1903), 16–17. See also Mary L. Schapiro, "Jewish Dietary Problems," *Journal of Home Economics* (February 1919): 47–59.
22. Fishberg, *Health and Sanitation*, 16.
23. Ibid.
24. Bernheim, "The Dietary Laws and Health."
25. See also Rev. Dr. Moses Hyamson, "The Jewish Method of Slaying Animals: From the Point of View of Humanity," *American Jewish Year Book* 25 (1923–24): 163–79; Jacob Cohn, *The Royal Table: An Outline of the Dietary Laws of Israel* (New York: Bloch, 1936).
26. Aronstam, *Jewish Dietary Laws*, passim. See also "Jewish Hygiene Exhibit at Dresden," *American Hebrew*, September 8, 1911, 548.
27. Aronstam, *Jewish Dietary Laws*, 13.
28. Ibid., 24.
29. Macht, "Scientific Aspects," passim.
30. Ibid., 219.
31. Quoted in Susan Strasser, *Satisfaction Guaranteed: The Making of the American Mass Market* (New York: Pantheon, 1989), 14.
32. *Hebrew Standard*, February 20, 1920, 7.
33. *Jewish Charities* 8, no. 10 (February 1917): 259.
34. *Hebrew Standard*, February 20, 1920, 7.
35. Quoted in Barbara Kirshenblatt-Gimblett, "Kitchen Judaism," in Susan Braunstein and Jenna Weissman Joselit, eds., *Getting Comfortable in New York: The American Jewish Home, 1880–1950* (New York: Jewish Museum, 1990), 93.
36. General Foods Corporation, *Customs and Traditions of Israel* (New York, 1934), 3.
37. Jacobs, *The Jewish Culture*, passim.
38. Ibid., 19.
39. Ibid., 21.
40. Washburn-Crosby Company, *Gold Medal Cook Book* (Minneapolis, 1921), 4, 5.
41. Procter & Gamble, *Crisco Recipes for the Jewish Housewife* (Cincinnati, 1935).
42. Quoted in Kirshenblatt-Gimblett, "Kitchen Judaism," 85.
43. *Jewish Examiner Prize Kosher Recipe Book*, iii.

44. Betty Greenberg and Althea O. Silverman, *The Jewish Home Beautiful* (New York: Women's League of the United Synagogue of America, 1941), 88.

45. *Jewish Examiner Prize Kosher Recipe Book*, iii.

46. Mordecai M. Kaplan, *Judaism as a Civilization* (New York: Macmillan, 1934), 441.

47. Ibid.

48. Ibid.

49. Ibid.

50. Sklare, *Conservative Judaism*, 204. Ironically enough, it seems that Kaplan did not always practice what he preached. According to an entry in his diary dated October 7, 1948, Kaplan ate nonkosher food for the first time more than ten years after having published his *Judaism as a Civilization*. Calling the meal an "ordeal," Kaplan wrote, "I went through it unscathed and the better for having had the courage to live up to my conviction on the matter." Mordecai M. Kaplan Diaries, Jewish Theological Seminary, New York.

51. Sklare and Greenbaum, *Jewish Identity on the Suburban Frontier*, 52.

52. Greenberg and Silverman, *Jewish Home Beautiful*, 88, 109.

53. Bellin, *Jewish Cook Book*, xv.

54. Ruth Glazer, "West Bronx: Food, Shelter, Clothing," *Commentary* (June 1949): 581. See also Jenna Weissman Joselit, "A Set Table: Jewish Domestic Culture in the New World, 1880–1950," in Braunstein and Joselit, *Getting Comfortable*, passim.

55. Aluminum Goods Manufacturing Company, *Passover Cook Book: Traditional and Modern Recipes in Keeping with the Jewish Dietary Laws* (1936), 4–5.

56. Jacobs, *The Jewish Culture*, 16 (my emphasis).

57. "Cookery," *Jewish Encyclopedia* (New York, 1903), 254. See also, Jenna Weissman Joselit, *New York's Jewish Jews: The Orthodox Community of the Interwar Years* (Bloomington: Indiana University Press, 1990), chapter 5.

58. Greenberg and Silverman, *Jewish Home Beautiful*, 13.

59. Ibid., 14.

60. Ibid., 65.

61. Ibid., 32.

62. Ibid., 13–14.

63. Deborah Melamed, *The Three Pillars of Wisdom: A Book for Jewish Women* (New York: Women's League of the United Synagogue of America, 1927), 40–41.

PART FIVE

The Impact of the Women's Movement

CHAPTER 16

Feminism and American Reform Judaism

Ellen M. Umansky

Over 150 years ago in Germany, a group of "like thinking, progressive rabbis" convened a series of conferences through which the ideology of the nascent Reform movement began to take shape.[1] Among the issues discussed was the role of women in Jewish religious life. At the Breslau conference of 1846, a commission appointed to reevaluate women's traditional roles in the light of modernity recommended that "the rabbinical conference declare woman to be entitled to the same religious rights and subject to the same religious duties as man."[2] Although no formal vote was taken, neither were any objections voiced to David Einhorn's pronouncement that it was nothing less than their "sacred duty" as Reform rabbis "to declare with all emphasis" men's and women's complete religious equality.[3]

In 1907, American Reform rabbi David Philipson concluded that while the commission's report was neither discussed nor voted upon, "in practice" the commission's various recommendations as to how women's equality might best be achieved "have been carried out in reform congregations, notably in the United States."[4] Philipson pointed to the abolition of a separate women's gallery in the synagogue and the introduction of mixed seating by Rabbi Isaac Mayer Wise in Albany in 1851. Indeed, in his prayerbook, *Minhag America*, published in 1857 and revised in 1872, Wise went so far as to describe the *minyan*, the quorum necessary for public worship, as comprising "ten adults, males or females."[5] Similarly, Kaufmann Kohler, president of Hebrew Union College, told members of the

Central Conference of American (Reform) Rabbis (CCAR) gathered together at the historic Pittsburgh Convention of 1885[6] that "Reform Judaism will never reach its higher goal [of spiritual and moral elevation] without having first accorded to the congregational council and in the entire religious and moral sphere of life, equal voice to woman with man."[7]

Yet, Classical Reform's commitment to women's equality was more theoretical than real. As Riv-Ellen Prell has observed,

> The Reformer's concern for women was an inevitable outgrowth of their commitment to the Enlightenment's values of equality, reason, and humanism. That the role of women in Judaism was not actively addressed until the last decade of feminist activism in America, despite its prominence in Reform's initial program, is as much because social reality lags behind ideology as it is because the women's issue for Reformers was a logical consequence of their ideology, not a central cause.[8]

My own research on the roles and status of women in Reform Judaism bears out Prell's assessment. Despite early pronouncements of commitment to women's equality in Germany and in the United States, "it was not until the late 1960s, as the burgeoning feminist movement [in the U.S.] began to create new expectations among women themselves," that Reform women began to press for and achieve significant change.[9] Thus, even though members of the CCAR overwhelmingly passed a resolution as early as 1922 maintaining that women could not "justly be denied the privilege of ordination," it was not until 1972 that women gained entrance into the Reform rabbinate.[10]

In attempting to ascertain why this was so, it is instructive to examine more closely the 1922 CCAR Resolution and the discussion preceding its adoption. Rather than arguing for women's ordination (perhaps on the basis of Reform's understanding of progressive revelation or of the need to create a Judaism more in line with the spirit of the modern age), supporters of the resolution maintained that, given all that Reform stood for (or did not stand for, including strict observance of traditional Jewish practice), there were no legitimate reasons for denying women the opportunity to become Reform rabbis. When the CCAR recommendation was overturned by HUC's Board of Governors a year later, the Board did so not because it disagreed with the CCAR but because its members felt that practical considerations outweighed philosophical ones. Given that women as religious leaders in (Protestant) America were the exception rather than the rule and that Jewish women were not clamoring for entrance into the rabbinic school, there seemed to be no reason to "change the present practice of limiting to males the right to matriculate for the purpose of entering the rabbinate."[11]

In 1956, a CCAR committee was formed to reconsider the issue. A number of mainline Protestant denominations in the United States had begun to admit women into their seminaries and to ordain them as ministers, while a few women had begun to seek admission either to Hebrew Union College or to Stephen Wise's Jewish Institute of Religion (which merged with HUC in 1950).[12] At least two women, despite their lack of rabbinic training, had already succeeded in becoming Jewish religious leaders. The first, Tehilla Lichtenstein, assumed spiritual leadership of the New York–based Society of Jewish Science, a Jewish countermovement to Christian Science, in 1938. While Jewish Science did not formally affiliate with Reform, its major proponents, including the Society's founder, Tehilla Lichtenstein's husband Morris, were Reform rabbis and members of the CCAR. Throughout the 1920s and 1930s, some of them attempted with little success to induce the CCAR to endorse its understanding of spiritual healing as central to Jewish religious life. Therefore, members of the Central Conference in 1956 were not unaware of Tehilla Lichtenstein's achievements. Indeed, by then she had been leader of the Society for almost twenty years—a position that she retained until her death in 1973.

Perhaps more influential was Paula Ackerman, who assumed spiritual leadership of Reform congregation Beth Israel in Meridian, Mississippi, in 1951, following the death of her husband, the congregation's rabbi. Ackerman continued to lead the congregation through the fall of 1953. During her tenure, she regularly led services, preached sermons, and officiated at weddings, funerals, and conversions. According to Ackerman, members of the Reform rabbinate treated her with great respect.[13] Correspondence between Rabbi Maurice Eisendrath, then president of the Union of American Hebrew Congregations (the association of Reform synagogues) and Sidney Kay, president of Temple Beth Israel, concerning the congregation's request that Ackerman serve as their leader, seems to indicate that initial approval of this request reflected a desire, at least by some Reform rabbis, including Eisendrath, to determine whether women could gain congregational acceptance as religious leaders.[14]

This interpretation of rabbinic interest in Ackerman's tenure at Temple Beth Israel is strengthened by Michael Meyer's claim that by the end of the 1940s "the Hebrew Union College found itself hard pressed to keep up with the demand for rabbis." Responding as best it could to Reform's congregational growth, HUC introduced a more active recruitment program and in 1950 merged with the Jewish Institute of Religion. Consequently, Meyer writes, "from less than 500 rabbis in 1943, [CCAR] membership rose to 850 in 1964 and grew even more rapidly thereafter."[15]

Finally, a new receptiveness in 1956 to the idea of women as rabbis may be attributed to new leadership. Certainly, the membership of the Board of Governors had changed since 1922, as had the presidency of the College. Even before the CCAR voted to reaffirm the 1922 resolution supporting the entrance of women into the Reform rabbinate, Nelson Glueck, then president of the Hebrew Union College–Jewish Institute of Religion (HUC-JIR), publicly expressed his support for this proposal and stated that the Reform seminary would ordain any woman who passed the required courses.[16]

Yet it was not until the late 1960s, when Sally Priesand, after receiving a joint B.A. degree from HUC-JIR and the University of Cincinnati, decided to continue her studies at HUC, that the doors to the Reform rabbinate were finally opened to women. It should be noted that Priesand's decision to enter HUC's rabbinical program came with little fanfare.[17] That Priesand completed her rabbinical studies and received ordination testifies both to her tenacity and to the support of members of the faculty and administration, most notably Glueck and Alfred Gottschalk, who succeeded Glueck after his death in 1971 as president of HUC-JIR.

In short, it was not a change in Reform ideology that led to the ordination of women as Reform rabbis; it was the changed social climate of the late 1960s.[18] Female religious leaders were gaining acceptance within Protestant denominations; qualified women were interested in entering the rabbinate; there were indications that congregations might be willing to accept them; and the Reform movement was in need of more rabbis to serve its congregations.

Feminism does not seem to have directly led to the entrance of women into the Reform rabbinate. Indeed, in the late 1960s, when Sally Priesand entered HUC's rabbinical program, the second wave of American feminism, spurred by the publication of Betty Friedan's *Feminine Mystique* in 1964, was still in its infancy. In contrast to the controversy about women's ordination in the Conservative movement ten years later, public discussion did not refer to the admission of women in the Reform rabbinate as a "bow to feminism."

Nonetheless, the impact of feminism on the ordination of women as Reform rabbis since the early 1970s cannot be underestimated. Feminism insured that once women were granted the privilege of ordination, a sufficient number of qualified women would seek to enter the Reform rabbinate with all of its personal and professional demands. Since the mid-1980s, feminism has taken deeper root in the Jewish community. As women rabbis within the Reform movement have become more visible and accepted, standing on the *bima* beside equally visible women cantors who gained entrance into the Reform cantorate in 1975, feminist expectations have begun to transform the Reform rabbinate.[19]

In an essay entitled "How Women Are Changing the [Reform] Rabbinate," Rabbi Janet Marder points out that, as of June 1991, few of the 168 women ordained by HUC-JIR "have achieved prominent positions of leadership in the movement":

> None heads a thousand-member congregation; only three serve as senior rabbis of congregations larger than 300. But it would be wrong to conclude that women's impact on the [Reform] rabbinate has been minimal. On the contrary, one senses in conversations with women rabbis that we are witnessing the beginning of a profound transformation within the rabbinate—a change brought about by distinctive values and goals women have brought to this once exclusively male enterprise.[20]

Many women rabbis, she maintains, consciously see themselves as "agents for change" and are attempting to reshape the role of the American Reform rabbi. Most, she continues, share a commitment to three fundamental values, all of which can be described as feminist: balance, intimacy, and empowerment.

While American feminism of the late 1960s and early 1970s may have viewed the struggle for women's equality as the gaining of equal pay for equal work, by the 1980s increasing numbers of white, middle-class feminists (including Jewish feminists) began to rethink the notion of equality. If equality meant working eighty hours a week at a high-pressure job at the expense of one's health, family, and friends, perhaps the concept needed to be redefined. While the goal of equal pay for equal work was not abandoned, increasing numbers of feminists began to claim that the demand for equal access did not mean that women wanted to be "just like men." Although this realization initially helped create the phenomenon of the superwoman—a woman with a high-powered career who also attempted to be a superb wife, mother, gourmet cook, housekeeper, and so forth—by the mid-1980s, as Gloria Steinem put it, increasing numbers of American middle-class women came to realize that "having it all" meant "doing it all."

Consequently, many feminists of the late 1980s and early 1990s replaced the notion of "having it all" with that of "achieving balance." While not all of the 168 women ordained as Reform rabbis would identify themselves as feminists, the feminist emphasis on balance has proved to be appealing not just to the vast majority of women rabbis but to a small but growing number of male rabbis as well. Marder notes that "many younger male rabbis are trying to make family time a priority." While some of those she interviewed doubted whether this was a realistic expectation, I have observed, as a former faculty member at HUC-JIR in New York and as a lecturer or scholar-in-residence at dozens of Reform congregations throughout the country, that Marder's observation is accurate. I have heard an increasing number of Reform rabbis, male and female, ask, "How can I teach my congregants about the importance that Judaism attaches to family life and then sacrifice my own?"[21]

This question is related to the two other feminist values that Marder describes in her essay: intimacy and empowerment. As psychologist Carol Gilligan, theologian Catherine Keller, and others have noted, women seem to place greater value than do men on human relationships, a value that Keller calls "connectedness" and that Gilligan identifies as an "ethics of care."[22] Whether biologically or culturally based (or both), concern for others is reflected in what Marder describes as intimacy: the desire among many of the women rabbis whom she interviewed to form close relationships with their congregants, leading them to choose small congregations in which it was easier to create a sense of community. Feminism has claimed that intimacy and connectedness, long identified as "feminine" inasmuch as they are supposedly rooted in women's eternal nature, have been used by men, most notably in the last two hundred years, to relegate women to hearth and home. But connectedness is an important human value that, in the Jewish context, affirms that caring for others, recognizing the uniqueness and absolute worth of each person, and working in community move us closer to the repair of the world, *tikkun olam.*

Has the feminist emphasis on relatedness as an important human value led increasing numbers of male and female rabbis to seek smaller congregations in which greater intimacy is possible? Not only is there no evidence that supports this claim, but the data seem to point to a different conclusion. While women on the whole do not seem to be seeking larger pulpits, most male rabbis still hope to move to larger, "more prestigious" congregations.[23] Certainly the desire for greater intimacy is not the only reason why the majority of women rabbis have not aspired to larger pulpits. Nor do male rabbis who aspire to larger congregations necessarily fear or lack interest in intimacy. But if feminism has influenced the decision of many women rabbis not to seek larger, more prestigious pulpits, it has also meant that there are few if any women rabbis today who can be considered among the leaders of American Reform.

Some might attribute this both to the relatively short period during which women have been in the rabbinate and to the average youth of women rabbis in comparison to male rabbis. Yet, as long as greater prestige is attached to serving larger congregations (in the words of Joseph Glaser, executive vice-president of the CCAR, as long as our society continues to believe that "big is beautiful")[24] and as long as most women rabbis opt out of the conventional path of "upward mobility," few women will serve on the CCAR's most important committees, few will hold offices, and few will be invited to speak at CCAR conventions or to serve as spokespersons for the

Reform movement, either in the United States or at international meetings.

If women seek a style of rabbinate that precludes many of them from gaining public recognition as "leaders of Reform," their greatest impact in the United States may not be exerted "from above" but rather "from below." Women serving as pulpit rabbis have already had enormous influence on their congregants. Those serving as educators, directors of Hillel foundations in American colleges, or in other ways with Jewish youth have had impact upon students, while those working in communal positions have had effect on a great number of lay people.

The third value emphasized by many women rabbis has been empowerment. Even those who do not identify themselves as feminists speak about replacing hierarchical structures with shared responsibilities, privileges, and power. Some might label this "network model of leadership"[25] as female or feminine (rather than feminist) because it is self-consciously critical of current male models of leadership. It is, however, a form of leadership that many women rabbis have already experienced in explicitly feminist settings (for example, in consciousness-raising groups, college women's centers, feminist organizations). In my view, using these nonhierarchical models to empower others (without sacrificing one's self in the process) is most certainly feminist.

Increasingly, lay committees are creating new Friday-night liturgies;[26] growing numbers of congregants are participating in the Torah service (and adult women are becoming *benot mitzvah*); congregants are leading daily *minyanim*; parents are writing babynaming ceremonies for sons and especially for daughters;[27] twelve-year-old boys and girls are creating, with their parents, special *bar mitvah* or *bat mitzvah* services for themselves. Scholars-in-residence are frequently selected by a lay committee that invites the scholar and works with him or her in selecting topics to study.[28] To be sure, not all of these developments have been initiated by women rabbis, but growing numbers of Reform rabbis and congregants have been influenced by feminism's understanding of empowerment as essential to self-realization.

Indeed, the increasing number of women who have assumed leadership roles within their congregations testifies to the impact that feminism has had on the Reform movement. As early as 1970, 96 percent of all Reform temples in the United States had elected a woman to their congregational boards. Since then, the numbers of women serving on boards and as officers of their congregations has increased further. By the mid-1970s, it was no longer unusual for a woman to serve as synagogue president.

While much of the leadership of the Union of American Hebrew Congregations (UAHC) remains male, women have increasingly assumed positions of leadership within the movement as a whole. Since 1973, for example, when the UAHC elected its first woman vice-chair, several women have been elected to this position.[29]

Eleanor Schwartz, the former executive director of the Women of Reform Judaism (formerly known as the National Federation of Temple Sisterhoods), has argued that feminism is currently having a positive impact upon the organization. She maintains that sisterhoods, always "radical in goal if not in style," recently have begun to attract younger, college-educated, professional women who would not have considered joining the sisterhood of their congregation twenty years ago.[30] According to Schwartz, temple sisterhoods seem to be "undergoing a renaissance" as the participation of women in Reform congregations has increased, as more women have taken on leadership roles in their synagogues and in the secular world, and as feminism has reasserted the importance of women's organizations and of women's forming social, professional, and spiritual bonds with one another. To be sure, not all local sisterhoods are flourishing, but Schwartz predicts that the number of local chapters throughout the United States will rise.[31]

Feminism has also affected religious education within the Reform movement. By the mid-1970s religious school textbooks "began to present female role models other than mothers and teachers."[32] Growing numbers of women have gained full-time positions within the last decade as education directors of Reform congregations, where they have become increasingly involved in selecting the textbooks being used. (However, the centrality of women in Jewish history and religious life does not yet seem to be a major priority among those developing curricula for Reform religious schools.)[33] In 1988 the six-hundred-member National Association of (Reform) Temple Educators (NATE) elected Zena Sulkes as its first woman president and, two years later, Robin Eisenberg to succeed her; the election of Sulkes and Eisenberg reflects both the increasing number of women entering the field of Jewish education and the growing influence of women educators within the Reform movement.[34]

Feminism can also be credited with changes in Reform's liturgical texts. Michael Meyer maintains that the increasing influence of the feminist movement accounts for beginning efforts to eliminate gender-based language:

> *Gates of Prayer* [published in 1975] in its English portions removed male language in reference to the worshipers: "all men" became "all"; "fellowship" became "friendship." One English version of the *Avot* prayer made reference to the "God of our mothers" as well as our fathers. Yet, although there were experimental substitutions of nongender names and pronouns also for God, the standard Reform liturgy in the 1970s continued to refer to deity as "our Father, our King" and as "He" and "Him." Moreover, the Hebrew prayers remained untouched by feminist criticism.[35]

By the late 1980s, references to God and the words of Hebrew prayers were no longer immune to feminist criticism. As a result of changes on the local level, including the creation of congregational gender-inclusive *siddurim*, it has become difficult to speak of a "standard Reform liturgy." In response to increased support from members of the Reform rabbinate, cantorate, and laity, the Central Conference of American Rabbis has finally revised some of the services in *Gates of Prayer* so that English references to God are gender inclusive and the mothers of Israel are mentioned in both Hebrew and English prayers. Similar changes were made to the CCAR Haggadah, originally published in 1974 and revised in 1982: while the earlier edition refers to God as "Lord" and "King of the universe," the later edition identifies God as the less gender-specific "YHVH" and "Sovereign of existence." All references to God as "He" are omitted. Two recent publications by the CCAR Press refer to God as "Adonai" and "Ruler of the Universe," scrupulously avoiding any reference to God in male terms. Both texts deliberately make reference to women as central to Jewish history and contemporary Jewish life.[36]

Thus far, the feminist call for a more radical revisioning of liturgy has met with resistance from the majority of Reform congregants. Judith Plaskow, Marcia Falk, and I, along with others, have

pointed out that gender-inclusive language is not in itself a sufficient rethinking of the underlying theological issues.[37] Although by
addressing God as "Sovereign of existence" we may have succeeded
in demasculinizing images of God, praying to God as "Sovereign"
or "Ruler" continues to designate the human-Divine relationship
as one of hierarchical domination. Emphasizing God as Ruler
makes it all too easy to lose sight of the human side in the encounter with the Divine.[38] Feminists have thus argued that there is a
need for new, nonhierarchical images of God (e.g., Co-Creator,
Co-Partner, Teacher, Friend) that reinforce the mutuality of the
covenant.

A suggested liturgical change that has already gained some support in the Reconstructionist movement—that of Marcia Falk—
proposes that the opening of the traditional blessings be transformed. Substituting "Nevarech" ("Let us bless") for the formulaic
"Barukh atah adonay eloheynu melekh ha-olam" ("Blessed are you,
Lord our God, King of the Universe") eliminates the exclusive male-
ness and anthropocentrism of the prayerbook's God language, while
at the same time claiming for the community the power of blessing.[39] Falk's *Book of Blessings*, published in 1994, may well lead to a
greater receptivity to such ideas within the Reform community.[40]
In the future Reform liturgists will hopefully struggle with new
ways of transforming the liturgy so as to create images of God that
reinforce the belief, so central to Reform Judaism, that the Jewish
covenantal partnership with God entails human action and
responsibility.[41]

There has been greater receptivity to the creation of feminist
midrashim. Long used by rabbis to make traditional texts come
alive, *midrash* has recently become a popular and effective means
of writing women back into biblical history. At the instigation of
Jewish feminists in the 1970s and 1980s, growing numbers of Reform
Jews are writing *midrashim* that explore the actions and feelings of
biblical women and their significance for today.[42]

Among other steps taken by the Reform movement in the 1980s
for which feminism should receive at least partial credit was the
adoption by the CCAR of the patrilineal descent resolution. Breaking with the halakhic principle that a child of an interfaith marriage is Jewish only if the child's mother is Jewish (unless the child

formally converted to Judaism), the resolution maintained that the child of one Jewish parent—mother or father—was "under the presumption of Jewish descent." A proviso was that the child's Jewishness would also be established "through appropriate and timely public and formal acts of identification with the Jewish faith and people." Influencing those CCAR members who voted in favor of the proposal in 1983 was the recognition that, given men's growing involvement in the raising of their children (itself a byproduct of the feminist movement), "the standing of the Jewish spouses and parents in mixed marriages" should be equalized. According to Rabbi Herman E. Schaalman in his 1987 report to the CCAR assessing the patrilineality resolution, "equalization of status between female and male . . . [was] the core of our 1983 statement."[43]

The CCAR adoption of an ad hoc committee's report on homosexuality and the rabbinate also reflects the impact of feminism. First created in 1986, the seventeen-member committee sponsored an information session at the 1987 CCAR convention, local consultations, and a plenary session followed by workshops at the CCAR convention in 1989. Finally, the committee's report was approved by the members of the CCAR at the 1990 convention in Seattle. The most widely publicized aspect of the report was an endorsement of HUC-JIR's newly introduced policy of viewing the sexual orientation of an applicant to HUC-JIR's rabbinic program "only within the context of a candidate's overall suitability for the rabbinate."[44] This policy reflected a change in the former policy of viewing heterosexuality as a necessary component of rabbinic suitability and therefore denying admission to openly gay or lesbian applicants.

The concern of many within the Conference about homophobia in American society and the Jewish community resulted in a call for "greater education and dialogue in our congregations."[45] More than a liberal commitment to pluralism, this also reflects a growing awareness, mainly through feminist writings, that religious and societal attitudes toward homosexuality, like religious and societal attitudes toward women, are culturally based. Within the liberal Jewish community, there seems to be a growing acknowledgment, as Judith Plaskow has written, that "the creation of Jewish communities in which differences are valued as necessary parts of a greater whole is the institutional and experiential foundation for the recovery of the fullness of Torah."[46] To be sure, neither the Reform rabbinate nor the laity is unanimous in its support of the ordination of gay and lesbian Jews. Those within the Reform movement who value difference do not agree on the kinds of differences that should be valued. Yet the feminist emphasis on naming and valuing differences echoes the liberal commitment to civil rights and "unity in diversity," as well as to the Jewish belief that all human beings have been created with equal dignity and worth. As such, it has clarified and strengthened among many Reform Jews the view that "homosexuality can be a legitimate expression of Jewish and human personhood" and that the Reform movement should accept homosexuals "as they are and not as we [i.e., those of us who are heterosexual] would want them to be."[47]

Last, feminism to a great extent can be held accountable for shifting relationships among the Jewish movements. Many feminist-influenced positions have led to a widening gap between the Reform and Orthodox movements at the same time as they have brought Reform and Reconstructionism closer. On the role of women in the synagogue, Reform and Conservatism have become more similar, whereas positions on conversion and patrilineal descent have underscored the differences between them. In short, feminism has become a crucial factor in Reform Judaism's ongoing understanding of itself as an authentic yet diverse movement that continues to occupy a significant place in contemporary American Jewish religious life.

Notes

1. David Philipson, *The Reform Movement in Judaism* (1907; New York: Ktav, 1967), 140.
2. Ibid., 219.
3. Ibid., 220.
4. Ibid., 219.
5. Isaac Mayer Wise, *Minhag America: The Daily Prayers for American Israelites* (Cincinnati: Bloch, 1872), 12, in the section introducing the morning prayers. I am grateful to David Ellenson for bringing this reference to my attention.
6. Out of that conference emerged the Pittsburgh Platform, the statement of the principles on which Classical Reform Judaism in America rested.

7. Kaufmann Kohler, "Conference Paper," in "Authentic Report of the Proceedings of the Rabbinical Conference Held at Pittsburgh, Nov. 16, 17, 18, 1885," reprinted in Walter Jacob, ed., *The Changing World of Reform Judaism: The Pittsburgh Platform in Retrospect* (Pittsburgh: Rodef Shalom Congregation, 1985), 96.

8. Riv-Ellen Prell, "The Vision of Woman in Classical Reform Judaism," *Journal of the American Academy of Religion* 50, no. 4 (December 1982): 576.

9. Ellen M. Umansky, "Feminism and the Reevaluation of Women's Roles within American Jewish Life," in Yvonne Yazbeck Haddad and Ellison Banks Findly, eds., *Women, Religion, and Social Change* (Albany: State University of New York Press, 1985), 482.

10. *Central Conference of American Rabbis Yearbook* 32 (1922): 51.

11. In Michael A. Meyer, "A Centennial History," *Hebrew Union College–Jewish Institute of Religion: At One Hundred Years* (Cincinnati: Hebrew Union College, 1976), 99.

12. Included among them was Helen Hadassah Levinthal, who actually completed the entire rabbinic course at JIR in 1939. The faculty seriously debated the issue of ordination but decided that the time was not yet right to ordain a woman as rabbi. As a compromise, she was given a Master of Hebrew Literature degree and a certificate in Hebrew designating that she had completed the curriculum. (Rabbi Israel Levinthal, letter, April 14, 1972, to Prof. Jacob Marcus, Correspondence File, American Jewish Archives, Cincinnati, Ohio).

13. This was repeated to me by Paula Ackerman on numerous occasions between 1984 and 1989 at her homes in Atlanta and Thomaston, Georgia.

14. In one letter, dated December 1950, for example, Maurice Eisendrath wrote to Sidney Kay,

> I will be especially interested in learning whether Mrs. Ackerman does accept [the congregation's offer] and will appreciate being kept informed as to the reaction in your congregation and community. . . . I wish to emphasize my genuine desire to hear from you as I may possibly make some comment on this step that you have taken in some future reference either by the spoken or written word. (Ackerman File, American Jewish Archives, Cincinnati, Ohio)

15. Michael A. Meyer, *Response to Modernity: A History of the Reform Movement in Judaism* (New York: Oxford University Press, 1988), 359.

16. *New York Times*, November 21, 1963.

17. Conversation with Rabbi Sally Priesand, Monmouth Reform Temple, Monmouth, New Jersey, on February 1, 1991.

18. I am grateful to David Ellenson for helping to clarify my thoughts here.

19. For a more detailed discussion of women's impact on the Reform cantorate, see Mark Slobin, "Engendering the Cantorate," in Deborah Dash

Moore, ed., *YIVO Annual*, vol. 19 (Evanston, Ill.: Northwestern University Press, 1990), 147–67.

20. Janet Marder, "How Women Are Changing the Rabbinate," *Reform Judaism* (Summer 1991): 5.

21. See, for example, "Thoughts of a New Generation: Rabbis of the 1990s," in *Reform Judaism* (Summer 1990): 9, in which male and female rabbinic students at HUC-JIR spoke of the importance of balancing family and work.

22. Catherine Keller, *From a Broken Web: Separation, Sexism, and Self* (Boston: Beacon, 1986); Carol Gilligan, *In A Different Voice: Psychological Theory and Women's Development* (Cambridge, Mass.: Harvard University Press, 1982).

23. Marder, "How Women Are Changing the Rabbinate," 7.

24. Quoted in Marder, "How Women Are Changing the Rabbinate," 8.

25. A description used by Reconstructionist Sandy Sasso in writing about women in the rabbinate, quoted in Marder, "How Women Are Changing the Rabbinate," 8.

26. I served on such a committee in 1990 and 1991 at the Jewish Community Center of White Plains, the Reform congregation to which I belong. I was the only member of the committee to have worked on liturgical change before. The process, for all of us, was an exhilarating one, and we have twice since used the service that we created (with members of the committee assuming leadership roles). In deciding to undertake this task, we were encouraged by similar work already accomplished in other Reform congregations.

27. Commenting in 1984 on the recent development of parents creating covenant ceremonies for their daughters, Reform Rabbi Cary D. Kozberg wrote,

> [These ceremonies] require greater legitimacy and more widespread acceptance. *Berit Milah* is a male-oriented ritual that carries with it the spiritual and emotional weight of several thousand years. Because of this tremendous weight, it has received more emphasis than the recent ceremonies for baby girls. Though I find it difficult to throw off this male emphasis, I do believe it is necessary to promote more vigorously these rites of passage for girls. Perhaps it is time to standardize them within the Jewish community. Certainly, it is time to infuse them with the "pomp and circumstance" and emotional energy that has always accompanied circumcision for males. (*Journal of Reform Judaism* [Summer 1984]: 8)

While these ceremonies have not been standardized, they have for the most part been successfully promoted by Reform rabbis in congregations throughout the United States.

28. Of the many Reform congregations in which I have served as scholar-in-residence over the past few years, approximately half have had such lay committees.

29. Conversation with Eleanor Schwartz, executive director of the National Federation of Temple Sisterhoods, August 5, 1991.

30. Temple sisterhoods were first established in the late nineteenth century as social, educational, and philanthropic organizations. By the second decade of the twentieth century, they were in existence in almost every Reform congregation in the United States and in 1913 they were coordinated on a national level as the National Federation of Temple Sisterhoods.

31. Conversation with Eleanor Schwartz, August 5, 1991.

32. Michael Meyer, *Response to Modernity*, 380.

33. Conversation with Nancy Bossov, Director of Education, Jewish Community Center of White Plains, White Plains, New York, August 6, 1991.

34. My thanks to Sherry Blumberg, assistant professor of education at HUC-JIR in New York for providing me with this information.

35. Michael Meyer, *Response to Modernity*, 380.

36. *Haneirot Halalu: These Lights Are Holy* (1990), a liturgy edited by Rabbi Elyse Frishman to be used at home in celebration of Hanukkah; *Seder Tu Bishevat: The Festival of Trees*, edited by Rabbi Adam Fisher for congregations or small groups gathering together to celebrate the renewal of nature. I would argue that the Hebrew "Adonai" (Lord) remains a male image of deity. The intention of the creators of these new liturgies, however, is to invoke an image that congregants do not consciously view as male, perhaps because they do not know Hebrew, perhaps because the word "Adonai" does not conjure up as easily the kinds of exclusively male, anthropomorphic images as does the English word "Lord."

37. See, for example, Judith Plaskow, *Standing Again at Sinai: Judaism from a Feminist Perspective* (San Francisco: Harper and Row, 1990); Marcia Falk, "Toward a Feminist Jewish Reconstruction of Prayer," *Tikkun* 4, no. 4 (July/August 1989): 53–57; and Ellen M. Umansky, "Creating a Jewish Feminist Theology," in Judith Plaskow and Carol P. Christ, eds., *Weaving the Visions: New Patterns in Feminist Spirituality* (San Francisco: Harper and Row, 1989), 187–98, and "Charting Our Future: Liberal Judaism in the Twenty-First Century," *Central Conference of American Rabbis Yearbook* 100 (1991): 63–69.

38. See especially Umansky, "Charting Our Future," 66.

39. See, for example, Marcia Falk, "Notes on Composing New Blessings: Toward a Feminist-Jewish Reconstruction of Prayer," in *Journal of Feminist Studies in Religion* 3, no. 3 (Spring 1987): 39–53.

40. Soon to be published by Harper and Row.

41. Certainly other Jewish movements see the covenant as central and affirm the importance of God and the Jewish people as covenantal partners. What my statement implies is that "covenantal theology," as articulated most clearly by Eugene Borowitz, has come to occupy a

central place in Reform theological teachings. While not all Reform Jews would agree with Borowitz's belief that being God's covenantal partner means that "somewhat greater priority must be given to Judaism in the balance of belief than to personal self-determination," most if not all theologically minded Reform Jews *would* agree, I think, that "the autonomous Jewish self derives its autonomy as part of the people of Israel's Covenant partnership with God. Such a Judaism knows no isolated, atomistic, worthy self. Rather, selfhood itself necessarily involves God, people and history" (Eugene Borowitz, "The Crux of Liberal Jewish Thought: Personal Autonomy," in Borowitz, ed., *Choices in Modern Jewish Thought: A Partisan Guide* [New York: Behrman, 1983], 269, 271).

42. Those interested in feminist *midrashim* might look at the first and second editions of *Taking the Fruit: Modern Women's Tales of the Bible*, ed. Jane Sprague Zones, published by the Woman's Institute for Continuing Jewish Education in San Diego (1982, 1989). Feminist *midrashim* can also be found in the pages of the *Melton Journal*, the *Reconstructionist*, *Tikkun*, and the *Journal of Reform Judaism* (now the *CCAR Journal*). As someone who writes feminist *midrash*, I have met dozens of Reform Jews throughout the country who are working to create feminist *midrashim*, often with the support and guidance of their rabbi. I have also received from numerous Reform rabbis, male and female, feminist *midrashim* that they have written and delivered in sermons to their congregation.

43. Herman E. Schaalman, "Patrilineal Descent: A Report and Assessment," *Central Conference of American Rabbis Yearbook* 97 (1988): 110.

44. Report of the Ad Hoc Committee on Homosexuality and the Rabbinate Adopted by the Convention of the Central Conference of American Rabbis, June 25, 1990, *Central Conference of American Rabbis Yearbook* 100 (1991): 111.

45. Ad Hoc Committee Report, *Central Conference of American Rabbis Yearbook* 100 (1991): 111.

46. Judith Plaskow, *Standing Again at Sinai*, 106.

47. Yoel H. Kahn, "Judaism and Homosexuality," *Homosexuality, the Rabbinate, and Liberal Judaism: Papers Prepared for the Ad-Hoc Committee on Homosexuality and the Rabbinate* (CCAR, 1989), 10, citing and affirming views originally presented to the CCAR in 1973 by Rabbi Sanford Ragins.

CHAPTER 17

Ezrat Nashim and the Emergence of a New Jewish Feminism

Paula E. Hyman

It is all the more difficult to address a contemporary phenomenon in historical terms when the historian in question has been a participant in the process she seeks to analyze. I am an engaged participant-observer of American Jewish feminism, and my reflections are the interpretation of a historian sensitive to feminist theory but, like most historians, eclectic in method and approach.

American Jewish feminism is about twenty years old. Its pioneers were largely well-educated young women deeply influenced by general feminist currents of the time. American feminism both provided evidence of the subordination of women in patriarchal cultures and championed a vision of equality between the sexes. Feminists who were deeply rooted in Judaism and Jewish culture recognized the applicability of the feminist cultural critique to their own heritage and community and proceeded to revision a Jewish community in which they could participate fully beyond the domestic sphere.

What we did not realize then was that we had predecessors. As recent historical scholarship has documented, for several generations American Jewish women had struggled to claim a place in Jewish communal life and to expand their possibilities for religious education and self-expression. Because Sunday School education and some forms of American philanthropy in the nineteenth century were considered appropriate to the female sex, middle-class

American Jewish women devoted themselves to the social housekeeping of their Jewish communities.[1] Through the national organizations that they created—the National Council of Jewish Women in 1893 and Hadassah in 1912—they asserted the right to place certain issues, such as white slavery, on the agenda of the Jewish community, to administer their own social welfare projects, even in the face of opposition from male communal leaders, and to develop their own political positions.[2] The early leaders of the National Council of Jewish Women also established their local chapters and programs with the aim of enhancing the Jewish knowledge of their members so that they could properly carry out their responsibility as agents of the transmission of Judaism to the younger generation.[3] In the Reform and Conservative movements the national associations of synagogue sisterhoods also did more than decorate the sanctuary for festivals and pour tea for congregants at Oneg Shabbats. Their leaders also called for increased participation of women in the ritual life of the synagogue.[4] The recovery of the past history of American Jewish women is itself one of the marks of the ongoing impact of feminism upon Jewish communal life, in this case upon Jewish scholarship.

Under the impact of the new American feminism, Jewish feminists of the 1970s forged a program that was based on concepts of gender equality more far reaching than any previously articulated by American Jewish women.[5] The earliest demands of Jewish feminists focused on questions of equalizing the status of women within Judaism, opening positions of power to them, and redressing the injustices that women suffered because of the patriarchal assumptions of halakhah. Thus, the small New York group that called itself Ezrat Nashim—perhaps the first contemporary Jewish feminist group to concern itself with religious as well as secular issues— publicly called upon the Conservative movement in 1972 to count women in the *minyan* and enable them to participate fully in public religious life, to train women to be rabbis and cantors, to encourage them to assume leadership roles in the synagogue and community, and to permit them to serve as witnesses and to initiate divorce. Recognizing that many of the halakhic disabilities that women experienced stemmed from their exemption from some *mitzvot*, Ezrat Nashim's "Call for Change" also asked for equal obligation of women in Jewish law.[6] The background statement accompanying Ezrat Nashim's press release declared that the group had come to the realization that change in the status of women in Judaism "could be brought about only through the concerted effort on the part of women such as ourselves to bring pressure upon American Jewish institutions."[7] Ezrat Nashim's manifesto drew upon the rhetoric of contemporary feminism; and the message of self-empowerment of the first stages of 1970s feminism spurred the ten women of Ezrat Nashim, the female activists of the North American Jewish Students' Network (who organized the Jewish Feminist conferences of 1973 and 1974), and numerous other Jewish women meeting in consciousness-raising groups to engage in political lobbying on behalf of the feminist agenda.

The message of early Jewish feminism fell upon a receptive community. Middle-class American Jews were sympathetic to ideologies that utilized a liberal discourse of egalitarianism and pluralism; they were aware that their own claim to equality in the modern world drew upon the premises of liberalism. Furthermore, they were urban and urbane, and more highly educated than the general American population. They were particularly sensitive to charges of discrimination and amenable to changes that could be made, at least at first, through symbolic actions rather than a real transfer of power.

There were specific factors in the development of American Judaism and in the character of Jewish feminism that facilitated the extraordinarily rapid achievement of most of the feminist goals enunciated in the early 1970s. The introduction of mixed seating in the Reform and Conservative synagogue and the promotion of equality of education for boys and girls in both denominations set the stage for greater participation by women in synagogue ritual. The sacred space of the non-Orthodox American synagogue had long been at least partly degendered, and the dismissal of women on the grounds that they were Jewishly unlearned could not be sustained in movements that had equally low educational expectations for children and adults of both sexes. Significantly, the appeal of Ezrat Nashim to the Conservative Rabbinical Assembly was all the more effective because the members of the group represented the elite youth of the movement. As the women of Ezrat Nashim stated in their "Call for Change," "To educate women and deny them the opportunity to act from this knowledge is an affront to their intelligence, talents and integrity. As products of . . . the Ramah camps, LTF [Leaders' Training Fellowship], USY [United Synagogue Youth], and the [Jewish Theological] Seminary, we feel this tension acutely."[8] In the Reform movement, which disregarded halakhic constraints, the logic of mixed seating and equal education led to the decision to admit women to rabbinic school in the late 1960s, before a Jewish feminist movement had crystallized. Sally Priesand was ordained as the first female American rabbi in 1972.[9]

In addition to their elite education, Jewish feminist activists also displayed a profound commitment to Judaism and the Jewish community that differentiated them from secular feminists of Jewish background. Not only did they focus their attention upon the Jewish community, but they also avoided the radical rejection of religious tradition that characterized some secular and Christian feminists. While Mary Daly, teaching at a Catholic college, developed her concept of women's "Exodus communities" that ultimately led her to break completely with the Church, Jewish feminists affirmed our Jewishness and rejected the notion of a static tradition whose sexism was fundamental to its message.[10] Because our identity was grounded as much in our religio-ethnic consciousness as in our gender, Jewish feminists were always conscious of the need to function within the Jewish community, even as we dissented from some of its behavior and ideology.

The focus on the community rather than the individual as the necessary locus for change facilitated the early, and ongoing, successes of American Jewish feminism. Jewish feminists also benefited, of course, from the fact that any ten adults can form a religious community and that there exists no ecclesiastical control over American Jewish life. The decentralization and localism of Jewish religious and communal affairs enabled Jewish feminists to press for change at the grass-roots level even as they addressed some issues in national institutions. It also enabled Orthodox feminists to meet their passionate need to approach the Torah directly in worship by establishing their own local *tefillah* (prayer) groups, sometimes with the support of sympathetic local rabbis, without

having to confront directly the formidable opposition of the Orthodox rabbinic establishment.[11] Some have faulted Jewish feminism
for having failed to institutionalize itself,[12] but one can argue in
rebuttal that the localism and diversity of Jewish feminism have
provided flexibility, enabling feminist activists to match their strategies to local needs and to gain adherents in a variety of communal
institutional settings.

The mechanisms that Jewish feminists have chosen to present
issues have also proven effective. The various baby-naming ceremonies for girls are a case in point. Meeting a felt need to welcome
daughters into the Jewish covenantal community with the same
excitement that greets newborn sons, the new rituals, which borrowed liturgically from the *brit milah* (circumcision) ceremony,
were disseminated through a variety of means. In the early 1970s,
those who participated in the new ceremonies, which were always
held amidst a crowd of family and friends, often passed word of the
new rite along to others and sought copies of ceremonies to use
when their own daughters were born.

Self-consciously seeking to create new rituals that, perhaps paradoxically, drew upon traditional Jewish themes, feminist parents
published accounts of the rationales for their ritual innovation and
for the traditional elements they had adapted. As a highly educated
and Jewishly literate group with connections to the Jewish counterculture of the late 1960s, they had access to such media as *Response* and the *Jewish Catalogues*; Ezrat Nashim even created, and
made available at low cost, a small pamphlet of feminist baby-
naming ceremonies (as well as a study guide and pamphlet of readings on women and Judaism).[13] So widespread among committed
Jews was the perception of injustice in the traditional response to
the birth of boys and girls that some Orthodox parents, who found
the new rituals too innovative for their taste, still developed welcoming ceremonies for daughters (even though the infant was not
formally named or entered into the covenant through them) or
adopted the Sephardi custom of the *seder zeved ha-bat* (celebration
for the gift of a daughter).[14] Sympathetic rabbis introduced the new
rituals to their colleagues and congregants. Thus, a combination of
informal networking and energetic dissemination of material in
print served to introduce and legitimate a feminist ritual. A similar

process, though on a smaller scale, occurred in the phenomenon of the adult bat mitzvah, in which a new rite was created to mark symbolically within a religious community grown women's assertion of their new-found equal status in the synagogue.[15]

Although the original feminist impulse originated outside the institutional framework of the organized Jewish community, supporters of equality for women were present at all levels within the institutions of the Reform and Conservative movements as well as within nonreligious Jewish communal organizations. Moreover, because of their rootedness within the Jewish community, Jewish feminist leaders were welcomed as speakers at synagogues and meetings of Jewish women's groups throughout the country. One of the first acts of the short-lived Jewish Feminist Organization, founded in 1974 in the wake of the second Jewish Feminist Conference, was the establishment of a speakers' bureau. Jewish feminists have also found a ready audience for the scholarly and popular literature that they have produced; feminist issues have been discussed regularly in Jewish magazines and journals, and feminists have succeeded in publishing the magazine *Lilith*, albeit somewhat irregularly, since 1976. The bibliography of writing on Jewish women and on women and Judaism in the past two decades is most impressive, especially in comparison with the paucity of material on those subjects in the preceding century.[16]

With the passage of time, feminists increasingly achieved positions of influence within important Jewish institutions. Less than twelve years after Ezrat Nashim presented its "Call for Change" to the Conservative movement, for example, two of its original members, Judith Hauptman and I, by then faculty members of the Jewish Theological Seminary, were able to take part in the vote to admit women to the movement's rabbinical school. Although the Association for Jewish Studies was established some twenty years ago by an all-male group of Judaic scholars, it now includes an active women's caucus of more than seventy-five members that, among other things, organizes panels for the association's annual conference. Many women staff local federations and their agencies, though generally at middle-management levels, and for the first time a woman, Shoshana Cardin, has served as president of the Council of Jewish Federations. The Union of American Hebrew

Congregations has had a Task Force on the Equality of Women in Judaism for many years, and the several hundred women who serve as rabbis and cantors in the Reform, Reconstructionist, and Conservative movements play an active role in their professional societies. In Reform and Conservative synagogues women increasingly serve as members of the board and as presidents.[17] This "infiltration" of feminists has served to raise women's issues quietly, and effectively, behind doors as well as prominently in public forums. An "old girls network" has taken its place alongside its male counterpart, thereby opening up the Jewish community to new perspectives.

Perhaps most important, through the activity of anonymous supporters, both female and male, of the feminist agenda of equal opportunity, the shape of the Jewish community has been transformed. For most Jews, a new social reality has eroded the psychological resistance that was the initial response to feminist innovation. In Reform temples and in Reconstructionist and the majority of Conservative synagogues, women participate fully in the ritual. My teenage daughters, graduates of day schools and regulars at *shul*, have lived their entire lives in an environment that takes gender equality for granted. Their peers, although they may be less observant or Jewishly educated, know that women can be rabbis and cantors, that the Torah is equally the heritage of women and men.

Although most Orthodox Jews reject feminist ideology, feminism has had an impact nonetheless in many sectors of the American Orthodox community. Most Orthodox rabbis have reacted with apologetics, scorn, or vituperation to the feminist critique of Judaism and its assertion of women's need for, and right to, equal access to Jewish learning, public religious expression, and leadership. In some Orthodox communities resistance to feminism—signaled by the raising of *mechitsas* and the lowering of sleeves—has become a benchmark of true piety. Yet the challenge of feminism has spurred moderate Orthodox rabbis like Saul Berman to explore the possibilities within the bounds of halakhah for enhanced participation of women in public ritual and for redress of the suffering of the *agunah* (chained wife).[18] It has led to increased emphasis upon advanced (albeit separate and gender-specific) Jewish education for women within Orthodox schools, even as Orthodox leaders denounce feminism. Just as feminist-inspired celebrations to mark the birth of a daughter have won acceptance in modern Orthodox communities, so, too, many girls in those communities mark their entry into adulthood with a bat mitzvah rite. Although the Orthodox bat mitzvah ceremony may be limited to a *devar Torah* (brief Torah lesson) delivered by the celebrant after conclusion of the formal religious services, still the girl coming of age has an opportunity to develop and display her learning and to be celebrated for it. Finally, the persistence of women's *tefillah* groups, even in the face of strong opposition, demonstrates the importance for some Orthodox women of the powerful experience of reading from the Torah and raising their voices together in prayer.

The issues of equal access represent only the first stage of Jewish feminism. From the late 1970s the feminist critique of Judaism has suggested that Judaism itself needed to be refashioned. Feminists argued that the Jewish tradition transmitted from one generation to another in the form of classical texts was incomplete, for it included no women's voices. The task of this generation was to create a woman's midrash, that is, to interpret the gamut of Jewish texts through the prism of women's experience. Feminists have also suggested the need to create new Jewish liturgies that reimaged God (in addition to modifying God-language) and that developed a new Jewish theology.[19]

On these profound, and more radical, issues Jewish feminists, for a variety of reasons, have had less success than on issues of equal access. First, there is no consensus among feminists themselves as to the necessity of the envisioned changes. Supporters of equal access, such as Arthur Green, the former president of the Reconstructionist Rabbinical College, have dissented from some of the experimental creativity that accompanies the development of a feminist Judaism.[20] Second, whereas communal support for egalitarianism remains strong, many Jews fear radical change in the nature of Judaism. Even those who do not share the theological premises of traditional Judaism may remain emotionally attached to traditional liturgy. Other American Jews, perhaps the majority, do not take Judaism as a religion seriously enough to struggle with the feminist call for its redefinition. On this theological and liturgical ground the perceived need for innovation clashes with the power of authenticity embedded in Jewish tradition. Finally, although feminists are prominent within the full spectrum of Jewish institutional life, for the most part the proponents of radical change in Judaism remain outside the central organizations of American Jewry. Indeed, they have introduced many of their liturgical innovations in small, often separatist women's communities; as yet, these innovations have not had much impact within the larger Jewish community.

No analysis of the impact of Jewish feminism, as well as its prospects for the future, would be complete without consideration of the resistance to change within the American Jewish community. The reluctance of some congregations to hire women rabbis, particularly as senior rabbis in large congregations or in the more prestigious pulpits, bespeaks a deep ambivalence about women in positions of authority. For some American Jews it is easier to accept women as cantors than as rabbis, because cantors are seen as subordinate religious functionaries. I have heard colleagues speak with horror about the "feminization" of the rabbinate and its consequent decline in status, even though women now comprise at least a third of students in such prestigious fields as law and medicine. Although women have entered Jewish communal service in large numbers, they continue to be clustered in the lower ranks and in middle management. Only a tiny percentage have attained the position of executive director of federations.[21]

Most disturbingly, many communal spokesmen continue to posit an inherent conflict between feminism and Jewish survival. From the middle of the nineteenth century, Jewish leaders have held women, especially mothers, responsible for defections from Judaism and the Jewish community, even though radical assimilation was far more common among males than females.[22] That tendency to project onto women communal guilt regarding assimilation continues, though in a muted form, when Jewish communal spokesmen attribute to women virtually sole responsibility for Jewish survival and criticize them alone for seeking self-fulfillment at the expense of Jewish communal goals.

The feminist task that confronts American Jewry as it prepares for the twenty-first century is less obvious than was the challenge of two decades ago. It calls for the sharing of power, and not merely equal access to the entry level of Jewish communal leadership, both lay and rabbinic. It necessitates confronting the challenges of liturgical change and accepting greater diversity of religious expression than American Jews have previously felt comfortable with. Most important, it requires a recognition that the struggle to define, and attain, equality is never permanently accomplished.

Notes

1. See, for example, Evelyn Bodek, " 'Making Do': Jewish Women and Philanthropy," in Murray Friedman, ed., *Jewish Life in Philadelphia* (Philadelphia: ISHI, 1983), 143–62.
2. On the National Council of Jewish Women, see Charlotte Baum, Paula Hyman, and Sonya Michel, *The Jewish Woman in America* (New York: Dial, 1976), 48–52, 165–70; and Faith Rogow, *Gone to Another Meeting: The National Council of Jewish Women, 1893–1993* (Tuscaloosa: University of Alabama Press, 1993). On Hadassah's independent stance within American Zionism, see Melvin I. Urofsky, *American Zionism from Herzl to the Holocaust* (Garden City, N.Y.: Anchor, 1975). On Jewish women volunteers, see Beth Wenger, "Jewish Women and Voluntarism: Beyond the Myth of Enablers," *American Jewish History* 70, no. 1 (Autumn 1989): 37–54.
3. Rogow, *Gone to Another Meeting*, 14, 20–21, 23–24, 59–72; and Sue Levi Elwell, "The Founding and Early Programs of the National Council of Jewish Women: Study and Practice as Jewish Women's Religious Expression" (Ph.D. diss., Indiana University, 1982).
4. Pamela Nadell, paper delivered at the Berkshire Conference of Women Historians, June 1990. On the important role of Orthodox synagogue sisterhoods in interwar New York, see Jenna Weissman Joselit, *New York's Jewish Jews: The Orthodox Community in the Interwar Years* (Bloomington: Indiana University Press, 1990), 97–122.
5. For a comprehensive survey of the relations between contemporary feminism and American Jewry, see Sylvia Barack Fishman, "The Impact of Feminism on American Jewish Life," *American Jewish Year Book* (1989): 3–62, and *A Breath of Life: Feminism in the American Jewish Community* (New York: Free Press, 1993). On the early years of American Jewish feminism, see Anne Lapidus Lerner, "Who Hast Not Made Me a Man: The Movement for Equal Rights in American Jewry," *American Jewish Year Book* (1977): 3–38.
6. "Jewish Women Call for Change," March 1972, my personal archive.
7. "Background Statement on Ezrat Nashim," March 1972, my personal archive.

8. "Jewish Women Call for Change," March 1972, my personal archive.
9. Michael A. Meyer, *Response to Modernity: A History of the Reform Movement in Judaism* (New York: Oxford University Press, 1988), 379–80; and Ellen Umansky, "Women in Judaism: From the Reform Movement to Contemporary Jewish Religious Feminism," in Rosemary Ruether and Eleanor McLaughlin, eds., *Women of Spirit: Female Leadership in the Jewish and Christian Traditions* (New York: Simon and Schuster, 1979), 333–54.
10. Mary Daly, *Beyond God the Father: Toward a Philosophy of Women's Liberation* (Boston: Beacon, 1973).
11. On women's tefillah groups and their reception, see Rivkah Haut, "From Women: Piety Not Rebellion," *Sh'ma*, May 17, 1985, 110–12; "Women's Prayer Groups and the Orthodox Synagogue," in Susan Grossman and Rivka Haut, eds., *Daughters of the King: Women and the Synagogue* (Philadelphia: Jewish Publication Society, 1992), 135–57; and Sylvia Barack Fishman, *A Breath of Life*, 158–66.
12. See, for example, Jack Wertheimer, "Recent Trends in American Judaism," *American Jewish Year Book* (1989): 155.
13. "Blessing the Birth of a Daughter: Jewish Naming Ceremonies for Girls," ed. Toby Fishbein Reifman with Ezrat Nashim, 1977; "Women and Judaism: Selected Readings," 1973; "Study Guide on the Jewish Woman," 1974; all from my personal archive. The Jewish Women's Resource Center in New York has a collection of more than fifty birth ceremonies for girls.
14. Examples of both may be found in the Ezrat Nashim pamphlet.
15. On the adult bat mitzvah see Susan Weidman Schneider, *Jewish and Female* (New York: Simon and Schuster, 1984), 142; and Ruth Mason, "Adult Bat Mitzvah: A Revolution for Women and Synagogues," *Lilith* 14, no. 4 (Fall 1989): 21–24.
16. On the resources available to Jewish feminists, on central issues of their concern, and for a selected bibliography, see Schneider, *Jewish and Female*.
17. Flyer of Jewish Feminist Organization, my personal archive; Anne Lapidus Lerner, "The Unfinished Agenda," *Judaism* 36, no. 2 (Spring 1987): 169–72; Fishman, "The Impact of Feminism," 10.
18. See, for example, Saul Berman, "The Status of Women in Halakhic Judaism," in Elizabeth Koltun, ed., *The Jewish Woman: New Perspectives* (New York: Schocken, 1976), 114–28.
19. On these issues, see especially Judith Plaskow, *Standing Again at Sinai* (San Francisco: Harper and Row, 1990), as well as her articles, "The Right Question Is Theological," in Susannah Heschel, ed., *On Being a Jewish Feminist: A Reader* (New York: Schocken, 1983), 223–33, and "Language, God, and Liturgy: A Feminist Perspective," *Response* 44 (Spring 1983): 3–14; Susannah Heschel, ed., *On Being a Jewish Feminist*, xiii–xxxvi; Marcia Falk, "Notes on Composing New Blessings:

Toward a Feminist-Jewish Reconstruction of Prayer," *Journal of Feminist Studies in Religion* 3 (Spring 1987): 39–53; and Ellen Umansky, "(Re)Imaging the Divine," *Response* 13 (Fall/Winter 1982): 110–19.

20. Arthur Green, "Keeping Feminist Creativity Jewish," *Sh'ma*, January 10, 1986, 33–35.

21. Fishman, "The Impact of Feminism," 33–35, and *A Breath of Life*, 201–29; Lerner, "Unfinished Agenda," 172.

22. See my "The Modern Jewish Family: Image and Reality," in David Kraemer, ed., *The Jewish Family: Metaphor and Memory* (New York: Oxford University Press, 1989), 188–90.

CHAPTER 18

Conservative Judaism: The Ethical Challenge of Feminist Change

Judith Hauptman

Jewish feminism has made American Judaism of the 1990s dramatically different from that of the 1960s.[1] Over the last few decades, women have become fully integrated into the religious life of the community. For the first time, they count as full-fledged members of a prayer quorum, read from the Torah in public, and assume such leadership roles as rabbi, cantor, and synagogue officer.

Why have American Jews, unlike most others around the world, welcomed Jewish feminism so warmly? Elsewhere, most notably in Israel, Jewish feminism has not captured the public imagination. The success of the Jewish feminist movement in the United States can be attributed to a number of factors, mainly the continuing popularity of liberalism, the openness of American society to new ideas, the coming of age of the Jewish community, and its pluralistic denominational structure. The last two require some explanation.

By the 1970s, many Jews were already well integrated into American social and professional life. Young Jews on the college campus were no longer seeking to suppress their ethnicity but instead were seeking to identify Jewishly and to assimilate for themselves the best of the secular and Jewish worlds. The proliferation of Jewish studies programs after the Six-Day War in 1967 had led to an increase in the number of young Jews conversant with classical Jewish texts and able to analyze them with rather sophisticated critical tools. When secular feminism became popular in the late sixties, it was individuals like these who were in a position to issue the first feminist critique of Jewish practice.[2]

The denominational structure of the American Jewish community also allowed the Jewish feminist movement to be accepted rapidly. Each of the three large denominations had a well-established network of affiliated synagogues, a sizeable membership, venerable rabbinical training institutions, and a distinct outlook on the practice of Judaism.[3] When challenged by the feminist critique, each movement responded differently.

Viewing halakhah as binding and stable, Orthodoxy found feminist change unthinkable. Since Orthodoxy seeks to insulate itself from its surroundings, viewing itself as an antidote to a morally bankrupt society, it is unlikely that feminist change will ever be instituted in this movement. Reform Judaism subscribes to the principle of personal autonomy, according to which each individual makes decisions for himself or herself about Jewish practice. Reform accepted most of the feminist critique willingly and is now beginning to grant women full, real equality in its main institutions.

Given the nature of Conservative Judaism and its history, feminism presents an interesting case study because it did not become the extensive battleground it could have been for feminist modification. Although there was heated debate, the feminist agenda was accepted earlier and changes occurred more rapidly than might have been expected.

First, the Conservative movement had already made a number of radical changes in ritual, one of the best known of which related to Sabbath observance. Following the post–World War II exodus to the suburbs, the Conservative movement found its synagogues nearly empty on Saturday mornings. Concluding (mistakenly) that the reason for this lapse was a reluctance on the part of many people to travel on the Sabbath, it issued a responsum in 1950 permitting riding to the synagogue and back home but nowhere else.[4] Although this did little to solve the problem of Sabbath attendance, it signaled to a generation of Jews that the Conservative movement viewed halakhah as a dynamic system, responsive to the changing needs of its members. Second, the movement had already adopted a number of measures that increased women's involvement in Jewish practice, such as replacing the *meḥitzah* with family pews[5] and giving girls in its summer camps and junior congregations an opportunity to fill leadership roles in the prayer service. Third, an open-minded approach to the study of classical Jewish texts permitted its rabbinic leadership to become aware of past change and the possibilities of future change. Anyone who took courses in Talmud at the Jewish Theological Seminary (JTS) in the sixties, as I did, had those points repeatedly driven home.

It is, therefore, not surprising that women who had learned about Judaism in Conservative circles and who had then become acquainted with feminism on the college campus were the first who attempted to explore the intersection of the two. It was they who discovered that a tradition that prided itself on its ingrained ethical stance did not apply the same high-minded principles to relations between the sexes. And it was they who discovered that Judaism, like other age-old religions, reserved the life of the mind and the spirit for men only. As enamored as these women were of Jewish observance, they were deeply frustrated by its entrenched male bias. Rather than spurn the whole system because of its sexism, they joined together in the fall of 1971, formed a consciousness-raising group called Ezrat Nashim, meaning "succor for women,"[6] and formulated a call for change. Their platform included a long list of demands, from counting women in the prayer quorum and ordaining them as rabbis to eliminating women's disabilities in the area of divorce.[7] The common thread running through most of their requests was that halakhah must change in order to restore ethical balance to Jewish practice.

The first feminist change in the Conservative movement actually predated the Jewish feminist movement by more than fifteen years. Halakhic norms for Conservative Jews are officially set not by individual rabbis but by the Committee on Jewish Law and Standards (CJLS), a group of twenty-five rabbis who study halakhic problems brought to their attention by members of the Conservative movement's Rabbinical Assembly. Any resolution approved by at least six of its members becomes an official position of the Committee and a legitimate option for a Conservative rabbi to implement in his congregation.[8] This committee had decided in 1955 to permit women to be called for an *aliyah* to the Torah.[9] The option was implemented in only a few synagogues in the Minneapolis area, a city with a strong liberal tradition, where women were apparently interested in fuller ritual participation.[10] Following the decision, little happened for more than a decade. But in the seventies, at a time when women across the United States were growing sensitive to the seemingly irreconcilable differences between feminism and Judaism, more changes were introduced.

In the spring of 1972, the members of Ezrat Nashim decided to bring their feminist critique to the public's attention by airing it at the annual convention of the Rabbinical Assembly. Their charges of sexism in halakhah, principally in the synagogue and in marital matters, resonated among rabbis and laypeople. I still remember the surprise felt by members of this group at the speed and enthusiasm with which its feminist position was endorsed.

One year later, in 1973, the CJLS voted to count women in the prayer quorum. This measure was hurried through the committee by a few rabbis who felt it was an opportune moment to inform the American public that the Conservative movement recognized the equality of women before the law and was able to change synagogue ritual accordingly. Word of the decision was rushed to the newspapers, so that most Conservative rabbis first learned of it from the pages of the *New York Times*.[11] In 1974, the CJLS adopted a series of proposals that equalized women and men in all areas of Jewish ritual.[12] As a result, a Conservative rabbi could, for instance, allow a woman to serve as *sheliah tzibbur* (prayer leader), count in the *zimmun* for *birkhat ha-mazon* (quorum for Grace), and function as a witness.

For the rest of the decade, synagogue after synagogue wrestled with the issue of ritual change. Many people saw feminism as an attempt to justify philosophically what they believed was an ongoing erosion of halakhic standards. They framed the underlying problem in simple terms as tradition and halakhah on the one hand versus the feminist critique on the other. In the eyes of many serious practitioners of halakhah, counting women in the prayer quorum or letting them read from the Torah was equivalent to eating unkosher food. Such a response made it clear that the forces of traditionalism had inculcated in many laypeople the belief that halakhah does not change, that continuity is immutability. Instead of viewing the feminist critique as an expression of ever-deepening commitment to halakhah and a natural outcome of serious analysis of its built-in mechanisms for change, they labeled the feminist critique as antinomian. Others saw feminism as a just social cause whose time had come. As a result, virtually every Conservative synagogue in the United States in the seventies and eighties accommodated feminism in some way, from merely letting a woman open the door to the ark to according full gender equality.[13]

The issue of ordaining women was first placed on the agenda by Ezrat Nashim in 1972 and debated for more than ten years. Allowing a woman to fill the pivotal role of religious leader of the synagogue seemed a greater break than allowing women to count in the *minyan*, which actually, halakhically speaking, was far more radical. A fact-finding commission was established, testimony was collected in Conservative synagogues across the United States, and a report summarized the various arguments.[14] The majority of those consulted, as well as of the commission members, favored the ordination of women. The minority opposed ordination because of its purported halakhic indefensibility.

Both the advocates and opponents of women's ordination agreed that most contemporary rabbinic functions, such as religious role model, teacher, preacher, and pastoral counselor, could be filled by women without making any halakhic adjustments. Although women had not engaged in these activities in the past, there were no explicit laws preventing them from doing so. The objections raised to ordaining women involved ancillary rabbinic roles—leading prayer services and serving as a witness at weddings, divorces, and conversions. Mishnah Megillah 4:3, the earliest law to address this issue, states that only men may count in the quorum of ten for prayer and discharge the prayer responsibilities of others. The Talmud and codes explicitly state that women do not qualify as witnesses.[15]

A number of JTS faculty members prepared position papers, some arguing in favor of ordination and others arguing against it. A responsum written by Rabbi Joel Roth proposed that women voluntarily accept the obligation to pray daily at fixed times, thereby equalizing their obligations with those of men;[16] upon doing so, they could count in the *minyan* and lead it in prayer.[17] Roth predicted that since only some women are inclined to accept such additional obligations, Jewish women would split into two groups: those who would continue to regard their requirement to pray as voluntary and those who would regard it as obligatory. Only women in the latter category could seek ordination.

As for women serving as witnesses, Roth declared that the rabbis of the Talmud, basing themselves on Deuteronomy 19:15 and 19:17, considered women ineligible and viewed them as unreliable. Since women's reliability was no longer in question, there was no longer any reason to exclude them. He therefore recommended invoking the ultimate halakhic act, abrogation of a biblical proscription.

In all, Roth proposed a reasonable plan for changing certain aspects of Jewish law in order to allow for the ordination of women. He insisted that male-female equality played no role in his thinking.[18] He meant that his conclusions were warranted by objective analysis of the law codes themselves and did not occur through a deliberate attempt to elicit leniencies or interpret the text from the a priori principle that women should be accorded equality. By implication, Roth held that looking actively for ways to solve social problems was unacceptable. But decisors and judges, both activists and those who exercise judicial restraint, have no choice but to read a text through the lens of their own life experiences. This has always been true of Jewish law and of secular systems. What distinguishes the Conservative approach to halakhah is an acknowledgment that the system is responsive to evolving ethical truths and, at the same time, that problems are soluble within the existing legal framework. Orthodox decisors, for political or personal reasons, claim that halakhic change in response to socially generated problems is impossible.

The various JTS faculty papers on the ordination of women[19] provided the basis for voting on the admission of women to the Rabbinical School. Although the issue was first brought to the faculty in 1979, deep rifts in its ranks—and also, I suspect, Chancellor Gerson Cohen's inner turmoil—caused the vote to be tabled. Seminary Rector and esteemed professor of Talmud Saul Lieberman had issued no statement whatsoever on the ordination of women but was assumed to be opposed.[20] In the fall of 1983, a few months after

Lieberman's death, Cohen brought the issue up again. Prodded by the chancellor, the faculty approved the admission of women by a substantial majority.[21] It did not predicate its decision on the acceptance of any particular position paper, but, when implementing the vote, decided in subcommittee to admit women as candidates for ordination only if they indicated that they had accepted upon themselves the same obligation to perform religious rituals as men accepted.

According to Anne Lerner, author of one of the faculty papers, the Roth responsum is followed mainly at the Seminary, while the general public posture is egalitarian. Most congregations ask women no questions about their personal practices and beliefs but simply count them in the *minyan* when they show up at the synagogue.

By the time JTS ordained its first female rabbi in May 1985, much of the Conservative community was ready to embrace this change, which did not, however, mean that jobs for women in the rabbinate were easy to find. A little less than half of each year's ordainees are women; some seek pulpits but many prefer other kinds of rabbinic positions. Smaller, outlying synagogues, which can only offer their rabbis relatively low salaries, find themselves faced with the choice of a qualified man and a more qualified woman who will not be employed by a larger or better-located congregation because of residual prejudice. Female rabbis report that these small congregations usually hire the best rabbi they can find regardless of gender; that is, women's integration into the rabbinate is coming about not because of laypeople's commitment to social justice or recognition of halakhic justification but because of the exigencies of the marketplace.[22] It is too soon to tell what changes women will make in the rabbinate. Opening the rabbinate up to twice as many people ought to produce twice as many talented leaders.

In 1987 women were invested as Conservative cantors. The four-year delay occurred, perhaps, because the newly appointed chancellor, Ismar Schorsch, felt that the community could not accept two such radical changes at the same time. The halakhic argumentation for ordaining women mainly concerned the permissibility of women serving as prayer leaders. In gaining employment, female cantors are encountering fewer significant problems than female rabbis. Because of a shortage of cantors, women are being offered high-salary positions in large congregations. It is still true, however, that many congregations will not even interview a female candidate. As cantors expand their role as a second spiritual leader and Jewish resource, rabbis often worry about competition, in particular from women. Half the enrollment in the JTS Cantors' Institute is currently female. It remains to be seen whether synagogues will be comfortable with hiring both a female rabbi and a female cantor.[23]

The other area mentioned in Ezrat Nashim's platform for change is marital law. According to Jewish law codes, only a man may initiate a divorce and prepare the necessary documents. This creates extreme hardship for women: a husband may extort large sums of money in consideration for granting a *get* (bill of divorce) or may simply decide not to issue one; he may then take a second wife without divorcing the first, but she may not remarry without benefit of a *get*. Prior to 1972 the Conservative movement made a number of attempts to solve this problem. In the 1950s, Saul Lieberman added a clause to the *ketubah* (wedding contract) that made it possible for a woman to sue a recalcitrant husband in civil court.[24] With pressure to remove women's marital disabilities growing even stronger in the seventies, a separate antenuptial agreement was instituted. Such an agreement was considered more enforceable than a religious document that could be challenged by the courts on church-state grounds. Should the husband who did not sign such a document at the time of marriage refuse to write a *get*, the wife could appear before the *Bet Din* (rabbinical court) of the Jewish Theological Seminary and ask to have the marriage annulled. An annulment, by definition, does not necessitate a *get*, but it does neutralize a husband's control of the wife's marital availability. In practice, then, if not in theory, women in the Conservative movement are no longer disabled in the matter of divorce.

A few feminist changes met virtually no resistance. In the mid-seventies Ezrat Nashim published a booklet entitled "Blessing the Birth of a Daughter"[25] to provide people with sample ceremonies for publicly inducting a baby girl into the Jewish religion. Not fraught with the same anxiety or historical symbolism as circumcision, this rite of passage rapidly became standard practice among Conservative and other Jews. Similarly, in the last twenty years, celebrating a girl's becoming a *bat mitzvah* in the synagogue with her reading publicly from the Torah and Prophets has become commonplace. More and more women have begun to cover their heads in the synagogue, to don *tallitot*, and to be called for an honor by both patronym and matronym (as have many men). Finally, issues of sexist language in the liturgy are now discussed at JTS as elsewhere.

In sum, the Conservative movement is assimilating feminist change with reasonable speed and without inordinate difficulty.[26] Not all of its members possess the requisite resilience. A small number of rabbis and laymen broke ranks in 1984 and formed a new branch, the Union for Traditional Conservative Judaism; they claimed to be motivated by the desire to stress observance of *mitzvot*. Because the rabbinical school that they opened will ordain men only, it would seem that the immediate cause of their action was their wish to distance themselves from feminism. In 1990 this group dropped "Conservative" from its title, hoping to make itself attractive to modern Orthodox Jews, who are now losing ground to the ultraright wing of Orthodoxy.

Despite these achievements, I am troubled that the Conservative movement, which has in feminism a golden opportunity to apply its founding principles to an issue of substance, is viewed by some as a movement no longer committed to halakhah. The law-making body of the Conservative movement has lost credibility in the eyes of the Conservative public; the leadership of the movement has made only weak attempts to inform the laity that there are numerous halakhic standards that need to be upheld by every Conservative Jew. Rabbis continue to make changes in synagogue ritual that cannot be viewed as consistent with halakhah and, in some cases, the move to egalitarianism has served as a catalyst for this process.

An ironic result is that even in those settings in which egalitarianism is practiced, the practitioners themselves often do not view their own actions as legitimate. There is a feeling in many egalitarian communities that they are doing what is right from an ethical perspective but that if examined objectively, their rituals and lifestyle would be found antihalakhic. Until people equate halakhah with principled change, and until they learn to distinguish between warranted and unwarranted change, the number of authentic Conservative Jews will remain small. The leadership of the movement needs to grasp that this is a propitious moment for creating a new understanding of the old slogan defining the Conservative position: "tradition and change." The challenge facing the Conservative movement is no longer to make itself palatable to acculturated American Jews but to portray itself as the modern reincarnation of Talmudic Judaism.

Probably the greatest contribution of feminism, therefore, has been to force serious, thoughtful Jews today to ponder the relationship between halakhah and ethics. If one recognizes that halakhah changes, and that one motivation for halakhic change is adjustment to evolving ethical insights, there is no choice but to endorse feminist change, unsettling as such change may be. But a deepening appreciation of feminism in secular and religious society is forcing men and women to evaluate dispassionately their behavior toward each other and the behavior of social and religious institutions toward both men and women. The outcome of this ferment will be change in time-honored practices and a more ethical, and therefore more appealing religion.

Will the legacy of today's Jewish feminists be modest or significant? Certainly no one will ever again dare to characterize traditional Judaism as an egalitarian religion. People may endorse or lament women's traditionally subordinate position, but they will no longer be able to ignore the critique of sexist elements in Judaism. A more enduring and substantive accomplishment is that Jewish feminists have brought about irreversible and wide-ranging accommodations in the synagogues, schools, organizations, minds, and hearts of most American Jews. Jewish life in the future will not resemble Jewish life in the past but will offer more people greater opportunities for involvement and religious satisfaction. As a result, Jewish life in the United States has become immeasurably strengthened.

Notes

1. I wish to thank Professor Richard Kalmin and Rebecca Jacobs for their comments and suggestions.
2. See Alan Silverstein, "The Evolution of Ezrat Nashim," *Conservative Judaism* 30 (Fall 1975), for a somewhat different understanding of the rise of Jewish feminism.
3. A fourth denomination, Reconstructionism, is so much smaller that I have not referred to it as a major American denomination. This movement was egalitarian from its inception in the 1920s. As with the other denominations, however, women did not become actively involved in synagogue ritual leadership roles until the 1970s.
4. See Elliott Dorff, *Conservative Judaism: Our Ancestors to Our Descendants* (New York: United Synagogue of America, 1977), 165–83, for two responsa, the first by rabbis Morris Adler, Jacob Agus, and Theodore Friedman, permitting riding to the synagogue on the Sabbath, and the second by Rabbi David Novak, written in 1974, objecting to this leniency.
5. The family pew was a source of tension between the lay organization and the rabbinic leadership for many decades. Rabbi Boaz Cohen, in his 1942 report as chairman of the Committee on Jewish Law (the forerunner of today's Committee on Jewish Law and Standards), responded to a question about the acceptability of mixed pews by saying that each congregation had to decide for itself, in the light of its own circumstances, whether or not to adopt this change. That is, this departure from traditional practice was permitted but not recommended (*Proceedings of the Rabbinical Assembly*, 1941–1944, 139–41.) In 1946 Rabbi Simon Greenberg further noted for the record that since segregation of men and women at prayer was only a custom (*minhag*), not a halakhic requirement, mixed pews were therefore within the purview of traditional Judaism (Minutes of Committee on Jewish Law, 4.3.46). For a full discussion of this issue, in both an Orthodox and a Conservative setting, see the entire Fall 1956 issue of *Conservative Judaism*.
6. The name is intended as a play on words: the literal meaning is "help for women." But *azarah* also means "gallery" and this term is usually used to refer to the women's gallery in an Orthodox synagogue. It was also the name of the gallery in the Temple in Jerusalem into which everyone entered, but beyond which women were not permitted to go.
7. Silverstein, "The Evolution of Ezrat Nashim," 44.
8. The number of votes needed to establish a legitimate minority opinion has varied over the years. It is also important to note that a standard only becomes binding on Conservative rabbis if 80 percent of the Com-

mittee members approve it and a majority of the Rabbinical Assembly convention votes in favor of it.

9. "An Aliyah for Women," *Conservative Judaism and Jewish Law*, ed. Seymour Siegel (New York: Rabbinical Assembly, 1977), 266–80.

10. A number of rabbis who served in the Minneapolis area at that time speculated, during phone conversations with me, that the community was receptive to enlightened leadership, in particular that of R. David Aronson. Aviva Comet-Murciano, in an unpublished doctoral dissertation entitled "Jewish Denominational Approaches to Religious Feminism" (Wurzweiler School of Social Work, New York, January 1992), notes that in the United States at that time there was a clearly defined trend toward giving women leadership roles in the churches. She also points out that in that same year Rabbi Barnett Brickner called on the Reform rabbinic leadership to reevaluate the ordination of women (74–75).

11. September 1, 1973.

12. For a full report on this series of decisions, see Aaron Blumenthal, "The Status of Women in Jewish Law," *Conservative Judaism* 31 (Spring 1977). An updated survey of decisions by the Committee on Jewish Law and Standards relating to women in the synagogue was prepared by Mayer Rabinowitz. See "The Role of Women in Jewish Ritual," *Conservative Judaism* 39 (Fall 1986).

13. A survey of twenty-eight branches of Women's League for the Conservative Movement, compiled by Edya Arzt and published in *Women's League Outlook* (Summer 1990): 20–21, shows that between 1987 and 1990 the number of synagogues honoring women with *aliyot* to the Torah and counting them in the prayer quorum increased substantially. By 1990 approximately two-thirds of the Conservative congregations were giving women *aliyot* and approximately one-half were counting them in the *minyan*.

14. *The Ordination of Women as Rabbis: Studies and Responsa* (New York: JTSA, 1988), 5–30. The report was issued on January 30, 1979.

15. BT Shevuot 30a; Maimonides, *Mishneh Torah*, Hilkhot Edut 9:1,2; *Shulhan Arukh*, Hoshen Mishpat 13,35.

16. Roth incorrectly assumes that women are exempt from daily prayer. Mishnah Berakhot 3:3, and commentators throughout the ages, uphold women's obligation. There is, however, a minority of codists who reduce a woman's obligation to merely uttering some petition each morning. See *Shulhan Arukh*, Orah Hayyim, 106:2, Magen Avraham *ad locum*.

17. *The Ordination of Women*, 127–87.

18. *The Ordination of Women*, 170.

19. These papers have been collected and published by the Jewish Theological Seminary in the volume mentioned above, *The Ordination of Women as Rabbis*.

20. Lieberman, in conversations with me, seemed sympathetic to women's desire to expand their options for participation in synagogue ritual. In his role as rabbi and decisor of the JTS synagogue, he permitted them to dance with a Torah scroll on Simhat Torah. Furthermore, without exhibiting any reluctance, he permitted me to enroll in his Talmud classes, which, in the early 1970s, were open only to rabbinical students. However, after his death, colleagues of his on the JTS Talmud faculty produced a written statement in his name, prepared several years earlier (in 1979), that indicated his opposition to the ordination of women. He comments, in the opening of this responsum, that he would have preferred not to deal with the question at all. He then goes on to say that it is stated clearly in the Jewish law codes that women may not serve as judges and render legal decisions. Therefore, since today's *semikhah* (rabbinic ordination) is, in essence, certification that an individual is fit to judge and render legal decisions, it follows that a woman may not receive rabbinic ordination (*Tomeikh KeHalakhah*, vol. 1 [New York: Union for Traditional Conservative Judaism, 1986], 15–18 [Hebrew], 20–22 [English]). It must be noted, however, that what JTS confers upon its rabbinic graduates is not *semikhah* but the degree of Rabbi, Teacher, and Preacher. I therefore think that Lieberman has (perhaps intentionally) sidestepped the entire issue.

21. Thirty-four faculty members voted in favor of admitting women as candidates for ordination to the Rabbinical School and eight voted against. The faculty's vote was an administrative decision, not a halakhic one.

22. Rabbi Margaret Wenig, a faculty member of HUC-JIR in New York, told me that in the Reform movement no woman is yet serving as head rabbi of a synagogue that has more than one rabbi on staff.

23. The source of this information is Rabbi Morton Leifman, dean of the Cantors' Institute at JTS.

24. For the text and translation of this modified *ketubah*, see Rabbi Jules Harlow, ed., *A Rabbi's Manual* (New York: Rabbinical Assembly, 1965), 35–38.

25. Toby Fishbein Reifman with Ezrat Nashim, eds., *Blessing the Birth of a Daughter: Jewish Naming Ceremonies for Girls* (Englewood, N.J.: Ezrat Nashim, 1976).

26. Silverstein, in his article on the evolution of Ezrat Nashim (see above, note 2), claims that since the group did not itself grow large or spawn an organization like NOW, its contribution to Jewish history is not very significant. But he seems to overlook the facts that Ezrat Nashim, even in 1975, was already responsible for significant changes in many Conservative synagogues in the United States, and, even more important, that Conservative women were electrified by its message.

PART SIX

Three Modes of Religiosity

CHAPTER 19

The Ninth *Siyum Ha-Shas:* A Case Study in Orthodox Contra-Acculturation

Samuel C. Heilman

In the multitude of people is the King's glory.

—Proverbs 14:28

Let us put aside our pain and bitter experiences and demonstrate for all the world to see that we are people of the Torah, blessed with eternal life.

—Eliezer Friedenson, *Beth Jacob Journal*, on the eve of the second *Siyum ha-Shas*, June 27, 1938

An issue underlying much of the Jewish experience in the New World has been whether acculturation can be accomplished without assimilation.[1] In America, religion and state are separate, and systematic or state-sanctioned exclusion absent, giving minorities like the Jews opportunities to enter the mainstream. American Jews for the most part embraced these opportunities to become part of their host culture, which, in spite of some practical obstacles, stood open in principle to their full participation. To what extent could they enter the mainstream without giving up their separate identity as Jews? To be sure, this issue was, by the nineteenth century, also a concern of many European Jews who took advantage of the changes that have come to be called "emancipation." In America, however, the question of acculturation and assimilation was there for Jews from their arrival on these shores.

Jews who held onto tradition tenaciously and perceived themselves as Orthodox were less comfortable than other Jews with the process of cultural change that America prompted. Indeed, while the Orthodox came to America, they did so with great reluctance. For them, it remained a Jewish wasteland, a *trefe medina*, an unholy place. Many stayed in Europe at the wellheads of tradition until they were destroyed in the Holocaust.[2] When the Orthodox did plant themselves in America, many accommodated to American ways while simultaneously trying to hold onto the punctilious observance of ritual and tradition.[3] They adapted their appearance and dress to look like Americans, accepted English as their language to sound like Americans, sent their children to day schools and universities to receive a secular education like Americans, and entered professions and adopted lifestyles that put them firmly into American culture. They even tacitly accepted pluralism in Jewish life as is sanctioned in American society. These people, who have come to be called "modern American Orthodox Jews," by all estimates make up the majority of American Orthodoxy.

Yet there were other Orthodox Jews who refused to endorse the cultural change, pluralism, and direction that American society seemingly specified. At the outset, these other Orthodox appeared little more than refugees of a lost world. A huge proportion had been destroyed in Europe, where they had stayed in compliance with the directives of leaders who warned them that America would be the death of their way of life. Stunned and disoriented, many arrived in America not understanding what had happened to them. How could their leaders and religious instincts have been so wrong? Coming to America just before, during, and after the Second World War, many of the most traditionalist Orthodox defined their existence as a way to demonstrate that they had not been abandoned by God or Jewish history.[4] They recreated the yeshivas of Europe in America, replanted the surviving rabbinic leadership on American soil, and developed new religious leaders who were *in* America but not *of* it. Given the acculturative environment, these efforts entailed considerable struggle. In the end, this type of Orthodoxy, which resisted assimilation and was wary of acculturation, has sustained itself, seeking vehicles to abet its existence and encourage its adherents to remain steadfast in their contra-accultura-

tive efforts. Nothing helped more to accomplish this end than traditions like the *daf yomi* (daily page) discipline that had its origins in
the pre-Holocaust way of life.

On an unseasonably warm evening in late April 1990, on *Rosh
Hodesh* (new moon) of the Hebrew month of Iyyar 5750, an event
took place that was to be the culmination of 2711 consecutive days
of preparation. During that interval, thousands of Jews from all
over the world had spent each workday of every week covering one
page at a time of the "Shas," an acronym for the "*Shisha Sedorim*"
(six divisions) and sixty-three tractates of the Babylonian Talmud.
For the ninth time since 1931, when the first such daily cycle was
completed, Jews would celebrate a *siyum*, the formal culmination
of one more cycle in this never-ending course of study.

Some had reviewed their pages of Talmud in small study circles
in synagogues; others had gathered to *lern* during morning or afternoon breaks or at home in their after hours. Some had even studied
by telephone, calling up "Dial-a-Daf," the 24-hour hotline that
provided an expert teacher in English or Yiddish who could guide
the student through each day's allotted, complex, often digressive,
and rather recondite page. Tonight, thousands of these students
were to gather in the time-honored ritual of Jewish study and celebrate their having gone through the entire Talmud at a mass meeting in Madison Square Garden, the huge arena in the heart of
Manhattan.

The idea of reviewing one page a day, "*daf yomi*," was formally
introduced at the first international Congress of Agudat Israel in
Vienna in 1923 by Meir Shapiro, a former member of the Polish
parliament and rabbi from Lublin. Still a young and relatively frag-
ile union of Orthodox Jews, Agudat Israel was searching for activities that would bind its members together and to the Jewish tradition as defined by Orthodoxy. In spite of their opposition to Reform
and assimilative trends, there was also much that divided the Jews
who shared the Agudah's Orthodox sympathies. When Shapiro,
head of the Agudat Israel Education Committee, "pointed out that
Jewish unity is visible on every page of Talmud, which includes a
Mishnah written in the land of Israel, a Gemara written in Babylo-
nia, the codes of the Rif written in Morocco, Rambam written in

Egypt, Rashi and Tosafos written in France and the Maharan written in Poland," and proposed that every Jew undertake each day to
study one identical page of the Talmud, the project struck many as
an idea around which all could rally. Everyone would symbolically
be united in a single class without walls. As Orthodox Jews, none
could oppose the idea of daily study of that most important text
that served for centuries as the pinnacle of Jewish scholarship.[5]

A few years after Rabbi Shapiro died in 1934 at the age of forty-
seven and on the eve of the Second World War, a crowd reported at
twenty thousand assembled at the yeshiva in Lublin to celebrate
the second *siyum* of the *daf yomi* program. After the war, the
relatively few who had survived the Holocaust tried to resurrect the
practices of Jewish life in the new soil in which they had been
transplanted in America and Israel, but *daf yomi* was difficult to
restart. Many thousands of dedicated Talmud students and scholars
had been wiped out and those who remained were often, in those
early years, among the walking dead. For a while, only a relative
few had kept up the practice of reviewing the daily page. In 1945,
at the third *siyum*, only three thousand were reported to have
assembled in Tel Aviv, site of the main celebration.

If unity had been one of the underlying themes of the *daf yomi*
program at its onset, after the war survival became its leitmotif.
With the center of Agudah activities shifting to the Land of Israel,
those assembled in 1945 heard an address by Joseph Kahaneman,
head of the Ponovezh Yeshiva (by then relocated from Lithuania to
Bene-Berak), who asserted that the study of the Torah and *daf yomi*
were the best and only true insurance for Jewish survival. The
occasion was more like a funeral for the millions lost than a celebration of study. To those who could not but ask themselves why so
few of the faithful had survived the gas chambers, Rabbi Kahaneman's declaration was a call to Talmud as a way of demonstrating
that one continued to keep faith with the tradition. The depleted
crowd dramatically underscored the losses the people of the book
had suffered, yet the fact that a *siyum* could be celebrated more or
less on time was also not ignored.

To be sure, *daf yomi* was not seen by everyone as the ideal
vehicle for resistance to acculturation. Leaders of the yeshiva world
who made study of the Talmud their life's task argued that re-

viewing one page a day was not sufficiently serious and absorbing; it was to Jewish learning what a quickly mumbled prayer was to true worship. They therefore eschewed quick fixes like a page a day, and focused rather on creating yeshivas and supporting them, a goal that most Orthodox Jews made a central concern of their organized existence both in Israel and in the Diaspora.[6]

For those who claimed that "the pressures of work and community involvement leave insufficient time for extensive periods of in-depth [Jewish] learning," but who nevertheless wanted to resist the seductive influence of non-Jewish life and sought moorings that attached them to the protective tradition, *daf yomi* was of growing importance. It allowed for an ongoing contact with the world of talmudic scholarship through limited but institutionalized ritual study.[7] And it provided an identity: "We're a *daf yomi* home," the participants could proclaim, including not only the man who does the actual studying but also, as one person put it, the "wife [who] encourages me to set aside evening and weekend time to catch up with the *daf*."[8] Participation in the program—joining a daily study circle, reviewing a portable mini-volume of Talmud on the train, listening to cassettes that rabbis have recorded of each day's page— and especially coming to the public event of the *siyum*—became a way of displaying openly a relatively high level of continuing Jew-ish commitment.

Daf yomi became perhaps an ultimate step in the democratiza-tion of the once elite practice of studying Talmud. What had been the province of the relatively few scholars who labored over every word was now something that masses could accomplish on the side and at an unprecedented speed. As one *daf yomi* supporter put it, "It enables everyone to achieve the Jewish dream of completing the entire Shas." Perhaps that too was a reason why the yeshiva people were at best ambivalent about it. For these champions of an intel-lectual elite of Torah, the idea that anyone could in a few minutes a day complete the entire Shas was a debasement of what true scholars did. Still, as the event at Madison Square Garden would illustrate, *daf yomi* would become a symbol of much more than a quick reading of an intricate text and would make even a *rosh yeshiva* into a grudging supporter.

After the war, the numbers gradually grew. In 1953, ten thousand were reported to have gathered in Jerusalem's Me'ah She'arim; in 1960 large celebrations were held in Israel, while the Americans met in a Catskill Mountains resort hotel. For nearly a generation, American Jewry's celebrations of the *siyum* remained in the shadow of Israel's. Nevertheless, Jewish life in the United States and Canada had not become the wasteland that many in Europe predicted it would when they warned the devout to stay away. In America, Orthodox Judaism—even its *haredi* forms—was far from disappearing.[9] Venerable European institutions of Jewish learning were replanted on American soil and new ones were founded. Orthodox Jews made their presence felt in other ways. Kosher food became ubiquitous. Popular magazines written from the Orthodox viewpoint were published in English. Thousands of kits were distributed, assisting Jews in performing everything from lighting Hanukkah candles to counting the forty-nine days between Passover and Shevuot; Jewish calendars were mailed out, ostensibly as fundraising devices but also as signals that Orthodoxy was alive and well. Orthodoxy made sure that everyone learned it was not losing its young in the same proportions as the other movements. Some gains were even made in attracting newcomers to traditional piety beginning in the 1960s.

Perhaps nothing so epitomized religious continuity after the Holocaust as the emphasis on universal daily study symbolically captured by the *daf yomi* idea. Jewish people who continued to review their Talmud demonstrated that they had not been chased away from their cultural core and religious treasures by the events of the twentieth century; the more who did this, the more dramatic their cultural resistance.

Nowhere was the connection to the Holocaust more clear than in America, the new center of the Diaspora. If the European concentration of Jews had ended in the death camps, the new one would not end thus. At a gathering in Manhattan in 1975 that about four thousand attended—a number far in excess of what many believed possible thirty years before—the Mo'etzet Gedolay ha-Torah (Council of Torah Sages) of the American Agudah formally declared the *siyum* to be a memorial for the Six Million. That the huge hall was overflowing and the turnout included not only survivors from among the old sages but also some of the new ones born or raised in America presumably reassured many of the future continuity of their way of life.

By 1982, as over five thousand squeezed into the Felt Forum, survivalism was evolving into an Orthodox Jewish triumphalism, a sense that "the people of the Torah were blessed with eternal life."[10] A hall usually reserved for far more profane activities of American culture was filled beyond capacity with Jews who claimed to have studied Talmud every day for seven and a half years. Here Jews showed the world that a new generation of Americans—not only wizened elders—was increasingly absorbing itself in Torah rather than being absorbed by contemporary American society.

The organizers recalled the remarks of the Klausenberger Rebbe at the last such gathering, when the rebbe "related how, when he had announced an award of $25,000 for anyone who could pass an examination on all of Shas with Tosafos [the major medieval commentary on the Talmud], he was called by a young man who said he was prepared to take the test but would need to have the questions asked in English because he knew no Yiddish!" The message was clear: the study of Talmud in the Diaspora had survived the transition to America; despite a switch from Yiddish to English, the essence remained.

Now the question was how to go "from strength to strength," as many put it. What would be an even greater triumph? The decision was made to meet in the main arena of Madison Square Garden itself, the tabernacle of profanity. Prefigured by the 1982 crowd at Felt Forum, the 1990 gathering in the main arena had to be more than a *siyum*. As many involved in the planning surely recognized, this raised the stakes. Failure to gather a much larger crowd would be tantamount to conceding the weakness of Orthodoxy in America, so the *siyum* was meant to be a sign of triumph. Success was not a foregone conclusion; only by making it clear that Orthodox vitality itself was being celebrated could the organizers from Agudat Israel hope for a very large turnout. Seven and a half years later at the auditorium from which the Ringling Brothers, Barnum and Bailey Circus had to be displaced and where the National

Basketball Association Playoffs were about to begin, twenty thousand Jews assembled for what the organizers claimed was "the largest gathering for Torah ever seen in the Western Hemisphere."

What follows is an ethnographic account of the event. Describing the task of ethnography and the study of cultural behavior, anthropologist Claude Levi-Strauss explained, "Exploration is not so much a covering of surface distance as a study in depth: a fleeting episode, a fragment of landscape or a remark overheard may provide the only means of understanding and interpreting areas which would otherwise remain barren of meaning."[11] As a practitioner of this discipline, I am always in search of such events, of what Milton Singer called cultural dramas where one can not only see the "concentrated expression of the whole collective life" but can also find the point where it can be "readily examined by the detached observer."[12] The *daf yomi* gathering at the Garden was such a moment of concentrated collective life when the essential character of traditionalist American Orthodoxy was performed in a cultural drama of high order.

The ethnographer's goal is "to impress his experience of what he has *seen* so strongly, so vividly, on his readers that they cannot doubt its veracity." To do that he must make them see what he has seen. Description is key, for "it is the visual that gives authority."[13] "Ethnographic writing as a rule subordinates narrative to description," Mary Louise Pratt observes, but it grows far more vivid when it combines "personal narrative and objectified description."[14] Thus, while the account that follows is interpretive, it is also narrative, because both together offer the reader a better chance to see the coherence, order, and meaning of the celebration through the ethnographer's eyes. Observing the event on the canvas of ethnographic experience and description, the reader will begin to see this Jewish group's response to America, acculturation, modernity, and the Holocaust.

The Event

The Jewish invasion of the Garden began with thousands of men with beards and black hats streaming along West Thirty-Fourth Street. Subway trains from Brooklyn and Queens were filled with

Orthodox Jews headed for Manhattan. Buses loaded with yeshiva students jammed the avenues and pulled up at the entrances of the Garden. Many of those coming were the sorts of people who seldom if ever came to the Garden; when they parked their cars in nearby garages, they often asked for directions to their destination. "What's going on there tonight?" one of the attendants asked as I gave him the keys to my car. The stares on the subway, the questions by bystanders, all reinforced the feeling that this was a remarkable event.

Just before 6:00 P.M. scores of obviously Orthodox Jews milled about trying to find an extra entry ticket. Tickets for a seat on the court floor, at one hundred dollars each, had been sold out weeks in advance, and even the upper decks, reserved for the women, were full. Some people stood around chatting with friends, while others read the handbills and billboards. Printed in Yiddish, Hebrew, and English, one advertised a new edition of the Talmud. Another announced a new yeshiva in a distant county where "there are 18,000 Jewish youngsters of high school age, the vast majority of whom do not know the Aleph-Beis and are bereft of Torah and Mesoras Avos [the tradition of our fathers]," a school that "needs your support to grow and expand." Some bearded and sidelocked guardians of religion handed out fliers to the clean shaven, warning them in Hebrew and English that "according to all [rabbinic] opinions, there is an absolute prohibition to use of the Norelco Lift and Cut shaving machine or others like them, since the device contains knives that make direct contact with the skin and therefore is no different than a razor." (Orthodox Jews knew using razors was prohibited by Jewish law.) The handbill added a phone number to call "for more information" and an appended page with essential quotations from ten prominent rabbis, all of whom forbade shavers. This was a good place to market stringent interpretations of Jewish law.

Throughout the event, the emphasis was not only on *what* was to happen but also on the fact that it would occur for everyone to see in the center ring of the main arena of the major capital of contemporary culture. In an immense pleasure dome, where many of the profane amusements of the contemporary world take place, the "Greatest Show on Earth" and the basketball championships were being displaced in favor of Torah. This was a miracle. How

could the *daf yomi* people, who represent a way of life so antitheti-
cal to circuses and sports events, dream of capturing the arena?
That they—so often called fossils—could do it was proof, as the
program put it, of the *"siyata deshmaya,"* the help of Heaven. Only
thus could the success of such an attack on contemporary hedonistic culture be explained. This event was a *"kiddush ha-Shem* [sanc-
tification of God] of unparalleled dimensions" and "an effective
proclamation before the eyes of the world—and, most importantly
before the eyes of all Jewry—of the centrality of Torah-learning to
Judaism and Jewish life."[15] To be sure, it also took earthly power
and the "aid of a major Orthodox Jewish figure in the business
community" (a member of the Reichman family, an entrepreneur
whose wealth was legendary and whose attachment to Orthodoxy
was well known), a man who, according to gossip spread that
evening, spent $150,000 to rent the Garden and five thousand more
to have the smell of the circus elephants eliminated.[16] Power and
influence in the service of the tradition could, if not topple, at least
temporarily neutralize the powers of hedonistic darkness; that was
the message at Madison Square Garden that night.

The imagery was not lost on *Jewish Week* reporter Jonathan
Mark: "The Garden traditionally hangs a banner from its ceiling
proclaiming '613,' the number of victories by Knicks basketball
coach Red Holzman, but on this night the packed arena understood
that number to mean only the number of commandments in the
Torah." This was the sanctification of the profane, a victory far
greater than any ever celebrated in the Garden. Even the arena
refreshment stands offered only kosher snacks for the night.

Organizers had bussed in lots of yeshiva students, including
many from the more moderately Orthodox schools who were not
full-time participants in *daf yomi* but were sent to bear witness to
Orthodox revival. Like the rest of the crowd, they were proof, many
asserted in a proverbial verse repeated throughout the evening, that
"in the multitude of people is the King's glory."

For this the press, the eyes and ears of the world, had been
invited as witnesses. Organizers wanted not just the parochial Jewish press but also major television stations and newspapers to pass
the word everywhere. To make certain that the "right" message was
reported, organizers prepared press packets for outsiders to the

world of Agudat Israel. Attached was a list of eighty cities, most in America but some in Canada, Mexico, and Great Britain, from which representatives had come: the phenomenon was not only a New York but a national, even an international, movement. Inside the folder were neatly printed English pages, their style and much of their contents decidedly in contrast to the overwhelmingly Yiddish speeches that would be heard throughout the evening. In terms that outsiders could grasp, organizers provided "suggested angles for stories" that were supposed to help outsiders comprehend the meaning of the event. Under the heading of "human interest" were suggestions to stress the "unending quest for knowledge" that was "not restricted to rabbis and full-time scholars" and a story on the "people who do *daf yomi*," including those who have done it for more than one cycle. Another sheet explained that the *daf yomi* exemplifies the "living transmission of Jewish law and practice" and that "it was followed by an estimated one million Jews before the Holocaust and is enjoying tremendous resurgence today." Under the heading of "sociological perspectives" was the suggestion that "people who study [Talmud] with each other for years form unique relationships [and become] virtual family members sharing in life's problems, sorrows, and joys" and that *daf yomi* serves as the "instant connection anywhere in the world" when participants discover one other. The publicists suggested that *daf yomi* could also form an "inter-generational link." Finally, there were remarks about the ways in which modern technology was enlisted in *daf yomi* as well as a suggestion that the press write about the "central role of Torah study in Judaism" and its capacity to play a part in "shaping the Jewish mind."

Were these assertions arrived at only for a press release or were they part of the event itself? At the very least they were declarations of faith and reflections of a self-conscious awareness by the organizers that to be resolutely traditional and Orthodox in an age that appeared fashioned from other stuff was no small matter. Telling the story in the terms that outsiders could understand and perhaps could sympathize with was part of the effort to thrust tradition into active contention with modernity, while utilizing the mechanisms of the very modernity against which it strived. The assembly at Madison Square Garden was, therefore, from its inception an act freighted with meaning. It offered those who came together an opportunity to experience what anthropologists call a major "cultural performance," a chance for the assembled to make "visible, audible, and tangible beliefs, ideas, values, sentiments, and psychological dispositions that cannot [otherwise] directly be perceived" but that are held in common by all those who shared the *daf yomi* experience.[17] Attendance was an emblematic deed meant to signal clearly, if not to establish, the participants' identification with the process of Jewish study as the permanent center of Jewish life, evoking "unifying sentiments of loyalty and identity."[18] After seven and a half years, the gathering at the Garden would allow these people who had studied alone or in small groups, who had taken time out of the daily humdrum of profane existence, to feel and show themselves to be a part of a mass movement and living Jewish counterculture.

For all the general celebration of traditionalist Jewish culture, the evening left the participants with a great deal of room to stamp this triumph with their own template of what it meant to be a traditionalist. It allowed them to reinterpret the meaning of what they were doing according to their various needs, which they did, seizing upon their incipient or developed differences and displaying continuity with the past and differentiation in the present. Under the blanket of black suits and white shirts and beneath the broad umbrella of their wide-brimmed hats, the various groups in attendance displayed many colors.

The Spectacle

As each ticket holder entered the arena, he was given a copy of a souvenir booklet that outlined the program for the evening. The crux was the collective review of the final lines of the last tractate *Niddah* and the beginning of the first *Berachot* that together would mark the conclusion and commencement of the ceaseless cycle of Torah review characterized as an endless attachment to Jewish ways. The formal program also included recitation of psalms, speeches and sermons, songs and prayers to shape the event so that it resonated with the sacred and momentous. Madison Square

Garden would be made into a sanctuary larger than any in American Jewry.

Around all this activity was the informal but no less important matter of seeing and being seen, walking about, conversing and commenting—in short, the performance of what might be called "active assembly" that turned the giant amphitheater into a meeting room and inserted intimacy into it. This also made outsiders feel even more alien. For some who came only as observers—as was the case with many of the members of the press—the result was awe and estrangement. One Jewish reporter, writing for a general circulation newspaper, said that as he looked around him he felt as if he had entered a place where everyone came from somewhere else. He was right, of course. They came from a world of different values and alternative explanations. They had snatched their adherents from the world to which the reporter reported, and they wanted that story told.

Upon entering the arena, many participants rented little transmitters and headphones to be used for the simultaneous translations of the Yiddish, Hebrew, and English speeches to come. As people found their seats, shepherded into place by the many ushers who were part of the arena regular staff—personnel who seemed alternately bemused and overwhelmed by this odd crowd so unlike the Garden regulars—they seemed ready for the game that was about to begin.[19]

The Game

If tonight's proceedings had been a basketball game, the start would have probably come with an introduction of the players and the singing of the national anthem. That is the way tournaments that normally take place in Madison Square Garden begin. Yet even though the *siyum* was a game of an altogether different order, there was something strangely parallel in the way it started out. Perhaps it was the venue: place does have a way of shaping behavior and framing meaning. Seated in front of a phalanx of about 150 dignitaries and arranged in a line along an extended dais placed at midcourt and festooned with a long banner were the great rabbis and sages who would deliver the speeches. Although each of these luminaries would have his name and affiliation flashed in bright lights on the scoreboard when he stood to speak, the program listed them as well.

I asked the man seated next to me, an editor of one of the Agudat Israel publications, how it had been decided who would speak and when. "With great difficulty and after many hours of discussion," he replied with a grin. If the details of the order were not worth explaining to an outsider, it was necessary to point out that there was indeed an order. Tonight's game was neither random nor unplanned. The figures who would speak were chosen not only because of who they were but also because of what they symbolized.

First was Zvi Spira, the Bluzhover Rebbe, the recently ascended incumbent of this hasidic chair. Why the Bluzhover? To remain an important organization of the traditionalist Orthodox world, Agudat Israel needed to include within it representatives of the hasidic community, because hasidim made up perhaps the largest segment of those who these days maintained Jewish tradition. However, over the years, many of the hasidim had turned away from the organization, seeing it as too close to cultures they spurned. Besides, hasidim by and large did not need umbrella organizations like the Agudah, since each court was its own organization. This was certainly true in America, where hasidim found funds and support without the intervention of Agudat Israel. Here appeals by hasidic groups could be made directly to the Jewish Federations or to the local legislative or city council representatives.

To show that it still included all Orthodox Jews, the American Agudat Israel, however, still needed prominent hasidim at its celebration. Among its stars was the Bluzhover Rebbe, a special sort of hasid. When Zvi Spira's father, the previous rebbe, came to America as a refugee from Galicia and a victim of the war, he was—like many other Galician hasidic leaders who had been spared the fate of less fortunate hasidim who had not survived—a broken man without many followers. Rabbi Spira had, however, reestablished himself here, building a curious following. Many of his new American hasidim were people who had in practice left behind the hasidic way of life, though they retained a nostalgic, compartmentalized attachment to it. Others were Jews who had never really been hasidim but who, especially after the destruction of European

Jewry, felt a vague affinity for the idea of "rebbe." These orphans of history became part-time hasidim, people who lived and worked in contemporary America but yearned for a romanticized hasidic world that existed as much in their imaginative reconstruction of the past as it did in reality. The Bluzhover Rebbe became a *tzaddik* for these people, who could be hasidic vicariously through him. Although his supporters were not full-fledged hasidim, they were devoted to him, and no one doubted that he himself was a full-fledged hasid. When he died in 1989, he was the oldest American rebbe; no one questioned his legitimacy—even the *New York Times* called him the oldest "hasidic rebbe in America." He had been part of the Agudah. This evening his son stood in his place. To fill the void left by his father's passing, he would try to offer everyone a chance to feel like a hasid, if only for the few moments that he led them in the recitation of the Psalms, a kind of opening anthem.

Next was Chaskel Besser, chairman of the Daf Yomi Commission and an official of Agudat Israel. Besser represented the organization and would preside over the proceedings, introducing each of the speakers. He was the master of ceremony.

Rabbi Moshe Neuschloss, one of the oldest sages in America and a Holocaust survivor, would offer *divrei brocha*, "words of blessing." (It was not incidental that the program, printed in English, referred to these remarks and the others in Hebrew terms, in the language of the Jews rather than the verbal envelopes of the Gentiles.) Representing a convergence of various populations, Neuschloss, by virtue of his age and origins, stood for continuity with the prewar world of European Jewry. As a halakhic authority, a *rosh yeshiva* and decisor of Jewish law, a man who was a member of the Skver hasidic community, a group affiliated with some of the most insular and rejectionist elements in Orthodoxy, he could be placed at the crossroads between legalistic rabbinism and pietistic hasidism. Finally, as someone who reestablished a yeshiva in America after the war, he represented the phoenixlike resurgence of traditional Jewry.

Yosef Harari Raful, rabbinic head of the Ateret Torah Yeshiva, was the lone representative among the evening's speakers of the non-Ashkenazi Orthodox Jewish world. To the untrained eye, the bearded Raful in black coat and fedora looked like all the other sages on the podium; his years of education in Ashkenazi yeshivas had obviously cast him in their image. But Raful spoke in Hebrew, the only person to do so among the speakers, most of whom used Yiddish. His presence was meant to demonstrate that East and West were brought together this evening. To be sure, Raful was now in America and that even further mixed his identity and affiliations. In the Orthodox world, especially this evening, the melting pot was not an irrelevant metaphor.

Yaakov Perlow, the Novominsker Rebbe, was another of the ambiguous hasidic rebbes. There were few if any Novominsker hasidim, making him a rebbe not very different from the Bluzhover. As one of the relatively few hasidim in the crowd explained to me in Yiddish: "Er is nisht kayn rebbe" (he is not a rebbe). Perlow was American born, a graduate of the Chaim Berlin Yeshiva, an institution far from being hasidic. He was said as well to be a product of Brooklyn College and had studied at the bastion of Litvak (Lithuanian Jewish) thinking, Beth Medrash Govoha in Lakewood, New Jersey. For years Perlow had been affiliated with a yeshiva in New York City's Washington Heights that the German Neo-Orthodox community—a far cry from hasidim—had established.[20] Perlow was an amalgam of opposites. For the Agudah, he was the right blend, an exemplar of what American traditionalist Orthodoxy had wrought: a sage who was trained in a Lithuanian-style yeshiva who now headed such an institution but who called himself a rebbe even though he had few hasidim. He sat on the Mo'etzet Gedolay Ha-Torah, the Council of Torah Sages, which itself was a blend of blends. Yet unlike earlier sages whose positions on the council were reflections of their influence, Perlow's influence, many claimed, came from the fact of his being on the council.

Next was Rabbi Simon Schwab, for many years the rabbi of the Washington Heights Orthodox community, Kahal Adath Jeshurun. As emissary of this remnant of German Neo-Orthodoxy and now emeritus, Schwab was one of the last links in a chain that began with Samson Raphael Hirsch and his son-in-law Solomon Breuer, a cofounder of Agudat Israel. A native of Germany, product of Lithuanian yeshivas, and survivor of the Nazi terror, Schwab was a synthesis like so many of the new Americans. He was also the quintessential community rabbi.[21] From his first post in Ichenhausen, Germany, as well as during more than twenty years of service in Baltimore and finally in Washington Heights, he had led Jewish laity. Schwab's position on the program was to play the role of a bridge connecting the yeshiva and the lay community. The only congregational rabbi to speak this evening, he represented those for whom the primary nexus was the community synagogue. Schwab's would be the first full-blown address, really a sermon. He spoke in English.

The other formal address this evening came from Rabbi Elya Svei, a leading member of the American Mo'etzet Gedolay ha-Torah, a celebrated *rosh yeshiva*. If Schwab stood for the lay congregation, Svei embodied the rabbinical elite in the American incarnation of the Old World Lithuanian yeshivas. These were people who studied more than a page of Talmud each day and "meditated on it day and night." Born in Lithuania, Svei came as a child to the United States. Enrolled in American yeshivas, he was most prominently a product of Beth Medrash Govoha, the successor institution of the famed Slobodka Yeshiva. Even though (or perhaps because) he was a product of America and its putatively latitudinarian ways, Svei had become known as a zealot of the yeshiva world.[22] The Philadelphia Yeshiva, a sister institution of Lakewood, which he cofounded about thirty years earlier, was renowned as uncompromising in its religious demands on its students.[23] Svei was an indigenous *gadol*, an exemplar of what could be fashioned in America's yeshivas, proof that this postwar new Jewish America was not a Torah wilderness.

Following the two addresses from the rabbis came two speakers from dissimilar Orthodox worlds. Selected presumably for their ability to stir the assembled to an emotional pitch, their role was to offer what the program called *Divrei Chizuk*, "words of encouragement and support." First was Osher Greenfeld, a rabbinic leader of the Vizhnitz hasidim posted from his native Israel to the Vizhnitz community in Montreal. While Montreal was not a major center of Vizhnitzer hasidim, whose two primary communities were in Bene-Brak, Israel, and Spring Valley, New York, there was no question about Vizhnitz representing a major hasidic dynasty. Greenfeld, however, was on the program not only because of those affiliations but also because, as a press release put it, "through his outstanding leadership and dynamic oratory he has become known as one of the bright lights of a new generation of Torah scholars here in North America."

For those who could not get fired up by Greenfeld's Yiddish remarks, there was the tall and imposing young Aharon Dunner from Great Britain. A *dayan* (rabbinic judge) for the religiously right-wing Union of Orthodox Hebrew Congregations, the Hisachdus Kehillos Ha-Haredim, in Britain, as well as a congregational rabbi in the Tottenham section of London, he was also a product of postwar yeshiva Orthodoxy. Studying in England and later at Ponovezh in Israel, he had undergone Lithuanian yeshiva indoctrination and now was back serving the Jews from whom he had sprung. Like Greenfeld, Dunner was supposed to be a young and inspiring speaker, a representative of uncompromising Orthodoxy's capacity to regenerate itself. He spoke in English.

Finally, there would be those who would lead the prayers and offer songs. Indeed, while the focus was on text and the program was overwhelmingly composed of speeches, the prayers and songs seemed to move the crowd most. There would be no national anthems to start the game; these were "*golus* Jews," persons who had made exile a central existential element of their being and collective consciousness. America was at best a temporary refuge and Israel an unfulfilled hope. This was a crowd celebrating a refusal to acculturate, people who knew that "achieving a sense of *golus* in a world of freedom is extraordinarily difficult, for *golus* is not merely a set of observances but a state of mind [that] demands from every Jew not only a sense of estrangement from the secular world in which he lives but also a constant sense of unfulfilledness."[24] No singing of the "Star Spangled Banner" or "Hatikvah" would change that; their sole anthem was prayer and study, which was why they began the evening with a mass recitation of the afternoon prayers, *mincha*, and ended with *ma'ariv*, evening prayers. With more than twenty thousand people frozen into place, the sports arena was transformed into possibly the largest synagogue in America.

So overwhelmed were some that they saw the occasion in prophetic terms. A participant from Brooklyn, Meir Winkler, would later write that, as he ended his prayer and readied himself for what would follow, he sensed he was a witness to a "partial fulfillment" of the Talmud's interpretation (B.T. Megillah 6a) of the prophet Zechariah's promise that "in a foreign land, Judah shall be like a chieftain (7:6)," meaning that in the theaters and circus "arenas of the Gentiles . . . the princes of the Jewish people will eventually teach Torah to the multitudes."[25]

The Start of the Play

Because many people were still trickling into the hall during *mincha*, something more was needed to galvanize the crowd. That something was the Bluzhover Rebbe's impassioned recitation of two chapters of Psalms, echoed verse by verse by the multitude. Chapters 20 and 130 were both affirmations of trust in the power of the Almighty and pleas for salvation and redemption. Both psalms were part of the liturgy, the first recited near the close of the daily morning prayers and the second before the open ark during the Days of Awe, from Rosh Ha-Shanah through Yom Kippur. Together they could elicit the diurnal and extraordinary features of prayer.

As the Bluzhover Rebbe's voice broke over several verses that the scoreboard proclaimed were being intoned for the sake of Russian Jews in great peril, many in the crowd were visibly moved. No more holocausts. Everyone seemed to repeat the words, even echoing the leader's cadences and melody. As they did, they abandoned the passive role of observers and were drawn into an active role in the proceedings.

Now came the speeches. Setting a tone that the throng should share in a full awareness of the gathering as continuity with the past, Rabbi Besser reminded them that they were engaged in an extension of what the Jews had encountered at Sinai, a historic demonstration of Jews' acceptance of God's Torah. "Just as those who stood at Sinai for the honor of the Torah, so we do it honor here." We were heirs of the ancients and guarantors of the future, links in an unbroken chain. Our steadfastness would lead to the ultimate reward: the redemption. This was not simply another conclave; it was an act encircled in messianic hope. Besser concluded, "May we have the privilege of having the Messiah conclude the next Shas."

For the aged rabbi from Skver, Moshe Neuschloss, it was important to bear witness that from where he came, *daf yomi* was a part of daily hasidic life, with many filling the "cracks in their day with study of the day's *daf* in small impromptu groups, during the break before *tekias shofar* [the blowing of the shofar] on Rosh Hashanah, in the few minutes before the Rebbe joins them." Rabbi Raful reminded the crowd of its existential dilemma: "We stagger about in the exile." For Rabbi Perlow, Torah study transformed Jewish passivity as victims and exiles into activity of a higher order. If devotion had been demonstrated by Jews in their service at the Holy Temple in Jerusalem, now that "we do not have the Temple, we still do have the Torah." After the catastrophe of destruction, it became "the great monument of the Jewish people's survival in exile."[26] And there was a more recent destruction: the Holocaust, the latest of the never-ending catastrophes to befall the Jews. The turn toward Jewish study, Perlow asserted, had signaled a refusal to accept the finality of Jewish destruction. We were, as Perlow said once before, "a nation of orphans" who could find solace "only in God and his Torah."[27]

Perlow was assigned the task of completing the last lines of the Talmud. He briskly read through the text, a copy of which was in the program. This was a symbolic rather than an intensive, focused review. In a few moments he reached the last statement in the text, which reaffirms the religious logic that stands behind *daf yomi*: "Everyone who reviews *halakhot* [Jewish laws] each day has secured for himself the World to Come." "*Mazal tov*," he concluded. Congratulations echoed through the hall.

Slightly stooped, Simon Schwab, a frail and aging man, sat down in front of the microphone. He looked as if he might barely be able to speak, but his voice thundered. According to him, Torah study and this *siyum* were nothing less than an opportunity for each person to accept the Torah again from on high. Schwab asked rhetorically, where was this happening? He answered, scanning the sea of faces as if caught up in the wonder of it all, "Right here in the heart of New York City." The Torah was being received and honored in a place where no one could have believed it possible. Who was responsible? Schwab, community rabbi and champion of the lay learner, suggested that those who engaged in study not as a vocation (as yeshiva people did) but for the sake of "*Torah leshma,*

for no ulterior motives," were the heroes. When we recite the Talmud, Schwab told the crowd, we are not quoting someone who
lived long ago; whenever we repeat their words and follow their
logic, the disputants "are still having that discussion."[28] More than
just reading literature, this was personal engagement with a text.
"The Mishnah and Gemara are really talking to me." The words are
"going right into our hearts."

Schwab told his audience that once he encountered a student
from one of those "other seminaries," schools that did not share
this relationship with the texts and tradition, places corroded by
acculturative tendencies. Schwab asked the student what he was
learning. "I am doing *Baba Kama*," the young man answered, naming one of the most popular of the Talmud's tractates. "I said to
him," Schwab continued, sounding as if he were a hasidic rebbe
repeating a parable, "I have never done *Baba Kama*, but it has been
doing something to me for a long time." The crowd loved it.

What could the *daf yomi* do to us, who studied it properly and
faithfully without ulterior motives? It could bring us closer to one
another. "The *daf yomi* can remove the *mekhitsa* [partition] that
divides one Jew from another." Those who review the same text
and come together to celebrate their common experience create a
commonality. There are no orphans, no lonely people, among the
daf yomi crowd. Booming applause filled the arena.

If Simon Schwab played the role of community rabbi, Elya Svei
took the part of *rosh yeshiva*. He opened his Yiddish address by
asking, who was really responsible for tonight's celebration? As he
saw it, the true progenitor of Torah in America was his teacher, the
late Rabbi Aaron Kotler, a pioneer and visionary who had seen the
possibilities for Jewish study in this alien land. What Rabbi Kotler
taught us—Svei shouted so loudly that his words often became
distorted over the loudspeakers—was that while *daf yomi* was a
fine thing, it was not enough. The message was clear. Laymen who
satisfied themselves with little more than a brush with Talmud
were not truly doing what the Jew was called upon to do by God.
Only those who followed Rabbi Kotler and the rest of the yeshiva
into a dedicated life of Jewish study were fully living up to their
obligations as Jews.

Svei spoke for too long or perhaps his message was not one that this hall, filled with laymen, happy with their *daf yomi* experience, wanted to hear. Restless, offering misplaced applause or shouting "amen" at the end of every sentence, the audience began to signal that he should end. Svei subtly shifted his message to one that everyone could accept. The Torah had been given to this generation in flames, but the survivors of the Holocaust—by now all those in the hall could see themselves either as real or symbolic survivors—had created the possibility that exile could be an honor for God. They had done that by their activities on behalf of Torah. This was their consolation.

Those who tried to make sense of the suffering in the Holocaust so often asked, what of the silence of heaven during the horrors? Svei confronted the question implicitly with the best answer a man whose entire life is one of Torah study could give. The courage of those who steadfastly reviewed Torah under the most adverse conditions, risking torture and death, was indeed repaid by God. God had not been silent. "When a person prays," Svei informed his audience, "he talks to God, but when he reviews Torah, God talks to him."

As if on cue, the focus shifted to a black-hatted singing group, the Friends of Regesh, who began to chant in Hebrew in four-part harmony:

> Look down from the heavens and see,
> For we've suffered scorn and contempt from other nations,
> Thought to be like lambs to the slaughter,
> To be slain and destroyed,
> Assailed and shamed.
> And yet, despite all this,
> Your name we have not forgotten,
> Please, forget us not!

The words, carefully selected from the immense Jewish canon, delicately mingled a plea for divine attention and its consolations for a people with a special relationship with God along with resentments connected to the memory of Jewish suffering. "Like lambs to the slaughter" was the phrase often used to refer to the victims of the Holocaust, especially the most religious among them. Sung to a plaintive tune in a minor key, these lines from the morning prayers resonated Scripture from Isaiah to the Psalms, and reminded those present of the losses mourned this evening, ending with the call to God to look down upon those people who had remained faithful to Him.

For those who could read between the lines, there was something else, perhaps, embedded in this song. Not only had other nations looked upon these Jews with scorn and derision. Had not other Jews also looked down with contempt on those who had remained faithful when God turned away? Had not many of the Zionist pioneers, the warriors, accused the Orthodox Jews, who had so disproportionately been casualties of the Holocaust, of having acted too much like "lambs to the slaughter"? These Jews, who were like *goyim*, would now have to pay attention. Those here would not be forgotten. The last verse was repeated again and again.

Several hours had passed and the crowd was getting fidgety. A number of the day-school students in the upper decks, brought by their Talmud teachers to witness the evening's celebration, had already begun to leave. They were unmoved by the long speeches in a Yiddish few of them understood and that fewer chose to follow over their headphones. For them, the sea of black and white was largely foreign waters. The proceedings were already far too long for those who had come directly from a full day at school and had missed supper. This, they discovered, was not really their party.

But for Osher Greenfeld of Vizhnitz, the party was not yet over. With all the passion he could muster, he picked up on the songs sung by the Friends of Regesh and assured everyone that they could not imagine what an impression this evening and all that had led up to it made in Heaven. It remained for Aharon Dunner of London to fire up the congregation again for a final expression of solidarity and faith. He told stories of the rabbis that repeated the message that the only way to keep the faith was with constancy. Each day and each page had its appointed hour. "You think you will catch up what you have missed?" he asked, and answered in his British Yinglish, "You will never catch it up."

It was time to begin the penultimate part of the evening's formal play: the opening of the first volume of the Talmud, the tractate dealing with the proper hour for reciting the Shema, the testament of faith the Jew must repeat morning and night. Elya Fisher, a Gerrer hasid and head of its *kollel*, would perform the task, but first he reminded his listeners how the study of these texts protected them from the corrosive influences of America. It was a message characteristic of Ger, which had always emphasized scholarship and concern about the offensive temptations of lust that surrounded all those who made their way into the world outside the four cubits of Jewish life. "We here in America," Fisher warned, "have to protect and insulate ourselves from the corruption and sensuality of the world." How could one be so protected if not by the act of Talmudic review? The person in the subway who protects himself from the assault against his eyes by looking into his volume of Talmud, the constant students of Talmud who keep themselves from becoming otherwise engaged—all were bringing about a "spiritual sunrise." And with a new day dawning on Jewry came the opening words of the Talmud, whose first Mishna recalled that the evening Shema must be said before the twinkling of the dawn.

The Songs

Since the Bluzhover Rebbe's responsive readings, the assembled had remained passive. Announcement was made repeatedly that the evening would conclude with "one united minyan for *ma'ariv*," the evening prayers. Leading into those prayers was the recital of Kaddish, repeated "for the six million *kedoshim* (sanctified)." Everyone stood. Then, in mournful tones, Cantor Dovid Werdyger sang *El Mole Rachamim*, the traditional paean for the souls of the departed. Finally, Heshy Grunberger, a Holocaust survivor, stepped to the microphone and led the crowd in the repeated singing of *Ani ma'amin*, "I believe," the credo of faith in the Messiah's coming. The tune was one that had come to be associated with the Six Million; survivors had reported having heard the melody and words sung softly in the barracks at night. It was the faithful believers' anthem of their survival in the death camps.

At first few voices joined Grunberger's. But as he repeated the song three, five, seven times, the number of voices grew. By the end, nearly everyone seemed to be singing and a united mass of humanity swayed with the slow beat. Long after people would forget the speeches, they would recall the spine-chilling experience of the repeated singing of this testament of faith in a final redemption. As one participant put it, "That was definitely the highlight."

The blessing of *ma'ariv* was a coda to the song, a long, hushed sigh ending with the silence of the *Amidah* prayer, as a forest of thousands swayed and bowed silently toward Jerusalem. Then it was over.

The Aftermath and Conclusion

The thousands who had stayed until the end of the prayers streamed toward the exits, pressing into one another. Being swept up in this mass of humanity made the experience of being one with all those present vivid and palpable. Many found it hard to depart, and they lingered in groups on the street, touching and being touched. Others climbed onto the more than one hundred buses ringing the arena. Dozens of police on foot and horseback controlled traffic, while passersby on the busy street watched in wonder. For the contra-acculturative Orthodox Jews once thought to be a disappearing breed in America, the stares were sweet, for they reflected a realization by the world that "we are here and there are many of us."

The *daf yomi* and its celebration had transformed Talmud study from an activity with an inherent meaning that flows from scholarship itself and from meditation on the text into an act whose primary importance was symbolic. What was specifically being studied was not in itself important either this evening or at any other point in this page-a-day program. Content was secondary to the symbolic fact that something was being studied and that the entire Talmud had been reviewed nonstop. Substance became symbol.

If the *daf yomi* was the symbol of successful contra-acculturation and the triumph of religion in the profane palace, one victory did not necessarily mean the culture war was won. No image captured this better than something that caught my eye as, walking away, I took one last look back at the Garden. There, over the entrance, was a large electronic marquee announcing the night's event. In flashing lights were the words, WELCOME TO THE 9TH SIYUM HA-SHAS OF THE DAF YOMI. This was the glory of the King of Kings. On top of the sign were bigger, brighter lights that would remain lit no matter who took over the Garden for the night. They spelled out BUD, KING OF BEERS.

Who was the real king in America? Which culture would win the war here: *daf yomi* or Bud? Had the celebrants who took time out for a page of Talmud and their King triumphed by taking over Madison Square Garden, or, in the end, would those who took time out for a Bud, the king of beers, swallow the former, turning tonight into just one more ethnic event on the calendar of New York extravaganzas? The traditionalist Orthodox Jews believed they and their King would ultimately win in the place where Bud was king. Only time would tell which king would have the final glory in this contest of cultures.

Notes

1. For a discussion of this theme see Erich Rosenthal, "Acculturation without Assimilation? The Jewish Community of Chicago, Illinois," *American Journal of Sociology* 66, no. 3 (November 1960): 275–88.
2. Stephen Sharot suggests that many of those first-generation immigrants to America that in the three-generations hypothesis have been labeled Orthodox were not really that observant—that is why they were willing to come to the New World—and that indeed much of Orthodoxy and its institutional life is a post-Holocaust phenomenon in America. See Steven Sharot, "The Three-Generations Thesis and American Jews," *British Journal of Sociology* 24 (1973): 151–64.
3. See Samuel C. Heilman and Steven M. Cohen, *Cosmopolitans and Parochials: Modern Orthodox Jews in America* (Chicago: University of Chicago Press, 1989).
4. For a careful analysis of this process, see Menachem Friedman, "The Haredim and the Holocaust," *Jerusalem Quarterly* 53 (Winter 1990): 86–114. See also Samuel Heilman, *Defenders of the Faith* (New York: Schocken, 1992).
5. See *Encyclopedia Judaica*, vol. 14, 1299–1300.
6. As William Helmreich has catalogued these schools in America, they included places like the Telshe Yeshiva, founded in Cleveland in 1941; Beth Joseph, founded in Brooklyn in 1941; Beth Medrash Gevoha, founded in Lakewood, New Jersey, in 1943; Chofetz Chaim, founded in New York in 1944; the Mirrer Yeshiva, founded in Brooklyn in 1946; Beth Ha-Talmud, also founded in Brooklyn in 1949; and the Philadelphia Yeshiva, founded in 1953.

7. Jacob I. Friedman, "Reflections on Learning the Daf Yomi," *Jewish Observer* (April 1990): 12. Friedman is quoted below in the citation from the *New York Times*.

8. Ibid., 13–14. There has also been a move to encourage women to begin a modified form of *daf yomi* study (*Jewish Observer*, May 1990).

9. See Heilman and Cohen, *Cosmopolitans and Parochials*; and Jeffrey S. Gurock, "Resisters and Accommodators: Varieties of Orthodox Rabbis in America, 1886–1983," *American Jewish Archives* (November 1983): 100–187.

10. Eliezar Gershon Friedenson, *Beth Jacob Journal* (June 1938), quoted in Joseph Friedenson, "Remembering the Second Siyum Hashas," *Jewish Observer* (April 1990): 9.

11. Claude Levi-Strauss, *Tristes Tropiques*, trans. John Weightman and Doreen Weightman (1955; New York: Washington Square Press, 1973), 38.

12. Milton Singer, "The Cultural Pattern of Indian Civilization," *Far Eastern Quarterly* 15 (1955): 23–26; Emile Durkheim, *The Elementary Forms of Religious Life*, trans. J. W. Swain (1915; New York: Free Press, 1965), 466; and Clifford Geertz, *The Interpretation of Culture* (New York: Basic, 1973), 113.

13. Vincent Crapanzano, "Hermes' Dilemma," in James Clifford and George Marcus, eds., *Writing Culture* (Berkeley: University of California Press, 1986), 57.

14. "Fieldwork in Common Places," in *Writing Culture*, 33, 35.

15. Program, 16.

16. Program, 15. Whether the gossip was true or not, it was part of the spectacle, for, like everything else, it attested to the immensity of the event.

17. Victor Turner, *The Forest of Symbols: Aspects of Ndembu Ritual* (Ithaca, N.Y.: Cornell University Press, 1967), 450.

18. Milton Singer, "Emblems of Identity: A Semiotic Exploration," in Jacques Maquet, ed., *Symbols in Anthropology* (Malibu, Calif.: Udena, 1982), 124.

19. See Kenneth Pike, *Language in Relation to a Unified Theory of Structure of Human Behavior* (Glendale, Calif.: Summer Institute of Linguistics, 1955), 44–48. Pike makes use of the terms "spectacle" and "game" to organize his analysis of public events such as that which I am considering here. Yet while Pike uses these terms as metaphor, the events in Madison Square Garden seemed to make metaphor and reality merge.

20. William Helmreich, *The World of the Yeshiva* (New York: Free Press, 1982), 267.

21. Even though he was by this time the voice of German Orthodoxy, Schwab had not always been accepted in Washington Heights as a genuine heir of the German tradition. When first proposed for the post,

he was opposed by some of the Kahal Adath Jeshurun leaders who felt that a graduate of Lithuanian yeshivas could not fully share in their communal ethos. To accept him as the *moreh d'asroh* (community leader) seemed less than ideal. But the Breuer family, among others, endorsed Schwab's candidacy and that carried the day. They argued that, after the war, the Lithuanian-German divergences seemed moot. Indeed, a pious scholar and sensitive man, Schwab, in time, came to represent successfully everything the Orthodox Jews of Washington Heights and Agudat Israel believed themselves to be.

22. William Helmreich discusses the "right-wing" and *haredi* character of Svei, among others, in *The World of the Yeshiva*, 318.
23. See, for example, Samuel Heilman, *Synagogue Life: A Study in Symbolic Interaction* (Chicago: University of Chicago Press, 1976), 19–20.
24. Aaron Twerski, "Experiencing *Golus* in a Free Society: Can It Be Achieved? The Stumbling Blocks," *Jewish Observer* 13, no. 7 (December 1978): 6.
25. Meir Winkler, "Personal Reflections on Being There," *Jewish Observer* (May 1990): 9–10.
26. Samuel C. Heilman, *The People of the Book: Drama, Fellowship, and Religion*, paperback ed. with new preface (Chicago: University of Chicago Press, 1987), 5.
27. Yaakov Perlow, "Our Generation: Churban Plus One," *Jewish Observer* (June 1976): 8.
28. For an analysis of the cultural meaning of this practice, see Samuel C. Heilman, *People of the Book*.

CHAPTER 20

Americanism and Judaism in the Thought of Mordecai M. Kaplan

Mel Scult

Mordecai Kaplan was the quintessential ideologue for the second generation of American Jews.[1] His appeal, as well as his significance, were tied to his audience among the children of immigrants, especially in New York City, who spoke English and were beginning to feel at home in America.[2]

Pressures on second-generation Jews to integrate into American culture were intense, even though integration was hindered by the increased antisemitism of the Depression era. (To be sure, American antisemitism was less virulent than the European strain.) Total assimilation was a complex course that only a few followed. Most Jews remained poised between two cultures. The resulting tension, a subject of countless movies, novels, and short stories, became a primary concern of Jewish leaders.

As a rabbi, Kaplan was confronted by Jews who did not find their religion compelling. Their values, hopes, and even their sense of identity derived mainly from the domain of the secular. Children of immigrants found Old World Judaism obscure and oppressive. Like other ethnic and religious groups, Jews embraced the values of pluralism and toleration. The openness of American society constituted a threat to Jewish identity. The individual Jew, in search of life's meaning, was free to move in almost any direction, and this freedom often led to a fragmentation and attenuation that endangered the Jewish communal cohesion. Some Jews questioned the need for a Jewish community altogether in a society where economic and social opportunities were so great. Many of the functions of the traditional Jewish community had been appropriated by government, making it difficult to perceive what significant functions were left to the Jewish community.

Kaplan's empathy with Jews of the second generation flowed from personal experience. Having arrived in 1889 at the age of eight, he was educated in the public schools and yeshivas of the Lower East Side and came into his maturity just before World War I. By the 1920s, when most of the second generation of Jewish immigrants had reached their adulthood, he had worked out his philosophy within the framework of their special needs.

Primarily concerned with Jewish survival, Kaplan came to believe that a thorough rethinking of Judaism was necessary. He was deeply critical of both liberal and fundamentalist Jewish views. On the one hand, the Orthodox were rigid and intolerant; they revered the ceremonial more highly than the ethical and frequently were "ruthless and unscrupulous" in their business dealings. On the other hand, Reform Jews seemed to disassociate themselves from three thousand years of Jewish nationhood in order to turn Judaism into an abstract religious philosophy. "Philosophy fails as a bond of unity because of its static character; . . . that which influences the conduct of people is not this or that philosophy, but the civilization into which one is born, the complex of relationships and the sum of habits and ideals resulting from those relationships into which one's lot is cast when he comes into the world."[3]

Kaplan concluded that new institutions were needed to insure Jewish survival in America. This conviction first appeared in his writing while he was involved in establishing the Jewish Center in New York City between 1915 and 1918. He was troubled by the "thinness" of contemporary religiosity. Judaism had traditionally been bound up with the life of the community as a whole but, since the Emancipation, the Jewish religion had become for many Jews a "sometime" thing. Kaplan believed that the only way Judaism would survive was for the Jews to share much more than prayer. Community preceded religion and, indeed, gave rise to it; a thriving community inevitably craves religious articulation to give form and context to its joys and its sorrows.

Insistence that Judaism was a civilization rather than a religion carried with it certain implications. To state from the pulpit that "we have no beliefs that are fixed, no dogmas which may become the center of a new 'Orthodoxy'" meant to accept the implications of Nietzsche's assertion that God is dead. If Judaism was a living civilization, then it was constantly changing; no single belief or dogma could be static. Especially in modern times, Kaplan held,

> We have learned to regard no truth as finished and final. Whatever the teaching be and whomever its authority, it can never be above further research and inquiry. Such an attitude toward truth is entirely unthinkable with regard to any teaching which is believed to come directly from God.[4]

Kaplan was convinced that the values of Jewish civilization were perfectly compatible with those of American civilization. He was the spokesperson for those who wanted to be Jewish and American at the same time. There was a strong traditional element within the parameters of his Americanism, just as there was a strong American element within his Jewish ideology.

Of all the major ideologists of the twentieth century, Mordecai Kaplan is perhaps the most devoted to America as the embodiment of democratic principles. These principles not only entail a trust in the democratic process, the rule of law and the ideal of equality, but also assume the value of religion (to be sure, religion as separated from the state) in its ethical dimension. Kaplan's Americanism was so strong that at times he was ready to shift his main attention away from the Jews to American culture. In the 1920s he confronted the realization that it was American, not Jewish civilization into which most Jews were born and in which they lived. At times he despaired that Judaism as a civilization had no real future in America. Short of emigrating to Palestine—a possibility he rejected—the only option seemed to be a shift of context toward the creation of a "religion of American civilization." In light of the slow progress at the Society for the Advancement of Judaism, the synagogue that he founded in 1922, he speculated that he was asking too much of its members and that perhaps the only way effectively to influence the behavior of his congregants was to "utilize contemporary American needs to develop such spiritual values as might enable us to meet those needs in a rational and humane way." This change of direction would require transforming the SAJ into "the Society for the Advancement of the Religion of America." Jews were abandoning Judaism and even those who continued to support Jewish institutions did so in a perfunctory way. "The more I work, the less hope I have of seeing Judaism take root in this country." He would continue to adhere to Jewish practice in his own life but would cease to advocate the Jewish religion as the primary carrier of ethical and spiritual ideals.

In these statements, Kaplan was essentially advocating a civil religion for the United States. American culture would become the primary transmitter of religious values. Ethical teachings that appeared originally in the Jewish context would be transferred to general American culture. The American people would become the new people of God. "After all," he wrote in his journal, "God wants to choose America as the instrument of his will no less than he wanted Israel of old to act as an instrument of this kind." America could become the new Israel. "Would to God that I were granted the opportunity to serve the American people by demonstrating even in a small way that it can become chosen of God as Israel of old was chosen, and even on a more comprehensive and significant scale."[5]

The Americanism evidenced here survived Kaplan's periodic depressions and was discernible throughout his life. His book *The Faith of America*, an attempt to create a liturgy for the "Religion of American Civilization," contained readings, songs, and prayers, mainly from non-Jewish sources, for American holidays including Thanksgiving, Labor Day, United Nations Day, and Election Day. At the beginning of each section was a prayer, presumably written by the editors, emphasizing America as a religious ideal. For example, the text for New Year's Day opens with the exhortation, "O God, we have assembled here at the beginning of the new year, to rededicate our lives to the sacred ideals of America. . . . Disillusioned with ourselves and with our failure to rise to the height of our national ideals in the service of humanity, we entreat Thee to help us fulfill the promise of America."[6] It was America, its government, and its people who were the elect and the embodiment of the divine plan.

Kaplan's willingness to embrace non-Jews as the transmitters of religious ideals extended further. In an unpublished Bible commentary, he discussed the Israelite authors' propensity to reify qualities of the realities they described. (He himself advocated a return to a theological focus on qualities rather than objects, a mode of thinking now called predicate theology.) He preferred, for example, to discuss that which is divine in the world, rather than concentrate our thinking on God as an entity in and of itself. In certain passages of his commentary Kaplan adopted this notion of speaking with adjectives rather than nouns to Israel and the Torah. "*Divine* is, therefore, whatever possesses the quality of furthering man's perfection or salvation. *Torah-like* is whatever possesses the quality of rendering the Jewish people aware of its function to further the process of man's perfection or salvation. *Israel-like* is the people that identifies with that process." Kaplan's universalism meant that the means to attain salvation may be found almost anywhere. In fact, Kaplan's interpretation of Israel dissolves the covenant: "The teaching that Israel is God's chosen people should mean that God's chosen people is *any people* [my emphasis] that is consciously dedicated to the purpose of furthering the perfection or salvation of man."[7]

Kaplan's lifelong Zionism complemented and sometimes contradicted the universalist notions expressed above. Indeed, plagued by unconfessed doubts that the Zionist enterprise would ever bear fruit, he occasionally associated life in Palestine with the "prevalence of Orthodox Jews or hidebound Zionists," whereas life in America was associated with freedom and democracy. Sometimes he felt that to migrate to Palestine would be "to die in a losing battle with the worst obscurantism in the world." Kaplan's ambivalence about Palestine even surfaced in connection with his children. He brought up his daughter Judith to be a "Lover of Zion," but when he found her enthusiasm running too deep, he became upset. Wanting her to "think of herself" first, in a moment of panic he began feeding her anti-Zionist propaganda. "I thought that the arguments against Zionism would shake her faith in Palestine," he confided to his journal. "Instead, she seemed as ardent in her faith as before." He consoled himself that "of course, it is too soon to judge." His Zionist vision sometimes weakened, but his dedication to Americanism never wavered.[8]

In Kaplan's integration of American and Jewish identity, especially in his views on democracy and cultural pluralism, he reminds us of his well-known contemporary, Horace Kallen. Also, Kallen's biography resembles Kaplan's.

The son of a rabbi, Kallen was born in 1882 in a town in Silesia, a part of Germany now found in Poland. While Kallen was still young, his family settled in Boston, where he was educated in the public schools and eventually received a doctorate in philosophy from Harvard. Alienated from his father, he did not sit *shiva* nor recite the *kaddish*, despite a deathbed reconciliation. It was not only from his father that Kallen was alienated but also from Judaism. He did, however, return to the fold in a secular sense: "[Kallen] did not return to his father or his father's religion, but to the Jewish heritage of culture, thought, and values, to the feeling of membership in the Jewish people, to a lively sensitivity to the Jewish being and the Jewish experience."[9]

Kallen is remembered primarily for his doctrine of cultural pluralism. He believed that the Jew would not be free until he was free *as a Jew* and that democracy did not mean sameness but the "union of the different." The metaphor he advanced was not that of the melting pot but of the orchestra, where each instrument (that is, each ethnic group) retains its identity while contributing to the harmony of the whole. If people were truly free, the resulting diversity would enrich everyone. For Kallen, Judaism was a living culture that constantly changed. Zionism was a logical extension of the right of the Jews to a separate group life: he did not think of Zion as an answer to persecution but as an opportunity to revive the Hebraic Spirit (a notion that directly influenced Louis D. Brandeis).

Kallen and Kaplan were schooled in the same pragmatic tradition, both drawing heavily from William James and Josiah Royce and later finding their ideas confirmed by John Dewey. Both saw the ideals of Jefferson and the American Enlightenment as their own. Kallen and Kaplan believed in the freedom of individuals to live in a society that fostered diversity and pluralism. Yet their conclusions diverged significantly. Kaplan was a rabbi, a religious man who sought throughout his life to relate his ideology to his theological commitments and was concerned with the theological implications of his ideological categories. Kaplan's religious consciousness led him in directions absent from Kallen's worldview. An impulse toward universalism, although strong, was kept in check by Kaplan's passionate particularity.

Not only was Kaplan's Jewish consciousness intense but the traditional component of his mentality, so powerful when he was young, never left him. He lived at home until he was twenty-eight and studied Talmud regularly with his father, with whom he was very close. Israel Kaplan was described by his contemporaries as having a brilliant mind and considerable erudition in traditional sources. The elder Kaplan had received rabbinical ordination from important rabbis of his day, including Rabbi Isaac Elhanan Specktor and Rabbi Naphtali Zvi Judah Berlin (called *Ha-netziv*).

The relationship of Kaplan's traditionalism to his Americanism is evident in his ideas about democracy and the proper construction of the Jewish community in America. Kaplan first articulated his philosophy of democracy in an article published in 1916 on Jewish education that stated that democracy did not call for the amalgamation of all groups into a single general culture. He rejected the notion of a "melting pot" as "social tyranny" and self-segregation as a "menace to peace and progress," opting for a middle road that he called "partial segregation." The aims and function of groups, especially religious ones, were analogous to those of families. "The main claim that a religious community can put forth is that it is serving the same kind of purpose in the body politic as the family group though on a larger scale."[10] Such groups foster individual self-fulfillment, teach decency, and maintain necessary social controls. Group life is essential to a democratic society because subcultures become the bearers of societal and democratic values: the individual has a right to pursue his own happiness, which entails a right to organize to pursue a common goal.

The right of any group to separate existence would be meaningless were that group not granted the right to perpetuate itself, and this perpetuation takes place through education. The Jews should use their educational agencies and institutions to foster Jewish consciousness. Kaplan hoped that the Jew would become "so integrated with the House of Israel that he conceives for it a loyalty which gives meaning to his life and value to his personality." Such loyalty should not be construed as conflicting with the loyalty of the Jew to the larger society. Jewish consciousness would not endure, Kaplan believed, unless "by means of it, our children will make better citizens of the state, unless it will fit them spiritually for the larger world in which they must live, [and] unless it will give them worth and character." The goal of Jewish education was to foster "adjustment to environment and not to abstract principles." It must create "in the child a sense of warm intimacy with the Jewish people . . . and a sense of exaltation in those experiences of his people which have constituted for the human race the very footprints of God."[11]

Traditional societies exert powerful pressures on individual members because the sense of collective will is so clear. The traditional Jewish community survived precisely because it was able to enforce such a collective will on each individual Jew. But traditional Judaism evinced a strong commitment to authoritarian structures. Neither the Jewish community nor its ideology had ever been democratic. The intellectual and economic elites that ran the Jewish communities in pre-Emancipation Europe used coercion wherever they could and certainly never submitted their rulings to a plebiscite.

Kaplan's proposals for the creation of democratic, organic communities in the United States reflect an admiration for the clarity and discipline inherent in the traditional Jewish community. An apostle of liberty and freedom, Kaplan lamented the passing of the institutions that clearly expressed the collective will. At times he stood quite far from the democratic individualism that some ascribe to him—all the more unexpected, considering his own need for freedom and his belief in pluralism. He saw in the weakening of the collective will a serious threat: "Throughout the centuries, wherever the Jews were scattered, they lived in communities that were able to a large extent to enforce their will upon the individual. If Judaism is on the wane it is because there is no possibility of resorting to the collective mind or the collective will, thus showing that the Jewish people are disintegrating."[12]

Kaplan admired the cohesiveness of the Catholic Church, which enabled it to withstand the disintegrating forces of secularization in the modern period. Indeed, he sometimes felt that the Church could serve as a model for the Jewish community: "The Catholics have, of course, an incomparably stronger bond of unity which is re-enforced by all the prestige, authority and skill in organization and education characteristic of the Church of Rome." That this unity was in large part a result of the Church's authoritarian structure did not seem to deter him. "[Catholics] still operate with a powerfully cohesive force, a force whose decline in Jewish life has created the present problem of Judaism."[13] He realized, of course, that the most effective expression of the collective will among the Jews was the instrument of excommunication. While he did not advocate its reintroduction, he implored Jews to imitate certain other features of the Church: "The Catholic Church is the outstanding visible church, possessing visible and tangible manifestations of its international solidarity; . . . because visibility and tangibility are essential to keep any group spirit alive, we Jews should strive to achieve a community status which is analogous to that of the Catholic Church."[14]

Kaplan found a model for the kind of community he believed viable in America in the New York Kehillah—with some very significant modifications. Established in 1909 under the leadership of Judah Magnes, the Kehillah was an experiment in combining the cohesiveness of the traditional Jewish community with a democratic structure. Kaplan was one of a handful who continued to sing the praises of this unique adventure long after its demise.

In a sense, Kaplan's plan was an attempt to circumvent American voluntarism, a novum in Jewish history. In the pre-Emancipation past most Jews had no choice about being Jewish, but now they had a multitude of options. Subcultural groupings in America were associational in structure and there was "little external or internal compulsion to join or affiliate with the Jewish community." Kaplan proposed reintroducing elements of the traditional European Jewish communal structure into the American landscape, while creating a substantially new kind of structure appropriate for the new context.[15] The Jewish community in America was fatally flawed, he asserted, because it was based on organizations, primarily synagogues, that were not compulsory. In bad economic times, when the individual had to reduce his or her budget, support of the Jewish communal organizations was sacrificed first. If the Jews were to remain a distinct people in America, a significant measure of "involuntarism" must be introduced. In *Judaism as a Civilization* he stated that

> a person is a member of a nation not by choice, but by virtue of the pressure of the cultural group into which he is born. That pressure is exerted in the first instance through the family. If nationhood has played a useful part in the evolution of the race, it has been due, in no small degree, to this involuntarism which characterizes it. If, then, Jewish nationhood is to function in the Diaspora, its principal manifestation must be this very element of involuntarism character- istic of national life.[16]

Kaplan proposed a communal structure in which the overall councils or federations or Kehillot would be more than mere fund- raising organizations. They would be quasigovernmental structures controlling all other organizations. A Jew could not belong to any Jewish organization unless he or she was first a member of the federated community. A constitution would establish who could belong to the Jewish community or Kehillah and what the obliga- tions of each member would be.

> These might include . . . agreement to marry within the faith, or to proselytize the non-Jewish partner to a marriage, agreement to pro- vide for such Jewish instruction as the community may deem neces- sary, willingness to pay such communal taxes for Jewish purposes as the community may require. In turn, the member may then claim such privileges as permission to worship in any of the community's synagogues, religious education for his children, religious services in celebration of *Brith Milah, Bar Mitzvah*, marriage, burial in a Jewish cemetery and with Jewish rites. All these services would have to be denied to non-members.[17]

There were those who believed that the Kehillah experiment failed because it went too far in attempting to impose itself on the Jewish community as a whole; Kaplan believed that the Kehillah did not go far enough and wanted to carry the model much further. The Kehillah would pass "laws" that would govern the qualifications for rabbis, cantors, teachers, and social workers, and that "would authorize courts for adjusting violations of its rules and arbitrating conflicts for which no law exists."

Nevertheless, he remained a genuine pluralist. His communal structure would include every kind of Jewish organization, both religious and secular, as well as all Jewish denominations from the most sectarian Orthodox to the most liberal Reform. Jewish law would be reintroduced in the sensitive area of ritual, but congregations of whatever stripe would set their own rules for their members. In the case of the Orthodox, the traditional canons would be in force; each liberal group would have to devise its own laws concerning its mix of old and new rituals.

Thus, Kaplan desired the reinstitution of Jewish law within the context of a democratic polity. His ideology would take the Jewish community back to the European model of the early nineteenth century and, in some regards, to a pre-Emancipation model. The Emancipation had seemed to mean that Jewish law was dethroned in the Diaspora. Although the term "Jewish law" continues to be in wide use today, it is only in Israel that *halakhah* has the force of law. In America, as in other contemporary democratic societies, religious organizations must be voluntary. Yet Kaplan's idea that the Jews themselves constitute a special polity was not in itself illegal in America. It was not undemocratic, either, because at every point the rules governing the Jewish community were to emerge from a majority vote of the representative bodies recognized by the community. Not only would Jewish law be reintroduced in the center of Jewish life but also Jewish courts and sanctions to enforce their decisions. Kaplan, the most famous Jewish excommunicant of twentieth-century America, seemed on the verge of accepting that the new Kehillah expel people who did not conform to its basic requirements.

Kaplan's bizarre scheme appears to be a throwback to a structure of Jewish life that had all but disappeared since the Emancipation. It sacrificed a considerable degree of freedom to gain a remnant of the order of former times and to strengthen the collective consensus of the Jewish people. Kaplan proposed reinstating the sovereignty of the community as a significant force in Jewish life in order to counterbalance the sovereignty of the "autonomous individual."[18] He was ready to accept giving greater power to the community at the expense of limiting individualism as the price of Jewish survival. For Kaplan, community was more basic than freedom.

A few examples from Kaplan's life at the Society for the Advancement of Judaism illustrate his efforts to restore order and authority to Jewish life in America. In the early years of the SAJ he wanted to create a synagogue board of arbitration. In traditional Jewish communities, the rabbinical court, or *bet din*, dealt with conflicts involving marriages and divorces and other matters of personal status; it was also used as a kind of small-claims court in arbitrating disputes. In 1925 Kaplan recommended that a board of arbitration of seven members be established at the SAJ to arbitrate disputes between parties that consented to accept its authority. (According to the laws of the state of New York, any dispute could be submitted to arbitration with the written decision being "binding and irrevocable" under the law.) When Kaplan presented the proposal to reconstruct a quintessentially Orthodox institution within a non-Orthodox context, he described it as "a concrete embodiment of the ethical concerns of the Society." Unfortunately we have no records of how this experiment functioned nor the disputes it considered.

Another example of Kaplan's effort to make the Jewish community more effective was his call, in the 1960s and '70s, for a worldwide constitutional convention in order to resurrect the collective Jewish will. Although his proposals regarding community structure were not adopted by the Reconstructionist movement, they represent an essential aspect of his worldview. He longed for the unity that had characterized an earlier period and was unwilling to accept the anarchy he saw as the ruling principle of the American Jewish community.

Kaplan's attraction to the traditional functions of religion is also reflected in his theory of ethics, broadly parallel to his theories about community. The formation of virtuous character has often been considered one of the primary purposes of religion. Many contemporary liberals have ceased to regard religion as only a system of discipline and have viewed it as a means to self-realization, self-discovery, and personal liberation. Kaplan believed that religion should help the individual function at the highest level of his capabilities; in addition, however, faith should create good character and foster self-control.

Shifts toward a religion of self-expression or self-realization occurred in America during the 1920s and again in the 1960s, periods characterized by a polarization between morality and freedom. Such a polarization is simplistic. However much one values freedom, the need for self-restraint and the suppression of destructive behavior is undeniable.[19] In his discussion of ethical problems Kaplan treated the traditional function of religion as character builder in the context of the concept of the sovereignty of God. For Kaplan, acceptance of this sovereignty meant acknowledging that personal needs and wants were not ultimate; will is subordinated to a law higher than the law of self-gratification. For Kaplan, atheism was the "conscious belief that life and what it brings to us are ours to do with as we please." Kaplan spoke to the inner conflict between the urge to be free and to do as one pleases and the need to live effectively in society. Believing that the individual can forge ahead to higher levels of self-realization without renouncing social responsibility, Kaplan spurned the notion that the "indulgence of the natural impulses is the only means to the realization and development of the individual." There were those who claim that all conventions stifle natural instincts toward goodness and creativity, but "this view identifies all morality with artificial conventions which, by hindering the satisfactions of the appetites, prevent the realization of one's true personality."

If the traditional theology that served as the basis of virtue and character is discarded, what is put in its place to support self-denial and restraint? Kaplan urged the reinstatement of religion as builder of character. A compensatory religious element should stand alongside the ethic of self-realization that had become a defining element of the liberal heritage. Discipline and self-realization, seemingly contradictory, would harmoniously complement each other.

In the past, faith supplied a sufficient basis for "altruism, generosity, and holiness." What will be the contemporary liberal substitute for such a faith? People are moved to self-denial and self-regulation through community pressure. In traditional societies, where the collective will was clear and united, such pressure functioned effectively. In a democratic society, directing the collective mind away from the exaltation of self-gratification toward enlightened self-denial becomes problematic. Are there mechanisms of community pressure compatible with a liberal sensibility? Can ethical pressure allow people significant autonomy and independence?

Kaplan confronted this difficulty in various guises, especially in the rabbi's relationship to the congregation. He acknowledged that rabbis lacked worldly expertise. The rabbi was a layman with respect to all businesses and occupations except those of the synagogue. How can the rabbi legitimately advocate a particular behavior in the public workplace? The first step was for the democratic rabbi to become an impresario rather than an oracle. The rabbi should bring congregants together in small groups organized according to professions in order to draw up a list of ethical principles and practices to which they would adhere in their own lives. Then all synagogue members would assemble to explore ways in which they could pressure their fellows to conform to these codes. The various groups would meet periodically to discuss their progress and problems. Traditional Jews have had little difficulty elaborating the rules by which people ought to live; these modern ethical codes are another example of Kaplan's desire to reintroduce aspects of Jewish law in a nontraditional setting.

In common with young educated American Jews of the early twentieth century, Mordecai Kaplan believed in America and was optimistic about its future. He accepted the American pragmatic and functional idiom, an approach well suited to the American landscape of change, growth, and never-ending opportunity. He embraced an ethics of progress and was concerned mainly with what would work, rather than with self-contained, theoretical philosophical systems. He wanted a realistic religion and a God related to the actual experience of a twentieth-century person. He wanted Judaism to embrace freedom but was ready to introduce law and regulation in order to strengthen Jewish tenacity and stamina. Kaplan believed that the community could survive only if people accepted that their religion demanded action from them. The advent of an open society did not obviate the need for the individual to submit to the commandment, the *mitzvah*. However, for Kaplan *mitzvah* was not to descend from on high. It would be created through the democratic processes of a modern society.

Notes

1. Some of the material in this article appears in an altered form in Mel Scult, *Judaism Faces the Twentieth Century: The Biography of Mordecai M. Kaplan* (Detroit: Wayne State University Press, 1993).

2. On the second generation, see Deborah Dash Moore, *At Home in America: Second-Generation New York Jews* (New York: Columbia University Press, 1981), as well as Arnold M. Eisen's intellectual history of American Jewry in the second and third generations, *The Chosen People in America* (Bloomington: Indiana University Press, 1983). The best work on the immigrants in New York is Moses Rischin, *The Promised City: New York's Jews, 1870–1914* (New York: Corinth, 1964).

3. For his criticism of Orthodoxy, see "Why Combat Fundamentalism?"—an outline of a lecture delivered on February 15, 1924 (Kaplan Archive, RRC [Reconstructionist Rabbinical College]). For his attack on Reform, see "Why Is Judaism More Than a Philosophy?"—a sermon at Society for the Advancement of Judaism (SAJ), November 9, 1923 (Kaplan Archive, RRC).

4. "Is Judaism a Revelation or a Philosophy?"—a sermon at the SAJ, November 2, 1923 (Kaplan Archive, RRC).

5. "The Universal in the National"—a sermon at SAJ, January 11, 1924, and "The Unification of Mankind," a sermon at SAJ on Rosh Hashanah (September 23), 1922 (both in Kaplan Archive, RRC). The discussion on America as the civilization of choice is found in the Kaplan Journal, December 26, 1923 (Kaplan Archive, RRC).

6. See Mordecai Kaplan, J. Paul Williams, and Eugene Kohn, eds., *The Faith of America: Readings, Songs, and Prayers for the Celebration of American Holidays* (New York: Reconstructionist Press, 1963), 3.

7. Both quotations in this paragraph are from a manuscript in the Kaplan Archive (RRC), a running commentary on Genesis that I call "Torah and Salvation." For a further exploration of Kaplan and the Bible, see my essay "Kaplan's Reinterpretation of the Bible" in *The American Judaism of Mordecai Kaplan*, Emanuel S. Goldsmith, Mel Scult, and Robert Seltzer, eds. (New York: New York University Press, 1990), 294–319.

8. Kaplan Journal, March 16, 1926 (Kaplan Archive, RRC).

9. Milton R. Konvitz, "Horace Meyer Kallen (1882–1974): In Praise of Hyphenation and Orchestration," in *The Legacy of Horace M. Kallen*, Milton R. Konvitz, ed. (New York: Herzl, 1987), 17. These observations on Kallen are based mostly on this book.

10. Mordecai M. Kaplan, "The Function of the Jewish School," *Jewish Teacher* 1, no. 1:9. Benderly created the Jewish Teachers Association of New York, which published *The Jewish Teacher*. The journal was edited by Alexander Dushkin, with Isaac Berkson serving as business manager and Mordecai Kaplan, Julius Greenstone, and Harry Friedenwald serving as members of the advisory board.
11. Ibid., 11, 12.
12. Mordecai M. Kaplan, Sermon at the Jewish Center, March 1, 1919, Parshas Vayakeyl (Kaplan Archive, RRC).
13. Mordecai M. Kaplan, *Judaism as a Civilization*, 2d ed. (New York: Reconstructionist Press, 1957), 77.
14. Mordecai M. Kaplan, *The Future of the American Jew* (New York: Macmillan, 1948), 99.
15. Daniel J. Elazar, *Community and Polity: The Organizational Dynamics of American Jewry* (Philadelphia: Jewish Publication Society, 1976), 12.
16. Mordecai M. Kaplan, *Judaism as a Civilization*, 292–93.
17. Mordecai M. Kaplan, *The Future of the American Jew*, 395.
18. For a pointed analysis of this key concept, see Eugene B. Borowitz, "The Autonomous Jewish Self," *Modern Judaism* 4, no. 1:39–55.
19. The line of thinking here was suggested by Michael Novak, "Crime and Character," *This World* 14 (Spring/Summer 1986): 26–54.

CHAPTER 21

The American Mission of Abraham Joshua Heschel

Edward K. Kaplan

Because of his combination of intellectual substance and charisma, Abraham Joshua Heschel (1907–1972) became a revered and notorious public figure in the United States during the tumultuous 1960s.[1] In 1966 *Newsweek* wrote of him, "To recover the prophetic message of ancient Judaism, Heschel has built up a rich, contemporary Jewish theology that may well be the most significant achievement of modern Jewish thought," confirming Reinhold Niebuhr's prediction fifteen years earlier that "he will become a commanding and authoritative voice not only in the Jewish community but in the religious life of America."[2]

Heschel's unique presence in the United States is a result of his having personally integrated the spiritual and intellectual treasures of three capitals of prewar Jewish Europe: Warsaw (his birthplace), Vilna ("the Jerusalem of Lithuania," where he received a diploma from the Yiddish-language *Real-Gymnasium*), and Berlin (where he attended a liberal rabbinic school and a secular university). Reared in a devout community, Heschel was a child prodigy who mastered the immense body of basic Jewish texts; his *yikhus*, his distinguished Hasidic ancestry, is vaguely known and still incompletely studied.[3] His astounding memory of the Bible, Talmud, and Kabbalistic texts dates from his childhood in Warsaw. Then he went on to earn a doctorate in philosophy from the University of Berlin in 1933.

Heschel came to America in 1940 having already bridged the

traditional and modern worlds and having lived through the European cultural crisis following the First World War. He knew first-hand the Nazi rise to power but did not place in the *Shoah* a source of Jewish energy, as seems to have happened to many American Jews after the war. Heschel's theology represents a challenging alternative to Judaism redefined by the Holocaust and the State of Israel. (It implies that survival does not require Jews seeing themselves, even triumphally, as victims.)[4] Heschel recognized that American Jewry, despite its struggle with recent historical facts, could not derive enduring values and identity from the vicarious experience of events essentially foreign to its daily reality. Heschel's Judaism insisted upon the real presence of God and Torah, as well as that of the Jewish people.[5]

Heschel's major English works are addressed to observant and secular readers alike because he lived within the tensions between religious confidence and a harsh moral imperative. With his characteristic mixture of philosophical polemic and lush poetic prose, he interpreted at once universal religious experience and particular Jewish tradition. *Man Is Not Alone* (1951) and *God in Search of Man* (1955) led him to be viewed as "a *zaddik* (or holy man) of the 1950s." *The Prophets* (1962) and *The Insecurity of Freedom* (1966) established the theological sources of Heschel as a "prophet of the 1960s." *A Passion for Truth* (1973), published soon after his death, with an autobiographical preface, outlines a radical and realistic post-Holocaust faith.

Heschel acquired his modern scholarly and philosophical credentials at the Hochschule für die Wissenschaft des Judentums in Berlin and the Friedrich Wilhelm (now Humboldt) University. On January 30, 1933, Hitler became chancellor of Germany. On February 11, 1933, Heschel successfully completed the oral defense of his doctoral dissertation on prophetic consciousness, just weeks before Jews were expelled from the German academic system.[6] On February 27, the Reichstag building was set on fire in the course of an election campaign that was to enable the Nazis to seize total power in July of that year. That same year Heschel published his first and perhaps most intimate book, a collection of Yiddish poems, *Der Shem Ham'Forash—Mentsh* (Mankind—God's Ineffable Name), express-

ing the intense compassion of a pious Jew who, despite his modernity, lives in intimacy with the biblical God. The poem "Ikh un
Du" (I and Thou) proclaims an even more intimate reciprocity of
human and divine than the dialogical relation already celebrated
by Martin Buber: "My nerves' tendrils are intertwined with yours."[7]

It has been observed that the systematic exclusion of Jews from
Germany's bountiful cultural life after 1933 stimulated German
Jewish creativity. Many assimilated Jews returned to the synagogue
and enrolled in adult education courses in Judaism.[8] Publishing
houses owned by Jews, forbidden to print "Aryan" authors, issued
an impressive new list of books in Judaica. With a Ph.D. and a
liberal rabbinical degree (he was ordained at the Hochschule in
July 1934), Heschel began to present his point of view to the general
public in print and as a teacher.

In 1935 Heschel became a reader for the Erich Reiss Verlag in
Berlin and editor of its series on Jewish thought and history (*Judentum in Geschichte und Gegenwart*). Reiss published Heschel's biography of Maimonides in 1935 and his biographical essay on Don
Isaac Abravanel in 1937.[9] Heschel complemented these inspirational biographies of Jewish thinkers and activists in exile with
eight essays on Tannaim (for example, on Yochanan ben Zakkai,
Rabbi Gamliel II, Rabbi Akiba, and Rabbi Jehuda Hannassi) published in the Berlin Jewish community newspaper, *Jüdisches Gemeindeblatt*, in 1936, signed "Dr. Abraham Heschel."[10] He gave
lectures at the Berlin Lehrhaus and, in March 1937, Martin Buber
called him to Frankfurt-am-Main to succeed him as codirector of
the Central Organization for Jewish Education and the Jüdisches
Lehrhaus; it was there that the young Fritz Rothschild first heard
Heschel lecture on the Bible to a skeptical group of youth leaders.
After their eventual emigration to the United States, the two men
formed a lifelong professional tie.[11]

Heschel was expelled from Germany on October 28, 1938, with
about eighteen thousand other Jews holding Polish passports. After
a short stay at the border town of Zbaszyn he returned to Warsaw.
He lived with his mother and two of his sisters on Dzika Street and,
from November 1938 to June 1939, taught at the Warsaw Institute
for Jewish Studies. In the spring of 1939 he received an invitation
from President Julian Morgenstern to teach at Hebrew Union Col-

lege.[12] Awaiting approval of a nonquota visa to the United States, Heschel left Warsaw for London, writing to Dr. Morgenstern on July 28, "I would like very much to study the English language and to continue the work on a philosophical book on the prayer [sic]. Two chapters therefrom will be published before long in the book published in honour of Prof. Balaban . . . and the *Monatsschrift für die Geschichte und Wissenschaft des Judentums*."

"Das Gebet als Aeusserung und Einfülung" (Prayer as Expression and Empathy) appeared in the famous swan-song issue of the *Monatsschrift*, volume 82 (1939). This elegant essay, without footnotes, took its place among the more conventionally academic monographs by leading German-speaking Jewish scholarly luminaries. A Hebrew essay, "Al mahut ha-tefillah" (On the Essence of Prayer), originally written for the *Meir Balaban Jubilee Volume* (to be published in Warsaw in 1939, but confiscated and destroyed by the Nazis), did not appear until February 1941 in *Bitzaron*, a Hebrew monthly.[13]

On March 21, 1940, Heschel arrived in New York appalled by an intimate havoc. He remained acutely aware that his family and entire culture were being annihilated. Much later, in a 1965 lecture at the Union Theological Seminary of New York, he defined himself as a survivor:

> I am a brand plucked from the fire, in which my people was burned to death. I am a brand plucked from the fire of an altar to Satan on which millions of human lives were exterminated to evil's greater glory. [On this altar] so much else was consumed: the divine image of so many human beings, many people's faith in the God of justice and compassion, and much of the secret and power of attachment to the Bible bred and cherished in the hearts of men for nearly two thousand years.[14]

At the Hebrew Union College in Cincinnati Heschel was perceived as a modern but religiously observant scholar committed to spiritual issues. It was there that he refined his American mission: "how to share the certainty of Israel that the Bible contains that which God wants us to know and harken to; how to attain a collective sense for the presence of God in the biblical words."[15] Heschel's perception of God's reality and his response to human evil remained consistent with that of his years in Berlin. Grateful for their having rescued him, Heschel judged American Jews as being in the throes of a second Holocaust—what he called "spiritual absenteeism." He would attempt to transplant his still vibrant faith.

Heschel's American career can be divided into three phases: (1) from 1940 to 1950 he dealt with philosophical and theological foundations; (2) from 1951 to 1962 he elaborated a critique of contemporary Jewish philosophy and practice; and (3) from 1962 to his death in 1972 he became a prophetic activist.[16] Rather than summarize Heschel's religious philosophy or analyze his main books, I want to explore how Heschel's Jewish soul took root in America. Heschel's various writings and appearances became like the divine tree of Kabbalistic legend: its roots in heaven, its branches and leaves on earth.

Heschel did not find enough American Jews struggling with the reality of God nor responding to divine imperatives. After the war, American Jews were relatively safe from antisemitism, gaining social and political power, moving to the suburbs, building synagogues and schools, yet handicapped by reductionistic conceptions of God and of the Jewish tradition. For Heschel it was essential that the living God must not be cut down to mere symbols, nor halakhah (Jewish law) to "customs and ceremonies." Accordingly, he challenged the institutional versions of Judaism with biblical standards of truth, holiness, and justice.

During his first fifteen years in this country (1940–1955), Heschel's publications focused on prayer and faith. He sought, literally, to save our soul (the Jewish *neshamah*) from oblivion.[17] In Germany, he had already written on the spiritual crisis of the twentieth century and continued to see Nazism as but another, albeit an unspeakable, outbreak of a prolonged cultural emergency. In the *HUC Bulletin* of March 1943 he published an English version of a speech he had delivered to a Quaker group in Frankfurt, Germany, in 1938. "The Meaning of This War" opened, "Emblazoned over the gates of the world in which we live is the escutcheon of the demons. The mark of Cain in the face of man has come to overshadow the likeness of God."[18] Heschel blamed secular civilization—"us," not "them," including Americans—for distorted values and a feeble,

ineffective response to events: "The outbreak of war was no surprise. It came as a long expected sequel to a spiritual disaster."[19]
Nazism was but an extreme perversion of the callousness of modern
civilization:

> We did not sink into the pit in 1939, or even in 1933. We had de-
> scended into it generations ago, and the snakes have sent their venom
> into the bloodstream of humanity, gradually paralyzing us, numbing
> nerve after nerve, dulling our minds, darkening our vision. . . . In our
> every-day life we worshiped force, despised compassion, and obeyed
> no law but our unappeasable appetite. The vision of the sacred has
> all but died in the soul of man.[20]

Heschel tried unsuccessfully during the war to help European
victims, and it became clear that his main impact would be through
his writings.[21] Heschel's first articles written in (impeccable) English appeared between 1942 and 1944: "An Analysis of Piety," "The
Holy Dimension," and "Faith."[22] For an article on "Prayer," published in 1945, the author signed his name as "Abraham Joshua
Heschel, Associate Professor of Jewish Philosophy, Hebrew Union
College"; by signing his full name, the American academic had
discreetly reappropriated his Hasidic ancestry.[23] Soon after moving
from Hebrew Union College to Jewish Theological Seminary in
1945, he published "The Mystical Element in Judaism."[24] These
foundational articles anticipate Heschel's American program.[25]

Heschel's manner of marketing his ideas, even then, was quintessentially American. He understood that his credibility would benefit from recognition by professionals outside as well as within the
Jewish community, so he published articles in English with the
prestigious journals of Columbia University and the University of
Chicago and in Mordecai Kaplan's *Reconstructionist*, which then
reached a large, diverse readership.[26] Moreover, Heschel's consum-
mate literary style was, by necessity, addressed particularly to outsiders as well as insiders. Heschel's goal was to unveil, and make
poetically concrete, life's fundamental holiness. He understood that
American readers could not recognize his constant allusions (most
of them without direct citation of sources) to traditional texts and
that their cultural experience was not very open to divine reality.

The destruction of European Jewry made especially urgent
Heschel's commitment to transplant the Kabbalistic tree of heaven

in the New World. In a translation of a speech given in Yiddish to the YIVO annual conference in New York in January 1945, he insisted that

> romantic portraiture of Hasidism, nostalgia, and piety, are merely ephemeral; they disappear with the first generation. We are in need of Jews whose life is a garden, not a hothouse. Only a living Judaism can survive. Books are no more than seeds; we must be both the soil and the atmosphere in which they grow.[27]

His first American work of spiritual rescue, published in 1950, is an expansion of this speech in English titled *The Earth Is the Lord's: The Inner World of the Jew in East Europe*. Illustrated with exquisite woodcuts by Ilya Schor, also a Jewish refugee from Poland, this book is more than an idealization of Heschel's heritage and a *kaddish* to a civilization lost; it challenges Jews to a prophetic task:

> We are God's stake in human history. . . . There is a war to wage against the vulgar, against the glorification of the absurd, a war that is incessant, universal. Loyal to the presence of the ultimate in the common, we may be able to make it clear that man is more than man, that in doing the finite he may perceive the infinite.[28]

Heschel's reputation as the spiritual voice of American Jewry was established by 1951, when two more books appeared: *The Sabbath* and *Man Is Not Alone*.[29] It was at this time that the author was lauded in the *New York Herald Tribune* by America's leading Protestant theologian and social activist, Reinhold Niebuhr, as a definitive authority on Judaism and religion.

The polyphonic style of *Man Is Not Alone*, as well as of *God In Search of Man* (1955) and *The Prophets* (1962), combines poetically evocative metaphor, assonance, and rhythm with a sometimes surgically incisive theological and philosophical polemics to convey the authentic religious experience. He expected his words, addressed to religious and secular readers alike, to open minds to the divine presence.[30]

Having decided that Americans must at first participate in his spiritual reality vicariously, Heschel had no choice but to exploit a rhetorical strategy to stimulate readers' intuitions. He evokes ineffable experience beyond the limits of language so as to thrust readers beyond concepts to God's initiative. Reading him becomes a

religious odyssey. His writing can at times become a virtuoso performance, verbal acrobatics. At its best, however, Heschel's artistry
sensitizes us to holiness—in the prayerbook, in the Bible, and especially in everyday living. His style supplies both form and content
for readers who do not have the advantage of the author's biblical,
rabbinic, Kabbalistic, philosophical, literary background. For those
who share Heschel's daily liturgical observance and training, his
poetic renditions infuse their acts with new *kavvanah*, sacred
intention.[31]

In 1953, in a week of intra-Jewish shuttle diplomacy, Heschel
delivered two addresses within four days to the (Conservative)
Rabbinical Assembly of America meeting in Atlantic City and to
the (Reform) Central Conference of American Rabbis at Estes Park,
Colorado. He warned his Conservative colleagues about the spiritual emptiness of their well-ordered services; he urged the Reform
rabbis not to abandon halakhah. Both audiences expressed a mixture of outrage, embarrassment, and veneration.

Heschel's message to the Rabbinical Assembly, "The Spirit of
Jewish Prayer," began with a critique of current synagogue practice.
"Has the synagogue become a graveyard where prayer is buried?" he
asked. "We have developed the habit of *praying by proxy*."[32] Rabbis
must face honestly the frailty of their religious faith: "I have been
in the United States of America for thirteen years. I have not discovered America but I have discovered something in America. It is
possible to be a rabbi and not believe in the God of Abraham, Isaac
and Jacob."[33]

Heschel then pinpointed a crisis in theology. He criticized (some
would say caricatured) four contemporary approaches to religion
that subvert true prayer: (1) the agnosticism that claimed "that the
only way to revitalize the synagogue is to minimize the importance
of prayer and to convert the synagogue into a center"; (2) a religious behaviorism whose "supreme article of faith is *respect for
tradition*"; (3) the view that prayer was a social act, "built on a
theology which regards God as a symbol of social action, as an
epitome of the ideals of the group";[34] and (4) a religious solipsism
that "maintains that the individual self of the worshipper is the
whole sphere of prayer life. The assumption [is] that God is an idea,
a process, a source, a fountain, a spring, a power."

The affirmative part of his address provided a demanding standard. It began with a citation from an earlier work: "It is precisely the function of prayer to shift the center of living from self-consciousness to self-surrender."[35] People should strive to view reality from God's perspective, a way of thinking that the Hebrew prophets both evoke and exemplify. The books he subsequently published seek to effect a religious Copernican revolution; they comprise a vast apologetics meant to recenter our consciousness from the self to God.[36]

At the same time, Heschel's theology was fully aware of modern anguish. In response to the view that Judaism bestows a tranquil "peace of mind" and that religion makes us feel at home in the universe, he insisted that "we could not but experience anxiety and spiritual homelessness in the sight of so much suffering and evil, in countless examples of failure to live up to the will of God. That experience gained in intensity by the soul-stirring awareness that God Himself was not at home in the universe, where His will is defied, where His kingship is denied."[37] Religious observance can provide the elements of a remedy: "To pray, then, means to bring God back into the world. . . . God is transcendent, but our worship makes Him immanent."

Heschel seems to have considered the 1930s and 1950s as spiritually equivalent. Modern skepticism had undermined the ability to recall God's self-revelation at Sinai: "If [conviction in the reality of God] is lacking, if the presence of God is a myth, then prayer to God is a delusion. If God is unable to listen to us, then we are insane in talking to Him."[38] (Heschel, of course, holds to the objective reality of the biblical God; to many of us, however, if taken seriously, his shocking statement might tempt one to relinquish any pretense to religious, as opposed to ethnic or political, identity.)

Heschel's admonition to Reform rabbis two days later, "Toward an Understanding of Halacha," also confronts the implicit agnosticism or atheism of American Judaism.[39] After expressing his gratitude to Julian Morgenstern, who made Heschel's emigration to the United States possible, he reassured his Reform colleagues: "I, too, have wrestled with the difficulties inherent in our faith as Jews."[40] Heschel described his own life as paradigmatic of the journey of the modern Jew. Scion of generations of rabbis, the young man had arrived in Berlin in the fall of 1927 to study at the University; one day he "walks alone through the magnificent streets of Berlin" and suddenly notices that the sun has gone down. He had forgotten to pray! "I had forgotten God—I had forgotten Sinai—I had forgotten that sunset is my business—that my task is to 'restore the world to the kingship of the Lord.'"[41] The East European *hasid*, nourished in the hothouse of German intellectualism, uprooted once again and transplanted to America, reminds American rabbis of their true origin: "There is something which is far greater than my will to believe. Namely, God's will that I believe."[42]

Rejecting the secularism that defined Jewish observance as "customs and ceremonies," Heschel insisted on God's reality and the divine origin of the *mitzvot*. He challenged his Reform colleagues "to take *a leap of action* rather than *a leap of thought*." The current crisis of belief results from a false premise, namely, that the mind must first know God before serving God. The opposite is true: "In carrying out the word of the Torah [a Jew] is ushered into the presence of spiritual meaning. Through the ecstasy of deeds [a Jew] learns to be certain of the presence of God." Heschel concluded, "For many years rabbis have in speeches delivered at conventions of the Central Conference of American Rabbis voiced their sense of shock and grief at the state of religious chaos prevalent in modern congregations and have urged the members of this Conference to return to Jewish observance. May it be a return to a halakhic way of life, not to customs and ceremonies."[43]

In 1953, thirteen years after his arrival on our shores, Heschel celebrated his bar mitzvah as a New American by denouncing vicarious Judaism. Faith in a real God was an imperative and must be lived. Heschel demanded of his readers that they emulate the God of pathos, the biblical God who cares passionately about the quality of human life. God is the source of Jewish energy—not big synagogues, community centers, money, or deeply felt responsibility toward Israel. In *Man Is Not Alone* Heschel had named the standard:

> GOD. Not an emotion, a stir within us, but a power, a marvel beyond us, tearing the world apart. The word that means more than universe, more than eternity, holy, holy, holy; we cannot comprehend it. We

only know it means infinitely more than we are able to echo. Staggered, embarrassed, we stammer and say: He, who is more than all there is, who speaks through the ineffable, whose question is more than our minds can answer; He to whom our life can be the spelling of an answer.[44]

A full-scale intellectual and cultural biography would trace in detail what Heschel meant by "the spelling of an answer," yet it is possible to draw inferences from his works. His study of the Bible, *The Prophets*, defined the source of his public activism, the "theology of pathos" sketched in his 1933 Berlin dissertation and the Yiddish poetry that expressed his hypersensitivity to evil.[45] "The prophet is a man who feels fiercely. God has thrust a burden upon his soul, and he is bowed and stunned by man's fierce greed. . . . [The prophet makes] much ado about paltry things, lavishing excessive language upon trifling subjects."[46]

At the height of the Cold War, at the threshold of John Kennedy's Camelot and Lyndon Johnson's "Great Society," Heschel became a prophetic figure, which, depending on the politics of his colleagues, either enhanced or compromised his reputation.[47] Heschel first reached mass acclaim at the 1960 White House Conference on Children and Youth, and the next year at the White House Conference on Aging. In 1963, he presented the opening address at the National Conference on Religion and Race in Chicago, which began, "At the first conference on religion and race, the main participants were Pharaoh and Moses. . . . The outcome of that summit meeting has not yet come to an end. Pharaoh is not ready to capitulate. The exodus began, but is far from having been completed."[48] At the Chicago conference Heschel met the Reverend Martin Luther King, Jr., beginning their close association in civil rights matters.[49]

Heschel applied to all social and political dilemmas what I call a "sacred humanism" that demanded reverence for the individual as literally an image of God.[50] This theology of mankind was a response to the living God of concern, and he supports it with citations from the Bible, the Talmud, and other rabbinic and Kabbalistic sources. The prophets' sympathetic identification with the divine pathos most dramatically defined our social, political, and religious standard. For example, with regard to civil rights, "Racial or religious bigotry must be recognized for what it is: satanism, blasphemy."[51] In the realm of international politics (the question was the war in Vietnam): "Oceans divide us, God's presence unites us, and God is present wherever man is afflicted, and all of humanity is embroiled in every agony wherever it may be."[52]

In the 1960s, Heschel's increasing involvement in interfaith dialogue and cooperation made him a veritable "apostle to the gentiles," in James Sanders's rather startling formulation.[53] Two examples must suffice. Starting in 1961, as a consultant to the American Jewish Committee, Heschel established a close working relationship with Cardinal Bea, whom Pope John XXIII put in charge of the Declaration on Non-Christian Religions at the Second Vatican Council. Heschel's conversations in Rome, including a personal interview with Pope Paul VI, contributed significantly to the final version of *Nostra Aetate*.[54] Second, Heschel's relations with colleagues at the Protestant Union Theological Seminary culminated in his appointment in 1965 as Harry Emerson Fosdick Visiting Professor. By then Heschel was perceived as a Hebrew prophet—his activist friends William Sloane Coffin, Jr., and Daniel Berrigan called him "Father Abraham." Heschel's unshakable defense of the autonomy of the Hebrew Bible, Judaism, Israel, the Jewish people— and the God of Israel—allowed him both to affirm the spiritual value of other traditions and to make demands on their integrity.

Heschel's final two books written in English—*Israel: Echo of Eternity* (1969) and *A Passion for Truth* (1973)—both confront the disasters of twentieth-century history. In their own ways, these troubling and incomplete books challenge us to redefine our relation to the God of the Bible. Heschel's modern theology faces the inescapable discrepancy between religious ideals and the facts of persistent barbarism. Heschel's emphasis on human freedom and responsibility does not contradict his faith in a caring God who remains involved in a continuing human process of redemption.

My view is that Heschel's witness is valuable even for those who do not share his vigorous confidence in God's revelation at Sinai, because his manner of thinking keeps the relevant questions alive. His "depth theology" strengthens our drive toward faith and does not contradict a commitment to harsh truth. Heschel's demand that we live in a manner compatible with God's presence reinforces our resolve in the face of God's silence.

Heschel's most explicit response to the nihilism of our age appears in *Israel: Echo of Eternity*. (Its publication, sponsored by the Anti-Defamation League of B'nai B'rith, is an attempt to communicate to key Christian leaders the preciousness of the Holy Land and to help them understand Jewish fears of annihilation during the June 1967 War.) Heschel did not rationalize the Nazi destruction theologically by interpreting the Jewish state as an "atonement" either by God or by the United Nations. But the existence of the State of Israel does confirm that the Jewish people has overcome despair. The "rebirth of Israel" represents a partial answer to the question of faith after Auschwitz—but not the definitive one. Faith is not static, like a formulated creed, but an unending challenge, a way of thinking about unfinished redemption: "There is no answer to Auschwitz. . . . To try to provide one is to commit a supreme blasphemy. One can merely say that Israel enables us to bear the agony of Auschwitz without radical despair, to sense a trace of God's radiance in the jungles of history."[55]

Heschel loyally supported Israel and celebrated the reunion in 1967 of new and old Jerusalem. But he also thought critically about Israeli policies. In the late 1950s, he had warned against what might happen if religious law, spiritual authenticity, and democratic rights were to be confused: "It would be a fatal distortion to reduce Judaism to individualism. . . . At the same time, it would be suicidal to reduce Judaism to collectivism or nationalism. Jewish existence is a personal situation."[56] Heschel's own "passion for truth" afflicted him with the inability to accept expedient solutions or pious rationales.

Heschel pointed to the prophets' "theology of pathos" as training us to view human events from the perspective of the Eternal. At the same time, he insisted that ultimate meaning remains a mystery, an unknown. There is no panacea. Heschel did not reveal his own irreducible conflict until the preface to *A Passion for Truth*, delivered to the publisher weeks before his death. Two Hasidic extremists who guided his youth represented his lifelong ethical and spiritual tensions:

> In a very strange way, I found my soul at home with the Baal Shem
> Tov but driven by the Kotzker. Was it good to live with one's heart
> torn between the joy of Mezbizh and the anxiety of Kotzk? To live
> both in awe and consternation, in fervor and horror, with my con-
> science on mercy and my eyes on Auschwitz, wavering between
> exaltation and dismay? I had no choice: my heart was in Mezbizh,
> my mind in Kotzk.[57]

The Kotzker rebbe reflects Heschel's agony at moral decay, the
frailty of conscience, the trivialization of religious and ethical demands, in contrast to the Baal Shem's uncritical love for all creation. The radical post-Holocaust theology implicit in *A Passion for
Truth* accepts the challenge of absolute contradiction: commitment
to moral integrity and faith in a caring God who, creating free
human beings, allows them the power to destroy themselves.[58]

We can grasp the modernity of Heschel's apologetics only in its
dialectical relation to moral despair. Prophetic ethics challenges
our calloused conscience, just as faith challenges our frail confidence in the Divine: "Dark is the world to me, for all its cities and
stars. If not for my faith that God in His silence still listens to my
cry, who could stand such agony?"[59]

This is not a reassuring conclusion. Heschel confronts the tensions that lacerate modern religion: the secularization of revealed
Tradition, the reduction of God to symbols, the shrinking of prophetic ethics to the confines of institutional or nationalistic self-
interest. "Depth theology" insists that no position taken by the
mind is final. Insight, he reminded us, occurs within an individual's
consciousness: but God meets the person equally in the heart and in
the jungles of the world.

Notes

1. My thanks to Samuel Dresner, Aharon Appelfeld, Jonathan Sarna, Jacob Neusner, Fritz Rothschild, Arnold Wolf, and Byron Sherwin for
   conversations about issues relating to this paper. I began this paper
   before the United States started to bomb Iraq (January 17, 1991) and
   before Iraq launched missiles into Israel. My writing and revisions
   continued throughout the agonizing conflict. One test of any theology
   must be to provide an authentic and relevant model of Judaism at
   such times.

2. *Newsweek*, January 31, 1966; *New York Herald Tribune*, April 1, 1951, reviewing *Man Is Not Alone*.

3. For the best summary of Heschel's Hasidic background, see Samuel H. Dresner, introduction to *The Circle of the Baal Shem Tov: Studies in Hasidism*, by Abraham Joshua Heschel, ed. and trans. Samuel H. Dresner (Chicago and London: University of Chicago Press, 1985). See also Hillel Goldberg, *Between Berlin and Slobodka: Jewish Transition Figures from Eastern Europe* (Hoboken, N.J.: Ktav, 1989).

4. In this regard, I agree with Jacob Neusner that American Jewish institutions tend to validate themselves in relation to Israel or to the Holocaust—to the exclusion of knowledge of the multifarious Jewish worlds before World War II, and to the exclusion of religious imperatives. See Jacob Neusner, *Strangers at Home: "The Holocaust," Zionism, and American Judaism* (Chicago: University of Chicago Press, 1981); also Jacob Neusner, *American Judaism: Adventure in Modernity* (Englewood Cliffs, N.J.: Prentice-Hall, 1972).

5. See A. J. Heschel, "God, Torah, and Israel," in *Theology and Church in Times of Change: Essays in Honor of John Coleman Bennett* (Philadelphia: Westminster, 1970), 71–90.

6. The printed cover of *Das prophetische Bewusstsein* carries this information but not the other version, which is entitled *Die Prophetie*; both were published in 1936 by the Polish Academy of Sciences (Krakow) and Erich Reiss Verlag (Berlin).

7. Heschel's poem was first published in the New York Yiddish periodical *Zukunft* in 1929.

8. See Ernst Simon, "Jewish Adult Education in Nazi Germany as Spiritual Resistance," *Leo Baeck Institute Yearbook* 1 (1956): 68–104, for a study of the phenomenon.

9. See *Maimonides: A Biography*, trans. Joachim Neugroschel (New York: Farrar, Straus & Giroux, 1982); *Don Jizchak Abravanel* (Berlin: Reiss, 1937), 32 pages; abridged translation by William Silverman in *Intermountain Jewish News—Literary Supplement*, December 19, 1986, 5–13.

10. It would have been misunderstood, in Western Europe, if he had signed his full Hasidic name, Abraham Joshua Heschel Heschel—or with the abridgment that became famous in the United States. (His three given names commemorate his great-great-grandfather, the Apter Rebbe, Abraham Joshua Heschel [1748–1825], known as the *Ohev Yisrael*, the Lover of Jews.) Neil Rosenstein, ed., *The Unbroken Chain*, 2 vols. (New York; CIS, 1990) is the basic reference work.

11. Interview with Fritz A. Rothschild. Later Heschel would help Rothschild, a penniless immigrant, enter the Jewish Theological Seminary, and Rothschild, after joining the faculty, would publish an anthology of Heschel's writings, *Between God and Man: An Interpretation of Judaism* (New York: Free Press, 1959; most recent revision of bibliogra-

phy, 1975), a lucid systematization of his philosophy, making Heschel accessible to a wide readership.

12. The letter is dated April 6, 1939, and is found in the American Jewish Archives, Cincinnati, Ohio. My thanks to archivist Kevin Proffitt for his help. See the important article by Michael Meyer, "The Refugee Scholars Project of the Hebrew Union College," in Bertram W. Korn, ed., *A Bicentennial Festschrift for Jacob R. Marcus* (Waltham, Mass.: American Jewish Historical Society; New York: Ktav, 1976), 359–75.

13. These exploratory papers define the categories developed later in *Man's Quest for God: Studies in Prayer and Symbolism* (Scribner's, 1954; reprinted as *Quest for God*).

14. "No Religion Is an Island," *Union Seminary Review* 21, no. 2 (January 1966): 117–34.

15. *God in Search of Man* (New York: Farrar, Straus & Giroux, 1955), 246. The sentence that follows underlines the gravity of his endeavor: "In this problem lies the dilemma of our fate, and in the answer lies the dawn or the doom" (ibid.); see ibid., 252–53.

16. Especially useful analytical summaries are Fritz Rothschild's preface to *Between God and Man*; John C. Merkle, *The Genesis of Faith: The Depth Theology of Abraham Joshua Heschel* (New York: Macmillan, 1985), the most detailed analysis of Heschel's theology, including responses to principal critics and interpreters; and Donald J. Moore, *The Human and the Holy* (New York: Fordham University Press, 1989).

17. In 1949 Heschel published as a fifteen-page offprint an urgent call for Jewish spiritual survival, *Pikuach N'Shamah* (New York: Baronial Press). This little-known (and important) essay, written in rich allusive Hebrew, was probably given as a talk to the Union of Principals of Day Schools and Yeshivas in the New York Metropolitan Area, as the cover suggests.

18. I quote from the version published as the final chapter of *Man's Quest for God*, 147–51. The original English essay, "The Meaning of This War," first published in the *HUC Bulletin* (March 1943): 1–2, 8, was revised slightly and reprinted in *Liberal Judaism* (February 1944): 18–21. The original German version, entitled "Versuch einer Deutung" (An Inquiry about Meaning), can be found in Margarethe Lachmund, ed., *Begegnung mit dem Judentum: Ein Gedenkbuch. (Stimmen der Freunde [Quaker] in Deutschland)* (Bad Pyrmont, 1962), 11–13.

19. Ibid., 149.

20. Ibid.; this part was added in the 1944 version.

21. Heschel did not confine himself to writing. In 1941, 1942, and 1943, he attempted to get American Jews to send food to Jews under German control and help them in other ways. See his interview in Yiddish with Gershon Jacobson, *Day-Morning Journal*, 13 June 1963, quoted in

translation by Samuel Dresner, ed., *The Circle of the Baal Shem Tov*, xxv, note 30.

22. "An Analysis of Piety," *Review of Religion* (March 1942): 293–307 (published by Columbia University); "The Holy Dimension," *Journal of Religion* (April 1943): 117–24 (published by the University of Chicago); "Faith," *Reconstructionist*, November 3, 1944, 10–14, and November 17, 1944, 12–16 (edited by Mordecai Kaplan, an early acquaintance who soon became his colleague at the Jewish Theological Seminary).

23. This article appeared in the *Review of Religion* (January 1945): 153–68.

24. The article was begun at Hebrew Union College. After he moved to the Jewish Theological Seminary (1945), it appeared in Louis Finkelstein's widely read anthology, *The Jews: Their History, Culture, and Religion* (New York: Harper & Brothers; Philadelphia: Jewish Publication Society, 1949), 602–23. Heschel's article, with citations from the Zohar, appears in volume 1 of the two-volume edition and in volume 2 of the four-volume edition. Compare with chaps. 10 and 11 of *The Earth Is the Lord's* (New York: Schuman, 1950), "Kabbalah" and "Hasidism."

25. For example, "An Analysis of Piety" (*Review of Religion*, March 1942), became the concluding chapter of *Man Is Not Alone* (1951), which he entitled "The Pious Man."

26. Heschel also completed his studies of medieval Jewish philosophy, the staple of academic respectability, with a monograph combining rigorous historical and philological research and theological reflections on faith. "The Quest for Certainty in Saadia's Philosophy" was first published in the *Jewish Quarterly Review* 33, nos. 2–3 (1943): 263–313, and 34, no. 4 (1944): 391–408, and was later published as a little "book" or broadside by Philip Feldheim in 1944.

27. The original was published in the *YIVO Bleter* 25 (1945) and the English translation in the *YIVO Annual of Jewish Social Science* 1 (1946): 86–106.

28. *The Earth Is the Lord's*, 109. Chap. 10, "Kabbalah," outlines his theological system.

29. Both published by Farrar, Straus & Young, the second jointly with the Jewish Publication Society.

30. I have analyzed this issue in "Language and Reality in Abraham J. Heschel's Philosophy of Religion," *Journal of the American Academy of Religion* 41, no. 1 (March 1973): 94–113.

31. Heschel's role as "*zaddik* of the 1950s" comes together in the papers collected in *Man's Quest for God*, which includes his 1945 article on prayer and the English version of his 1938 address on the Hitler period to the Quakers at Frankfurt. Heschel announces his mission most dramatically, however, in its two central chapters (3 and 4), based on the two papers he delivered to the American rabbinate.

32. "The Spirit of Jewish Prayer," *Proceedings of the Rabbinical Assembly of America* 17 (1953): 151–77; discussion, 200–217; revised and reprinted in *Man's Quest for God*, chap. 3, "Spontaneity Is the Goal," 49–89.

33. "Spirit of Jewish Prayer," 159.

34. "Spirit of Jewish Prayer," 156, note 3. Heschel traces this "sociological fallacy" to the 1913 book by Josiah Royce, *The Problem of Christianity*, not to Mordecai Kaplan, whose *Judaism as a Civilization* first appeared as a book in 1934. During the discussion, Heschel makes a covert reference to Kaplan, whom he admired as a person and as a passionate Jew: "The strange thing about many of our contemporaries is that their life is nobler than their ideology, that their faith is deep and their views are shallow, that their souls are suppressed and their slogans proclaimed. We must not continue to cherish a theory just because we embraced it forty years ago" (ibid., 215).

35. From his 1945 article, "Prayer," published in the *Review of Religion*.

36. For a more detailed analysis of Heschel's Pascalian strategy, see my article, "Abraham J. Heschel's Poetics of Religious Thinking," in John C. Merkle, ed., *Abraham Joshua Heschel: Exploring His Life and Thought* (New York: Macmillan, 1985), 103–19.

37. "Spirit of Jewish Prayer," 163.

38. Ibid., 163.

39. "Toward an Understanding of Halacha," *CCAR Yearbook* 63 (1953): 386–409; revised slightly as "Continuity Is the Way," chap. 4 of *Man's Quest for God*, 93–114.

40. "Toward an Understanding of Halacha," 386. Then follows a passage about his student days in Berlin, which begins, "I came with great hunger to the University of Berlin to study philosophy." An important statement omitted in the version revised for *Man's Quest* traces the emptiness of rational religion—so compatible with the ideology of classical Reform—to neo-Kantian professors who regarded "religion as a *fiction*, useful to society or to man's personal well-being. [For them] religion is not a relationship of man to God but a relationship of man to the symbol of his highest ideals. There is no God, but we must go on worshipping his symbol" (ibid., 387).

41. "Toward an Understanding of Halacha," 390, quoted in Hebrew; *Quest*, 96.

42. "Toward an Understanding of Halacha," 391.

43. Ibid., 409.

44. *Man Is Not Alone*, 78.

45. *The Prophets* (Harper and Row and Jewish Publication Society, 1962).

46. *The Prophets*, 3. See Edward K. Kaplan, "The Spiritual Radicalism of Abraham Joshua Heschel," *Conservative Judaism* 28, no. 1 (Fall 1973): 40–49. The entire issue is devoted to tributes to Heschel soon after his death.

47. The specific goals of Heschel's activism can be found in his collection of addresses, *The Insecurity of Freedom: Essays on Human Existence* (New York: Farrar, Straus & Giroux, 1966). The acknowledgments section gives names and dates of the occasions on which the papers were delivered. Community issues such as Soviet Jewry, Israel and the Diaspora, and religious education are also explored in *The Insecurity of Freedom*. Papers published after this important and insufficiently studied volume should also be consulted: Heschel's illuminating conversation on Jewish education at the Solomon Schechter School, his charismatic speeches on Vietnam, and his lectures on interfaith dialogue, beginning with the inaugural lecture of 1965 at the Union Theological Seminary, "No Religion Is an Island." See Rothschild, *Between God and Man* for the specific references. See also the anthology edited by Jacob Neusner and Noam M. M. Neusner, *To Grow in Wisdom* (Lanham, Md., 1989).
48. *Insecurity of Freedom*, 85.
49. Martin Luther King, Jr., was invited to give the principal address at a gathering of the Rabbinical Assembly honoring Heschel on his sixtieth birthday: see "Conversation with Martin Luther King," in *Conservative Judaism* 22, no. 3 (Spring 1968): 1–19.
50. "The awareness of divine dignity must determine even man's relation to his own self. His soul as well as his body constitutes an image of God" (from the important essay "Sacred Image of Man," in *Insecurity of Freedom*, 155; see also "The Patient as a Person," "Religion and Race," and "Sacred Image of Man"; also Heschel's summary, *Who Is Man?* [Stanford, Calif.: Stanford University Press, 1965]).
51. *Insecurity of Freedom*, 86.
52. "The Moral Outrage of Vietnam," in *Vietnam: Crisis of Conscience*, with Robert McAfee Brown and Michael Novak (New York: Association Press, Behrman House, Herder and Herder, 1967), 52.
53. J. A. Sanders, "Abraham Joshua Heschel: An Apostle to the Gentiles," *Conservative Judaism* 28, no. 1 (Fall 1973): 55–60; also the important book edited by Harold Kasimow and Byron L. Sherwin, *No Religion Is an Island: Abraham Joshua Heschel and Interreligious Dialogue* (Maryknoll, N.Y.: Orbis, 1991), which contains Catholic, Protestant, Muslim, Hindu, and South Asian responses to Heschel's thought as well as a useful bibliography.
54. See Eva Fleischner, "Heschel's Significance for Jewish-Christian Relations," in Merkle, ed., *Abraham Joshua Heschel: Exploring His Life and Thought*, 142–64.
55. *Cross Currents* 19, no. 4 (Fall 1969): 423; first delivered at the St. Louis Symposium on "Theology in the City of Man" (October 1968). Compare:

    What should have been our answer to Auschwitz? . . . Our people's faith in God at this moment in history did not falter. At this moment in history Isaac was indeed sacrificed, his blood shed. We all died in Auschwitz, yet our faith survived. We knew that to repudiate God would be to enhance the Holocaust. . . . The State of Israel is not an atonement. It would be blasphemy to regard it as a compensation. However, the existence of Israel reborn makes life in the West less unendurable. It removes some of the weight from hindrances to believing in God. (422)

56. "Yisrael: Am, Eretz, Medinah: Ideological Evaluation of Israel and the Diaspora," *Rabbinical Assembly of America Proceedings* 22 (1958): 122; see also "The Individual Jew and His Obligations" (1957) and "Israel and the Diaspora" (1958), both reprinted in *Insecurity of Freedom*; "The Theological Dimensions of Medinat Yisrael," *Rabbinical Assembly of America Proceedings* 32 (1968): 91–103; discussion, 104–9. See Arnold Eisen, *Galut: Modern Jewish Reflection on Homelessness and Homecoming* (Bloomington and Indianapolis: Indiana University Press, 1986), 169–72, for an insightful placing of Heschel's views on Israel into their American context.

57. *A Passion for Truth* (New York: Farrar, Straus & Giroux, 1973), xiv.

58. See Edmond La B. Cherbonnier, "Heschel's Time-Bomb," *Conservative Judaism* 28, no. 1 (Fall 1973): 10–18; also Edward K. Kaplan, "Mysticism and Despair in Abraham J. Heschel's Religious Thought," *Journal of Religion* 57 (January 1977): 33–47.

59. "On Prayer," *Conservative Judaism* 25, no. 1 (Fall 1970): 7. See also *Man Is Not Alone* (1951), chap. 16, "The Hiding God," which cites (without attribution) Heschel's 1943 article on "The Meaning of This War."

PART SEVEN

Surviving as Jews in Twenty-First-Century America

CHAPTER 22

Modern Times and Jewish Assimilation

Paul Ritterband

Sociologists of the Jews have been classified as accommodationists or assimilationists—perhaps more simply and explicitly as optimists or pessimists. I am among the assimilationists-pessimists, not on ideological grounds but on the basis of my reading of the sociodemographic data.

To be fair to the optimists-accommodationists, we should note at the outset that no modern diaspora Jewish community has produced the quantity of scholarship and intellectual product as has American Jewry. We need only contrast the struggle of the fathers of *Jüdische Wissenschaft*, who sought unsuccessfully to enter the mainstream of German academic life, with the authors in this volume, who are almost all affiliated with secular universities and enjoy the unself-conscious, comfortable life of American academe. Furthermore, there are more students in advanced *yeshivot* in America and Israel than there were at the high point of the Lithuanian *yeshivot* during the nineteenth century. One-third of all children currently enrolled in Jewish schools in the United States are attending day schools and *yeshivot*. On a secular level, Jews in America are doing extraordinarily well. Of the four hundred richest Americans annually listed by *Forbes*, it is estimated that approximately 25% are Jews, even though Jews constitute only 2.5% of the American population.

Other examples abound. From a barely tolerated minority whose entrance to high places was controlled by a *numerus clausus*, Jews have become major figures in American academic and intellectual life. They are disproportionately employed in universities and, more significantly, the more distinguished the institution, the higher the proportion of Jews. Jewish professors publish more articles and books, secure more grants; by every standard measure of success in academe, Jews have arrived.[1] While for a generation no Jew served on the United States Supreme Court (perhaps reflecting the conservative bent of the appointers and the liberal stance of most American Jews, including presumably Jewish jurists), that situation has now been corrected, and the House of Representatives and Senate have three times as many Jews proportionately as their number in the population would predict. Perhaps the only significant public arena in which Jews are underrepresented is sports, but that is generally true of the urban, white middle class.

If things are so good, why worry? First, the Jewish community of the United States is becoming bimodal: the distribution of Jewish behaviors, beliefs, and attitudes is moving away from the common bell-shaped normal curve to a "camel-backed" two-humped curve in which the more committed Jews have increased their commitment while less committed Jews have more and more opened themselves up to the forces of assimilation. Thus, to mix metaphors, Jewish day schools are bursting at the seams, and intermarriage rates are going through the roof. American Jewish institutions and ideologies that grounded themselves in "centrism" find themselves in increasing trouble. The inertial force of the culture of the immigrant generation has been all but lost.

Second, individual success is not paralleled by collective success. Jewishness is attenuating. Jews are leaders in modernization and secularization, processes that inevitably lead to assimilation and demographic decline. The structure of belief, in which both Jews and non-Jews participated, a structure that effectively made the Jews an *imperium in imperio* for so many centuries, has withered away, accompanied by serious decline in the viability of the American Jewish community. In this essay, I will focus on three demographic changes emblematic of the devolution of the Jews in our time: fertility, intermarriage, and geographic location.

Jewish commitment to secularization and economic rationality has contributed to individual success but has wreaked havoc with Jewish collective life. The Jews of modernity are obsessed with modernity. Even among first-generation American Jews, it was a matter of pride to be considered modern and a compliment to call someone modern, as in "he keeps *shabbes* but he is modern." To modernize their children, immigrants gave their children "modern" names. No more Isaacs, but now Irvings. Gone were the Mottels, Moshes, and even Mordechais; in their stead came Mortons and Murrays. What Jews did not realize was that by transposing the surnames of WASPs into the first names (Christian names?) of their children, they were identifying them as Jews in WASP clothing. Another instance is the awkward term "Modern Orthodoxy." Do we find "Modern Methodism" or "Modern Islam" or "Modern Catholicism"? Why did Jerry Falwell call his television program the "Old-Fashioned Gospel Hour"? Why does one group of religious traditionalists call itself, with pride, "modern," and the other with equal pride call itself "old-fashioned"?

For Jews, modernity has meant the sloughing off of characteristics that non-Jews had defined as negative attributes of Jews. As a minority no longer protected by communal walls, Jews came to believe what gentiles said about them. They internalized the critiques of their enemies and putative friends. "Be a Jew at home and a human being abroad" became the watchword of Jewish enlightenment. If we could somehow save a kernel of the Jewish past, the essence of the Jewish experience, we would be able to eliminate the excrescences and become acceptable to non-Jewish society. A secular Messiah had arrived in the form of enlightenment and emancipation.

Jews did not assimilate to generic America: they assimilated to an America that exists only in the minds of a few, among them most Jews. America in the minds of the Jews is a culturally neutral society, one in which the public arena is secular, allowing space for Jews to enter not as Jews but as citizens. Further, Jews took secularization beyond the public sphere into their private lives. Thus, Jews have become the most secularized of all the ethnic groups in America of European origin.[2] Jews became secular, at least in part, so that they could become American. By doing so they became less American as well as less Jewish. Fertility is one critical indicator of this metamorphosis.

. . .

The secularization and modernization (the processes are inseparable) of the rank and file of Jews for almost two centuries have
become a major threat to diaspora Jewish continuity in the twentieth century. The demographic transition of the nineteenth century,
in which birth rates plummeted, was led by Jews and was in part a
consequence of increased secularity. I use the term "led" not to
indicate that the Jews were active propagandists for fertility control, leading Europe into the era of the small family, but rather to
indicate that in the aggregate, Jewish fertility declined far more
rapidly, more precipitously, and much earlier than did the fertility
of non-Jews. To paraphrase Heinrich Heine: as do the Jews, so do
the Christians.

Low fertility, a characteristic of Jews wherever they became
emancipated, was a corollary of their emergent modern status and
secular turn of mind. During the immediately premodern period
Jewish fertility was greater than that of the surrounding non-Jewish
populations.[3] The decline in fertility that became manifest for Jews
in the early nineteenth century in Germany (and that preceded
that of Protestants and Catholics by one and two generations, respectively) was concurrent with a wide variety of changes in the
status and culture of the Jews. Such changes included a rapid decline of Jewish religious observance and traditional Jewish culture.[4]
Jewish fertility remained high in the villages of South Germany
long after it had declined to subreplacement levels in urban centers.
Within the villages, premodern patterns of fertility were to be found
among the more traditional elements in the community. While
we do not have compelling evidence of the relationship between
secularity and low fertility for nineteenth-century populations,
such evidence does exist for twentieth-century Jews as well as
Christians (particularly Catholics), and there is reason to believe
that it was true for the earlier period as well.[5]

The Jewish lead in the demographic transformation continues to
have serious consequences for Jewish continuity. Given current life
expectancies and marriage frequency, it can be reasonably assumed
that 2.1 children per Jewish woman are necessary for the biological
continuity of the Jewish people (assuming no losses through intermarriage, of which more below). Western societies are reproducing

below replacement and the Jews lead the way, as they have for more than a century. The United States fertility rate in 1980 was 40% below what it was in 1950. Conforming to the well-established pattern, Jewish fertility (and nuptiality as well) was significantly below that of non-Jews. The March 1957 Current Population Survey reported that the number of children born to Jewish women forty-five years of age and older was 29% less than the number born to Catholics and 21% less than the number born to Protestants.[6] A study of college freshmen of the class of 1974 found that, by 1980, 42% of Jewish women were married, as compared with 57% of non-Jewish women. About one in twenty Jews were parents, compared with one in four of non-Jews.[7] Analysis of the 1990 National Jewish Population Survey showed that the fertility of Jewish women is significantly below that of non-Jewish whites and significantly below replacement.[8]

A counterargument asserts that Jewish women do not complete their childbearing years with fewer children than non-Jewish women; rather, they have their children later in life, so that their total fertility is underestimated. A 1982 data collection reported that Jews expect to have about 2.1 children, less than Protestants and Catholics but enough for replacement.[9] Both the 1975 and 1985 Boston population studies report that currently married Jewish women expected to have 2.2 children. Closer analysis of the 1975 Boston data shows that the 1949–1959 cohort expected to have 2.8 children, while the most recent marriage cohort expected a total completed fertility of 1.9 children.[10] Subjective fertility desires and expectations are, of course, subject to revision upward or downward. Panel studies that I have consulted show a significant downward trend of fertility desires for Jews and non-Jews.[11] That does not take into account what has been termed "effectively Jewish fertility"[12] (raising children as Jews, something quite problematic in the instance of exogamy), nor does it take into account infertility, divorce, death, and other impediments. Therefore, the actual fertility of ever-married Bostonian, and by extension American, Jewish women is likely to be significantly below replacement (taking into account decreased rates of nuptiality).

Jews have been committed to modernity (a mode of thought and behavior that includes, inter alia, commitment to the small nuclear family) since they stepped out of the ghettos and villages of Eastern and Central Europe. To be modern was the dream of the rank and file of Jews over the past century or more. For most Jews, to be modern meant to become secular and to be secular meant to bear few children.

For a long time, Jews could feel themselves insulated from the sociological model in which acculturation inevitably led to assimilation. Jews felt that they could take on the characteristics of the public culture (style of life, language, and other ethnic markers) without giving up the Jewish neighborhood, Jewish friendship circles, and, most significantly, endogamy. Jews saw themselves, and were seen by professional social scientists, as sui generis.[13] That sense of immunity from social forces was based upon reasonable evidence. The March 1957 Current Population Survey reported an intermarriage rate among Jews of only 4%, one-third that of Catholics and one-half that of Protestants.[14] Yet, there were signs of the breaching of the walls. A study of American college graduates, class of 1961, reported on religion-specific rates of intermarriage among those alumni who were married by 1964: while Jewish intermarriage rates were still relatively low (12% as compared with 16% for Protestants and 34% for Catholics), one could see portents of the future. Even at 12%, the vast majority of Jews did not choose their mates without consideration of Jewish criteria. With 2.5% of the population (not taking into account age squeeze in the marriage market) the 12% rate was far below the rate that would have occurred if total randomness had obtained. Distance from the immigrant generation was a powerful predictor (and probable cause) of intermarriage. Of those Jews who had no grandparents born in the United States, 11% intermarried; of those who had one to three grandparents born in the United States, 13% intermarried; while among those with all four grandparents born in the United States, 33% reported being intermarried. Generation (number of grandparents born in the United States) had little or no effect on Protestants and Catholics. Once again, for Jews Americanization has meant secularization, a phenomenon not found among Catholics and Protestants.[15]

The proportion of American Jews who are third- and fourth-generation Americans has grown enormously and with that growth there has been a substantial increase in rates of intermarriage and falling away from the community. Concurrently, there has been a decline in the community's inhibition about intermarriage so that we now have a joint age cohort and generational effect of intermarriage.[16] The most recent rate reported for intermarriage (that is, married between 1985 and 1990) was 52%, up from 9% for those married prior to 1965.[17]

While intermarriage may reflect disinhibition and a change in priorities, it need not constitute a threat to group continuity. If half of the children of the intermarried were to be reared without ambiguity as Jews, then intermarriage might be little more than an interesting social fact. Some scholars essentially claim that to be the case; they claim that intermarriage per se does not lead to Jewish population decline because a significant fraction of the intermarried rear their children as Jews. As I interpret the evidence, this is not so. Most intermarriages, as recorded in communal surveys, lead to syncretism or religious neutrality in the home, a state of mind that almost inevitably terminates in cultural Christianity. The growing intermarriage rate is accompanied by a low rate of Jewish retention of children of such marriages. In recent mixed marriages, 28% of the children are reported as being reared as Jews, 31% as being reared with no religion, and 41% as being reared in some non-Jewish religion (in most instances one can presume that the religion is the Christian faith of the non-Jewish parent).[18] If we examine the Jewish education and socialization of the children of intermarried parents, we can be even more pessimistic about the Jewishness of the grandchildren of intermarriage. Even when they are raised as Jews, their Jewish socialization is weak. This can be shown by the reports of Jewish education given to the children of the intermarried. What is not reported, because it is not asked, is the impact of the child's functioning in a mixed network of relatives. One side of the family may observe a Passover of sorts while the other side observes a Christmas of sorts. The child receives two messages as to who he or she is and what is expected of him or her. Moreover, because of the way in which the question is asked in most of the surveys (beginning with the introductory filter question, "Is anyone in the household Jewish?"), it is easy to miss those households where one of the partners was born or reared Jewish and is no longer Jewish, either through formal conversion to Christianity or through informal drift. More on this issue will emerge from the analysis of the 1990 National Jewish Population Survey.

While intermarriage and fertility are perhaps the most dramatic indicators of Jewish decline, geographic location is an equally sensitive, if less intrusive indicator. Jewish spatial distribution has undergone massive changes in the past two centuries. There were many forms of such resettlement: the mass migration to the Western hemisphere, the migration from villages to large cities all over Europe, migration within the United States from densely Jewish New York to less densely populated Jewish communities, and local migration from areas of first and second settlement to areas of lessened Jewish population density. The last two forms of migration will be examined in detail.

The significance of religio-ethnic population masses and density is, on the face of it, clear. Its apparent simplicity, however, is misleading. For the modern period, density has been shown to be significant on multiple levels, affecting the rate of endogamy, affiliation with the Jewish community, the creation and maintenance of Jewish communal institutions, and so on. Difficult to measure exactly is the extent to which mass concentration of Jews is conducive to the creation of a public Jewishness, the Jewishness of the street, a Jewishness that at least potentially gives Jews, particularly youngsters, a sense of who they are and that they constitute a significant group. In premodern society, from the Middle Ages to the early nineteenth century, there were few large cities in Europe and none in which there were large Jewish populations. As late as the beginning of the nineteenth century, only three cities in the world—Amsterdam, Salonika, and Constantinople—had Jewish populations of at least ten thousand. The vast majority of the world's Jews then lived in small towns and provincial cities in whatever country they called home. (Remember that the Rhenish Jewish communities of the High Middle Ages numbered Jewish populations in the tens, or at most, the hundreds, and that the famous Gluckel of Hamelin's family was one of only two Jewish families in town at the end of the seventeenth century.)

Small and scattered communities had their problems but were able to maintain basic Jewish institutional life: a school for children, a burial society, often a yeshiva. Despite the small numbers of local eligibles, intermarriage was not a problem because by definition and common consent, marriage with Christians was neither desired nor feasible in the vast majority of instances.

That small Jewish communities (small, that is, by the standards of the twentieth century) could survive and even flourish demographically and culturally was a function of Jewry as an international theocracy, tightly regulated by the revealed law. The Jews constituted a recognized corporate, self-regulating body. Modernity shattered that idyll. At least in theory, Jews became individual citizens with free choice of domicile, association, and mate. Given the freedom offered by modern society, geography took on more significance. In the absence of communal cultural and psychological walls, sheer density became a crucial factor in group maintenance.

Jews poured into the major cities of Europe and later of America, forming a critical mass that permitted a semblance of Jewish life to continue, albeit on a weakened institutional basis. Concentration in major cities made it possible for Jews, even the unbelievers among them, to interact largely with other Jews and to choose their mates from among Jews, by the sheer force of numbers and propinquity. In the American case, German Jewish immigrants in the middle nineteenth century spread across America rather evenly. With the flood tide of East European migration, Jews became more concentrated in the cities of the Northeast, particularly New York. I estimate that in 1880, 28% of America's Jews lived in New York City, a proportion that rose to 52% by 1910. From 1920, the New York fraction of American Jewry declined steadily so that by 1980, 19% of America's Jews lived in New York City.

Another way of viewing the same phenomenon is to measure the scatter of Jews over the inhabited area of the United States. In 1880, the Jewish population of the United States was more scattered than was the American population in toto. By 1910, the American Jewish population reached the lowest point in its scatter over the one-hundred-year period being examined, while the American population continued to steadily increase its scatter. Beginning with

World War I, whatever was keeping the Jews together spatially on the national level was weakening. By 1980 the Jewish population was almost four times as dispersed as it was in 1910.

In New York City, the largest single urban conglomeration in all of Jewish history, a similar story emerges. Taking as our statistical measure the proportion of Jews who would have to move to secure a random spatial distribution of Jews, we find that, in 1925, 59% of the Jews would have had to shift residence in order to achieve a random spatial distribution. By 1981, that proportion had dropped more than half, to 27%. It could be argued that with the emergence of telecommunication, good roads, and other forms of communication, spatial propinquity is not as necessary for the maintenance of communal ties. While this may be true to a limited extent, it remains the case that Jews were less likely to feel the need to live with Jews in the 1980s than they felt in the 1920s. The power and salience of Jewish identity have been weakened, allowing for the centrifugal force of geographic dispersion. Jews have less in common with other Jews, need them less, are more likely to choose residence, friends, and spouse based upon criteria that give less weight to Jewishness. The densely Jewish neighborhoods in which Jews born before the Second World War grew up are largely gone. The major exception is the Orthodox settlements in Brooklyn.[19]

The decline in Jewish population density, as is the case with intermarriage, is a two-edged indicator. First, it expresses the lessened interest Jews have in associating with other Jews. In choosing a neighborhood, as in choosing a spouse, we make our choices in accordance with a scale of preferences that reflect our priorities. Not choosing to live with Jews and not choosing to marry a Jew both reflect the declining salience of Jewishness. In addition, they also make it significantly less likely that the current Jews will act out their Jewishness and that their children will be raised within a Jewish milieu. Inter alia, the rates of exogamy are significantly higher in the newer areas of Jewish settlement and in relatively small settlements. In the absence of strong religio-cultural walls, communal size has emerged as a significant factor in maintaining the Jewishness of individual Jews and the Jewish household.

.   .   .

For the past two centuries, world Jewry has attempted to come to terms with modernity. For the most part, it has collectively failed, though Jews have prospered individually, particularly in America. Modernity has produced many social, political, and religious answers to the questions of why and how Jews shall remain Jews. In Eastern Europe, there were the movements of social reform, including Yiddishism, Territorialism, and Zionism, of which only the last can be considered to have been at least partially successful. Diaspora nationalism failed, not only because of the brutality and thoroughness of the Germans and their many friends but also because it was built upon illusions, as was made manifest in the subsequent history of East Central Europe.

In the West, coming to terms with modernity generated religious movements to which American Jewry has become heir. Although American Jewry is overwhelmingly East European in origin, the society in which it finds itself is multireligious rather than multiethnic, having more in common with Western Europe than with Eastern Europe. Attempts to transfer East European secularist diaspora nationalism in any of its forms have been noteworthy in their failure to attract a significant fraction of second- and third-generation American Jews. While American Jews are overwhelmingly secular in that transcendent religious ideas and sentiments play a small role in their lives, they are not ideologically or institutionally secularist. The religious movements have been a success institutionally. On the level of individual commitment and loyalty to Judaism in whatever form, these movements have been a failure, despite claims to the contrary.

In the first generation, Orthodoxy was the default or residual category for American Jews; in the second generation, Conservatism; and in the third, Reform. Few Jews of the first generation were ideologically Orthodox, as few second-generation Jews were committed Conservative Jews, and few third-generation Jews are Reform by conviction. Unlike in the Christian denominations after which the American Jewish pattern by and large is modeled, ideology has played a very small role in American Jewish religious life— except for a small layer of religious professionals and an even smaller proportion of the laity.

The possible exception to the rule is a newly aggressive and self-confident Orthodoxy, which, while few in number (7% of the religiously self-identified American Jewish population), constitutes a "fighting force," unlike the other denominations, which are armies of generals without troops. Jacob Katz has summarized the Orthodox experience in two telling phrases. Rather than being the totality of the Jewish people, Orthodoxy has become "a section of Jewish society" in which "loyalty to tradition was the result of conscious decision."[20] In becoming a willed community, with a sense of being besieged and needing to defend itself not only from an increasingly intrusive gentile society but from Jewish society as well, Orthodoxy retreated within the four cubits of the law, ignoring or denying the messianic ferment that ultimately produced the third Jewish commonwealth.

Conservatism initially saw itself as the heir to the mantle of tradition. At the time of the founding of the Conservative union of synagogues (1913), Solomon Schechter, president of the Jewish Theological Seminary, referred to the new body both as Conservative and as Orthodox. Schechter and his colleagues hoped to create a united front of traditionalists that would oppose the radicalism espoused by Reform. The newly founded Orthodox Union established itself as the leader of the Americanizing traditionalists, while the Seminary remained traditionalist and so did many of its alumni who served in Conservative pulpits.[21] For the mass of Conservative Jews, however, the driving force of the movement was less a matter of ideology than of nostalgia, albeit in cleaned-up and decorous form. A leading Conservative rabbi remarked, "The suburban synagogue is not a *shul*, and it has become a service center for its affiliate members rather than a communal center."[22] The functioning Conservative movement actually placed its bet—a bet that it is coming to lose—on the force of sentimentality for an increasingly passive laity and on *Wissenschaft* as the core of the rabbinic curriculum.

The Reform movement is rapidly becoming the modal Jewish religious identity for the mass of American Jews. However, looking beyond the sheer weight of numbers, one finds thinness and superficiality. Those who identify with the Reform movement tend to affiliate when their children are of an age to attend Sunday School and disaffiliate shortly thereafter. (This is true to a somewhat lesser degree of the Conservative movement and is not true of Orthodoxy.) As Leonard Fein has noted, "As long as the young are 'taken care of,' the temple is, to most of its members, too peripheral an institution for them to get very excited about."[23] A child-centered movement that is not taken seriously by the parents will ultimately not be taken seriously by the children either. In the New York area, one in seven males affiliated with a Reform synagogue attends any given Sabbath service, as compared with one in four among the Conservatives and four out of five among the Orthodox. The costly services of Reform and Conservative congregations (high salaries for rabbis, cantors, choir leaders, often professional choirs and organists) capture the imagination and loyalty of few of their supporters, while the stripped-down, bargain-priced, pipe-rack Orthodox *minyan* does much better.

Thus, while there are some significant "survivalist" bright spots, the immediate prospects are not too bright. Philanthropy, once the much-admired hallmark of the Jewish people, has been shifting away from Jewish causes. As Jews become wealthier and further removed from the immigrant period, a larger proportion of their philanthropic dollar goes to non-Jewish causes. While the propensity of Jews to give remains constant, their targets have been shifting away from Jewish purposes.[24] At one time, for the large fraction of Jews who would give (and still does), Jewish communal causes were the only game in town. Now that Jews are welcome participants in major cultural and educational institutions, recognition has become available from those who count in America. Jews wanted to be integrated into American society, but that integration is exacting a price.

Several years ago there were predictions of a Jewish population in the United States late in the twenty-first century of about 2% of its present size. To be sure, extrapolation from current behavior is a dubious enterprise: given the high fertility and statistical insignificance of intermarriage among ultra-Orthodox *haredim* in contrast to most of the rest of the Jews, it would not be more unreasonable to predict that by an arbitrarily chosen year, most American Jewish males will wear *peyot* and all married American Jewish women will wear wigs. With a birth rate of about five to six children per woman (assuming no attrition through assimilation), the ultra-Orthodox population will double in twenty to twenty-five years.[25] Assuming that they now number about one hundred thousand, they would number about 3,200,000 by the year 2110.

With the historians, I feel much safer in predicting the past. If forced to become a prophet, however, I cannot with confidence predict a rosy future for American Jewry as a functioning collectivity.[26] This is not a matter of being a member of the "pessimist school" as opposed to the "optimist school" or the "accommodationist school" as opposed to the "assimilationist school." The data themselves do not make one optimistic. If the Jews are to be understood as an ethnic group, then it is likely that they will enter into what Richard Alba has so felicitously termed the "twilight of ethnicity."[27] They will engage in episodic acts of "symbolic ethnicity" rather than a sustaining regimen of life.[28] Jewish self-definition is that of a religious group, but few Jews are believers in any significant way. As a Reform rabbi stated, "Prayer is still the pretext, but the justification of the act, the real purpose, is now achievement of community, the sense of belonging."[29] Prayer may lead to community, but only for believers or those capable of becoming believers. When the latent function of prayer is made manifest, its transforming power is lost.

As Jews lost the historic stigmata of Jewishness, they created a Jewish culture with new stigmata that they substituted, consciously or not, for the old. More concretely, at one time a Jew could be recognized by what went into his stomach, the clothes on his back, the cut of his hair and beard, the language that came out of his mouth. Now, if we find a group of individuals who are politically liberal, resolutely secular in values, well-educated and prosperous, patrons of the arts (members of museums, art auction attenders, concert goers), devotees of the various forms of psychotherapy, there is a better-than-chance probability that we have come upon a group of Jews. The boundaries of the newer forms of Jewishness are permeable to a far greater degree than were the older. The holy community, the building block of the larger Jewish society, has been shattered. Almost gone is a sense of transcendent Jewish obligation, what the tradition terms *mitzvah*. The purposes for which Jews gather are less frequently peculiarly Jewish (lest they be seen as parochial and not modern) and, ultimately, centrifugal force spins them out of the Jewish orbit. Modernity and secularity, the great loves of modern Jewry, have turned to ashes.

Notes

1. Seymour Martin Lipset and Everett Carl Ladd, Jr., "Jewish Academics in the United States: Their Achievements, Culture, and Politics," *American Jewish Year Book* 72 (1971): 89–128.
2. Compared with the Italians, the contemporaries of Jews during the period of great migration, Jews are almost twice as likely to be secular (sample-run based upon the data of the 1990 National Jewish Population Survey, no date).
3. While for the earliest period we have no direct evidence of the magnitude of Jewish fertility, the enormous growth of Jewish population from the end of the seventeenth century to the beginning of the twentieth century must have been due to very high fertility, higher even than that of the surrounding gentile populations. See Arthur Ruppin, "The Jewish Population of the World," in *The Jewish People Past and Present*, vol. 1 (New York: Jewish Encyclopedia Handbooks, 1946), 348–60. See also Alice Goldstein, "Some Demographic Characteristics of Village Jews in Germany: Nonnenweier, 1800–1931," in Paul Ritterband, ed., *Modern Jewish Fertility* (Leiden: Brill, 1981), 112–43.
4. John Knodel, *The Decline of Fertility in Germany, 1871–1939* (Princeton, N.J.: Princeton University Press, 1974). See also Massimo Livvi-Bacci, "Social Group Forerunners of Fertility in Europe," in Ansley Coale and Susan Cotts Watkins, eds., *The Decline of Fertility in Europe* (Princeton, N.J.: Princeton University Press, 1986), 182–200.
5. U. O. Schmelz, *Modern Jerusalem's Demographic Evolution* (Jerusalem: Institute of Contemporary Jewry, Hebrew University, 1987); Steven M. Cohen and Paul Ritterband, "Why Contemporary American Jews Want Small Families: An Interreligious Comparison of College Graduates," in Ritterband, ed., *Modern Jewish Fertility*, 209–31. On the relationship among secularity, traditionalism, and fertility among European Christians, see Ron Lesterheghe and Chris Wilson, "Modes of Production, Secularization, and the Pace of Fertility Decline in Western Europe, 1870–1930," in Coale and Watkins, eds., *Decline of Fertility*, 261–92.
6. Sidney Goldstein, "Jews in the United States: Perspectives from Demography," *American Jewish Year Book* 81 (1981): 3–59. For an analytic review of Jewish fertility, see Sergio DellaPergola, "Patterns of American Jewish Fertility," *Demography* 17 (1980): 261–73.
7. Geraldine Rosenfield, "Jewish College Freshmen: An Analysis of Three

Studies," in Sidney Goldstein, ed., "The Demographics of American Jewry," typescript (Providence, R.I.: Brown University, 1986).

8. Barry A. Kosmin, et al., *Highlights of the CJF 1990 National Jewish Population Survey* (New York: Council of Jewish Federation, 1991), 15. It should be clear by now that this is not a peculiarly American phenomenon. Both historical and contemporary evidence from other countries points in the direction of demographic decline for Jewry. The Jewish historical record for late Imperial Germany was similar. See Felix A. Theilhaber, *Der Untergang der deutschen Juden: Eine Volkswirtschaftliche Studie* (Munich, 1911). France serves as a useful contemporary example. Ignoring the problem of intermarriage and whether children are being reared as Jews, we find that as of 1979, Paris Jewry showed a total fertility rate of 2.4, well above the replacement level. However, the total fertility for Parisian Jewish women born in North Africa was 3.1, for women born in other parts of Europe, 2.8, and for native-born Parisian Jewish women, 1.7, significantly below replacement and not far from the total fertility of American Jewish women. Examining the fertility of North African–born Jewish women by marriage cohorts reveals that for those married in the first decade after World War II, fertility was 1.74 times that of native French Jews; for the next decade (1956–1965), it was 1.26; and for the 1966–1975 cohort, the fertility of North African–born Jewish women was exactly equal to that of the native born. Doris Bensimon, "Tendances démographiques des populations juives d'Europe occidentale," paper prepared for the World Jewish Population Symposia, Jerusalem, 1987, typescript.

9. Calvin Goldscheider and Frances K. Goldscheider, "Family Size Expectations of Young American Jewish Adults," in U. O. Schmelz and S. DellaPergola, eds., *Papers in Jewish Demography, 1985* (Jerusalem: Institute of Contemporary Jewry, Hebrew University, 1989), 133–47.

10. Calvin Goldscheider, *Jewish Continuity and Change: Emerging Patterns and Change in America* (Bloomington: Indiana University Press, 1986), 97.

11. Cohen and Ritterband, "Why Contemporary American Jews Want Small Families"; Goldscheider and Goldscheider, "Family Size Expectations." On the question of expectations more generally, see Sidney Goldstein, "Jews in the United States," 190.

12. U. O. Schmelz, "Jewish Survival: The Demographic Factors," *American Jewish Year Book* 81 (1981): 70.

13. Erich Rosenthal, "Acculturation without Assimilation," *American Journal of Sociology* 66, no. 3 (November 1960): 275–88.

14. U.S. Bureau of the Census, "Religion Reported by the Civilian Population of the United States, March 1957," *Current Population Reports*, series P-20, No. 79, 1958.

15. Fred Solomon Sherrow, "Patterns of Intermarriage among American College Graduates" (Ph.D. diss., Columbia University, 1971), 111.

16. There is a marked decrease in inhibition concerning intermarriage among younger Jews. Goldscheider, *Jewish Continuity and Change*, 15, says that those over sixty years of age were twice as likely to be negative about intermarriage as were those eighteen to twenty-nine years of age.

17. Kosmin, et al., *1990 National Jewish Population Survey*, 14. Without question, from the perspective of American Jewish history the current rate of Jewish exogamy is very high, even though, when compared with other ethnic groups, Jewish intermarriage does not appear to be extraordinarily high. Thus, among Italians, as of the 1980 census, for the cohort born during or before 1920, 58% married Italian spouses while for the cohort born after 1950, 15% married Italians. The comparisons are being made with persons of single ancestry. Taking into account the fact that there are about twice as many Italians as Jews in the United States and that small groups show higher rates of exogamy (since much marriage is random with respect to ethnicity), the "true" Jewish rate is even lower. Richard Alba, *Ethnic Identity: The Transformation of White America* (New Haven, Conn., 1990), 13.

18. Kosmin, et al., *1990 National Jewish Population Survey*, 16. Taking the effects of intermarriage, and thus effectively Jewish fertility, into account, we arrive at an estimate of the *net* reproduction rate of American Jews as of the late 1960s of 0.7 as compared with a net reproduction rate of 1.2 for American whites generally. A rate of 1.0 indicates zero population growth (net of migration). Clearly the Jews are subzero, that is, the excess of Jewish deaths over births leads to a decline in population (not counting the migratory balance, which at this point in time is a small component). For further discussion of this issue, see U. O. Schmelz, "Jewish Survival," 61–117. With the further increase in intermarriage and decrease in fertility in the twenty years since the 1970 NJPS, it is more than likely that the net reproduction rate of the Jews of America will have declined even further. For a very different perspective on the amount and impact of intermarriage, see Steven M. Cohen, *American Assimilation or Jewish Revival* (Bloomington, Ind., 1988), particularly 25–42 and 110–25.

19. Paul Ritterband, "The Geography of the Jews as an Element in Jewish Social History: New York, 1900–1981 and the United States, 1880–1980," paper presented at the Faculty Seminar of the Center for Israel and Jewish Studies, Columbia University, February 13, 1981, typescript. The proportion having to move is a function of the number and size of units being used in the calculation. In these calculations, I am using the Revised Statistical Districts first developed by C. Morris Horowitz and Lawrence J. Kaplan in *The Jewish Population of the New York*

Area (New York, 1959), mimeo. These are large districts; if we were to use census tracts, all the numbers would be increased but the trend would remain the same.

20. Jacob Katz, "Orthodoxy in Historical Perspective," in Peter Medding, ed., *Studies in Contemporary Jewry*, vol. 2 (Bloomington: Indiana University Press, 1986), 3–17.

21. Herbert Rosenblum, *Conservative Judaism: A Contemporary History* (New York, 1983), 21–23; Abraham Karp, "The Conservative Rabbi: Dissatisfied but Not Unhappy," *American Jewish Archives* 35, no. 2 (November 1983): 209.

22. Stanley Rabinowitz, "Where Do We Stand Now," *Judaism* 26, no. 3 (1977): 276.

23. Leonard Fein, *Reform Is a Verb* (New York, 1972), 22.

24. A recent collection of papers dealing with changes in philanthropic behavior may be found in Barry A. Kosmin and Paul Ritterband, eds., *Contemporary Jewish Philanthropy in America* (New York: Rowman & Littlefield, 1991).

25. That the ultra-Orthodox *haredim* have achieved high levels of fertility is not a matter of their innocence of the theory and practice of contraception. Rather, it is a conscious, willed commitment to a constructed, idealized past. See Susan Harlap, "Contraceptive Use by Jerusalem Mothers with Special Reference to Orthodoxy, Ethnic Group, and Husband's and Wife's Education," in U. O. Schmelz, et al., *Papers in Jewish Demography, 1977* (Jerusalem: Institute of Contemporary Jewry, Hebrew University, 1980), 329–39. See too, Menachem Friedman, "Life Tradition and Book Tradition in the Development of Ultraorthodox Judaism," in Harvey E. Goldberg, ed., *Judaism Viewed from Within and from Without: Anthropological Studies* (Albany: State University of New York Press, 1987), 235–55.

26. Forecasts of American Jewish population size vary widely but in the main predict decline. See, for example, Elihu Bergman, "The American Jewish Population Erosion," *Midstream* (October 1977): 8; Samuel S. Lieberman and Morton Weinfeld, "Demographic Trends and Jewish Survival," *Midstream* (November 1978): 9–19.

27. Richard D. Alba, *Italian Americans: Into the Twilight of Ethnicity* (Englewood Cliffs, N.J., 1985).

28. Herbert Gans, "Symbolic Ethnicity: The Future of Ethnic Groups and Cultures in America," in *Ethnic and Racial Studies* 2 (1988): 1–20.

29. L. A. Hoffman, "Creative Liturgy," *Jewish Spectator* 40 (Winter 1975): 42–50, cited in Frida Keerner Furman, *Beyond Yiddishkeit: The Struggle for Jewish Identity in a Reform Synagogue* (Albany: State University of New York Press, 1987).

CHAPTER 23

Jewish Continuity over Judaic Content: The Moderately Affiliated American Jew

Steven M. Cohen

All American Jewry is divisible into three parts.[1] One part consists of those most intensively involved in Jewish life, among whom are the religiously observant and pro-Israel activists. At the other extreme are those who are most peripheral to conventional Jewish life, including many who have married non-Jews. This group engages only in occasional acts of Judaic involvement and maintains relatively few informal links to other Jews and few formal ties to organized Jewry. Between these two groups is situated the vast middle of American Jewry. They are formally affiliated with Jewish institutions, engage in a variety of Judaic practices throughout the year, but are not nearly as active in organized Jewish life or Jewish ritual practice as those in the most Jewishly active group. For convenience, the most active group may be termed the "Involved," and the least active may be called the "Peripheral." I will refer to the intermediate group as the "Jewish middle" or the "Moderately Affiliated."[2]

The Moderately Affiliated are a pivotal group, especially with respect to the long-standing debate among scholars and practitioners over the vitality of American Jewry.[3] Participants in this debate range from optimism to pessimism regarding the American Jewish present and future. At one pole are those who project the widespread "assimilation," in the colloquial sense of the term, of most American Jews, excepting only the Orthodox and a small

395

number of other highly involved Jewish families. At the optimistic end of the spectrum are those who see many signs of a persisting cohesive community.

Most learned observers of American Jewry would probably agree that those who are most Jewishly involved stand the greatest chance of producing Jewishly identified progeny three and four generations hence. At the same time, even the so-called optimists concede that the mixed-married and others among the most peripheral Jews stand a very good chance of having their children and grandchildren leave the Jewish group. Thus, one's projection for the future of American Jews essentially turns on an assessment of the Jewish staying power of the American Jewish middle.

We have some degree of confidence as to why involved Jews are committed and why peripheral Jews are relatively indifferent to conventional Jewish ritual and communal life. Far more enigmatic to most of us who closely follow developments among American Jews is the nature of Jewish commitment among those in the middle. If these Jews really do care about being Jewish, how is it that they are not more involved? Alternatively, if they are nearly indifferent toward their Jewishness, why do they even bother to engage regularly in several acts of Jewish affirmation? In short, why is there a Jewish middle—why do the Jews of the middle not join the ranks either of the highly involved or of the more peripheral?

The debate over the American Jewish future can be largely reduced to differences over the nature and strength of the Jewish commitment of the Moderately Affiliated. Is their Jewish commitment, such as it is, transmittable to their children and sustainable over several generations? Or are they living out an eroding vestige, a progressively paler reflection of a once intensive but now fading ancestral Jewish past? To address these and related questions, this paper tries to advance our understanding of the Moderately Affiliated, those situated in the middle of the Jewish identity spectrum.

How do the Peripheral, the Moderately Affiliated, and the Involved Jews differ? The answer may be found in two simplifying catchwords: commitment to Judaic *content* and commitment to Jewish *continuity*.

As the analysis below demonstrates, many of those in the Peripheral segment may be nearly indifferent to their families' Jewish continuity; by definition their lives are relatively devoid of what Judaic specialists of almost all ideological stripes would regard as serious Judaic content. In contrast, Involved Jews are certainly deeply committed to Jewish continuity, but their commitment extends beyond continuity. They are also committed to a particular brand of Jewish culture and community, be it Orthodoxy, Conservatism, Reform, Reconstructionism, Zionism, secularism, political liberalism, or something else. Often, their commitment to these particular strands is so profound that they regard abandonment of their own ideological camp for another as a betrayal. Passionate members of particular communities can be heard to remark that they would prefer that their children drop Judaism altogether than that they defect to what they would view as a particularly odious style of Jewish living.

In contrast with the Peripheral, most of the Moderately Affiliated Jews are committed to the continuity of the Jewish group and to their families' connection to that group. In contrast with the Involved segment of the population, the Moderately Affiliated generally exhibit far less ideologically motivated dedication to any particular brand of Jewish life. Hence, to abbreviate (and to overstate): the Peripheral are nearly indifferent to both Jewish continuity and Judaic content; the Moderately Affiliated are committed to continuity but generally not to a specific content; the Involved are committed both to content and to continuity. The details follow.

The issues raised above are explored below using data based on a mail-back questionnaire completed by 944 Jewish respondents nationwide in 1989. The Jewish Communal Affairs Department of the American Jewish Committee sponsored the research, and the survey was fielded by the Washington office of Market Facts, Inc. These respondents are members of the company's Consumer Mail Panel, a group of 250,000 individuals who have agreed to be surveyed from time to time on a variety of concerns. After the data are weighted to account for the underrepresentation of the Orthodox, the frequency distributions for the major sociodemographic and standard Jewish identity variables resemble those found in recent population studies of major metropolitan Jewish communities.[4]

The questionnaire was unusual in that it contained scores of questions on Jewish beliefs and attitudes as well as the usual number of questions on ritual practice, communal affiliation, and other behaviors. The analysis presented is, in effect, an extract of the larger analysis upon which this paper is based. Thus, inferences below that are drawn from the answers to just a few survey questions actually derive from a much larger number of items in the original analysis.

The thrust of the analytic method is to discern distinctions among the three key subpopulations: the Involved, the Moderately Affiliated, and the Peripheral. For analytic purposes, the three groups were defined by their answers to just a few key indicator survey questions. The Involved group was defined as those who meet any one of the following conditions. The Involved Jews

1. attend synagogue twice a month or more, *or*
2. have visited Israel at least twice, *or*
3. maintain two sets of dishes at home for meat and dairy products (in accord with Jewish dietary laws).

The Peripheral group consisted of those who meet all of the following qualifications. The Peripheral Jews

1. attend synagogue only on the High Holydays (if then), *and*
2. do not fast on Yom Kippur, *and*
3. have never been to Israel.

Moderately Affiliated Jews are those who fail to meet the criteria of either the Involved or the Peripheral. This means that they attend synagogue less often than twice a month, that they have never visited Israel or have visited it only once, that none maintain meat and dairy dishes, and that most fast on Yom Kippur. Less than half of the weighted sample fell into the Moderately Affiliated group, about a third are in the Involved group, and a quarter qualify as Peripheral (first row, table 23.1 in the appendix).

Table 23.2 in the appendix enlarges upon the description of these three groups by presenting measures not directly used to construct the boundaries among them. The Involved group is predominantly

Conservative (43%) and Orthodox (29%). Almost all attend a Pass-over seder, light Hanukkah candles, and, if married, are married to a Jewish spouse. Substantial majorities (about two-thirds to three-quarters) of this group belong to synagogues, belong to other Jewish organizations, and have close friends who are almost always Jew-ish. About two-fifths give at least one hundred dollars to the local federation or UJA campaign, and an equal number sit on the board or a committee of a Jewish organization. As a whole, this group is certainly active in Jewish life, both at home and in the public sphere.

In contrast, most (58%) in the Peripheral group identify with no major Jewish denomination. Majorities report marriage to a Jewish spouse (80%), attending seders (59%), and lighting Hanukkah can-dles (67%), but these are the only Jewish identity traits in table 23.2 that characterize most Peripheral Jews. Almost half (46%) report that most of their closest friends are non-Jews. Just a few belong to synagogues (16%) or other Jewish organizations (19%), or give at least one hundred dollars to the UJA (15%). Only 3% serve on any Jewish organizational boards or committees. Certainly these are very inactive Jews.

The large middle group is, in all respects, intermediate between the Involved and Peripheral segments. The Moderately Affiliated are almost equally divided between Conservative (37%) and Re-form (34%) identities. Their ritual and communal activity levels are not quite as high as those of the Involved Jews, nor as low as those of the Peripheral Jews. Significantly, with the lone exception of the near-absence of the Orthodox, the Moderately Affiliated group's characteristics are nearly identical to those reported by the entire sample (see the "total" column in table 23.2 in the appen-dix). In this sense, we may speak of the Moderately Affiliated as "typical" Conservative and Reform Jews.

We may now proceed to examine how the Involved, Moderately Affiliated, and Peripheral groups differ with respect to such critical issues as belief in God, commitment to Jewish law, ritualism, Zion-ism, and Jewish learning. To measure these attitudes, I constructed several indices, each built out of just two survey questions. Each pair of questions used to construct an index consisted of a "hard" and an "easy" question. An easy question is one that elicited affirmative responses from about two-thirds to three-quarters of the total sample; a hard question is one to which only about a fifth to a quarter of the sample responded affirmatively. As a general rule, easy questions distinguish the Moderately Affiliated from the Peripheral Jews; hard questions set off many of the Involved Jews from the vast majority of the Moderately Affiliated. The five indices below consist of three levels: the highest level answered both hard and easy question affirmatively; the second level answered only the easy question; the lowest level answered neither question in a manner signifying Judaic commitment of one sort or another.

The questionnaire asked respondents whether they accept or reject nine statements expressing traditional beliefs about God. Most respondents said they definitely believe that God exists and that God is a force for good in the world. However, only small minorities could express unqualified support for such statements as "God intervenes in the course of human events" or speak of God as answering prayers, punishing sin, rewarding good deeds, and having a special relationship with the Jewish people. In other words, while most American Jews believe God exists, only a minority are sure He does anything. It may be said that most American Jews (and, as we shall see, most Moderately Affiliated Jews) believe in what has been called the "Watchmaker God," a God that constructed the world and set it in motion but has little to do with keeping it in good and working order.

From the answers to two questions (one hard, one easy), we are able to distinguish three sorts of approaches to God. Some Jews believe in an active God; others, labeled simple "believers," believe in God's existence but doubt that He has a special relationship with Jews (emblematic of their doubts about an active and personal God, as expressed in their answers to several other survey questions). The "skeptics" doubt God's existence, as indicated by their failure to answer "definitely yes" when asked whether God exists. By these definitions, over a third of the Involved group believe in an active God, as opposed to half as many among the Moderately Affiliated and hardly any Peripheral Jews (table 23.3 in the appendix). Most Moderately Affiliated Jews believe God exists but are doubtful about God's active involvement. In contrast, Peripheral Jews are almost evenly divided between simple "believers" and outright "skeptics."

In short, Moderately Affiliated Jews tend to believe in God more than Peripheral Jews. Compared with the Involved Jews, fewer of the Moderately Affiliated believe God is active in the contemporary world. We may infer that for many of the Moderately Affiliated, God exists, but, for much of the time God does not matter very much.

Traditional Judaism is a legal system. Obedience to the ancient law as given to the Jewish people at Mount Sinai and as interpreted by the ancient rabbis is the cornerstone of the traditional conception of what being Jewish means. In contrast, modern Western notions of religion (heavily influenced by the Protestant model) emphasize such concepts as individual autonomy and personal faith rather than active obedience to an obligatory law. For many modern Jews, the traditional customs and rituals have become voluntary rather than mandatory, presenting available options to be exercised when and if they are personally meaningful.

Two survey questions are especially relevant to these sorts of distinctions. One asks whether respondents are committed to keeping at least some Jewish traditions (53% feel this commitment to a great extent); the other asks about their commitment to obeying Jewish law (just 25% feel this commitment to a great extent). Nearly half (45%) of the Involved Jews are committed to both keeping traditions and obeying the law, as opposed to just 16% of the Moderately Affiliated and hardly any Peripheral Jews. The median or typical Moderately Affiliated Jew proclaims commitment to Jewish traditions but rejects commitment to Jewish law. In contrast, a large majority of Peripheral Jews express commitment neither to Jewish law nor to keeping Jewish traditions.

The rejection of obligation occurs elsewhere in the survey. Fully 90% of the total sample (though less among the Involved) agree that "a Jew can be religious even if he or she is not particularly observant." Just 20% of the sample (and more among the Involved) see Jewish law as "extremely important" to their sense of being Jewish. Less than a quarter regard keeping kosher, a key indication of compliance with traditional Jewish law, as even desirable to being a good Jew.

As Charles Liebman has observed, the emphasis of voluntarism over obligation closely parallels another distinction: celebration over ritual. To the extent that American Jews view the tradition as a collection of customs and symbols that they may voluntarily appropriate when personally meaningful rather than as a corpus of Divinely ordained obligations, they also will be more attracted to acts of celebration than to ritual performance. The very term "ritual" connotes actions that are repeated, obligatory, and precisely defined and regulated. "Celebration" connotes voluntary activity with a very broad definition of which sorts of actions are acceptable or meaningful.

Not surprisingly, far more American Jews profess a commitment to celebrating Jewish holidays than to practicing Jewish ritual. Moreover, among Involved, Moderately Affiliated, and Peripheral Jews the distribution of these commitments varies predictably. The Involved divide almost evenly between those who are just committed to celebrating Jewish holidays and those who are also committed to practicing Jewish ritual. Among the Moderately Affiliated, only a minority (20%) are ritually committed, and a sizable majority (76%) feel committed to celebrating Jewish holidays. Hardly any Peripheral Jews are committed to ritual practice; the vast majority feel committed to celebrate certain holidays and a small but notable number are not even strongly committed to celebrating Jewish holidays.

In broad terms, the Involved Jewish population segment includes a substantial number (perhaps nearly half) who feel strongly committed to obligation, Jewish law, ritual commandments, and related traditional Jewish principles. The Moderately Affiliated segment contains few such people. By and large, and more than Peripheral Jews, the Moderately Affiliated feel attracted to Jewish customs, traditions, and holidays.

Traditional Jewish norms emphasized frequent and intensive study of religious texts. Ideally, Jewish men were to maximize the time devoted to text study; moreover, in the premodern Jewish community, those who were especially proficient in the art achieved prestige, social status, and wealth. For today's American Jews, the contemporary understanding of what it means to be a Jew maintains the importance of some study, some learning, and some knowledge of Judaism. But as with the other dimensions presented above, we can distinguish different sorts of commitment of varying degrees of magnitude.

To elaborate, most respondents place some value on Jewish learning. Thus, almost all (88%) think that in order to be regarded as a good Jew, it is at least desirable (if not essential) to give one's children a Jewish education. About the same number (90%) think it desirable to know the fundamentals of Judaism. Almost as many (78%) say it is very important for their children to understand what it means to be a Jew. Two-thirds (68%) say it is at least very important for them to give their children a Jewish education.

These findings are evidence of high levels of support for statements expressing a broad commitment to Jewish education and learning, albeit loosely conceived. In contrast, far fewer respondents endorse more specific, narrower, and more intensive statements of commitment to Jewish learning. Thus, just over a quarter (28%) say it is very important for them to engage in some form of adult Jewish education. Less than half (41%) say it is at least desirable for a good Jew to study Jewish texts; just 21% say it is even desirable for good Jews to send their children to a Jewish day school.

These results suggest that most American Jews recognize the importance of some amount of learning, schooling, study, and Judaic familiarity. On the other hand, only a minority even approach the traditionalist principle of a maximalist commitment to intensive Jewish study for its own sake.

As with the dimensions presented earlier, we divide the respondents into three groups, using two key indicator survey questions. The group most intensively committed to Judaic study is defined as those who regard giving one's children a Jewish education as essential and who regard the study of Jewish texts as desirable or essential. The middle group accept their children's Jewish education as essential but reject text study as desirable. Those least committed to Jewish education are those who do not even regard children's Jewish education as essential.

Using these operational definitions, almost half of the Involved group is highly committed to Jewish learning. This compares with only a fifth of the Moderately Affiliated and only a handful of the Peripheral group. The Moderately Affiliated respondents are most typically committed to their children's Jewish education but not to text study. In contrast, most Peripheral Jews are not highly committed even to giving their children a Jewish education.

Once again, we observe clear distinctions among Involved, Moderately Affiliated, and Peripheral Jews.

It is certainly correct that the State of Israel enjoys widespread support among American Jews.[5] In several surveys of American Jews, roughly two-thirds say, in various ways, that they care deeply about Israel. Israel is undoubtedly the major mobilizing issue in the American Jewish political domain.

Yet, several analyses have argued for a more qualified view of the place of Israel in the American Jewish psyche.[6] They suggest that while Israel may dominate the public sphere of American Jewish life, it is largely marginal in the private sphere. The cause of Israel certainly pervades Jewish organizational life, but it has little real impact on the more intimate activities conducted with family and friends. For most American Jews, Israel plays little or no role in the celebration of Passover, High Holydays, Hanukkah, bar mitzvahs, marriages, baby namings, and *brit milah* ceremonies. (It is hard to imagine that most Jews relate seriously to the frequent mention of Israel, Zion, and Jerusalem in much of the liturgical material connected with the holidays and family life-cycle events that they do celebrate or that they are even aware of such references.) The art, literature, and music of Israel remain unfamiliar to the vast majority of American Jews. In the everyday conduct of their Jewish lives, American Jews maintain little substantive connection with Israel.

Parallel with this distinction between Israel's importance in the public and private spheres, several observers have noted that while American Jews may be pro-Israel, not many are Zionists in the classical sense.[7] Zionists are distinguished from pro-Israel Jews not merely in the depth and intensity of their passion for Israel but also in their understanding of the meaning of Israel. More than those who are merely pro-Israel, Zionists (1) see contemporary Israeli society as presenting a challenge to their Jewish life in the Diaspora; (2) believe Israel offers a greater chance of a fulfilling and secure Jewish life; and (3) are confronted with the possibility of settling in Israel and attracted to it. Thus, while most American Jews are pro-Israel, far fewer are Zionists in the classical sense.

The widespread support for Israel is demonstrable by the large majority (73%) who say support of Israel is at least "desirable" for their conception of a good Jew. Evidence of the far smaller minority who care most deeply about Israel is found in the much smaller number (19%) who regard such support as essential to their conception of a good Jew.

The operational distinctions between Zionist, pro-Israel, and those relatively indifferent to Israel are drawn by way of answers to two questions. Zionists are defined as those who might have given some thought to living in Israel (to making *aliyah*) and who say that caring about Israel is an important part of their being a Jew. The pro-Israel segment are those who care about Israel without having thought of *aliyah*. The indifferent group does not even claim to care strongly about Israel.

While most Involved Jews can be classified as merely "pro-Israel," it is only among them that we find a sizable minority (almost a third) who qualify as *aliyah*-oriented Zionists. Among the Marginally Affiliated just 10% are Zionists, and among the Peripheral the figure drops to 5%. Using the definitions outlined above, most of the Moderately Affiliated are pro-Israel while most of the Peripheral are relatively indifferent to Israel.

We have seen several ways in which the Involved segment differs from the Moderately Affiliated. More than the latter, Involved Jews believe in an active and personal God, accept Jewish law as obligatory, feel committed to Jewish ritual life, value Jewish text study, and maintain a Zionist orientation to Israel. The Marginally Affiliated also differ from the Peripheral segment. More than the latter, the Marginally Affiliated believe in God, feel attracted to Jewish traditions and customs, are attached to Jewish holidays and celebrations, believe in the importance of some familiarity with Jewish life, and care about Israel.

At the same time, most American Jews, no matter what their level of involvement, share certain elements in their Jewish identities. For example, Involved, Moderately Affiliated, and even Peripheral Jews all avow a certain pride in and stubborn connectedness to their identity as Jews. Vast majorities of the respondents agree with the following statements:

I am proud to be a Jew (97%).

Jews are my people, the people of my ancestors (95%).

Jews have had an especially rich and distinctive history, one with special meaning for our lives today (94%).

Being Jewish is so much a part of me that even if I stopped observing Jewish traditions and customs, I still couldn't stop being Jewish (91%).

Being Jewish is something special (87%).

Even among Peripheral Jews, agreement with these statements reaches rather high levels, ranging from 74% to 93% (see table 23.4 in the appendix). Moreover, with respect to the proportions simply agreeing with these views, the Moderately Affiliated and the highly Involved hardly differ.

The three segments do differ considerably, however, with respect to the number who "agree strongly" with these views. For each measure of strong agreement with an expression of ethnic pride, the Involved significantly outscore the Moderately Affiliated, who, in turn, exceed the Peripheral segment.

"Agree strongly" answers suggest a more passionate expression of Jewish pride and attachment than the simple "agree" answers. Accordingly, we may conclude that less involved Jews share with their more involved counterparts at least some measure of pride in their ethnic heritage. However, the salience of that identity and the potency of that pride climbs with increasing Jewish involvement. In short, almost all Jews are proud of being Jewish; the more involved are simply prouder.

. . .

Aside from a generalized pride in being Jewish, the vast majority of Jews from all three levels of involvement also express a keen affection for Jewish holidays, family, and food. Moreover, the three objects of their affection are often intertwined.

Thus, at least 80% of the respondents agreed with each of these statements (table 23.5):

The major Jewish holidays make me feel connected to my Jewish heritage and traditions (92%).

I find the religious significance of the major Jewish holidays very meaningful (80%).

For me, Jewish holidays are a time to be with the family (92%).

During major Jewish holidays, I feel a desire to make sure my children feel connected to Jewish traditions (86%).

Certain Jewish holidays evoke in me some very fond childhood memories (85%).

Some of my best feelings about the major Jewish holidays are connected with certain foods (80%).

Holidays are meaningful in part because they connect Jews with their current immediate family, their family memories (parents), and their family aspirations (children). The appeal of special foods consumed around holiday seasons derives to some extent from their consumption in emotionally charged family settings. This interplay of family, food, and holidays characterizes other American ethnic groups as well.[8] Slavic, Italian, German, and Irish interviewees report special feelings connected with certain foods once prepared by their mothers and grandmothers during major holidays. Even if they were unsure whether the foods were genuinely associated with their particular ethnic group, they report a special affection for dishes linked in their memories with family celebrations of major holidays.

While family, food, and holidays enjoy affection among majorities of all three Jewish involvement segments, the extent to which such emotions are reported varies along familiar lines, ranging from

Involved to Moderately Affiliated to Peripheral Jews. For the most part, with respect to affection for Jewish holidays, family, and food, the Moderately Affiliated more closely resemble the Involved than the Peripheral segment.

Feelings about historic Jewish persecution, the Holocaust, and contemporary antisemitism constitute yet another important feature in the group identity of American Jews on all levels of involvement. Peripheral Jews appear to feel quite strongly about these issues.

American Jews are nearly unanimous in their recognition of historic Jewish victimization and in believing that prior victimization influences Jews today (table 23.6 in the appendix). As many as 99% agree that "Jews have been persecuted throughout history," and almost as many (93%) agree that "Jews are united by their history of persecution." When given a list of thirteen diverse Judaic concepts and symbols and asked to state their importance to their sense of being a Jew, respondents ranked the Holocaust first and American antisemitism third, just behind Rosh Hashanah and Yom Kippur and just ahead of God. Fully 85% regard the Holocaust as very or extremely important to their sense of being Jewish and 80% feel likewise about American antisemitism. The sensitivity to persecution and antisemitism is hardly less widespread among Peripheral than among Involved Jews. Even the most Peripheral Jew who has "forgotten" an erstwhile attachment to Jewish family, people, and holidays "remembers" the centrality of victimization to the Jewish experience.

We return to the question posed at the outset. Who are the Moderately Affiliated Jews, and what constitutes their Jewish consciousness? The results presented above suggest the outline of an answer.

The Moderately Affiliated consist of those Jews situated in the vast middle of the American Jewish identity spectrum. They are neither the most involved nor the least involved in Jewish life at home or in the wider community. For the most part, they identify as Reform and Conservative Jews who, by and large, attend services only on the High Holydays and for family life-cycle celebrations. They celebrate Rosh Hashanah, Yom Kippur, Hanukkah, and Passover in some fashion, while generally ignoring most of the other holidays on the Jewish calendar. The great majority of their close friends and (if married) their spouses are Jewish.

By and large, they refrain from adopting the commitments that typify the more involved Jews. Moderately Affiliated Jews tend to believe in God, but they tend to feel God is inactive and noninterventionist. They eschew the traditionalist religious conceptions of obligatory law and punctilious ritual observance. Instead, they feel attracted to a body of available religious activities from which they feel free to select in accord with their sense of personal relevance and meaningfulness. The historic emphasis on maximal study of religious texts has little appeal for them. Instead, they espouse a modicum of familiarity with what they regard as the fundamentals of Judaism, both for themselves and their children. While most Moderately Affiliated are certainly pro-Israel, very few have a vivid conception of Israel presenting an option for a fuller, richer Jewish life.

Certainly the Moderately Affiliated part company from the Involved Jews in many features of Jewish identity. Yet, at the same time, in several important areas the Moderately Affiliated share some things in common with their more involved Jewish counterparts. Perhaps most fundamentally, they express great pride in their group identity. In the private sphere, the key elements for Moderately Affiliated Jews revolve around family, food, and celebration of certain major holidays. In the public sphere, their key issue is antisemitism, the long history of Jewish persecution, and response to contemporary threats to Jewish survival and security.

In short, they are dedicated to the continuity of Jewish identity both in their families and among the Jewish people generally. However, they tend to lack a commitment to a well-defined Judaic ideology. Hence, we may arrive at the catchword expression of "continuity over content."

Is the Jewish identity of the Moderately Affiliated, such as it has been described, rich and attractive, or shallow and unappealing? Is it sustainable and, if so, for how long? Certainly these questions are interesting and intriguing. But ultimately their answers lie beyond the scope of this paper.

Appendix

TABLE 23.1
Variables Used to Define Involved, Moderately Affiliated, and Peripheral Jewish Groups
(Entries Are Percentages)

	Involved	Moderately Affiliated	Peripheral	Total
Distribution	36	41	23	100
Visited Israel				
Twice+	35	0	0	12
Once	24	38	0	24
Never	41	62	100	63
	100	100	100	100
Attends Service				
2+/month	56	0	0	20
Once/month	4	9	0	5
5–10/year	19	33	0	21
1–4/year	18	46	52	37
Never	2	12	48	17
	100	100	100	100
Fasts on Yom Kippur	82	76	0	60
Owns Meat & Dairy Dishes	60	0	0	22

Key: Involved Jews: Visited Israel twice or attend services at least twice a month or own separate dishes for meat and dairy products.

Peripheral Jews: Never visited Israel, attend services only on High Holydays or less often, do not fast on Yom Kippur, and do not own meat and dairy dishes.

Moderately Affiliated: Qualify neither as Involved nor as Peripheral Jews.

TABLE 23.2
*Denomination and Selected Jewish Identity Activities by Jewish
Involvement Classification
(Entries Are Percentages)*

	Involved	Moderately Affiliated	Peripheral	Total
Identifies as . . .				
Orthodox	29	2	3	12
Conservative	43	37	11	33
Reform	16	34	28	26
Just Jewish	12	27	58	29
	100	100	100	100
Attends a Seder	96	85	59	83
Lights Candles Hanukkah	95	86	67	85
Synagogue Member	78	52	16	53
Jewish Org'n Member	71	44	19	48
Gave $100+ to the UJA	41	29	15	30
Jewish Org'n Committee or Board Member	37	17	3	21
Closest Friends Who Are Jewish				
Almost all	63	47	29	48
Most	26	29	25	27
Half or fewer	10	24	46	25
	100	100	100	100
Spouse Is Now Jewish	97	89	80	90

TABLE 23.3
Major Dimensions of Jewish Attitudes by Jewish Involvement Classification
(Entries Are Percentages)

	Involved	Moderately Affiliated	Peripheral	Total
Faith in God				
Active God	35	17	6	21
Believer	44	58	52	52
Skeptic	21	25	42	27
	100	100	100	100

Key: Do you believe that there is a God? (Definitely yes.) Do you believe that God has a special relationship with the Jewish people? (Definitely yes.)

	Involved	Moderately Affiliated	Peripheral	Total
Keeps Traditions vs. Obeys Jewish Law				
Both	45	16	6	24
Traditions	28	40	19	31
Neither	27	44	75	45
	100	100	100	100

Key: To what extent do you feel a commitment to keep at least some Jewish traditions? (A great extent.) To what extent do you feel a commitment to obey Jewish law? (A great extent.)

	Involved	Moderately Affiliated	Peripheral	Total
Celebrates Holidays vs. Practices Rituals				
Both	51	20	5	28
Celebrates	49	76	81	67
Neither	0	4	14	5
	100	100	100	100

Key: To what extent do you feel a commitment to celebrate Jewish holidays? (A great extent.) To what extent do you feel a commitment to practice Jewish religious rituals? (A great extent.)

	Involved	Moderately Affiliated	Peripheral	Total
Children's Jewish Education vs. Adult Study of Texts				
Both	47	20	7	27
Children only	33	41	37	37
Neither	20	39	56	36
	100	100	100	100

Key: To be a good Jew one must give one's children a Jewish education. (Essential.) Study Jewish texts. (Essential or desirable.)

Attitude toward Israel

"Zionist"	32	10	5	16
Pro-Israel	55	65	45	57
Neither	13	25	50	27
	100	100	100	100

Key: Caring about Israel is an important part of my being a Jew. (Agree.) Have you ever seriously considered living in Israel? (Yes; not sure.)

TABLE 23.4

Expressions of Pride in Being Jewish by Jewish Involvement Classification
(Upper entries are the percentages who "agree" or "agree strongly"; lower entries are the percentages who "agree strongly")

	Involved	Moderately Affiliated	Peripheral	Total
Proud to Be a Jew	99	97	93	97
	81	69	47	68
Jews Are My People	96	95	93	95
	62	44	31	47
Jews Have a Rich History	96	93	90	94
	58	45	35	47
Couldn't Stop Being Jewish	95	93	83	91
	52	44	36	45
Being Jewish Is Special	93	88	74	87
	70	56	36	56

Key: I am proud to be a Jew.

Jews are my people, the people of my ancestors.

Jews have had an especially rich and distinctive history, one with special meaning for our lives today.

Being Jewish is so much a part of me that even if I stopped observing Jewish traditions and customs, I still couldn't stop being Jewish.

Being Jewish is something special.

TABLE 23.5
Expressions of Affection for Major Jewish Holidays by Jewish Involvement Classification
(Upper entries are the percentages who "agree" or "agree strongly"; lower entries are the percentages who "agree strongly")

	Involved	Moderately Affiliated	Peripheral	Total
Make Me Feel	97	85	81	92
Connected	64	50	20	48
Meaningful	91	82	60	80
	56	40	14	39
A Time to Be	97	94	80	92
with Family	67	52	25	51
Make Sure Kids	94	89	68	86
Are Connected	57	46	18	43
Fond Childhood	87	86	79	85
Memories	43	45	30	41
Best Feelings	69	72	68	80
about Foods	21	26	18	23

Key: The major Jewish holidays make me feel connected to my Jewish heritage and traditions.
I find the religious significance of the major Jewish holidays very meaningful.
For me, Jewish holidays are a time to be with the family.
During major Jewish holidays, I feel a desire to make sure my children feel connected to Jewish traditions.
Certain Jewish holidays evoke in me some very fond childhood memories.
Some of my best feelings about the major Jewish holidays are connected with certain foods.

TABLE 23.6
Expressions of Centrality of Jewish Persecution by Jewish
Involvement Classification

	Involved	Moderately Affiliated	Peripheral	Total
Persecuted	98	100	99	99
Jews United	92	95	89	93
Holocaust Important	89	86	77	85
Antisemitism Important	83	83	72	80

Key: Jews have been persecuted throughout history.
Jews are united by their history of persecution.
"The Holocaust" is very or extremely important to your sense of being Jewish.
"American antisemitism" is very or extremely important to your sense of being
  Jewish.

Notes

1. Someone once quipped that there are two types of people—those who
   divide the world into two and those who do not. For most analytic and
   policy-oriented purposes, it usually makes more sense to divide the
   world into three. The usual practice of distinguishing "affiliated" Jews
   from "unaffiliated," or "religious" from "secular," erroneously suggests
   a rigid bifurcation of American Jewry. A three-part division more
   readily connotes the dynamic quality of the identity and involvement
   of most American Jews.
2. In earlier works I called this group "marginally affiliated" Jews. See
   Steven M. Cohen, "Outreach to the Marginally Affiliated: Evidence
   and Implications for Policymakers in Jewish Education," Journal of
   Jewish Communal Service 62, no. 2 (Winter 1985): 147–57.
3. For contrasting views on this matter, see Charles Silberman, A Certain
   People: American Jews and Their Lives Today (New York: Summit,
   1985); Calvin Goldscheider, Jewish Continuity and Change: Emerging
   Patterns in America (Bloomington: Indiana University Press, 1986);
   Calvin Goldscheider, "American Jewish Marriages: Erosion or Transfor-
   mation?" in Israel: State and Society, 1948–1988, vol. 5, Studies in
   Contemporary Jewry, Peter Medding, ed. (New York: Oxford Univer-
   sity Press, 1989), 201–8; U. O. Schmelz and Sergio DellaPergola, "Basic
   Trends in American Jewish Demography," in Facing the Future: Essays
   on Contemporary Jewish Life, Steven Bayme, ed. (New York: Ktav and
   American Jewish Committee, 1989), 72–111; Steven M. Cohen, "Reason
   for Optimism," in The Quality of American Jewish Life: Two Views
   (New York: American Jewish Committee, 1987); Steven M. Cohen,

American Assimilation or Jewish Revival? (Bloomington: Indiana University Press, 1988); Charles Liebman, *Deceptive Images: Toward a Redefinition of American Judaism* (New Brunswick, N.J.: Transaction, 1988). Also see Steven M. Cohen and Leonard J. Fein, "From Integration to Survival: American Jewish Anxieties in Transition," *Annals* (July 1985): 75–88.

4. For more details, see Steven M. Cohen, "Content or Continuity? Alternative Bases for Commitment" (New York: American Jewish Committee, 1991).

5. See the following works by Steven M. Cohen: *American Modernity and Jewish Identity* (New York and London: Tavistock, 1983); "Attitudes of American Jews toward Israel and Israelis: The 1983 National Survey of American Jews and Jewish Communal Leaders" (New York: American Jewish Committee, 1983); "The 1981–82 National Survey of American Jews," *American Jewish Year Book* (1983): 89–110; "From Romantic Idealists to Loving Realists: The Changing Place of Israel in the Consciousness of American Jews," in *Survey of Jewish Affairs, 1985*, W. Frankel, ed. (Rutherford, N.J.: Fairleigh Dickinson University Press), 169–82; "Ties and Tensions: The 1986 Survey of American Jewish Attitudes toward Israel and Israelis" (New York: American Jewish Committee, 1987).

6. Steven M. Cohen, "Are American and Israeli Jews Drifting Apart?" (New York: American Jewish Committee, 1988); Charles Liebman and Steven M. Cohen, *Two Worlds of Judaism: The Israeli and American Experiences* (New Haven, Conn.: Yale University Press, 1990).

7. For example, Steven M. Cohen in *American Modernity and Jewish Identity*.

8. Mary Waters, *Ethnic Options* (Berkeley: University of California Press, 1990).

CHAPTER 24

From an External to an Internal Agenda

Egon Mayer

What might American Judaism look like in the twenty-first century? Who will be America's Jews a generation from now, say in the year 2015? How many Jews will there be? What will be their manner of communal and religious organization? These are but a few of the questions that leap to mind as one tries to imagine the future of American Jewish identification and affiliation in the decades ahead.[1]

In developing a profile of the American Jewish future, several caveats loom large. First, the chastening words of Rabbi Yochanan in the Talmud: "From the time that the Temple was destroyed, the gift of prophecy was taken away from the prophets and given over to fools and children" (Bava Kama 12b). There is an element of childishness in believing that just because one would like desperately to "envision the future," one can do so.

Then there is the caveat taught by history. In 1938, we would have made poor visionaries attempting to imagine the Judaism and Jewries of 1948 or 1958 or 1995. There is no reason to expect that we would be any better at envisioning how our community will look in 2015.

I am mindful that in 1938, just a little over fifty years ago, neither my parents nor my grandparents imagined that their lives would be radically altered in a few short years, first by the Holocaust, then by the birth of the State of Israel. They were deported by the Nazis from Budapest in the spring of 1944, just months after my parents married. After a stint in a displaced persons compound in Switzerland, my parents returned to Hungary, only to be stranded behind the Iron Curtain until 1956, while my grandparents emigrated to Israel.

Had even more of Eastern European Jewry followed the "prophetic" visions of the Orthodox rabbinic leadership who had admonished against emigration in the earlier decades of the century, even more Jews would have perished in the *shtetlach* and ghettos, and American Jewry would never have assumed its present importance. And Israel might never have been reborn. The vision of the radical Reformers of the late nineteenth and early twentieth centuries fared no better: witness their stands on Zionism, the use of Hebrew in prayer, and the role of ritual and spirituality in Jewish life.

There is also the caveat that warns us against thinking that the meaning of terms like "religion," "community," and "identity" remains constant over long periods of time. In fact, they do not. At least part of our difficulty in imaging the Jewish future stems from our inability to know what these concepts will mean to our grandchildren twenty years from now.

As a Jewish sociologist involved for nearly twenty years in the empirical observation of the demography, conduct, and public opinion of America's Jews, I project a vision of the future of American Jewry that is rooted partly in available research and partly in my (somewhat wishful) interpretation of that research. I took the invitation to prepare this paper as an opportunity to be imaginative within the parameters of sociological realities, because I recognize that the present moment can result in very different futures. I consider some of those alternatives more desirable than others. Most important, I believe that in the forecasting of social character, culture, and identity, *sof ma'aseh bemahshavah tehilah:* real outcomes are often the function of what was imagined in the first place.

My thesis is that the cultural and institutional configuration of contemporary American Jewry represents a successful adaptation to the challenges to survival under the conditions of the late nineteenth and early twentieth century, including violent antisemitism, mass migration, rapid technological and economic change, and a shift of venue from monolithic and authoritarian societies to a pluralistic and egalitarian one. Meeting these challenges has resulted in a Jewish survivalist agenda oriented essentially to the hazards of the external environment and the public domain of community life. But whether Judaism can survive as successfully in the America of the next century will depend on its ability to overcome the unanticipated consequences of its successes in the current century. Therefore, a survivalist agenda may well be inadequate to the tasks of the next generation. Those tasks appear to be framed by challenges within the private domain.

It is within the context of these reflections that I will examine the social trends of the recent past and attempt to project the complexion of American Jewry in 2015. I turn first to intermarriage and outreach.

The proportion of Jews who marry gentiles has increased without letup over the past two generations, as shown in table 24.1 in the appendix.[2] With the almost unlimited opportunities for assimilation in America, group survival is challenged in a uniquely intractable manner by intermarriage. The private nature of marriage, along with the fact that it seems to spring from subjective values such as love, the desire for personal fulfillment, and a commitment to egalitarianism deeply cherished by contemporary American Jews, has made intermarriage a far more difficult challenge than the more familiar ones that Jews have had to face in their previous struggles for survival.

One of the findings of a study I conducted of Jewish identity patterns among 450 intermarried couples, published by the American Jewish Committee in 1979, was that, rather than intermarriage causing assimilation (and thereby threatening Jewish survival), assimilation causes intermarriage. Jews with a weakly grounded sense of Jewish identity are especially likely to intermarry and are often unable to transmit Jewish identity to their children. One of the key problems involving intermarriage, therefore, is that those American Jews who are doing most of the intermarrying are ill-prepared to perpetuate Jewishness in their own families. By the same token, the Jewish community is ill-prepared to help them with that challenge, having devoted most of its (failed) efforts to trying to prevent such marriages from taking place.

More than a dozen years of my own research on intermarriage, as well as research by others, have shown that intermarriage does not erode Jewish identity and family life in the simple, linear fashion that figured so prominently in the alarmist literature of earlier decades. It is probably fair to say that in just a few years these studies have helped change the climate of Jewish opinion about intermarriage from outrage to outreach.

Changes in the perception of intermarriage have gradually led to changes in the Jewish communal response to it. In 1979 the Task Force (subsequently the Commission) on Reform Jewish Outreach was created by the Union of American Hebrew Congregations as the first modern attempt to alter the course of what had seemed, a decade earlier, to be the inexorable direction of American Jewish history. By the mid-1980s a variety of Jewish outreach programs to the intermarried had begun to be developed in such institutional contexts as Reform temples, Jewish family service agencies, and Jewish community centers.

As outreach has become a more common response to Jewish intermarriage, it raises numerous questions of strategy, practice, purpose, and method. Does outreach serve as a legitimation of intermarriage, thereby increasing its likelihood? Does it threaten to dilute the integrity of the community by including those Jews-by-choice whose Jewish authenticity is not universally accepted? Should outreach be undertaken with the explicit goal of converting the non-Jewish partners in intermarriages? Regardless of the answers to these and other questions, all current forms of outreach have been marked by a common focus on a Jewish "internal agenda" (that is, on Jewish survival and issues of institutional strategy). Regardless of sponsorship or purpose, they have concentrated on program and curriculum (for example, how to introduce the non-Jew or Jew-by-choice to Jewish life-cycle and holy day celebrations, to synagogue practice and etiquette). Or these outreach efforts have devoted considerable attention to matters of recruitment, personnel, and methods and settings for instruction. But none has really addressed the broader but crucial question of how outreach relates to the long-standing commitment of most Jews to public invisibility, the usual way American Jews as individuals comport themselves vis-à-vis their gentile neighbors, and the way the organized Jewish community has tended to represent itself in public.

I believe that if Jewish outreach is to have more than episodic relevance to a limited number of individuals, it must reject the posture of Jewish social and cultural invisibility that has been the lot of Jewry in modern America. It must take public both Judaism as a religion and Jewishness as a civilization; it must energetically articulate its claim to a fair share of the public's attention.

Some of the ways that Judaism might be taken public are suggested by recent struggles of Blacks, Hispanics, and gays to improve their image. Pressures brought to bear on advertising agencies, media executives, publishers, and educational policymakers have clearly borne fruit in changing the public image of those communities in the last few years. Jews might well consider advocating the following: (1) more positive, identifiably Jewish characters, themes, and images in television and radio programs developed by the major networks (particularly in urban markets where Jews constitute a significant segment of the consumer population); (2) greater Jewish content in high school and college textbooks and courses in the humanities and social sciences; (3) restoration of Hebrew as a language option in high schools and colleges; (4) more inclusion of Judaica in the holdings of local libraries, in the exhibition schedules of museums, and in the programs of community-sponsored theaters and symphonies; (5) greater cultural exchange with Israel and other significant Jewish centers around the world.

It is unlikely that these strategies would have an effect on the rate of intermarriage, but they are likely to enhance the self-image of Jews in ways that are public and accessible to non-Jews as well. Thus, in the long run they will constitute an open door to Jewish civilization through which those who wish to enter may do so.

Even though the soaring intermarriage rate among America's Jews since the end of the 1960s has wrought a veritable demographic revolution in the Jewish community, intermarriage has not been the only force transforming the American Jewish population. At the dawn of the twentieth century, American Jewry was characterized by a growing homogeneity as a result of the mass migrations from Eastern Europe. The rapid resettlement between 1880 and 1924 of approximately two million Jews from the Russian Pale to the urban ghettos of New York, Chicago, Philadelphia, Boston, and other cities resulted in configuring an American Jewry whose primary concerns were economic survival, social acceptance, and the perpetuation of an ethnic culture with a religious core. The relative homogeneity of the community was insured by a low incidence of intermarriage, dense Jewish settlement, and shared experiences of economic, social, and geographic mobility.

The grandchildren of immigrants, however, grew up with a high degree of security and material advantage, together with a low degree of personal familiarity with the social, cultural, or religious concerns of their forebears. Their coming of age is producing a community whose basic Jewish homogeneity—with all the commonalities that such homogeneity implies—can no longer be taken for granted. The social and geographic mobility of American Jews has resulted in an American Jewry whose tastes, ideas, and ideals are becoming as heterogeneous as that of Americans in general.

One of the distinctive features of American Jewish identity is its denominational character. Unlike prewar European Jews, who classified themselves either along a continuum of greater or lesser religious observance or as Hasidim or as secular Zionists, Communists, or universalistic "free thinkers," and unlike contemporary Israelis, who continue to identify themselves along these lines (with a few additional political wrinkles), American Jews have identified themselves overwhelmingly as Orthodox, Conservative, or Reform (as well as with the Hasidim and the Reconstructionists and other small religious groups).

In a 1954 report on American Jews in suburbia presented to the Conference on Jewish Relations, Marshall Sklare concluded that 80% described their grandparents as Orthodox, but only 20% described their parents as Orthodox.[3] In 1970, the authoritative National Jewish Population Study (NJPS) showed that about 10% of America's Jews identified themselves as Orthodox, about 30% as Reform, and about 40% as Conservative. (The balance identified themselves as having a preference other than the three main branches of American Judaism or as having no denominational preference at all.) In 1986, in a widely cited public opinion survey of American Jews, based upon a large national sample, Steven M. Cohen found that 11% of the respondents identified themselves as Orthodox, 25% as Reform, 33% as Conservative, and 1% as Reconstructionist; nearly one-third of the respondents (31%) reported themselves as "just Jewish"—without any specific denominational preference.[4]

If one compares the later Cohen survey with the earlier NJPS, it appears that the Orthodox branch has managed to stem the defections characterizing it for the first six decades of this century; statistics confirm the widely held impression that Orthodoxy has been enjoying a degree of unexpected hardiness. On the other hand, the data show little more than that Orthodoxy has stopped hemorrhaging. It is still the smallest branch of American Jewry (not counting the Reconstructionist movement, which in origin is mainly an offshoot of Conservatism). Orthodoxy is certainly far from becoming a major force in the life of the overwhelming majority of American Jews, nor does Orthodoxy show signs of becoming that over the next twenty years.

At the same time, however, the data on denominational trends show a startling decline in the percentage of American Jews who continue to identify themselves with the two largest branches. If one compares Cohen's 1986 figures with the 1970 NJPS figures, it appears that the greatest growth has occurred among those who regard themselves as "just Jewish" and identify with no particular branch of Judaism. Lest these figures be taken to suggest an overall decline in the willingness of America's Jews to identify themselves as such, it should be noted that no survey indicates any evidence that there has been a general trend toward apostasy or disaffection from generic Jewishness. Rather, there appears to be disenchantment among a large and growing segment of the American Jewish public with the denominational labels that served as identificational reference points for their parents and grandparents.

This decline in associational Jewishness, as expressed in lowered denominational identification, seems to correspond to a trend to "invisible Jewishness": a privatized sense of longing, belonging, and meaning that is more psychological than communal, more felt than articulated in words and deeds. "Invisible religion," in Thomas

Luckmann's concept, draws on the same wellspring of collective symbols and memories as institutionalized religion. But it refuses to be constrained by the boundaries and social controls of formal institutions, such as synagogues, Jewish organizations, and Jewish schools, that claim to specialize in the perpetuation of a particular (Jewish) system.[5]

Equally important as a social trend is the growing divergence between the official positions of the major branches of American Judaism on key issues of Jewish identity and the opinions expressed by large segments of their members.

In a followup analysis of his 1986 survey sample, Steven Cohen looked into the opinions of American Jews on the much-debated issue of "patrilineal descent."[6] The Reform and the Reconstructionist movements have decided that a child of a mixed marriage is presumed to be Jewish even if the mother is not Jewish and the child did not undergo formal conversion to Judaism, as long as the father is Jewish and the child is reared as a Jew. Both the Orthodox and Conservative movements have vigorously opposed this position. The percentage of people who indicated acceptance of the patrilineal definition of Jewish identity were as follows: 83% of the Reform, 47% of the Conservatives, 12% of the Orthodox. Note that almost half the Conservative respondents do not subscribe to the standard of their movement on the issue. When Cohen asked, "Would you be upset if your child married a non-Jew?" the affirmative response was as follows: 39% for the Reform, 68% for the Conservative, 85% for the Orthodox. However, when Cohen phrased the question, "Would you be upset if your child married a patrilineal Jew?" the affirmative response was 11% for the Reform, 33% for the Conservatives (an even greater divergence from the official standards of the movement than in the previous question), and 78% for the Orthodox (indicating a high degree of consistency).

Noting that 70% of the nondenominational Jews in Cohen's survey accept the patrilineal definition, it appears that, except for the Orthodox (who are a small minority), most American Jews— including many Conservative Jews—accept patrilineal descent as a legitimate basis of Jewish identity. Thus, Conservative Judaism has to face the prospect that close to half its members are voting differently in their hearts, and their children are voting very differently in their ultimate mating choices, from the official ideology of the movement.

The Reform movement is in a similar situation with respect to rabbis officiating at marriages between a Jew and a non-Jew. In a 1987 study of some twenty-seven hundred delegates to the biennial convention of the Union of American Hebrew Congregations, investigators found that the respondents to their survey were evenly split on whether they agreed with the statement "A rabbi should officiate only if the prospective bride and groom are both Jewish."[7] (The Central Conference of American Rabbis, the rabbinical body of the Reform movement, has gone on record as disapproving of rabbis officiating at mixed marriages.) Upon further questioning, the research found that while the great majority of respondents were opposed to rabbis officiating at a mixed marriage if the wedding were to be held in a church (90% were opposed), or if the couple said that they want to expose their children to both religious traditions (63% were opposed), the majority of the respondents approved of rabbis officiating if the couple joined the temple (53% approved) or promised to rear their children as Jews (58% approved).

A large-scale survey of American Jewish leaders, conducted by this writer in the summer of 1990 under the sponsorship of the Jewish Outreach Institute, confirmed both of the above points, as shown in tables 24.2 and 24.3 in the appendix.

A question on whether respondents would consider their own grandchildren Jewish if their son married a non-Jewish woman and the grandchildren were being reared as Jews produced the results shown in table 24.2, indicating that overwhelming sentiment in the American Jewish community—except for the Orthodox—is to consider children Jewish if one parent is Jewish by birth and if the children are, in fact, being reared as Jews. (One can speculate, however, that these results indicate the profound desire on the part of American Jewish parents to deny the possible consequences of intermarriage, on the one hand, and to assure themselves of Jewish grandchildren, on the other.)

While the great majority of Orthodox gave a negative (that is, the traditional) response to the question, and while the great majority of Reform gave an affirmative answer (an answer in this case consistent with the ideological stance of their movement), the

Conservatives appear to be deeply divided among themselves, a division that reflects a split between their leadership and laity as well.

The survey also asked respondents in what type of ceremony they would prefer to see the couple marry: a civil ceremony only or one in which a rabbi officiates. (See table 24.3 in the appendix.) Moreover, they were asked whether, if they did prefer to see a rabbi officiate, the ceremony should be conditional on a commitment to rear the offspring as Jews or whether no conditions should be attached to the rabbi's agreement to officiate. Those who preferred a civil ceremony were queried as to whether they would help to give the ceremony some Jewish content. (It should be noted that both the Orthodox and the Conservative movements have been steadfast in their opposition to rabbinic officiation at a marriage between a Jew and a gentile, regardless of whether the Jew in question is a man or a women and regardless of whether the prospective couple have made a commitment to rear their children as Jews.)

In order to put the issue of intermariage in an even more personal context, respondents were then asked, if they themselves were rabbis who had been approached by a couple like "Ruth" and her gentile fiancé or by "Michael" and his gentile fiancée, would they officiate (or would they like their own rabbi to do so)? The response alternatives were (1) no, under any circumstances; (2) no, but I would help with a civil ceremony; (3) no, but I would refer the couple to another rabbi; (4) yes, if children were to be reared Jewish; (5) yes, without any conditions.

Although intermarriage is contrary to the Jewish tradition, only about 31% of the sample would refuse any rabbinic involvement at all with the marriage of the hypothetical couple. About 16% would recommend a civil marriage ceremony with "some Jewish cultural content." About 15% would refer the couple to another rabbi who might officiate. Nearly a quarter of the respondents would officiate themselves, or they would want their own rabbi to officiate if there was a commitment by the couple to rear their children Jewish. Finally, 14% favored officiation without any conditions. (Table 24.3 in the appendix explores these responses in further detail by distinguishing between rabbis and nonrabbis among the three major denominational bodies.)

Here, as elsewhere, one sees a high degree of consistency in the responses of the Orthodox, be they rabbis or lay leaders. However, such is not the case among Conservative and Reform respondents. About 36% of Reform rabbis would officiate at an intermarriage. (Twenty-four percent stipulate they would do so only if there is a commitment to rear the children as Jews.) Nearly 62% of Reform lay leaders want them to officiate in such a situation. Likewise, only 4% of Conservative rabbis said they would officiate at an intermarriage (and then only if there were a commitment to rear the children as Jews). Yet nearly 38% of Conservative lay leaders would prefer to have their rabbis officiate at such marriages.

In short, the popular attitudes of members of both major movements of American Judaism reveal serious departures not only from historic concepts of Jewish identity but also from the currently professed positions of those movements. Over the course of the next twenty years, these departures will very likely increase disaffection from the existing patterns of denominational Jewishness, exerting great pressure on the major movements for change in their understanding of Jewish identification toward more acceptance of the social process already underway, and for greater syncretism. But such departures may also pave the way for the emergence of schism, new movements, and countermovements.

Currently, only about half of America's Jews report themselves as being affiliated with synagogues and temples or other Jewish organizations. This pattern seems to have been well fixed for the past forty years.

Citing figures from 1953, Will Herberg noted that about 50% of American Jews replied affirmatively in a nationwide survey to the question, "Do you happen at the present time to be an active member of a church or a religious group?" The National Jewish Population Study of 1970 found that 47% of its respondents reported belonging to a synagogue. In the 1986 Cohen survey, about 51% of the respondents indicated belonging to a synagogue. Given the apparent stability of the rate of synagogue affiliation over the past forty years, there is little reason to doubt that about the same proportion (approximately 50%) of America's Jews will continue to maintain some type of formal affiliation with the organized Jewish community. There is also little reason to expect any significant rise in that proportion. Given the current demographic revolution, the mixture of people who constitute the Jewishly affiliated families of America will probably include ever greater numbers of intermarrieds, non-Jews, half-Jews, and patrilineal Jews.

Attendance at synagogue services, like affiliation, has also shown constancy over the past thirty years. A Gallup poll dealing with attendance at religious services in January 1956 asked a cross-section of Americans, "Did you happen to attend any Sunday or Sabbath services during the last twelve weeks?" Forty-four percent of Jews answered in the affirmative.[8]

In 1970, the NJPS report showed that 18% of America's Jews attend synagogue service "regularly"; 28% indicated that they attend only on the High Holydays; another 26% indicated that they "attend occasionally" and the remaining 28% indicated that they "never attend."[9] The 1986 Cohen study found that about 26% of the nationwide sample of American Jews reported attending synagogue service "at least once a month."

While synagogue attendance might have been somewhat more common among America's Jews in the mid-1950s (perhaps owing to the postwar baby boom), it was certainly lower than the incidence of affiliation. The decline from the 44% reported by Gallup in 1956 to the 26% figure reported by Cohen in 1986 may be more apparent than real because of the phrasing of the questions. The Gallup question that generated the 44% figure inquired into religious service attendance "during the last twelve weeks." When Gallup asked the question in terms of religious service attendance "in a typical week during the last year," the pattern of response was 27% for Jews—a figure that is virtually identical to the Cohen finding some thirty years later.

With synagogue attendance low, the main forum for Jewish expression will probably continue to be the Jewish home, and central acts of identification are likely to be carried out within the private lives of those who consider themselves Jewish. As we shall see below, however, those acts are more likely to be of the heart and thought rather than deeds linked to the formal mitzvah system of institutionalized Judaism.

Studies of Jewish practice indicate a greatly diminished sphere of Jewish activity within the daily lives of most American Jews. In his 1986 survey, Cohen found that 84% of his respondents attended a Passover seder in the past year and 82% reported lighting Hanukkah candles. Only 20% use separate dishes for meat and dairy (a requirement for a kosher home). In his 1983 survey, Cohen also found that 34% of respondents have Sabbath candles lit in their homes.

Lest one jump to conclusions about the recency of a decline in the level of observance among America's Jews, it is worthwhile to recall some of the earlier studies of American Jewry. For example, a 1955 study of the Orthodox community of Milwaukee found that 66% had Sabbath candles lit in their home on Friday nights and 62% had separate dishes for meat and dairy. In the same sample it was found that 66% ate meat in nonkosher restaurants and 88% would handle money on the Sabbath. Moreover, only about 2% indicated that their married sons are as observant as they.[10]

One Jewish activity that seems to have increased appreciably over the last twenty years is travel to Israel. According to the 1970 NJPS, about 16% of America's Jews had visited Israel at least once. According to the 1986 Cohen survey, about 33% of America's Jews have visited Israel at least once. Though the current crisis in Israel, coupled with the declining value of the dollar, has cut into the travel of American Jews to Israel, there is reason to expect that over the next twenty years larger proportions of American Jews will visit there. The declining significance of Eastern Europe as the reference point of Jewish ethnicity will help to bolster the ethnic magnetism of Israel as the homeland of the Jews.

Change is perhaps most likely in certain observances that have not yet surfaced in Jewish community surveys, including such ceremonials as baby naming (for daughters especially), adult bat and bar mitzvah (particularly for women who came of age at a time when the bat mitzvah ceremony was not yet popular), and conversion to Judaism. Another area of future study is consumption habits of American Jews aimed specifically at expressing and enhancing identificational impulses. An erstwhile preference for kosher-style foods and Yiddish humor has been supplemented, if not supplanted, by some of the following: acquisition of Jewish ceremonial and art objects (largely from Israel), frequenting of restaurants run by Israeli and Russian immigrants, political activism on behalf of Israel, foreign travel to sites of Jewish interest in the Old World as well as the New, and allocating time to films, theatrical productions, and TV productions of Jewish cultural relevance. These forms of Jewish self-expression build upon the consumerist tendencies of a gentrified Jewry seeking to express its commitments not merely with a bow toward tradition but also with the élan of educated good taste. This is of relevance to a population whose majority within the next twenty years will have the benefit of considerable postsecondary education, high levels of discretionary income, and a relatively low birthrate, making investment in life quality a key personal and family value.

Up to this point, the "futurology" in this presentation has remained close to the shoreline of available data concerning patterns of Jewish identification. The remainder of this paper suggests a more speculative look at some wider social forces, both structural and cultural, as to their possible impact on Jewish identification in the next twenty years. I refer first to the changing roles of women.

Probably no social force has had a greater impact on our understanding of human identity than the growing equalization of gender roles. With the large-scale entry of the postwar baby-boom generation of women first into higher education and then into the labor force, all Americans have had to adjust their gender-based expectations. Given the high mobility aspirations of Jewish women, this aspect of the sexual revolution has resulted in an influx of women into the rabbinate to the point where some now refer to the feminization of that profession, much as education and social work were feminized several decades earlier. Yet the number of women seeking to enter the rabbinate is minuscule compared with the number of their sisters who have sought careers in the professions such as medicine, law, accounting, and business management. While this trend has produced considerable stress within the American Jewish family, as well as in the synagogue, over the next twenty years it may have a salutary effect upon the American Jewish identity.

Large-scale entry of Jewish women into the labor force has meant that more Jewish children are exposed to a greater amount of Jewish fathering. Whatever advantage in Jewish education Jewish fathers have had over Jewish mothers (there is evidence of some), it can be expected that children's greater exposure to their Jewish fathers may yet have a positive effect on their children's Jewishness twenty years hence. The large-scale entry of Jewish women into the labor force has also compelled modern Jewish families to make greater use of child-care services (including Jewish child-care facilities) and of available Jewish grandparents. There is reason to expect a correspondingly favorable impact upon the Jewish identification of the grandchildren over the course of the next generation.

The equalization of the role of women in the synagogue, most notably the emergence of a significant body of female congregational leaders and rabbis, has gone hand in hand with greater involvement by women in serious Jewish learning and has opened up new modes and opportunities for their Jewish self-expression. At the very least, the trend has doubled the numbers of Jews who engage in the social production of Jewish identification, be it from the pulpit, in the classroom, or from other venues we have not yet even imagined.

Second only to the changing role of women among current social trends is the expanded market demand on leisure time. The increased education and economic well-being of American Jews has made them an ever-growing target of merchants of leisure-time use. Jews are susceptible, as an elite market segment, to the general purveyors of products and services, from health clubs to unique cultural programs to exotic vacations. As an aging community with high disposable income, they are much sought after by those who market to the retirement population. The changing Jewish socioeconomic profile is bound to present a serious challenge to traditional Jewish institutions (Jewish centers, synagogues, clubs, fraternal organizations, and the like), which must now compete, as never before, for the time, money, and loyalty of their constitutents.

Each of the challenges faced by American Jews—new educational opportunities, career possibilites, and residential options— has been posed to Jews as individuals by the non-Jewish world. Having successfully met these various personal challenges, many thought that the collective well-being of Jewry was also secured. Perhaps for the better part of the past forty years that equation of the personal and collective has held fast. Another element reshaping collective Jewish life at present is the growth of the electronic frontier.

With the tremendous diffusion of television, VCRs, computers, and other forms of electronic technology, the challenges to Jewish identity are no longer merely the encounters between tradition and modernity, between science and religion, or between ethnicity and mobility. The coming twenty years will test the Jewish community on another level. Above all, it will involve integrating the visual and sound images and data needed to perpetuate Jewishness into the massive flows of information to which all modern Jews now have access.

The prospect that people born or reared in American Jewish families in the closing decades of the twentieth century will constitute a vital American Jewry in the twenty-first century are excellent. Even as associational and denominational ties have become attenuated for so many of America's Jews, there is reason to believe that there remains a powerful appetite for the symbolic universe of Judaism and for the texture and values of *Yidishkayt*. We see this longing for Jewishness reflected time and again in Jews who flock to Woody Allen movies or to films with more explicit Jewish content like *Crossing Delancey* or to the wildly popular one-man show of Jackie Mason. We see it in the halting moves of young men and women intrigued by the Lubavitch "mitzvah tanks" and in the emotionally charged conversations of Jews who come with their gentile spouses into "self-help" workshops to understand why they feel stressed about how they will rear their children. We recognize the longings that these and other human expressions mirror, even though we cannot see the forms of social belonging that they will engender. But those who share the same longings and expressions constitute a community that perpetuates itself.

I believe that from deep and ancient stock fresh branches of Jewishness sprout in each generation in response to the ever-changing Jewish milieu. The branches are forever tearing through the now-threadbare canopy of the past. Looking at the tears, some lament that the sky is falling. Others, through the openings, see a reaching toward new forms of a common and ancient destiny. The outer tips of the branches are slowly intertwining, already forming the contours of the canopy of the future.

Appendix

TABLE 24.1
Percentage of Currently Married Jews-by-Birth Marrying Various Categories of Spouses, by Year of Marriage

	Year Persons Got Married			
	Pre-1965	1965–74	1975–84	Since 1985
Jew-by-Birth	89	69	49	43
Jew-by-Choice	2	5	7	5
Non-Jew	5	19	37	47
*(A) Non-Jew	4	6	8	5
	100	100	100	100

*Refers to marriages of apostate Jews to non-Jews
Source: 1990 NJPS; calculations by author.

TABLE 24.2
"Would You Consider Your Own Grandchildren Jewish?"
(Father Jewish–Mother Gentile)
(By Role and Denomination; Numbers Are Percentages)

	Orthodox		Conservative		Reform	
Category of Respondent	Yes	No	Yes	No	Yes	No
Rabbi	7	93	41	59	94	6
Synagogue Lay Leaders	5	95	49	51	93	7
Communal Professionals	7	93	62	38	94	6
Communal Board Members	17	83	79	21	96	4
Laity	10	90	78	22	100	0

TABLE 24.3
Would Respondent Officiate? By Role and Denomination
(Numbers Are Percentages)

	Rabbi			Not Rabbi		
	Orthodox	Conservative	Reform	Orthodox	Conservative	Reform
No, under Any Circumstances	94.2	58.3	21.3	85.1	24.9	9.9
No, but Help with Civil Ceremony	5.8	26.0	13.2	9.4	23.3	14.2
No, Refer to Another Rabbi		11.5	27.6	3.3	14.1	14.2
Yes, If Children Jewish		4.2	24.5	1.1	29.2	37.2
Yes, without Conditions			13.4	1.1	8.5	24.5

Notes

1. Since this essay was completed before the publication of the 1990 National Jewish Population Survey, the data referred to herein do not include the most current findings. However, this author has found nothing in the recent NJPS that would contradict the trends outlined in the present paper.
2. On this and other issues discussed in this paper see the following: Barry A. Kosmin, Nava Lerer, and Egon Mayer, *Intermarriage, Divorce, and Remarriage among American Jews, 1982–87*, Family Research Series, no. 1 (New York: North American Jewish Data Bank, 1989); Egon Mayer, *Intermarriage and the Jewish Future* (New York: American Jewish Committee, 1979); Egon Mayer, *Children of Intermarriage* (New York: American Jewish Committee, 1983); Egon Mayer, *Conversion among the Intermarried* (New York: American Jewish Committee, 1987); Marshall Sklare, "Intermarriage and the Jewish Future," *Commentary* (April 1965): 37, 46–52; Marshall Sklare, "Intermarriage and Jewish Survival," *Commentary* (March 1970): 43, 51–58.
3. Marshall Sklare, "Forms and Expressions of Jewish Identification," cited in Will Herberg, *Protestant-Catholic-Jew* (New York: Doubleday, 1955), 204.
4. Steven M. Cohen, *Ties and Tensions: The 1986 Survey of American*

Jewish Attitudes toward Israel and Israelis (New York: American Jewish Committee, 1987).

5. Thomas Luckmann, *The Invisible Religion* (New York: Macmillan, 1967).

6. Steven M. Cohen, "Jewish Attitudes to Issues of Jewish Unity and Diversity," unpublished report to the American Jewish Committee, November 1987.

7. Mark L. Winer, Sanford Seltzer, and Steven J. Schwager, *Leaders of Reform Judaism: A Study of Jewish Identity* (New York: Union of American Hebrew Congregations, 1987), 55.

8. Cited in Herberg, *Protestant-Catholic-Jew*, 49.

9. Gary A. Tobin and Alvin Chenkin, "Recent Jewish Community Population Studies: A Roundup," *American Jewish Year Book* (1985).

10. Howard W. Polsky, "A Study of Orthodoxy in Milwaukee," in Marshall Sklare, ed., *The Jews* (New York: Free Press, 1958), 325–35.

CHAPTER 25

Jewish Survival, Antisemitism, and Negotiation with the Tradition

Charles S. Liebman

The record of social scientists in predicting the future is not a reassuring one. The concluding chapter of my book *Deceptive Images* elaborates on the inadequacies of my profession in this regard.[1] Nevertheless, I am led to offer some thoughts about the future, not out of any conviction that what I predict will come to pass but as a way of exploring the present condition of American Jews as it affects the prospects for their survival.

I understand Jewish survival in the United States to mean the continued presence in the United States of a group that defines itself as Jewish and that is recognizably Jewish. I encapsulate Judaism in my definition of Jewish survival. I define Jewish survival as the survival of a group whose Judaism exhibits significant continuity with the Judaism of previous generations and with the Judaism of Jews throughout the world. I would not only exclude Jews for Jesus and Black Jews claiming to be the only true Jews and Christians claiming to be the true Israel; I would also argue that there will be no Jewish survival if American Jews continue to identify themselves as Jews but the ties that bind them to the Jewish tradition and to Jews in the rest of the world become attenuated beyond a certain point. In other words, we have to consider the possibility that a collective group of Jews might retain their identity as Jews—a variety of political or social or economic reasons might encourage the maintenance of ethnic ties—but become so assimilated that they are culturally unrecognizable as Jews.

In my book *Deceptive Images*, I have suggested that this is the direction in which American Judaism is moving at present, which is not the same as saying that this will finally occur. I now want to suggest that certain contrary tendencies are likely to become evident in the next generation. These tendencies are the outcome of what I fear will be growing antisemitism in the United States and a continued drop in the percentage of Jews within the total population of the United States.

I think that we are likely to see rising levels of antisemitism in the United States over the course of the next decade or two. I hazard this guess on the following basis. First, Blacks are likely to become increasingly antisemitic as their level of resentment and frustration continues to rise. A rise in the level of their frustration is inevitable, given the conviction, reinforced by the media and virtually all political leaders, that the cause of their relative disability stems from prejudice and discrimination in American society at large. Since, as far as I can tell, the basic cause for the relative disability of Blacks comes from an unwillingness or inability to order their own lives, no amount of lessened prejudice and discrimination will resolve their problems. Yet the political facts of life are that few Blacks and even fewer Whites will speak openly about this. Indeed, I gather that, outside the circles of the political Right, the very discussion of the issue is grounds for being charged with racial prejudice. The result is an accumulation of grievances, grievances likely to be directed increasingly at Jews, since they are relatively easy targets for Blacks. Furthermore, I think that Blacks sense, rightly or wrongly, that Jews are hypocritical about the black condition and how it can be ameliorated. Jews pay lip service to the notion that black disability is the result of prejudice, but Jews insist on maintaining independent structures and institutions and in pursuing their own interests even when these interests conflict with those of Blacks. Blacks, therefore, feel that Jews are less eager to accommodate Blacks than they proclaim. I suspect that the success and high status that Jews presently enjoy undermines the convictions of the black community about the prejudiced nature of American society. That Jewish leaders scrupulously avoid calling this to the attention of black leaders, or for that matter to anyone else, is, I suspect, viewed as another instance of Jewish paternalism rather than any appreciation for Jewish sensitivity to the condition of American Blacks.

Black antisemitism is especially significant because Blacks, unlike, for example, Hispanic-Americans or Asian-Americans, occupy the special position that Jews once occupied in that attitudes toward them are deemed to be litmus tests of one's humaneness and morality. Hence, as others have already noted, black antisemitism legitimates hostility toward Jews on the part of other Americans— at least as long as black spokesmen are clever enough to moderate raw expressions of Jew-hatred. This seems to me to have been the lesson that Jesse Jackson learned between 1984 and 1988.

No less important in explaining the projected growth of antisemitism is the breakdown of the center, a characteristic of modern life in general and American life in particular. I am conscious of how often this has been said—not only about American society but also about the modern world since the French Revolution. Historians of the classical world probably find these same sentiments expressed in ancient Greece; I know they are to be heard in the classical literature of ancient Rome.[2] So I must treat my own prophecies of gloom with a touch of skepticism. But I respond to what I see around me, filtered, I readily admit, through my subjective vision. And what I see around me, in my extended visits of a few months in the United States every three or four years, is a society that increasingly lacks a sense of collective purpose, a vision of the future, and even self-conscious roots in the past. The overthrow of Communist regimes in Eastern Europe and the disappearance of the Soviet Union as a threat to American security will only quicken this process. Anticommunism did provide a focus, a convenient symbol around which one could mobilize energy and effort on behalf of some larger goal. The disappearance of this focus of collective purpose will further enhance centrifugal forces in American society and further undermine images of order that protect us from our baser instincts. I doubt if such domestic threats as drugs, AIDS, or problems of the homeless are adequate substitutes (although the environment might end up filling the bill) because the definition of the problem and the solutions that have been offered are so divisive. It might be argued against me that the really divisive opinions on AIDS, drugs, and the homeless are effectively silenced in public debate. Whereas this silence reduces the level of divisiveness, it may make solutions more difficult to achieve.

The breakdown of the center is enhanced by increased politicization of subgroups—the assertiveness of various ethnic, racial, religious, professional, environmental, and other groups demanding recognition and affirming their own interests, not only as part of what was once defined as an American national interest but also as alternatives to it. In a model society, an overarching sense of national purpose moderates the demands that subgroups raise. But the very term "national interest" seems to have lost symbolic legitimacy. The decline of a sense of national purpose, therefore, raises the specter of increased political unrest in which Jews provide convenient targets because of their disproportionate presence in the most visible arenas of power and status in the United States.

Social forces of this nature engender their own counterreactions. My fear is not only that the increased loss of a sense of order and moral purpose in American society will occasion antisemitism but also that the effort to recapture a sense of purpose will do so as well. I do not believe that the increased level of antisemitism will endanger Jewish lives or property in more than a marginal sense. It is its effect on the nature of Jewish life and American Judaism about which I will speculate.

Is antisemitism a help or a hindrance to strong Jewish identity? The question is not easily answered. Observers as disparate as Schneur Zalman of Lyady[3] and Jean-Paul Sartre[4] were convinced that antisemitism strengthened Jewish identity and religious sensitivities. The former, commenting on the likely consequences of a French victory over Tsar Alexander, observed that "riches will increase among the Jews . . . but they will be estranged from God," whereas if the Russian tsar won, "the Jews will become impoverished but their heart will be joined with God."[5] Experience in the United States has been that antisemitism abroad strengthens American Jewish identity and a sense of collective Jewish purpose. Antisemitism, or perceived threats of antisemitism within the United States, is an important instrument for mobilizing American Jewry and generating political and financial energies on behalf of Jewish needs and organizations. Thus it can serve as a stimulus for Jewish unity.

On the other hand, Charles Silberman has made the opposite case.[6] He argues that the decline of prejudice and discrimination against Jews in the United States and their acceptance into virtually every stratum of society removed the disabilities to being Jewish and thereby encouraged American Jews to strengthen their Jewish identity, albeit in new forms. He reminds us that many Jews prominent in American life sought to conceal their Jewish identity. It is not far-fetched to attribute the growth and support of classical Reform Judaism in the United States—especially its effort to excise elements of Jewish particularism and to stress the notion of a universal Jewish people lacking ethnopolitical interests, its slavish imitation and acceptance of upper-middle-class liberal Protestant norms and values, and its alienation from the masses of Jewish immigrants to the United States and their traditions—to fears of antisemitism. In accordance with this notion, at least some Reform Jews believed that by disassociating themselves from the Russian Jewish immigrants at the turn of the century they could protect themselves from the force of antisemitism.[7] My view is that the relationship between antisemitism and Jewish commitment has not been satisfactorily resolved and, as I hope to show, may never be.

Assumptions that the relationship between antisemitism and Jewish identity is unidirectional may be too simplistic.[8] I suspect that antisemitism may strengthen Jewish commitment among some Jews and weaken it among others.[9] Levels of expectation with regard to antisemitism, one's prior Jewish identity, and one's social goals could be all keys to the difference. In other words, the consequences of antisemitism on Jewish identity may be a polarization. In a more profound sense, the question about the relationship between antisemitism and Jewish identity is, perhaps, the wrong question to ask. Jewish identity or commitment may be sustained independently of antisemitism, or alternately, the impact of antisemitism on Jewish identity may be indirect rather than direct. Two better questions are the following: Do different forms of antisemitism (pogroms, mass slaughter, sporadic physical attacks, legal discrimination, economic exclusion, social prejudice, and so forth) affect Jewish identity in different ways? What images of Judaism and the Jewish tradition are reinforced by the presence or absence of antisemitism? I am concerned in particular with the second question.

I believe that American Jews will experience rising levels of hostility as a result of increased polarization within American society. This new antisemitism is rooted in group rivalry rather than an image of the Jew as estranged from the central elements of a dominant American culture or at least peripheral to them. The new antisemitism projects the Jew as competitor rather than outsider. In this respect, the hostility that I foresee is a less dangerous form of antisemitism in two ways. First, it is less likely to insist upon the destruction of Jews or even their removal from American society than might, for example, an antisemitism arising out of fundamentalist Protestantism. Second, this form of antisemitism is more likely to strengthen Jewish identity, at least among a significant number of American Jews. The alternative form, characteristic of Europe, pictured the Jew as alienated from the dominant culture. It not only heaped disabilities on the Jew but also imposed a negative image that many Jews also internalized—the image of the alien, inferior Jew who could overcome his or her disabilities if he or she adopted the dominant culture. It was this antisemitism that tempted individual Jews with assimilation and collective Jewry with self-reform in the image of the dominant culture. Assuming that my prognosis is correct, the new antisemitism reminds the Jew of his or her Jewish origins but holds out little hope for collective acculturation because there is no dominant culture into which to acculturate. In fact, I suspect that one focus of resentment among some American minorities may be that what passes for the dominant American culture has become so Judaized. On the other hand, the possibility of individual assimilation is likely to remain viable, a partial tribute to the impact of Jews on American society. Despite my prognosis of assertive minority groups increasingly hostile to one another, I do not believe that all other types of identity groups will disappear. Jews who wish to avoid the constraints of ethnic identity will continue to find that many professional societies and certain occupational groups offer an alternative mode of identity. The notion of the "work group as family" may seem absurd to the vast majority of Americans but not to those engaged in highly specialized occupations, especially occupations like the media or the academic world, with their espousal of cosmopolitan moralism and self-expression as the ultimate virtue. In other words, Jews will not be forced to be Jews. But those who do choose to be Jewish are likely to form images of Judaism based on the experience of antisemitism. Among those who retain their Jewish identity, antisemitism will shift their priorities in the matter of private versus public concerns. In the private realm antisemitism is likely to reinforce Jewish particularism, ethnocentrism, and ritualism. I now want to consider both these matters in greater detail, but I must first deal briefly with the falling proportion of Jews in the total population.

I assume that the number of Jews as a percentage of the total American population will continue to decline as a result of relatively low birthrates and high rates of mixed marriage leading to assimilation. The most important consequence of this decline, I suspect, will be that Jews and issues of Jewish concern will play a lessened role in the American public agenda. The most important consequence, for our purposes, is a decreased status for Jews; that is, being Jewish will no longer confer the honorific status that it presently does. Furthermore, decreased attention paid Jews in the media will mean that a major source of Jewish identity in contemporary America will taper off. Media attention reinforces the Jewish identity of many American Jews. Bringing Jewish labels and concerns to their attention reminds American Jews that they are Jewish and that being Jewish is not a trivial matter—after all, even the mass media make note of it.

There are two models or paradigms to explain the Jew's relationship to Judaism in the modern era. I mean to suggest not that these two modes of relationship are mutually exclusive but rather that they are conceptually distinct. Furthermore, I believe that we can identify most Jews by the model or paradigm that best describes their relationship to Judaism. Elsewhere I have referred to these two models as "public" and "private." By "public" Judaism I mean the Judaism that conceives of the Jew as part of a collective entity— the Jewish people—with obligations and responsibilities toward other Jews and toward the collective interests of the Jewish people. Most nonsectarian Jewish organizations define their Judaism in public terms. Concern for Israel, Soviet Jewry, or the political interests of American Judaism is a reflection of public Judaism. Private Judaism, on the other hand, reflects a regard for the meaning Judaism has for the individual Jew. The Jew who defines his or her Judaism in private terms is concerned with what patterns or answers Judaism provides for stages of life, for calender events, for personal crises, and for a need to celebrate aspects of life. The Jew who sees his or her Judaism in personal terms is more likely to think of Judaism in religious terms, whereas the Jew who defines his or her Judaism in primarily public terms is more readily categorized as an "ethnic" Jew.

The 1970s and especially the 1980s witnessed the surge of private Judaism at the expense of public Judaism for a number of reasons. First, private Judaism, more concerned with self, is more compatible with the style of modernity in general and American life in particular; second, from an objective point of view the public concerns of the Jewish people in the 1980s (whether of Israel, of Soviet Jews, or within the United States) were less than riveting and the solutions for them by no means clear. The problems that confronted the Jewish people in the 1980s did not compare in magnitude or severity to the problems that confronted other groups about whom American Jews felt at least some responsibility. In addition, assuming one felt a sense of responsibility to the collective Jewish people, and assuming that one wanted to do what is best for that collectivity, it was by no means clear what one ought to do or what position one ought to adopt with respect in the 1980s to the two major issues of Jewish public concern: Israel and Soviet Jewry. I anticipate that the growth (or even a perceived growth) of antisemitism will shift the balance between private and public Judaism again toward the greater importance of the latter. Furthermore, this may have an impact on the intermarriage rate. (I will return to this at the close.)

.   .   .

I suggest not only that the present emphasis on private as contrasted with public Judaism may shift but also that, in a related development, the very nature of Judaism, as it is interpreted in the private realm, is likely to undergo reformulation. In the volume I coauthored with Steven Cohen, *Two Worlds of Judaism*,[10] I argued that those American Jews who chose to retain their links to the tradition had reinterpreted it in accordance with values of individualism, voluntarism, universalism, and moralism. It was inevitable, Cohen and I asserted, that Jews would reinterpret the tradition, given the markedly different conditions under which American Jews lived in comparison with those under which the tradition emerged. In the concluding chapter of the book, therefore, we were not so concerned that the contemporary interpretation of Judaism in the United States constituted a radical departure from that tradition (although we made no secret of our unhappiness—mine in particular—on this point), but rather that it seemed to set American Judaism on a trajectory that was distancing it from Israeli interpretations of Judaism. I want to return to that point. I bent over backwards, perhaps at the prodding of my coauthor, in distinguishing my preferences from my analysis. In doing so, I conceded a survival capacity to American Judaism of the 1970s and 1980s that it may not merit. I can best explain what I think is likely to occur in the next few decades by elaborating upon my image of American Judaism at the present moment.

Jews relate to or accommodate themselves to or reappropriate the Jewish tradition in one of three ways. The tradition can constitute a kind of museum. Artifacts of the tradition are admired and enjoyed at one's pleasure but without making demands upon one's life. In that case, aspects of the tradition are culled out and relocated in a setting that facilitates a purely object-subject relationship.

A second mode of relationship is best described by the term "submission." According to this relationship the tradition is imagined as a series of commandments as well as customs to which the Jew is required to submit. That not all Jews who relate to the tradition submissively do in fact observe everything the tradition demands of them is immaterial, as long as they assume that submission is the appropriate norm and do not project deviations from this norm as legitimate. The relationship of "submission" raises

questions about the proper interpretation of the tradition and there
are differences of opinion on this score. But characteristic of those
Jews who relate through the mode of "submission," that is, mostly
Orthodox Jews, is that none believe they can interpret the tradition
merely as they see fit. Authoritative interpretation is a matter for
those who are masters of sacred texts and are versed in its
interpretation.

The third mode of relationship to the tradition is best described
as "negotiation."[11] In this mode of relationship the tradition is
conceded as having a certain degree of authority but an authority
limited in a number of ways. It is limited, in the first instance, by
what the individual or his community members know. For example, most Conservative Jews do not *choose* to violate laws of family
purity; they simply do not know they exist. Second, it is limited by
what the individual or his community rejects. Conservative Jews
are aware of the roles that the tradition allots exclusively to men
but have rejected this gender differentiation. Third, it is limited by
the manner in which the individual or his community chooses to
interpret those aspects of the tradition that are accepted, especially
by perceptions as to who has the right to interpret. Unlike the
Orthodox, the "negotiators" do not necessarily pay deference in
matters of interpretation to the masters of sacred text.

I take "negotiation" to be the mode of relationship worth discussing in greater detail not only because it is the most complex but
also because I suspect that it characterizes the way in which the
majority of committed Jews in the United States would define their
relationship to Judaism. As indicated earlier, I am less interested in
the noncommitted, the roughly 25 percent of American Jews who
define themselves as "just Jewish" and display no interest in Jewish
life, public or private; they may or may not be lost to Judaism, but
their behavior has only an indirect effect on the collectivity of Jews
in the United States. The same is true of "museum" Jews. They are
an important segment of American Jews and include the wealthiest
and most successful Jews in the United States. It is not coincidental
that Jewish museums enjoy great success in their fundraising efforts, whereas most Jewish organizations, rabbinical schools, and
schools of Jewish education are in financial straits. But the category
of "museum" Jew is not, I believe, a stable one. To expand the

metaphor, either the "museum" Jew is likely to become obsessed with his collection, in which case it will begin to affect other aspects of his life and he will relate to the tradition either as a negotiator or as submissive, or the "museum" Jew will devote himself to other collections. The "submissives," at the other end of the continuum, are a numerical minority. I have sympathy for them and I think that their passion and dedication can serve as models for other kinds of Jews. Under proper condition they will inspire twinges of guilt among the rest of us. But I do not believe that their mode of relationship is suitable to the vast majority of American Jews even under conditions of moderate antisemitism and a subtle retreat from the acceptance to which American Jews have become accustomed. Therefore, it is "negotiation" as a mode of relationship to which I turn my attention.

First, Judaism itself, or the tradition that I take as synonymous with Judaism, is not neutral about how one relates to it. Negotiation as a self-conscious mode of relationship automatically redefines the nature of the tradition. It imposes a flexibility on the tradition, especially on the structure of authority within the tradition and on the centrality of sacred texts, that undermines one of its central pillars. Negotiation assumes that the tradition is negotiable. This posits a very different image from that which the model of submission suggests. The tradition has always been negotiated and the modern era is not unique in this respect; what is unique is that this is happening in a self-conscious manner.

Second, "negotiation" as it has proceeded in the past two decades subverts the tradition by the terms under which it takes place. I would single out three principles (though one can surely find more) by which increasing numbers of American Jews in the seventies and eighties negotiated the tradition. These principles are anchored in the styles and mores that characterize the professional and intellectual strata of America, and they may have a deeper basis in the nature of the modern experience. But they also reflect peculiarly Jewish roots, because they can be understood as a revolt against the patterns of synagogue life and ritual codes that had heretofore dominated American religious life. One finds them in full flourish in the *havurah* movement, but they have increasingly penetrated Conservative and Reform synagogues (and even some Orthodox synagogues) as well as their rabbinical seminaries. The principles to which I refer are informality, egalitarianism, and ethicism.

Informality is a style, but it is also a mode of consciousness. It includes the manner in which Jews enter the synagogue, seat themselves, approach the Torah and the ark, and even address the rabbi. Its most obvious reflection is the way in which increasing numbers of Jews dress during synagogue services. This constitutes, I believe, a statement about the meaning of the service within the synagogue: that the Jew has not come to the synagogue to stand before God the King, but to join his or her peers in some shared enterprise. It is consistent with another observation about synagogue services—the increased emphasis on communal singing and the decreased time devoted to silent prayer.

The second principle by which Jews in the United States negotiate the tradition is "egalitarianism," which is related to the principle of informality. Egalitarianism refers to more than the equality, really the interchangeability, of the sexes. Not only are differences between men and women to be ignored for purposes of observing or celebrating the folkways of Judaism but differences between young and old, married and unmarried, knowledgeable and ignorant, pious and impious, observant and nonobservant are also ignored. All these are categories to which the tradition ascribes significance in the assignment of roles but that American Jews disregard.

This in turn relates to the third principle, "ethicism," which is the opposite of ritualism. It matters not whether the folkways of Judaism are or are not observed in the proper manner; what matters is the proper intention. It does not matter whether the individual called upon to lead the congregation in prayer or deliver a homily or read from the Torah knows how to do it properly; all that counts is that the person, male or female, young or old, married or unmarried, indeed, at its most extreme Jew or gentile, wants to participate in the service and wants to play a role in the synagogue.

What I find threatening to Jewish survival in all this is not the deviation from tradition but rather the direction in which the tradition is moving—the terms under which it is being negotiated. Each of these three principles, especially when they are combined, undermines the central pillar of the Jewish tradition, the awesome and authoritative God whom Jews are obliged to obey. They substitute a Judaism focused upon the legitimation of self and the kind of lives American Jews have chosen to lead. They serve to strengthen the nuclear Jewish family and foster small communities of mutual support based on those who have made similar choices. Maintaining family and building community are necessary conditions for Jewish survival but are not substitutes for Judaism. What is emerging is a "religion" suitable for highly educated and materially successful young professionals who are unwilling to compromise their own moral assumptions and political worldview—indeed, who never even consider assessing the validity of these assumptions. This "religion" provides, in a sense, a foundation stone for the construction of American Judaism. But its focus on self-legitimation and its refusal to recognize an authority beyond the self carries within it the seeds of Jewish (Judaic) destruction.

A rise of antisemitism and a situation where Jews are less than the high-status people that recent years have accustomed them to being may undermine this version of Judaism. First, as I indicated, it will probably shift the focus of Jewish attention (at least among those Jews who continue to identify with Judaism) back to the public realm. Second, it will probably restrain the universalist and ethicist component of Judaism and restore greater sensitivity toward Jewish particularism and ritualism. A worldview that is a product of perceived gentile hostility is no longer a worldview that conceives the cosmos as open ended with unlimited choices. The world is now a place where, at least to some extent, destiny plays a role and ascribed characteristics determine one's status. This kind of worldview is more sensitive to formality rather than informality, status rather than egalitarianism, ritualism rather than ethicism. I do not for one moment believe that the peculiar formulation of American Judaism in the 1970s and 1980s will be entirely overturned, but I do hold that it will be reformulated in a way more compatible with the thrust of the tradition itself.

Finally, the growth of antisemitism is likely to lessen the desirability of Jews as marriage partners. Part of the impetus for the growth of private Judaism may have been that public Judaism is less meaningful to the intermarried Jew and especially to the non-Jewish partner, whether that partner does or does not convert to Judaism. The shift in emphasis from public to private Judaism and the reformulation of Judaism in more traditional or particularistic terms will also make Judaism less desirable to the non-Jew and may influence the ability and desirability of the Jewish community to absorb intermarried couples. This will certainly strengthen its capacity for survival.

As indicated at the outset, I am wary of making predictions, but I am very concerned about the state of American Jewish life. I do not believe that anything now taking place forestalls the disappearance of American Jews as a numerically significant and Jewishly identifiable collectivity. I do hold that something important will have to change if Judaism is to survive substantively in the United States. My essay suggests that an increase of antisemitism in the United States might constitute one such change. What other social-cultural fluctuations might reduce the attractiveness of Jews as marriage partners to non-Jews (or vice versa) and might lead American Jews to strengthen their Jewish commitments and reorient their notions about the nature of Judaism? That is a question I have difficulty in answering. If enough Jews were disturbed about the fundamental issues, the situation would be better. I worry about the attitude that a basically sound Jewish community in the United States need only introduce this organizational change or that tactical strategy in order to "reach out" to the intermarried or coopt greater numbers of young Jews. The popularity of such a doctrine signals the continuing decline of Judaism in the United States.

Notes

1. Charles S. Liebman, *Deceptive Images: Toward a Redefinition of American Jewish Life* (New Brunswick, N.J.: Transaction, 1990).
2. As George Steiner notes, "The image we carry of a lost coherence, of a centre that held, has authority greater than historical truth. . . . This appears to be an almost organic, recursive process. Men of the Roman Empire looked back similarly on utopias of republican virtue; those who had known the *ancien régime* felt that their later years had fallen on an iron age" (*In Bluebeard's Castle: Some Notes towards the Redefinition of Culture* [London: Faber and Faber, 1971], 16–17).
3. Cited in Lucy Dawidowicz, ed., *The Golden Tradition* (New York: Holt, Rinehart, and Winston, 1967), 95.

4. Jean-Paul Sartre, *Portrait of the Anti-Semite* (London: Secker and Warburg, 1948).

5. Dawidowicz, *The Golden Tradition*.

6. Charles Silberman, *A Certain People* (New York: Summit, 1985).

7. Michael Meyer does not say this, but nothing he says would contradict this notion. He observes, "The heyday of classical Reform Judaism was also the period of massive immigration by East European Jews." Further along he notes, "One reaction of German Jews in the United States was to make their Reform synagogues bastions of Americanism setting them apart from the uncouth un-Americanized greenhorns regularly disgorged from the steerage ships reaching New York" (*Response to Modernity: A History of the Reform Movement in Judaism* [New York: Oxford University Press, 1988], 292).

8. This point comes through very sharply in Todd Endelman, *Radical Assimilation in English Jewish History, 1656–1945* (Bloomington: Indiana University Press, 1990).

9. In the case of Jews striving for integration into gentile society and frustrated by a rise in antisemitism, the result may even be apostasy (Todd M. Endelman, introduction to *Jewish Apostasy in the Modern World*, ed. Todd M. Endelman [New York: Holmes and Meir, 1987], 1–19). This was a minority option. On the other hand, although I do not know of any study on the topic, I have heard it said that many Polish Jews who aspired to acceptance in Polish society and were frustrated in this desire by the rising wave of antisemitism in the 1930s joined the ranks of the Revisionists, the most militantly Zionist party.

10. Charles S. Liebman and Steven M. Cohen, *Two Worlds of Judaism: The Israeli and American Jewish Experience* (New Haven, Conn.: Yale University Press, 1990).

11. I first heard the term used by Martin Marty in a talk delivered at the Jewish Theological Seminary in November 1989 to describe the relationship of most American Christians to the Christian tradition. I do not know whether Marty invented the term. I find it most apt to describe the behavior of an important segment of American Jews.

CHAPTER 26

American Jewry in the Twenty-First Century: Strategies of Faith

Arnold Eisen

I am not quite sure just how prophetic I am meant to be. The twenty-first century, after all, is almost upon us, and we can presumably hang on tight in the nineties; the end of the next century, especially given the enormous changes that have overtaken us in this one, seems far away indeed—and certainly beyond my meager powers of imagination. With God, for God, concerning God, all things are possible—so how is one possibly to predict them? I have decided to focus on faith and, as a Conservative Jew ever in search of elusive middle ground, I will direct my attention halfway between the immediate and the far off, the forecast that is doable and that which might be interesting. I will draw upon recent research into the state of American Judaism during the past few decades in order to guess at what may lie ahead in the next few. I am far from alarmed about our prospects, as you will soon see, but neither do I discern much cause for celebration.

Let me begin by noting that our theme is *American* Judaism rather than Judaism in general. I see little hope of convergence with patterns of faith in either Europe or Israel, even if I agree with Charles Liebman and Steve Cohen that it is premature, even silly, to speak of Israeli Judaism as a separate entity altogether.[1] If Max Weber had anything at all to teach us, it is that the shape of a society and polity impinges heavily on the configuration of its faiths. The State of Israel—soon to possess a majority of world

Jewry, perhaps, and certainly more Jews than America—will continue to develop the holiness of space, while we insist that Jews sanctify only time. Messianism will continue to agitate hearts and minds there, and only terrify us from afar. The attempt to have the social order directed in some way by Torah, even if it be through the notion of *mishpat ivri*[2] rather than halakhah per se, will remain high on their religious agenda and be kept off ours by the commitment to separate church and state. Finally, the denominational dynamics of the two Jewries will likely remain distinct, and the theological developments that I am about to predict for America will likely not appear among Israeli Jews, or hardly faze them. Having said that, let me add at once that Israeli and American Orthodox Jews especially will still have much in common, that the Reform and Conservative footholds in Israel will likely remain, and that Israel will no doubt continue to be existentially crucial to committed American Jews—even as it grows more problematic politically and more distant culturally. We are set upon distinct but intersecting paths, in religion as in so much else.

I take it, second, that we in America have already emerged from the period in which Jewish thought was dominated by the two themes that have preoccupied it for most of the post-1967 period: covenant theology and confrontation with the Holocaust.[3] A new generation of theologians is already upon the scene, declaring, like the previous one, its intention to reorient theological discourse substantially. Covenant, for reasons I have discussed elsewhere,[4] has proven a difficult vehicle for theology in a community disinclined to submit to the "yoke of Torah," however liberally defined, and bereft of any satisfactory notion of revelation, particularly "after Auschwitz." The theologians who have made the Holocaust central, meanwhile—Emil Fackenheim, Irving Greenberg, Arthur Cohen—have themselves urged the move from or through encounter with the "rupture" or "caesura" of "Auschwitz" to *tikkun*: renewed Jewish commitment, "the Jewish way."[5] The question becomes what sort of commitment—and, increasingly, the nature of Jewish community. Two examples of recent thought illustrate the point rather nicely.

Arthur Green, a student of Abraham Heschel and expert on Hasidism who assumed the mantle of Mordecai Kaplan as president of the Reconstructionist Rabbinical College, is working on a synthesis that puts the emphasis upon personal religious experience or "awareness." Jews must admit the gap that separates them from traditional symbols and beliefs, but they can, like countless generations of their predecessors, particularly the Hasidim, seek "spiritual wakefulness and awareness, . . . cultivation of the inner life." Judaism demands intensity of vision, searchings of the soul. *Mitzvot* are the way Jews live a life "in constant striving for . . . relation to the transcendent and in response to the demands made by it." The search is undertaken with others of similar commitment—in other words, in Jewish communities.[6]

For Judith Plaskow, author of a groundbreaking effort to formulate a feminist Judaism, the way around the tradition's general exclusion of women's concerns and consciousness is for contemporary Jewish women to "stand on the ground of our experience, on the certainty of our membership in our own people." Note that authority rests with the experience of a particular community, and its "God-wrestling." Feminist history, midrash, and ritual must be created to provide forms and content for that search. The effort is revolutionary, Plaskow argues, but so was the transformation of biblical Judaism accomplished by the rabbis of old following the cataclysmic destruction of the Second Temple.[7]

This is not the place for a detailed review of either thinker's work. I only want to suggest that the trends that the two represent—experiential, communal, spiritual, feminist—will be long-lasting if the atomization of our communities, our liberal suspicion of authority, our search for individual meaning, and the successes of the women's movement in recent decades prove enduring. Feminist reinterpretation of the tradition is part and parcel of modern revision more generally, and even attacks on "patriarchalism" seem tied to the democratization of "god-talk" evident throughout the modern period, never more so than in America in recent decades. Tocqueville would hardly have been surprised by these developments, and neither should we be.[8] Our theological directions will keep pace with the social changes that underlie them.

In a sense, these directions provide a framework rather than specific content. They describe a kind of thinking, an approach to thought, rather than supplying hard-and-firm answers to questions about God and God's plans for the world. American Jews have never seemed particularly interested in theology, and not much systematic Jewish religious thought has been produced here—a trend likely to continue. Consider the various strategies of faith that predominate among us: (1) "compartmentalization," which thrives by separating issues of faith from daily life and the scientific perspective that organizes it; (2) the parallel division of faith from reason as Martin Buber's I-Thou is divided from I-It, as Abraham Heschel's realm of wonder and mystery is divided from the world in which we "measure and weigh," and as Joseph Soloveitchik's "covenantal man" Adam the Second is divided from his Adam the First of mastery and honor;[9] (3) translation of traditional concepts such as Jewish chosenness into images that move us not by the logic of belief but by the pictures they present to the mind and heart; and (4) most prevalent of all, the move from questions of what is true to considerations of what is meaningful, which I call the strategy of tradition. We feel free to participate in rituals and textual study without feeling compelled to give assent to the words we utter. "Blessed are you, Lord our God, King of the Universe, who has commanded us" need not deter those who do not believe in a commanding God, or in God's ordinance of this particular observance, so long as they can supply an interpretation to their behavior that seems both meaningful and authentic.

I take this to be the most widely practiced strategy of faith in current employ, outside of traditional Orthodoxy, and it—even more than the other strategies just named—sets theological questions aside in favor of the experience of transcendence, profundity, and community. It will likely remain such. The elites of the various movements seem disinclined to focus on age-old questions of belief, let alone resolve them with any consensus, while Jewish laypeople seem quite happy with the notion that tradition is a legacy for them to use as they see fit, even piecemeal, rather than a coherent and binding set of obligations—let alone a belief system to which they must assent. I would be willing to bet that this emphasis on the flexibility and pluralism of tradition and the de facto autonomy of the individual Jew will grow in coming decades. A community with our intermarriage rate, our internalized concern with the good opinion of certain highly secularized gentile Americans, our desire to balance particularist "survival" with harmony and integration and not, God forbid, to go too far in either direction—this is not a community about to undertake a theological move to the "right." Even inside modern Orthodoxy, where the behavioral norms seem ever more demanding, Jewish belief coexists precariously with the demands of the world beyond and inside the walls. The sources of strain in that situation, and in American Judaism generally, are far more evident than any tendency to abandon secular America wholesale—or adapt it in a new and convincing Maimonidean synthesis.

There is perhaps one exception to this rule: we may well find Jewish mysticism ever more appealing in coming decades, both because people are more and more comfortable with myth, having learned to read it in a way that does not make literal claims about what is true, and because the science of the coming century may converge decisively with the most mythic, least rational elements of our tradition. One reads Stephen Hawking's *Brief History of Time*, perhaps a sign of things to come, and the affinities with Kabbalah are striking. There is little room anymore for Mordecai Kaplan's judgment of our inheritance by a rationalist, scientistic standard. The scientists themselves increasingly have recourse to mythic language (e.g., the big bang), and the belief that science can master nature, let alone harness it for the benefit of the species, seems at century's end naive at best and at worst a cruel delusion. Theological symbols that have cosmic rather than social reference, spiritual rather than political implications, may experience a renaissance of meaning. In this respect, we may have license to think boldly. Our grandchildren may look back at us as having inhabited a time of conflict between religion and science that they no longer know. They may have the luxury of other problems.

In conclusion, I cannot escape noticing that we met to discuss the American Jewish future in the relatively humdrum week of *Tazri'a-Metzora*, interposed between the eternally terrifying drama of the deaths of Nadav and Avihu in *Shemini* (a *parasha* that always coincides with *Yom ha-Shoah*) and the eternal challenges of *Aharei-Mot* and *Kedoshim*. One must choose a standpoint, in faith as in sociology. I find that these weekly Torah readings from Leviticus provide me with a landmark of sorts from which to view our present—indeed, any Jewish present. They tell me where I am and have been (like Aaron, relatively "silent" about the awful events just behind us, and mainly concerned to get on with the job of being a holy people). They remind me, too, where we as a community need to go, even if none of us ever gets there entirely and many of us do not get there at all. It is also extremely comforting, when doing Jewish futurology a mere forty-six years after the Holocaust, to have no fear for the survival of the Jewish people; and, forty-three years after the creation of the Jewish state, to have no fear for the existence of Israel; and, after decades of predictions about the imminent demise of American Jewry, to worry not a bit that our descendants will not be able to convene in scholarly conferences a hundred years from now and worry about *their* descendants. A few decades ago, I could hardly have been this optimistic. Perhaps, then, we should conclude each rehearsal of anxiety for what might come in a tone of blessing for what is already here and has not been lost.

Notes

1. Charles S. Liebman and Steven M. Cohen, *Two Worlds of Judaism: The Israeli and American Experience* (New Haven, Conn.: Yale University Press, 1990). See in particular chapter 7.
2. Literally, "Hebrew law"—i.e., the entire history of Jewish legal practice, now the name of a movement to align current Israeli legislation with that precedent.
3. I draw here upon my survey, "Jewish Theology in North America: Notes on Two Decades," *American Jewish Year Book* (1991): 3–33.
4. Ibid.
5. "Tikkun" is Fackenheim's phrase; see Emil Fackenheim, *To Mend the World* (New York: Schocken, 1982). *The Jewish Way* is the title of a volume by Irving Greenberg (New York: Summit, 1988).
6. Arthur Green, "Rethinking Theology: Language, Experience, and Reality," *Reconstructionist* (September 1988): 8–11. See also his book *Seek My Face, Speak My Name* (Northvale, N.J.: Jason Aronson, 1992).
7. Judith Plaskow, *Standing Again at Sinai: Judaism from a Feminist Perspective* (San Francisco: Harper & Row, 1990). I have cited an article that serves as a précis of the book: Judith Plaskow, "Standing Again at Sinai: Jewish Memory from a Feminist Perspective," *Tikkun* 1, no. 2 (1986): 28.

8. I refer of course to the great nineteenth-century survey of American mores and institutions: Alexis de Tocqueville, *Democracy in America*, 2 vols. (New York: Schocken, 1961).

9. See Martin Buber, *I and Thou*, trans. Walter Kaufmann (New York: Scribner's, 1970); Abraham Heschel, *Man Is Not Alone* (New York: Harper Torchbooks, 1966); and Joseph Soloveitchik, "The Lonely Man of Faith," *Tradition* (Summer 1965): 5–67.

Index